THE GULF WAR OF 1980-1988

THE IRAN-IRAQ WAR IN INTERNATIONAL LEGAL PERSPECTIVE

This publication was produced in co-operation with the
Netherlands Institute of Social and Economic law Research (NISER)
University of Utrecht, The Netherlands.

T.M.C. ASSER INSTITUUT
THE HAGUE

The Gulf War
of
1980-1988

The Iran-Iraq War
in International Legal Perspective

edited by

Ige F. Dekker
Harry H.G. Post

MARTINUS NIJHOFF PUBLISHERS
DORDRECHT/BOSTON/LONDON

T.M.C. Asser Instituut — Institute for Private and Public International Law, International Commercial Arbitration and European Law
20-22 Alexanderstraat 2514 JM The Hague, the Netherlands — tel. (0)70-3420300 — telex: 34273 asser nl, telefax: (0)70-3420359

Director: C.C.A. Voskuil

The T.M.C. Asser Instituut was founded in 1965 by the Dutch universities offering courses in international law to promote education and research in the fields of law covered by the departments of the Institute: Private International Law, Public International Law, including the Law of International Organisations, Law of the European Communities and International Commercial Arbitration. The Institute discharges this task by the establishment and management of documentation and research projects, in some instances in co-operation with non-Dutch or international organisations, by the dissemination of information deriving therefrom and by publication of monographs and series. In addition, the Institute participates in the editing of the Yearbook Commercial Arbitration and in the editing and publishing of, *inter alia*, the Netherlands International Law Review and the Netherlands Yearbook of International Law.

The Institute provides the nine university law faculties in the Netherlands with a research assistant's post-graduate course in international and European law, and assistance to *Asser College Europe*, a partnership venture with eastern and central European countries which offers a framework for the organization and implementation of research and educational projects.

Cover Photograph: ANP Foto

ISBN 0-7923-1334-8

Published by Martinus Nijhoff Publishers, P.O.Box 163, 3300 AD Dordrecht, The Netherlands. Kluwer Academic Publishers incorporates the publishing programmes of Martinus Nijhoff Publishers.

Distributors
---
for the United States and Canada: Kluwer Academic Publishers, 101 Philip Drive, Norwell, MA 02061, U.S.A.
for all other countries: Kluwer Academic Publishers Group, P.O.Box 322, 3300 AH Dordrecht, The Netherlands.

Copyright

© 1992, T.M.C. Asser Instituut, The Hague.

PREFACE

Unlike the 1991 Gulf War, which was in nearly every way unprecedented, the Gulf War of 1980-1988 in most respects was a highly traditional armed conflict between two States. In fact, since World War II it is one of the rare examples of a classic war between States that was conducted for a considerable number of years and where all the relevant rules of dispute-settlement, of humanitarian warfare, of the law of neutrality and finally of state-responsibility and personal criminal responsibility passed in review. All the rules were there to prevent the outbreak of that war, to nip it in the bud once hostilities had broken out, to bring armed conflict to a speedy end, to mitigate its effects for combatants and non-combatants, to safeguard the rights of non-parties to the conflict and — possibly — to bring to justice those who had so rampantly violated those rules. All the rules were there and nevertheless they conspicuously failed to serve their purpose.

The Gulf War was an ugly war, it was an inhuman war, and it was a senseless war. If anything was able to show its utter futility, it was the handing over of the spoils of that war by Iraq to Iran in the early days of the second Gulf crisis in 1990. But it was also a unique war in that it presented an opportunity to analyse why the rules which had been drawn up precisely for this type of war did not work satisfactorily. It is often said that one of the set-backs of the laws of warfare is that rules are always drawn up for the regulation of yesterday's war instead of for the regulation of tomorrow's war. That cannot be said, however, of the Gulf War because that war was a nearly exact replica of yesterday's war. And, therefore, the legal aftermath of the Gulf War will be with us for a considerable time to come. Important parts of the law of international armed conflict like, *e.g.*, the law of neutrality, means and methods of warfare, armed conflict at sea, have to be re-examined in order to make them more effective, and ultimately, to enable them to serve better their final goal, *viz*, the mitigation of the evils of war.

In order to analyse the various legal issues involved a colloquium was convened in November 1990. It was pure coincidence that it took place at a time when the Gulf area was again the focal point of world-attention. A great number of highly qualified experts attended this colloquium and either introduced a report or ventured their opinion on these reports. The present book contains the reports and the comments which have been adapted by their authors in the light of the discussion that took place at the colloquium.

Peter H. Kooijmans
Professor of Public International Law,
University of Leyden

ACKNOWLEDGEMENTS

Before writing their definitive texts, the contributors to this book had the opportunity to submit their views to a learned audience at the 1990 Asser Colloquium on International Law, entitled 'The Gulf War in International Legal Perspective', which took place on the 23rd of November of that year at the Dutch Ministry of Foreign Affairs in The Hague.

This Colloquium was organized by the Institute of Public International Law of the University of Utrecht, the Faculty of Public Administration of the University of Twente and the T.M.C. Asser Instituut in The Hague. On behalf of the organizing committee, the editors gratefully acknowledge the generous organizational and/or financial support the Colloquium and the production of this book received from the following Institutions:

> The Dutch Ministry of Foreign Affairs
> The Dutch Ministry of Defence, Naval Staff
> The Legatum Visserianum
> The Royal Netherlands Academy of Arts and Sciences.

The quality of a book is, of course, first and foremost determined by its authors. When the editors put forward the idea of an international legal study on the 1980-1988 Gulf War, it was enthusiastically received, in particular by those scholars who at the time (1988) were among the few international lawyers who already had examined aspects of the Iran-Iraq War. Many of them agreed to submit original essays.

Many people encouraged this project and although it is always hazardous to single out some of them in particular, we will nevertheless do so because without their participation, this book and the Colloquium might have been of a completely different nature or, indeed, might never have seen the light of day.

Professor Frits Kalshoven was among the first to whom the whole undertaking was outlined. His warm support from the very beginning and his willingness to contribute a paper at the Colloquium and later a chapter to the book, strongly stimulated the realization of both. Also at an early moment in the conceptual phase, Professor Peter Kooijmans' invaluable suggestions and observations strongly stimulated us to pursue the project. Furthermore, he was prepared to act as President of the Colloquium and opens this book with a Preface. To both Frits Kalshoven and Peter Kooijmans, we are greatly indebted.

Our sincere gratitude should be extended to His Excellency Mohammed Bedjaoui, Judge in the International Court of Justice. We had long hesitated whether or not to invite him to conclude the Gulf War Colloquium with an address to be included in this book. In view of the subject matter and his high office, we realized, how difficult it might be for him to decide upon such a request. Far better than can be done here, Judge Bedjaoui himself explains these difficulties and his considerations with regard to them in the introductory sentences to his contribution (the concluding Chapter 9 of the book). Judge Bedjaoui's address proved to be the main event of an also otherwise most successful Colloquium and will be vividly remembered by all who were present.

We also wish to thank the Chairmen of the Workshops at the Colloquium, Professors Leo Bouchez, Cees Flinterman, Ko Swan Sik and Alfred Soons, who greatly contributed to its scientific success. The rapporteurs at the Colloquium have made a sincere effort to use the observations made during the workshops, in order to transform their reports into the chapters of this book. In particular, the remarks by special commentators have often been most beneficial to this end. As far as their comments have not been, or could not be, included in the chapters of the book, they have been reworked into separate comments for each chapter. We are, of course, greatly indebted to our co-authors and the commentators, whose contributions built up the Colloquium and now form the core of this book.

Members of staff of the T.M.C. Asser Instituut undertook the realization and publication of the present book. In this respect the editors also gratefully wish to mention the professional and patient assistance of Jacqueline Smith and Carla Groenestein of the Netherlands Institute for Social and Economic law Research (NISER) in Utrecht, who prepared the manuscripts for publication.

Further legal studies of the 1980-1988 Gulf War are undoubtedly necessary. The editors hope that this work will be a valuable stimulus for such studies, and thereby, will provide a (modest) scientific contribution towards peace in the area. In that case, as regards the publishing of this book, we may conclude with a variation of a saying by a great Dutch novelist: 'It was an idea - but it was a good idea'.

Enschede/Amsterdam, October 1991   Ige F. Dekker
                                                     Harry H.G. Post

TABLE OF CONTENTS

Comments

PART II
The *Ius in Bello*

Chapter 3

Comments

Comments

PART III
Armed Conflict at Sea and Neutrality

ABBREVIATIONS

A/RES	Resolution of the General Assembly of the United Nations
AFDI	Annuaire Français de Droit International
AJIL	American Journal of International Law
ARES	ARES Défense et Sécurité
ASIL	American Society of International Law
BFSP	British and Foreign State Papers
BYIL	British Yearbook of International Law
Can.YIL	Canadian Yearbook of International Law
CDDH	Diplomatic Conference on the Reaffirmation and Development of International Humanitarian Law Applicable in Armed Conflicts, 1974-1977
CDI	Commission de Droit International
cf.	compare
CICR/ICRC	International Committee of the Red Cross
Doc.	document
e.g.	for example
EEZ	Exclusive Economic Zone
EPIL	Encyclopedia of Public International Law
et.seq.	and the following
etc.	et cetera
FRG	Federal Republic of Germany
Hague Recueil	Recueil des Cours (collected courses), Hague Academy of International Law
HMSO	Her Brittanic Majesty's Stationery Office
i.e.	that is
ibidem	in the same place
ICJ	International Court of Justice
ICLQ	International and Comparative Law Quarterly
ICRC/CICR	International Committee of the Red Cross
idem	the same
ILC	International Law Commission
ILM	International Legal Materials
ILR	International Law Reports
infra	below
IRRC	International Review of the Red Cross
JDI	Journal du Droit International
LNTS	League of Nations Treaty Series
loc.cit.	in the place cited
LOSC	Law of the Sea Convention 1982
NATO	North Atlantic Treaty Organisation
no.	number

NYIL	Netherlands Yearbook of International Law
O.R.	Official Records
ODIL	Ocean Development and International Law
Official Journal	Official Journal of the League of Nations
op.cit.	in the work cited
PCIJ	Permanent Court of International Justice
RBDI	Revue Belge de Droit International
Rev. belge	Revue Belge de Droit International
RGDIP	Revue générale de droit international public
supra	above
Syracuse J.Int'l L. & Com	Syracuse Journal of International Law and Commerce
UN Doc.	United Nations Document
UNESCO	United Nations Educational, Scientific and Cultural Organisation
UNIIMOG	United Nations Iran-Irak Military Observer Group
UNTS	United Nations Treaty Series
USN	United States Navy
Virg.JIL	Virginia Journal of International Law
WEU	Western European Union
ZaöRV	Zeitschrift für ausländisches öffentliches Recht und Völkerrecht
ZDv	Zentrale Dienstvorschrift

INTRODUCTION

Like all wars, the war that raged in the Gulf from 1980 to 1988 was repulsive and inhuman. However, due to its length and the way it was conducted this war shall probably be counted among the most vicious of modern times. Both in terms of the number of victims among soldiers and civilians – estimated at over a million – and in view of the virtually immeasurable material damage caused, the years between 1980 and 1988 were been extremely costly, in particular, of course, for the belligerents.[1] Moreover, it can safely be assumed that the Iraqi invasion of Kuwait in August 1990 and the military and other reactions triggered by that operation, can only be fully understood in the light of the Iraqi experiences and losses in the war with Iran.

Although any war, almost by definition, can be said to be among the most unfortunate of human undertakings, the 1980-1988 War appears particularly tragic because in the end it is very difficult to perceive any positive results for either party. Even in terms of the territorial issue that to a great extent served Iraq as a most classic *casus belli*, nothing seems to have been gained or lost: in 1991 both parties occupy the same territorial positions as they did in 1980.

In several respects and certainly in terms of international law, the 1980-1988 War was a 'traditional' war. It was an almost classic *international* war, not a colonial liberation war or an internal armed conflict with international implications, of which the world had seen so many varieties since the Second World War. This international war had virtually been 'declared' in September 1980. Such open resort to military action was rather unexpected in view of the general prohibition on the use of force laid down in the Charter of the United Nations.

Analysts have often argued that in the modern age, with its rapid communications and strongly interwoven interests, an international military conflict can no longer be contained and kept from spilling over into other 'theatres'. Yet, for a considerable period of time, in fact until in 1984 the 'tanker war' really transformed the Iran-Iraq War into a Gulf War, hostilities remained limited to the two belligerents.

As the War continued, an increasing number of states needed to redefine the nature of, in particular, their economic relations with Iran and Iraq. In defining this aspect of their foreign policy they could derive little benefit from any guidance offered by the United Nations. The world organization did not appear able to take effective action regarding the War (nor did any other international organization, for that matter). More or less on their own, third states were thus forced to make clear whether or not they supported one or other of the belligerents or stood aside from the conflict. As long as the War remained limited in nature, a neutral position was logical and attractive. Later, when the scope of the War had widened, it became more difficult to maintain such a

---

1. The United States Secretary of State estimated the number of victims over the first seven years of the War to be one million (*cf. Department of State Bulletin*, no. 2126, September 1987, p. 75). The number killed in these years is estimated to be over 377,000.

neutral stand. Nevertheless, most third states, including those in the region, continued, at least formally, to prefer neutrality.

From 1984, after the tanker war had started to affect the interests of an increasingly large part of the world community, concerted international action grew in relevance and, in the end, also in effectiveness. Rising tensions in the Gulf due to continued attacks on (neutral) merchant shipping and the substantial naval presence of the most important maritime states also seemed to draw more attention to the source of the conflict. A greater awareness of the dangers involved in the prolongation of the War now that the direct involvement of other states was becoming more likely, resulted in an increasing media coverage of events including more attention to the way the belligerent parties conducted themselves in their air and ground operations. Publicity for the atrocities of the War (missile attacks on cities, the employment of chemical weapons, the use of child-soldiers, *etc.*,) and the ensuing discussions, not least in the Arab and Muslim world, on the justification of the means and methods employed, undoubtedly also contributed to the decisive drive within the United Nations, after seven years, to bring an end to the War. This process culminated on 20 July 1987 in the adoption by the Security Council of Resolution 598. It still took more than a year (often with fierce fighting) before a cease-fire between Iran and Iraq came into force. Only as late as August 1990, immediately after the Iraqi Government had decided to invade Kuwait, could the two neighbouring states agree on a withdrawal of their armies behind international boundaries and on the exchange of tens of thousands of prisoners of war. At the time of writing (August 1991), there are no indications of steps towards a more definite peace settlement.

The following collection of essays aims only at addressing a number of the most important international legal aspects of the Gulf War of 1980-1988. There is no pretension to provide an exhaustive legal analysis of the War and even less to examine it from other scientific points of view. The latter are only touched upon if the international legal analysis so requires. The perspective of the international lawyer suffices here in particular because, until relatively recently, this War has drawn such remarkably little attention from that corner.

The need for more thorough international legal reflection, however, seems obvious. In the first place, there are the border disputes between Iran and Iraq, in particular regarding the Shatt-al-Arab waterway, which for such a long time have affected their mutual relations and have formed one of the most important reasons for the outbreak of the hostilities in September 1980. The significance of the several border agreements between Iran and Iraq in any assessment of the legal position of the two belligerents has been emphasized by the parties themselves. Their attitude with regard to these agreements raises, at the same time, several important international legal questions, such as whether or not an appeal to the law on the termination of treaties is acceptable, or what is the status of the *Thalweg* line in international law.

As the War progressed beyond its initial stages, many more states than just Iran and Iraq became affected by it. This was due in particular to the extensive activities of the belligerent parties which were detrimental to the shipping of non-belligerent states. The involvement and acts of this greater number of states has also broadened the potential implications of the conflict for the state of international law. The hostilities eventually came to an end in August 1988 (but only with a cease-fire!), but for a prolonged period of time the international community will have to cope with its international legal aftermath.

More fundamentally perhaps from a scientific perspective, the Gulf War has refocussed the interest of international lawyers on some matters that for a long time seemed to have lost their place of prominence. Important examples are the law of neutrality and some parts of the law of international armed conflict, in particular the law of naval warfare and several aspects of the law governing the conduct of war (regarding missile attacks on the civilian population, or on the recruitment and use of child-soldiers).

Perhaps most crucial in terms of law and justice, the conduct in this horrible War of the states involved, their governments, their leaders and their soldiers, have raised numerous questions of morality and responsibility. Violations of the general prohibition on the use of force and of fundamental principles of humanitarian law have brought to the fore with increased force the subject of (individual) criminal responsibility for such deeds.

As the Gulf War of 1980-1988 was, primarily, a war between two Islamic states, its conduct also gave a new impetus to the analysis of legal orders existing beside the universal legal order, an analysis which perhaps may provide rules that prevail over the rules of general international law.

The contributions in this volume are divided in four parts. Part I, *casus belli* and the *ius ad bellum*, begins with an essay (chapter 1 of the book) by Harry H.G. Post addressing, within the context of the Iran-Iraq border regime, what perhaps has been the most salient cause of the 1980-1988 War: the dispute over the frontier in the Shatt-al-Arab waterway. This essay provides a review of the legal history of the boundaries between Iran and Iraq and a study of some of the international legal questions still not fully analysed in the available literature, like those involving aspects of the law of treaties and the law regarding the determination of frontiers. Erik Franckx and Gerard Tanja have added their commentaries.

The other pages of this Part deal with what traditionally was called the *ius ad bellum* or the *ius contra bellum*: the international principles and laws on the use of force. The essay by Kaiyan H. Kaikobad (chapter 2) involves an analysis of the principles and laws concerning the prohibition of aggression and intervention and the right of self-defence, as well as their application to the situations created by the actions of the parties to the conflict. This essay has been commented on by Rob C.R. Siekmann and Marc Weller. The latter also added a detailed discussion of the response to the use of force by the United Nations Security Council addressing, in particular, the significance of the resolutions of the Security Council in regard to the right of self-defence.

Parts II and III of the book examine issues of, again speaking in traditional terms, the *ius in bello*, including the law of neutrality. The first essay in Part II by Frits Kalshoven (chapter 3), with comments by Rainer Lagoni and Gert-Jan van Hegelsom, focusses on the means and methods of warfare used in the 1980-1988 Gulf War in the light of the rules applicable in this War. In the last pages of his essay, the author discusses the repercussions in the outside world, such as the response of the International Committee of the Red Cross and the United Nations, to some of the modes of waging war employed by the belligerents.

Paul Tavernier follows (chapter 4) with a review in the light of humanitarian law of the distinction between, and the treatment of, combatants and non-combatants during the War. Two very controversial issues in particular are dealt with, namely, the issue of prisoners of war and the issue of child-soldiers. Judge George H. Aldrich, on the one hand, and Louise Doswald-Beck and Maria Teresa Dutli, on the other, have provided commentaries.

Part III concerns aspects of the law of armed conflict at sea and the law of neutrality. It opens with an imaginative chapter on targeting theory in the law of armed conflict by Francis V. Russo, Jr. The author discusses the shortcomings of the traditional principles and rules of naval warfare and how they must be interpreted in the light of modern naval capabilities and practices. The consequences of this theory are illustrated by reference to the tanker attacks during the Gulf War. This essay has been commented on by Dieter Fleck and Terry D. Gill.

Chapters 6 and 7, the other essays in Part III, deal with the law of neutrality. Michael Bothe's essay (chapter 6) discusses neutrality at sea, with comments by Christopher Greenwood and Adriaan Bos. The main points discussed in this chapter are the concept of neutrality and the effects of the *ius ad bellum* on the development of this concept. Special attention is paid to the legality of military actions by neutrals against belligerents and by belligerents against neutral shipping.

In the third and last essay in this Part (chapter 7), Andrea Gioia and Natalino Ronzitti examine third states' commercial rights and duties, aspects of international law which previously have not been of great concern in the literature on the Gulf War. This essay focusses on the following questions: the right of neutrals to trade with belligerents and the limitations to that right, measures taken by belligerents which interfere with neutral commerce and measures taken by neutrals in order to enforce freedom of commerce. Ove Bring has added his comments to this essay.

The fourth and last part of the book consists of two chapters: one on questions of criminal responsibility and the other on an Islamic international legal perspective. In chapter 8, followed by Eric David's and Peter Malanczuk's comments, Ige F. Dekker addresses the sensitive subject of criminal responsibility for the initiation of the Gulf War in September 1980. The author discusses the – still emerging – concepts of criminal responsibility of states as well as of individuals for the initial use of force and he applies his analysis to the military activities and the official justifications of the parties in the first stage of the War. In this respect the question is examined whether President Saddam Hussein of Iraq should be held responsible for a crime against peace.

Part IV, and the book, are concluded by Judge Mohammed Bedjaoui's detailed essay in which, after a succinct review of the catalogue of violations of international law by the belligerents and the role of international organizations and third states, he undertakes 'the search for another cipher key' to the 1980-1988 Gulf War by reviewing it in terms of an Islamic conception of international law.

Ige F. Dekker
Harry H.G. Post

Part I

Casus Belli and the *Ius ad Bellum*

Chapter 1

BORDER CONFLICTS BETWEEN IRAN AND IRAQ: REVIEW AND LEGAL REFLECTIONS

Harry Post[*]

I   INTRODUCTION

The legal history of the boundaries between Iran and Iraq will be reviewed in the following chapter. This history has already largely been written, in part also with the needs of an international lawyer in view.[1] In the pages that history will be covered only in the perspective of an international legal analysis of the behaviour of the states involved.

At first sight, much attention to the older border agreements between the two countries may seem somewhat superfluous. However, for an understanding of the nature of the border conflicts, which were generally referred to as among the main causes of the Gulf War 1980-1988, a perception of their legal history is indispensable. Moreover, in view of the recurring practice of both Iran and Iraq (unilaterally) to denounce boundary agreements, even today the status of the older agreements is or can be of vital legal significance.

With regard to the demarcation of the Iranian-Iraqi boundary, the crucial question is – and not only in that regard! – whether or not the 1975 Treaty 'system' is still in force. Although a viewpoint on that question is presented here, it must be qualified in the light of a 'classic' problem of the analysis of border issues: the uncertainty about the adequacy of the facts. Although this problem is largely remedied by strong reliance on official documents in general, and on the official statements by the Iranian and Iraqi authorities in particular, it cannot be entirely avoided. Therefore, if on the basis of evidence other than that which is used in this chapter the conclusion, should be drawn that the 1975 demarcation is no longer in force, the 1913/1914 demarcation – with its obscurities and in the light of subsequent modifications – should be considered to determine the location of the boundary. Hence, in order to assess the current international boundary regime, an occasionally rather detailed account is given of both full-scale attempts at demarcation.

Along the historical legal path that is followed, several important and complicated international legal questions will be faced, like whether or not an appeal to rules on the termination of treaties is acceptable, or what the status of the *Thalweg* line in

---

* H.H.G. Post, Senior Lecturer in Public International Law, University of Utrecht.

1. Kaikobad, K.H., *The Shatt-al-Arab Boundary Question; A Legal Reappraisal*, Oxford 1988 and, in particular, U. Gehrke and G. Kuhn's 'classic', *Die Grenzen des Irak*, Stuttgart 1963.

I.F. Dekker and H.H.G. Post, eds., The Gulf War of 1980-1988
© 1992, T.M.C. Asser Instituut, The Hague

international law is. The analysis of such controversial matters will often remain at the level of legal reflections: full-scale studies of jurisprudence and state practice fall outside the scope of this paper. Unfortunately requirements of scope also prevent any treatment of (at least) two subjects that perhaps should have been covered in this chapter: the Iran-Iraq maritime boundaries and the navigational regime of the Shatt-al-Arab or Avand Rood.

Sections II, on Land Frontiers, and III, on the Frontier in the Shatt-al-Arab, are chronologically divided according to the major boundary agreements. Section IV, on the Current Border Regime focusses on questions of treaty denunciation and termination. Some concluding remarks are made in section V.

II   BOUNDARY AGREEMENTS; LAND FRONTIERS

The Treaty of Zohab, a Treaty of Peace and Demarcation of Frontiers, signed in 1639 between Sultan Murad IV of the Ottoman Empire and Shah Safi of Persia delimited, rather unspecifically, a common border located between the Zagros Mountains in the East and the Tigris in the West.[2] Usually, the Zohab Treaty is taken as the starting-point of boundary delimitation between Iran and Iraq. Its territorial division was been reaffirmed until the beginning of the 19th century, including in the first Treaty of Erzeroum of 28 July 1823. However, due to the important changes it brought for the common boundary, the second or 1847 Treaty of Erzeroum really must be taken as the starting-point of any analysis of the current Iranian-Iraqi boundary regime.

A   The 1847 Treaty of Erzeroum

The Treaty of Erzeroum of 1847 is not only the basis for the modern frontiers between Iran and Iraq, but it also marks the beginning of the most persistent – and violent! – of the Iranian-Iraqi border conflicts: that on the Shatt-al-Arab waterway.

According to Article II of the Treaty of Erzeroum, the border between Persia and the Ottoman Empire in the South-Eastern sector, will follow the Shatt-al-Arab waterway along the low water line on the eastern – Persian – bank. Before this Treaty entered into force, on 31 March 1848, in this sector the boundary used to follow the Bahmanshir River, situated to the north of the Shatt-al-Arab (and running roughly parallel to it – see the map in Annex B, *infra*). The territory between the two waterways which the Treaty transferred to Persia, consisted of Khizr (now Abadan) Island. Furthermore, Persia acquired the Ottoman city of Muhammara, now Khorramshahr.[3]

---

2. *British and Foreign State Papers* (1912), pp. 763-766 (further: *BFSP*). *Cf.* map in Annex A, *infra*.

3. The relevant provisions of Article II are as follows: 'Le Gouvernement ottoman s'engage formellement à ce que la ville et l'échelle de Mohammara, l'île de Khizr, le lieu d'ancrage, et aussi les terrains de la rive orientale, c'est-à-dire de la rive gauche du Chatt-el-Arab, qui sont en la possession des tribus reconnues comme relevant de la Perse, soient dans la possession du Gouvernement persan en pleine souveraineté.' *Cf.*, *BFSP* (1947/8), pp. 874-875; also: Kaikobad, *op.cit.* (note 1), pp. 119-120.

Persia had obtained these territorial gains in the South in exchange primarily, for territory in its northern provinces of Zohab and Suleimanié. Article II provides:

> 'II. Le Gouvernement de Perse s'engage à abandonner au Gouvernement Ottoman tous les terrains plats, c'est-à-dire, les terrains de la partie occidentale de la province de Zohab; et le Gouvernement Ottoman s'engage de son côté à abandonner au Gouvernement Persan la partie orientale, c'est-à-dire, tous les terrains montagneux de la province de Zohab, avec la vallée de Kerrind.'[4]

Although the Treaty of Erzeroum embodies an over-all settlement on the mutual borders, several specific issues are phrased rather vaguely, in particular in respect to the Shatt-al-Arab region. For the Turkish Government in particular, the agreement laid down in Article II was less than crystal clear: Turkey wanted (*inter alia*) to be sure that the agreement did not allow Persia to claim territory outside Muhammara. Therefore, before signing the Treaty, the Turkish Government asked Great Britain and Russia – as mediating powers involved in the negotiations – for a *Note explicative*. This 'note', indeed, was drawn up, and solved the Turkish worries.[5] The remaining problem, however, was the Persian consent to it. Apparently, the Government of the Shah was unaware of the existence of the explanatory note.[6] After the Persian and Turkish representatives had signed the Treaty on 31 May 1847, the Shah ratified without changes or additions on 26 June 1847.[7] However, problems arose at the subsequent exchange of ratification documents in Constantinople. The Turkish Government declared that, before the exchange could take place, the Persian Government should officially recognise the British/Russian explanatory note. Only after strong pressure on the Persian representative by the two mediating powers, did the latter give his consent to the note.[8] On 31 March 1848, the ratification documents were eventually exchanged, and the Treaty entered into force.[9]

However, this conclusive step did not constitute full clarity. Upon being informed of the explanatory note and the consent to it by the Persian representative, the Persian Government declared both to be null and void. With regard to the representative's

---

4. *Idem* (see also footnote 12, *infra*, and the literature mentioned there on the interpretation problems this text has caused).

5. For the text of this 'Note explicative': see Document 21, at p. 44 of the 'Dokumenten-Anhang' to Gehrke and Kuhn, *op.cit.* (note 1).

6. *Cf.*, Gehrke and Kuhn, *op.cit.* (note 1), p. 179. Kaikobad's research of the unpublished documents of the India House Library and Records, confirms their account (in: Kaikobad, *op.cit.* (note 1), pp. 17-26).

7. Gehrke and Kuhn, *op.cit.* (note 1), pp. 179-180; source: *Official Journal of the League of Nations* (1935), p. 114 (further: Official Journal).

8. The Persian representative was 'threatened' with causing the disruption of diplomatic relations with Russia and Great Britain. See Gehrke and Kuhn, *op.cit.* (note 1), p. 180.

9. After the acceptance by the Persian representative (in a letter of 31 January 1848), the Turkish Government still hesitated. The exchange could take place only after renewed pressure by the mediating powers, this time on Turkey. The nature of the pressure seems unknown (see: Harari, M., *The Turco-Persian Boundary Question*, Ph.D.-Diss., Columbia University, New York 1958, p. 86).

consent, it declared that he had grossly overstepped his instructions: his powers were limited to the exchange of ratification documents.[10]

Although, a boundary commission – again, involving also Russia and Great Britain[11] – nevertheless began to determine the exact course of the boundary, disagreement on the frontier in the area immediately to the North of the Shatt-al-Arab, to the West of Muhammara, and, as far as Turkey was concerned, even to the East of that town, appeared unsolvable.[12]

B   The 1911 and 1913 Protocols

Legally, the most relevant results of the successive attempts in the 19th century at a resolution of the remaining problems, of which those in the Southern area proved to be the most important, were a *status quo* agreement of 1869, which did not provide additional clarity regarding the disputed areas, and the so-called 'carte identique'. This map was a joint British-Russian cartographic undertaking also made public in 1869. It showed a 'frontier zone' within which the two mediating powers considered the boundary to be located. The 'carte identitique' appeared relevant in the first successful attempt to reach a legal settlement which took until the first decennium of the 20th century to materialize.[13]

After pressure by the – by now – traditional mediating powers, Great Britain and Russia, the two contesting neighbouring states in 1911 agreed to the Protocol of Tehran. This agreement provides a 'framework' on the basis of which an over-all legal settlement of the remaining border conflicts was supposed to be reached. The Protocol has therefore, primarily a general and procedural nature. It established a Mixed Commission at Constantinople charged with reaching agreement on the boundary as a whole. Article 3 of the Tehran Protocol states that the Treaty of Erzeroum will be the basis for the work of the Commission; it does not prescribe any more specific principles or interpretations. Neither does it contain any reference to specific areas, such as the vital Southern area of the border.[14]

---

10. For the text of the Persian note, see *Journal Officiel de la Société des Nations* (1935), pp. 217-218.

11. *Cf.* Articles III and IV of the Treaty of Erzeroum: *BFSP* (1847/8), p. 874; or Kaikobad, *op.cit.* (note 1), p. 119.

12. The Turkish claim extended to a line far north to, and parallel with, the Bahmanshir River (see the map in Annex B, *infra*). *Cf.* Kaikobad, *op.cit.* (note 1), figure 1, at p. 21. Attempts to solve this dispute have been undertaken over a prolonged period of time. See Gehrke and Kuhn, *op.cit.* (note 1), pp. 181-184, and Kaikobad, *op.cit.* (note 1), pp. 18-23; the latter gives a detailed report on the development of the dispute in the southern region.

13. For the *status quo* agreement reached on 3 August 1869, see: Gehrke and Kuhn, *op.cit.* (note 1), 'Dokumenten-Anhang', p. 51 (Doc. 24); or, for the English translation, Parry's *The Consolidated Treaty Series*, Vol. 139, pp. 425-426. Kaikobad, *op.cit.* (note 1), at pp. 24-25 reproduces the 'carte identique' which, along the full length of the Turkish-Persian border, shows a frontier zone with a width '... ranging from twenty to fifty miles, ...'

14. Article 3 of the 'Protocole de Téhéran' says: 'Les Travaux de la Commission mixte qui se réunira à Constantinople auront pour la base les clauses du Traité dit d'Erzeroum conclu en 1263 ...' Source: *Official Journal* (1935), p. 226; also in: Gehrke and Kuhn, *op.cit.* (note 1), 'Dokumenten-Anhang', p. 70 (Doc. 27), in: Kaikobad, *op.cit.* (note 1), p. 121, and in Parry's *Consolidated Treaty Series* (1911/12), p. 138.

Seen in a broader perspective, the most remarkable article in this Tehran Protocol is its compromissory clause (Article 4). It stipulates an obligation to submit all matters of interpretation and application regarding provisions of the Treaty of Erzeroum on which parties could not agree '... à la cour arbitrale de la Haye afin que la *question entière soit ainsi définitivement tranchée.*'[15] This clause marks, in a sense, the beginning of a range of attempts legally to 'contain' agreements on the Turkish/Iraqi-Persian/Iranian boundaries by means of agreements or treaty clauses on the pacific settlement of disputes. Finally, this trend culminated in Article 6 of the 1975 Baghdad Treaty, the most comprehensive provision of this sort.

Article 4 of the Tehran Protocol, apparently played a role in the matter of the acceptance by Persia of the 'note explicative' of 1847. As already noted above, the rejection by Persia of the 'note' was a major stumbling bloc in the negotiations following the conclusion of the Protocol. Only after considerable pressure by Russia in particular, was Persia eventually willing to accept this explanation of Article II of the Treaty of Erzeroum.[16] The argument which convinced the Persian negotiators was, according to Ulrich Gehrke, that Turkey appeared prepared to apply Article 4 of the Tehran Protocol. In that case the Hague Permanent Court of Arbitration would be empowered to decide on *all* the boundary issues. Apparently, at the time, such a solution did not seem very attractive to Persia.[17]

The Persian acceptance of the 'note' opened an avenue towards agreement, which indeed was reached and laid down in the 'Protocole de Constantinople' concluded on 17 November 1913 by Great Britain, Russia, Persia, and Turkey. This most important Protocol gave a detailed determination of more than three quarters of the Persian-Turkish border. For the parts on which no agreement could be reached, Article II forsaw the establishment of a 'Commission de Délimitation' composed of representatives of the Four Powers.[18] On the basis of several specified instructions, the Commission obtained remarkable powers to decide on the parts of the boundary which were not yet delimited: in case of a divergence of opinion among its members '... sur le tracé de telle ou autre partie de la frontière, ...' Article IV allowed the Russian and British representatives to decide the issue. Their decision would be binding on all four Governements.

This provision could be even more important in view of Article V, which says that as soon as part of the frontier has been delimited: '... cette partie sera considérée comme fixée définitivement et ne sera susceptible ni d'examen ultérieur ni de revision.' And

---

15. Source: *cf.* the preceding footnote (emphasis added). In view of the year 1911, the 'cour arbitrale de La Haye', of course, can only be the 'Permanent Court of Arbitration'.

16. This acceptance did not find expression in the Protocol of Constantinople, itself (see, in particular, its Preamble containing an overview of relevant steps in the process of negotiation). The *Journal Officiel de la Société des Nations* (1935), p. 219, gives the following text: the Persian delegation '... *déclare accepter la note collective* desdites puissances, en date du 14/26 avril 1847, et reconnaître les explications y contenues comme faisant partie inégrante du traité d'Erzeroum.'

17. See Gehrke and Kuhn, *op.cit.* (note 1), p. 235. However, neither Kaikobad, *op.cit.* (note 1), p. 31, nor Khalid Al-Izzi, *The Shatt-al-Arab River Dispute in Terms of Law*, Baghdad 1972, give this reason for the Persian agreement.

18. This Commission was the 'commission technique' already forseen in Article 2 of the Tehran Protocol.

Article VI added to the practical relevance of the work of the Commission by stating: 'A mesure de l'avancement des travaux de délimitation, les Gouvernements ottoman et persan auront le droit d'établir des postes sur la frontière.'[19]

According to Article III of the Constantinople Protocol, the Commission was supposed to do its work on the basis of the '... dispositions du présent Protocole; ...', and according to a '... Règlement intérieur de la Commission de Délimitation en annexe (A) au présent Protocole'. This internal regulation provided in its Article II that the 'carte identique' of 1869 would serve as the topographical basis for the delimitation.[20]

Apart from a survey of notes exchanged during the period of negotiations which serves as a Preamble, the text of the Constantinople Protocol mentions only at two places negotiations which had taken place since the conclusion of the Treaty of Erzeroum. For the Kotur, a Protocol of 15 July 1880 was applied, whereas in the Zohab sector a British-Turkish declaration made in London on 29 July 1913 was to be used as starting-point for the Delimitation Commission.[21]

The Constantinople Protocol left the Delimitation Commission with six specific parts of the boundary to determine, and, at the end of Article I, contained the following general clause:

'Les parties de la frontière non détaillées dans le tracé susmentionné seront établies sur la base du principe du statu quo, conformément aux stipulations de l'article 3 du Traité d'Erzeroum.'[22]

For two of the specific matters, the text also instructs the Commission to use the *status quo* principle, described there as 'général' and as 'accepté'. Furthermore, in the area north of Sirvan, the Commission was allowed, explicitly 'à titre exceptionnel', to delimit the frontier by taking into consideration the 'changes' that might have taken place between 1848 and 1905 (however, what kind of changes is not indicated). Finally, more to the South, the Commission is supposed to make up a special arrangement for a division of waters of the Gengir (or Soumar), and to delimit the border area in the Zohab sector according to the 1913 Declaration of London, just mentioned above. With regard to the border in the Shatt-al-Arab, see further section III.B, *infra*.

19. Article VII also reveals a special interest on the side of the British in the matter of this boundary: it contains a specific guarantee for a concession the Anglo-Persian Oil Company had been granted in 1901 by the Shah of Persia.

20. For the text of the 'Règlement intérieur', see Gehrke and Kuhn, *op.cit.* (note 1), 'Dokumenten-Anhang', pp. 63-66 (Annex to the Protocol of Constantinople, Doc. 25).

21. See on the specific issue of the boundary in this sector, Kaikobad's detailed account of the negotiations, *op.cit.* (note 1), pp. 40-49.

22. Protocole relatif à la délimitation de la frontière turco-persane. Source: *Official Journal* (1935), p. 206; or in Gehrke and Kuhn, *op.cit.* (note 1), 'Dokumenten-Anhang' p. 62 (Doc. 25); or in Kaikobad, *op.cit.* (note 1), p. 128. It does not become entirely clear what is meant by this principle, but as the boundary has never before been demarcated, it can hardly refer to anything else than to the *de facto* situation at the time. To determine what the factual situation in 1914 was, is what the Commission seems to have done.

The Delimitation Commission completed its work between January and November 1914.[23] Apparently, it did not face very grave problems.[24] As it was supposed to do according to its 'Règlement intérieur', the Commission marked the boundary on location and drew the demarcated line on the 'Carte Identique'.[25] Due to the outbreak of the First World War, the states involved never gave their opinion on, or consent to, the proceedings. Later, this lack of explicit consent was referred to by Iran, in particular, to deny the validity of the Protocol of Constantinople. However, the Protocol itself does not give any indication that such consent is required in order to make the Commission's specific demarcations binding for the Parties. Article V of the Protocol (see *supra*) indicates the contrary: as soon as the Commission has delimited a part of the boundary, that part is fixed definitively. Moreover, according to Article VI, the parties are immediately allowed to erect posts along the thus delimited parts of the boundary.[26]

After the First World War, when Iraq, as one of the successor states, had assumed the international rights and duties of Turkey,[27] in particular, the arrangement of the Constantinople Protocol with regard to the Shatt-al-Arab gave rise to problems (as will further be discussed in section III.B, *infra*). In the early 1930s, the Iranian demands to come to new agreements regarding the border between the two countries became increasingly more pressing. In 1933 and 1934 several incidents – even involving the

23. The Commission's decisions were laid down in 'minutes'. These minutes were not published, but were made available for the archives of the League of Nations in Geneva. However, some of the most relevant minutes regarding the land frontiers are published in the *Official Journal* (1935), at pp. 235 *et seq*. E. Lauterpacht describes the most important minutes of relevance to the boundary in the Shatt-al-Arab in his "River Boundaries: Legal Aspects of the Shatt-al-Arab Frontier", in: *ICLQ* (1960), pp. 212-214.

24. Kaikobad, *op.cit*. (note 1), p. 52, notes that by 28 October, the whole boundary had been demarcated, with a small section in Kotur as the only exception. Why this demarcation did not take place – notwithstanding the fact that it had been included in the Constantinople Protocol as one of the special tasks of the Delimitation Commission – he does not record. From the minutes it seems clear that a lack of time was the main problem; in principle the delimitation was possible, but it awaited instructions of the Turkish Grand Vizier (see *Official Journal* (1935), pp. 235 *et seq*., at p. 237). Kaikobad uses unpublished source materials from the India House Library and Records (see his Bibliography, at p. 143).

25. However, in a 1974 report to the Secretary-General of the United Nations, a special representative stated that in the region Zain al-Qos, he found the frontier inadequately demarcated. In his view this was due to a failure of either the 1914, or the 1937 delimitation commissions (*cf. UN Doc*. S/11291, with annex).

26. Perhaps, the first sentence of Article I of the Constantinople Protocol, can be said to plead against this reasoning: 'Il est convenu que la frontière entre la Perse et la Turquie *sera* tracée comme suit: ...' (emphasis added). However, it is otherwise clear from the Protocol's text that pending the 'technical' demarcation on the spot, the frontier described in quite some detail in the Protocol is binding on the Parties to it (notwithstanding the subsequent demarcation).

27. After British occupation during the First World War Iraq was proclaimed a British mandatory territory (by Great Britain) in 1920. This led to a revolt by the population of Iraq, which, eventually, resulted in the coronation of King Faisal on 23 August 1921, a date which is often considered as the beginning of Iraqi independence. Nevertheless, in 1924 the Council of the League of Nations agreed to a (modified) British draft mandate. On these grounds Iraq has been occasionally referred to as a quasi-mandatory territory. In 1932 Iraq was accepted as a member of the League of Nations. In the statement to the Council of the League of Nations of 14 January 1935 by the Iraqi Minister of Foreign Affairs Nuri As-Said, Iraq was, *e.g.*, presented as one of Turkey's successor states (in: *Official Journal* (1935), pp. 113 *et seq*.)

new Iranian navy – took place.[28] During 1934 tension increased to such an extent that on 29 November of that year, Iraq submitted a complaint to the Council of the League of Nations.[29] This complaint not only concerned the dispute over the Shatt-al-Arab, but also included other territorial matters. Iraq stated that Iranian police posts had been set up in Iraqi territory, it referred to a border dispute in the small area of Sarkushk[30] and to the division of waters of the Gunjan Cham river.[31] However, as Gehrke notes, these matters were of no weight in comparison to the Shatt-al-Arab issue.[32]

The Iranian answer to the Iraqi complaint was rather sweeping:

> '... que pour la détermination de la frontière, le Traité d'Erzeroum de 1847, le Protocole de Constantinople de 1913 et, par suite, le tracé de la Commission de délimitation de 1914 sont, en droit et en équité, dépourvus de toute valeur.'[33]

The legal justification that Iran presented was based on its view that the Treaty of Erzeroum had not been validly drawn up due to the fact that, at the time, the Persian negotiator had exceeded his powers when he agreed to the 'note explicative' (see, *supra*, section II.A). As the Constantinople Protocol, and the work of the Delimitation Commission (and also the 1911 Tehran Protocol) had all been based on the Treaty of 1847, the Iranian position, in fact, was that the boundary with Iraq was not regulated by a treaty regime.[34]

However, whatever truth there is in the argument that the consent to the 'note explicative' had been invalid under international law,[35] and cannot, in principle, be held against Iran, of overriding legal importance are the subsequent acts of the parties

---

28. For more details see, Gehrke and Kuhn, *op.cit.* (note 1), pp. 225-232, or Schofield, Richard N., *The Evolution of the Shatt Al-'Arab Boundary Dispute*, Outwell, Wisbech 1986, p. 54.

29. In a letter to the Secretary-General of the League of Nations, Iraq based its action on Article 11(2) of the League's Covenant (*cf. Official Journal* (1935), pp. 196-197).

30. *Official Journal* (1935), p. 213.

31. *Cf. idem*, pp. 213-215.

32. Gehrke and Kuhn, *op.cit.* (note 1), p. 233. An examination of the documents referred to in the two preceding footnotes leads only to agreement with that judgment (the Binawa Suta dispute seems to resemble a village brawl).

33. In a letter of 8 January 1935 to the Council of the League (source: *Official Journal* (1935), p. 217; also in: Gehrke and Kuhn, *op.cit.* (note 1), p. 234).

34. Iran did not refer to older written agreements between the Ottoman and Persian Empires, like the 1823 First Treaty of Erzeroum or the 1639 Treaty of Zohab.

35. In the light of the accounts made public a case could be made in favour of the Iranian/Persian position. The consent of the representative of Persia, most likely, could not bind Persia. Apparently, the relevant limits to the powers of the representative were quite obvious to Turkey (and to Great Britain and Russia, for that matter). For the Law of Treaties, Article 47 of the 1969 Vienna Convention on the Law of Treaties, codifies for such a case the applicable rule of international law (however, whether the law of treaties at the time had already developed to this extent, is quite unlikely). Moreover, there might even be enough evidence for the application of Article 51 of the Vienna Convention ('Coercion of a representative of a state'). Another matter is, of course, what the consequences of the (possible) invalidity of the 'note explicative' are for the validity of the Treaty of Erzeroum itself. There might be some room for debate on the Iranian position that the Treaty is 'dépourvu de toute valeur'. In view of the subsequent developments, the answer to questions like these, however, is, primarily, of academic significance.

concerned. As mentioned above, in 1912 Persia had after all consented to the explanation which the 'note explicative' gave of Article II of the Treaty of Erzeroum. During the League of Nations' debates, Iran did not deny this consent. Its arguments focussed on the pressure the mediatory powers had exerted during the negotiations preceding the agreement on the Constantinople Protocol.[36] Moreover, in the Iranian view, the Protocol, in fact, was an entirely new agreement conflicting with the Treaty of Erzeroum. The principles of the Treaty could not be said to serve as the basis of the Protocol, which according to Article 3 of the Tehran Protocol, they were supposed to do. Furthermore, Iran argued, Turkey had not abandoned or transferred territory which it should have handed over in accordance with the Constantinople Protocol.[37] Perhaps somewhat surprisingly, Iran's argument did not so much serve as a complaint against Turkish behaviour but as further proof that, like Iran, Turkey did not recognize the boundary delimitation.

Finally, Iran advanced a constitutional argument to support its thesis that the Protocol is not valid. Due to the far-reaching nature of the Constantinople Protocol, the Persian Constitution required that it be approved by Parliament (in fact, a similar argument would hold for Turkey). However, the Protocol never received such approval.

As a result of the invalidity of the Erzeroum Treaty regime and the Protocols of 1911 and 1913, in the Iranian view the border in the Shatt-al-Arab was to be drawn on the basis of customary law. This position was of particular relevance for the boundary in the Shatt-al-Arab. According to Iran, the *Thalweg* principle had to be applied there because it was mandatory in such a situation (see further, *infra*, section III.C).

Iraq, of course, did not agree with this interpretation of the boundary regime. The Iraqi representative, Nuri As-Said, replied that Iraq considered that Article II of the Erzeroum Treaty determined the border in the Shatt-al-Arab: '... implicitement en tout cas, que c'est la rive gauche du Chatt-el-Arab, et non le *Thalweg*, qui constitue la frontière de la Perse dans le secteur sud.'[38] A fundamental argument for this point of view was, that from 1848 to 1914, both countries had actually behaved in accordance

36. The 'Règlement intérieur' of the 1914 Delimitation Commission (*cf.* the text, *supra*), shows, *e.g.*, that Iran has some grounds here (see also footnote 19).

37. Iran did not specify which territory was meant here (*cf. Official Journal* (1935), p. 220). The allegation was repeated by the Iranian Minister of Foreign Affairs, Kazimi, in the League Council, during its session of 15 January 1935. Then, however, the argument got a different twist because he stated that 'The non-execution of a treaty by one of the contracting states gives the other state the right to regard that treaty as cancelled.' So Iran appealed to the principle of *non adimpleti contractus*. In terms of the modern law of treaties, it could be argued that Turkey was accused of a 'material breach' (see Article 60 of the 1969 Vienna Convention of the Law of Treaties, and the arguments in respect of this rule presented in sections II.C and IV.A, *infra*). However, Iran did not point to the breach of a specific obligation, but argued, rather debatably, that 'The application of the 1913 line on the ground in 1914 was not complete, but was hampered by the opposition and resistance of the Ottomans' (both citations in *Official Journal* (1935), p. 118).

38. *Journal Officiel de la Société des Nations* (1935), p. 114.

with the relevant provisions of the Treaty. Furthermore, the constitutional objections of Iran regarding the Protocol of Constantinople were convincingly rejected.[39]

Proposals were made in various quarters, including by the British delegate Anthony Eden, to submit the matter to the Permanent Court of International Justice. However, mediation by the Italian Baron Aloisi, led to direct negotiations between the two Parties. The ultimate result was the 'Traité de Frontière entre Le Royaume de L'Irak et L'Empire de L'Iran', signed at Tehran on 4 July 1937.[40]

C   The 1937 Treaty of Tehran

The Treaty of Tehran, in the first place, confirms older agreements. In Article 1 of the Treaty, the High Contracting Parties state that the Protocol of Constantinople and the 1914 Minutes of the Delimitation Commission 'sont considéré valables'. With regard to the work of the Delimitation Commission, the Article adds: 'Vu les dispositions du présent Article et sauf ce qui est prévu à l'Article qui suit la ligne frontière entre les deux Etats est telle qu'elle est définie et tracée par la susdite commission.'[41]

Article 2 provides for some changes in the border line in the Shatt-al-Arab. Furthermore, Article 4 stipulates rules and principles for the use and maintenance of the Shatt, whereas in Article 5 the Parties undertake to conclude a separate Convention on these subjects. A Protocol annexed to the Treaty contains a time-schedule for the conclusion of this Convention (see, further, *infra*, in this section and in section III.C).

Article 3 provides for a commission to erect the frontier marks already determined by the 1914 Delimitation Commission. The Protocol annexed includes a further instruction for that commission.

At the end of 1938, the commission was indeed installed, but, in 1940, after virtually fruitless attempts, its work came to a definite stand-still due to irreconcilable disputes between the Iraqi and Iranian members.[42] With regard to the land frontiers the

---

39. The most important argument in international law was that because the Protocol did not require ratification, the absence of such ratification had no effect on its validity (see, *idem*, p. 116). On the matter of the actual behaviour of both states, see also section II.C, *infra* (especially note 72).

40. The exchange of ratifications took place in Baghdad on 20 June 1938. Text in 190 *League of Nations Treaty Series* (1938) (further: LNTS), pp. 242 *et seq.* (French official text); the English translation follows at pp. 256 *et seq.* See for the English text also: 8 *International Legal Materials* (1969), pp. 478 *et seq.*, or Kaikobad, *op.cit.* (note 1), pp. 130 *et seq.* (Annex 4). Gehrke and Kuhn, *op.cit.* (note 1), 'Dokumenten-Anhang', pp. 72 *et seq.* (Doc. 28) give the French text.

41. *LNTS* (1938), p. 242.

42. See Gehrke an Kuhn, *op.cit.* (note 1), pp. 249-250; or Kaikobad, *op.cit.* (note 1), pp. 63-64. On 24 July 1937, Iran and Iraq had also concluded a 'Traité pour le Règlement Pacifique des Différends entre le Royaume de l'Irak et l'Empire de l'Iran' (Source: *LNTS* (1938), pp. 270 *et seq.*). This treaty which entered into force on 20 June 1938 states in its first Article: 'Les Hautes Parties contractantes s'engagent à soumettre à une procédure de règlement pacifique, de la maniére prévue au présent traité, tout différend qui pourrait s'élever entre elles et qu'il n'aura pas été possible de régler par la voie ordinaire des négociations diplomatiques.' In the following article, the Permanent Court of International Justice is mentioned as the judicial institution to decide on the differences, unless the Parties prefer arbitration. However, in Article 2(3), (among others) disputes which arose before this Treaty came into force, and disputes concerning the territorial status of the Parties, are excluded. The Treaty also includes a conciliation procedure which is not hampered

demarcation executed by the 1914 Delimitation Commission and laid down in the 'minutes' thus remained the valid demarcation.[43]

Attempts to revive contacts on the border disputes, in particular in the mid fifties, and again in the early sixties when for a short period the relations between both countries had improved considerably, did not lead to any conclusive results.

The Iraqi revolution of July 1968, which brought the *Ba'ath* party into power, led to a rapid deterioration of relations with Iran. On 27 April 1969, the Iranian Government officially announced that it considered the 1937 Treaty to be null and void. The Iranian arguments used in 1969 resemble, to some extent, the arguments of the Iranian representatives put forward in the League of Nations Council meetings in 1935.

In the first place, Iran points to numerous violations of the 1937 Treaty on the part of Iraq. However, as has already been argued, for the unilateral termination of the Treaty this argument can hardly be sufficient because, *inter alia*, from its entry into force both parties seem to have considered the Treaty to be the basis of their relations. In 1963 Kuhn also reached this conclusion after a survey of relevant events and a careful analysis of the many (possible) violations of the Treaty up to that year. The events that took place between 1963 and the Iranian declaration of 1969 do not justify a different interpretation.[44]

Among Iraqi violations, Iran emphasizes one in particular, one which would enable it to terminate the Treaty on the basis of the exception *non adimpleti contractus*. Due to Iraqi unwillingness, the Convention on navigational matters regarding the Shatt-al-Arab, forseen in Article 5 of the 1937 Treaty, never materialized. According to Iran, the absence of such a convention allowed Iraq '... to turn to its own and to refuse to account to its Treaty partner in the regulation of navigation on the Shatt-al-Arab for the large sums of money it has collected in dues from vessels using that common waterway.'[45]

---

by the restrictions just mentioned. However, the conciliation procedure is not 'waterproof' (see: Lauterpacht, *loc.cit.* (note 23), p. 233).

43. That is: including possible differences of opinion on the interpretation of the 'minutes'.

44. *Cf.* Gehrke and Kuhn, *op.cit.* (note 1), pp. 289 *et seq.*, and in particular, p. 340 (see also Al-Izzi, *op.cit.* (note 17), pp. 89 and 90). Under international law, the unilateral termination of a (bilateral) treaty on the basis of violations by the other Party is subject to strict conditions (*cf.* Article 60 of the Vienna Convention on the Law of Treaties, and, notably, Bruno Simma's analysis of the pertinent rule in his "Reflections on Article 60 of the Vienna Convention on the Law of Treaties and its Background in General International Law", in: *Österreichische Zeitschrift für öffentliches Recht* (1970), pp. 5 *et seq.*). In this respect it is also of some interest that the Iranian-Iraqi Traité pour le Règlement Pacifique des Différends (...), to which we referred in footnote 42, was still in force in 1969 (*cf.* also Lauterpacht, *loc.cit.* (note 23), especially his footnote 70). As said, in Article 2 this Treaty provides for the compulsory settlement of disputes by the PCIJ/ICJ, at least for *non-territorial* disputes. There is no evidence that Iran has made any attempts to solve its disputes with Iraq – particularly those on navigational matters seem to be appropriate examples – by these means. See for a somewhat different view regarding the actual behaviour of the parties before the First World War, Wilson, A.T., *Persia*, London 1932, p. 124 (further: footnote 67, *infra*).

45. *UN Doc.* S/9190 of 1 May 1969 (reproduced in *ILM* (1969), pp. 489-492, at p. 490). In its Article II, the Protocol annexed to the 1937 Treaty, allowed an extension with one year (to be decided by common accord) of the period to conclude the convention (for Article II: see p. 18, *infra*). The Government of Iran did not agree to an extension of this period, because it would also mean an extension to the Iraqi privilege (see *idem*).

Moreover, in the Iranian view, the collected sums were not used, as the 1937 Treaty stipulates, for the maintainance, improvement, *etc.* of the Shatt.[46]

It is difficult to determine whether either of the two neighbouring states, and in particular Iraq, frustrated the conclusion of this convention to such an extent that Article 5 of the 1937 Tehran Treaty, or Article II of the Protocol annexed to it, has been materially breached. However, a decisive preliminary problem in that respect is the difficulty of reading a specific obligation of Iraq (or of Iran, for that matter) in the text of, in particular, Article II of the Protocol. The Articles do not contain more than a common engagement:

> 'Les Hautes Parties contractantes s'engagent à conclure la convention prévue à l'Article 5 du traité [the 1937 Treaty-HP] dans le courant d'une anneé à partir de l'entrée en vigueur du traité. Si malgré la diligence prodiguée par elles, cette convention ne venait pas à être conclue dans le courant de l'année, ce délai pourra être prolongé par accord commun des Hautes Parties contractantes.'[47]

Iran also complained about the character of the Treaty of Tehran. Because, at the time of its conclusion, Iraq was 'the protégé of the imperialist power in the region' Iran was pressed to accept 'the iniquitous boundary provisions of Articles I and II'.[48]

A similar argument is advanced in a declaration by the Iranian Government in the (Iranian) Senate, but there it is linked with the principle of *rebus sic stantibus*.[49] In view of the strict conditions for the applicability of this principle, and the generally accepted exception in respect to border treaties, this ground for unilateral termination of the 1937 Treaty does not seem sufficient.[50]

---

46. *Cf. idem.*

47. *LNTS* (1938), p. 244 (for the English translation, p. 258). Nevertheless, if a deliberate frustration by Iraq could conclusively be shown, it might be possible to construct an interesting case. Of course, here again, the argument with regard to the Traité pour le Règlement Pacifique, *etc.* might be applicable (see *op.cit.* (note 42)).

48. *UN Doc.* S/9190, p. 491. In the same letter: 'If this principle of equality was observed, how is it that the Talweg Line, or the median line principle, always recognized as the frontier line where a large river is the common frontier of two countries, has not been adhered to ...?' Although not entirely explicit, Iran uses an 'unequal treaty' argument here. Neither in the Law of Treaties, as a ground for the termination of a treaty, nor in international law, in general, has such an argument found much support (*cf.* O'Connell, D.P., *International Law*, 2nd ed., London 1970, p. 240). Moreover, such arguments are usually directed against the pressure exerted *by* the other party to the treaty, whereas here the pressure *on* the other party is at stake. Moreover, Kuhn's argument that the parties for a prolonged period of time behaved in accordance with the provisions of the treaty, is here also relevant (see, *supra* (note 44). In section III.C, *infra*, the question whether or not it is (or was, at the relevant period of time) mandatory for neighbouring states to delimit their common river boundary in accordance with the *Thalweg* (or median line) principle, will be answered negatively (on the Articles I and II, also, see section III.C).

49. In *ILM* (1969), pp. 481 *et seq.* an unofficial translation of this statement is given. *Cf.* pp. 483-484 for the appeal to *rebus sic stantibus*.

50. *Cf.* Kaikobad, *op.cit.* (note 1), pp. 85-87 (particularly p. 86) for a detailed analysis of this Iranian argument. Article 62(2)(a) of the Vienna Convention on the Law of Treaties is generally considered declaratory of International Law. See, *e.g.*, Sinclair, Sir Ian, *The Vienna Convention on the Law of Treaties*, Manchester 1984, pp. 192-196; Bastid, S., *Les traités dans la vie internationale: conclusions et effets*, Paris

In view of the documents available, and the facts known, the arguments Iran used for its unilateral denunciation of the 1937 Tehran Treaty, do not appear to be convincing in terms of international law and, hence, the Treaty cannot be considered as being terminated.

Remarkably shortly after the crisis of 1969, both states decided in 1975 on a new over-all agreement. The urgent need for Iraq to obtain Iranian co-operation in finding a solution to the Kurd rebellion is usually mentioned as the most important reason. In particular, at the end of 1974 the battle against the Kurds had developed into a deadly threat to the Iraqi Government.[51]

On the 6th of March, at the OPEC Summit meeting in Algiers after mediation by Algeria, a first agreement on principles was reached. Like the 1937 Tehran Treaty, this Algiers 'Communiqué Commun' in its first Article refers to the Constantinople Protocol and the Minutes of the Delimitation Commission. However, in the Communiqué the Parties do not confirm these documents as they did in the 1937 Treaty. In the first Article they agree '[D]e procéder à la démarcation définitive de leurs frontières *terrestres* sur la base du Protocole de Constantinople de 1913 ...' and the 1914 Minutes.[52]

Article 2 reveals the reason for this more limited reference to the 1913/1914 documents. Iran got its way on a very important point: it was agreed that the 'frontières fluviales' will now be drawn along the *Thalweg* (on this latter point: *infra*, section III.C).[53] In the 'Communiqué', the two states further undertook '... to exercise strict and effective control over the frontiers with a view to the complete cessation of all subversive infiltration from either side ...' They agreed to the establishment of a Mixed Iranian-Iraqi Commission to implement the decisions taken.[54]

This Mixed Commission consisted in fact of three Committees, established by a Protocol concluded 17 March 1975: 'le Comité chargé de la démarcation de la frontière terrestre', 'le Comité chargé de la délimitation de la frontière fluviale', and 'le Comité militaire'. Each of the three committees shall produce a final protocol. These three final Protocols constitute an indivisible whole. The Protocol of 17 March says in section IV:

'Les deux Parties concluront un traité sur la base du Communiqué d'Alger et des Protocoles susmentionnés (section III). Ces Protocoles, étant indivisibles et partie intégrante du Traité, seront signés en même temps que celui-ci.'

1985, pp. 211-212. Also: the International Court of Justice in its *Temple of Preah Vihear* decision (*ICJ Reports* 1962, pp. 34 *et seq.*). From the analysis by Anna Wyrozumska in "Treaties Establishing Territorial Regimes", in: *Polish Yearbook of International Law* (1986), pp. 251 *et seq.*, at pp. 263-264, some doubts on the general acceptance of Article 62(2)(a) can be inferred.

51. See, further, Dekker, I.F., and Post, H.H.G., "The Gulf War from the point of view of International Law", in: *NYIL* (1986), pp. 82-83, and the literature mentioned in the footnotes to these pages.

52. *United Nations Treaty Series* (further: *UNTS*) (1976), no. 14903, p. 118 (emphasis added).

53. For the text of the 'Communiqué', see *UNTS* (1976), no. 14903, p. 118, for the English translation: *idem*, p. 196.

54. In view of the criteria mentioned in Article 2(a) of the Vienna Convention on the Law of Treaties, there cannot be much doubt that the Communiqué is a treaty.

In the 'Procès-verbal' of 30 March 1975 of the Committee to Demarcate the Land Frontier, the Parties authenticated the minutes and maps of the 1914 Delimitation Commission and declared that these documents '... définit le tracé de la frontière terrestre entre l'Iran et l'Irak.'[55]

On the 13th of June 1975, Iran and Iraq, in Baghdad, concluded the 'Traité relatif à la Frontière et au Bon Voisinage entre l'Iran et l'Irak', which a year later, on 22 June 1976, entered into force.[56]

D   The 1975 Treaty of Baghdad

As was said above, in a Protocol of 17 March 1975, Iran and Iraq had, on the basis of the Algiers Communiqué, decided to conclude a Treaty and three Protocols annexed to it: on the Land Frontier, on the River Frontier, and on military (security) matters.[57] In Articles 1-3 of the Treaty, these three subjects are, indeed, mentioned, each with a reference to one of the three Protocols which contain the material provisions.[58]

In the 'Protocole relatif à la Délimitation de la Frontière Fluviale..,' the border in the Shatt-al-Arab is, as agreed in Algiers, delimited along the *Thalweg* (further, see *infra*, section III.D).

Article 1 of the 'Protocole relatif à la Redémarcation de la Frontière Terrestre...' mentions the following documents as those on which the re-demarcation of the *land* frontier is based: the 1913 Protocol of Constantinople and the Minutes of the 1914 Delimitation Commission, the 'Protocole de Téhran' of 17 March 1975 and three 'procès-verbaux' already referred to above.[59] Furthermore, Article 1 refers to a great number of maps indicating the frontier, constituting annex 2 to the Protocol as an integral part of it and superseding all existing maps.[60] The description of the land frontier (and the set of maps) show that the Parties have reached complete agreement. This agreement seems to include the parts of the land frontier which were a source of dispute up to that time. Moreover, the demarcation on location seems to have been

---

55. See for the texts of the 'Protocole' of 17 March 1975, and of three 'Procès-verbaux' of 30 March, 20 April and of 20 May 1975, *UNTS* (1976), pp. 119-134, and pp. 198-212 (for the English translation).

56. *Idem*, pp. 56 *et seq.*, and, for the English translation, pp. 135 *et seq.*

57. Section IV of the Protocol of 17 March 1975 (*cf.* (note 55), *supra*).

58. 'Protocole relatif à la Délimitation de la Frontière Fluviale...', *UNTS* (1976), at pp. 58 *et seq.* (the English translation at pp. 138 *et seq.*); 'Protocole relatif à la Redémarcation de la Frontière Terrestre...', at pp. 61 *et seq.* (the English translation at pp. 140 *et seq.*); the 'Protocole relatif à la Securité à la Frontière...', at pp. 111 *et seq.* (the English translation at pp. 190 *et seq.*). The Protocols are followed by Annexes.

59. Another document referred to, is a descriptive record of the land frontier dated 13 June 1975. It is added as Annex 1 to the Protocol (and constitutes an integral part of it). This Annex 1 was replaced by a similar description signed 21 December 1975 (reproduced in *UNTS* (1976), pp. 63 *et seq.*; the English translation is at pp. 142 *et seq.*). Finally, under Article 1(8) a document giving the co-ordinates of the frontier marks is listed (reproduced in *idem*, pp. 84 *et seq.*; the English translation is at pp. 162 *et seq.*).

60. The maps are inserted in a pocket at the end of 1017 *UNTS* (1976). They are not easily accessible without a good working knowledge of Arabic. Within a year, all these maps are supposed to be replaced by new maps '... sans que ceci préjudicie à la mise en vigueur du traité dont le présent Protocole fait partie intégrante' (Article 1(C) of the Protocol). Whether this has taken place is not clear from the documents published.

executed as well.[61] The disputes regarding the use of watercourses, mentioned *supra* (in section II.B), have legally been solved in one of the Treaties, concluded on 26 December 1975.[62] Finally, in Article 6 of the Protocol, the two Contracting Parties have agreed that the provisions of the Protocol '... règlent désormais toute question de frontière entre l'Iran et l'Iraq. Elles s'engagent solenellement sur cette base à respecter leur frontière commune et définitive.'

The 'Protocole relatif à la Securité à la Frontière...' aims to exercise a strict and effective control over the entire length of the common frontier 'en vue de la cessation de toutes infiltrations à caractère subversif'. To this avail the Parties have agreed on detailed measures of information and cooperation. For example, in Article 3 specific 'infiltration points' likely to be used by subversive elements have been identified. They are put under specific observation by the Parties. Furthermore, the handling of 'subversive persons' by the authorities is agreed upon. Although much broader in scope, in the 'Accord entre l'Iran et l'Irak concernant les Commissaires de Frontière' concluded 26 December 1975, Iran and Iraq have agreed on further measures regarding order and security in the frontier zones.[63]

Articles 4 and 5 of the Baghdad Treaty emphasize the finality and permanence of the provisions agreed upon; they confirm, in particular, that the course of the frontiers shall be inviolable, permanent and definitive. Moreover, Article 4 states that the provisions of the Protocols and their annexes '... constituent les éléments indivisibles d'un règlement global. Par voie de conséquence, toute atteinte à une des composantes

61. For example, once more, the frontier in Zohab is included in the demarcation; moreover, the dispute on Binawa Suta (Sarkushk), which Iraq complained about in 1935 (see *supra*, section II.B) has been agreed upon. The demarcation in the Kotur, the only issue the 1914 Commission had not solved, has now also taken place. Probably the demarcation also includes the marshy lands between marks no. 14A and 15, referred to in Article 1(B) of the Protocol as 'still to be completed'. The adaptation of the Description of the Land Frontier, signed 21 December 1975 (see *UNTS* (1976), gives no indication of the contrary, nor does a concluding 'Procès-verbal' of 26 December 1975 (*idem*, at pp. 110 or pp. 188-189), indicate any remaining difficulties of this sort.

62. The 'Accord entre l'Iran et l'Irak concernant l'Utilisation des Cours d'Eau Frontaliers', *UNTS* (1976), pp. 256-257, and, for the English translation, pp. 258-259, which entered into force 22 June 1976, says in its Article 2: 'Les deux Parties Contractantes sont convenues des dispositions suivantes: a) Partage en deux parts égales entre les deux pays des eaux du Bnava Souta, du Kourétou et du Guenguir. (...) b) Le partage entre les deux pays des rivières Alvend, Goudjan-Tchem, (*etc.*) se fera sur la base des procès-verbaux de la commission de délimitation frontalière irano-ottomane de 1914 et la coutume.' Disputes concerning the interpretation or application of the Agreement shall be settled according to the procedure of Article 6 of the 1975 Baghdad Treaty (see this section, *infra*).

63. For the text of this Agreement which entered into force on 22 June 1976, see *UNTS* (1976), pp. 216 *et seq.*, and p. 222 for the English translation. In particular, Article 6(II) and (III) seems relevant. Article 6(VIII) refers to investigations regarding frontier incidents and stipulates an extensive list of kinds of incidents. As a whole the agreement is an impressive attempt to maintain security and order in the frontier zones; in principle, the commissioners should have sufficient powers to perform their tasks, but, of course, the primary presumption for an effective execution of the agreement is good faith on either side. Remarkably enough, this Agreement does not contain a reference to Article 6 of the Baghdad Treaty (see this section, *infra*), or to any other 'closed' pacific dispute settlement clause. Disagreement, according to Article 19, shall be resolved 'par la voie diplomatique'.

de ce règlement global est, de toute évidence, incompatible avec l'esprit de l'accord d'Alger.'[64]

Article 6 – the last material Article of the June 1975 Treaty – is by far the longest Article of the Treaty. It is an elaborate, and above all conclusive, compromissory clause, which at the end of the year was made even more sophisticated by an 'Additif':

'1. En cas de différend relatif à l'interprétation ou à l'application du présent Traité, des trois Protocoles ou de leurs annexes, ce différend sera résolu dans le respect strict du tracé de la frontière irako-iranienne visé aux articles 1er et 2 ci-dessus ainsi que dans le respect du maintien de la sécurité à la frontière irako-iranienne conformément à l'article 3 ci-dessus.

2. Ce différend sera résolu par les Hautes Parties Contractantes en premier lieu, par voie de négociations bilatérales directes dans un délai de deux mois à partir de la date de la demande de l'une des Parties.

3. A défaut d'accord, les Hautes Parties Contractantes auront recours, pendant une période de trois mois, aux bons offices d'un Etat tiers ami.

4. En cas de refus de recours aux bons offices par l'une des deux Parties ou d'échec de la procédure de bons offices, et dans un délai n'excédant pas un mois à compter de la date du refus et de l'échec, le différend sera réglé par voie d'arbitrage.

5. En cas de désaccord des Hautes Parties Contractantes sur la procédure d'arbitrage, l'une des Hautes Parties Contractantes pourra avoir recours, dans les quinze jours de la constatation du désaccord, à un tribunal d'arbitrage. Pour la constitution du tribunal d'arbitrage et pour chaque différend à résoudre, chacune des Hautes Parties Contractantes désignera l'un de ses ressortissants comme arbitre et les deux arbitres choisiront un surarbitre. Si les Hautes Parties Contractantes ne désignent pas leur arbitre dans un délai d'un mois après que l'une des Parties aura reçu de l'autre la demande d'arbitrage, ou si les arbitres ne parviennent pas à un accord sur le choix du surarbitre avant l'expiration du même délai, la Haute Partie Contractante qui aura demandé l'arbitrage a le droit de prier le Président de la Cour Internationale de Justice de désigner les arbitres ou le surarbitre, conformément à la procédure de la Cour Permanente d'Arbitrage.

6. La décision du tribunal d'arbitrage a un caractère obligatoire et exécutoire pour les Hautes Parties Contractantes.

7. Les Hautes Parties Contractantes supportent chacune la moitié des frais d'arbitrage.'

ADDITIF

'... Le dernier passage du paragraphe 5 de l'article 6 du Traité susmentionné, savoir «conformément à la procédure de la Cour Permanente d'Arbitrager», sera supprimé et remplacé par les paragraphes suivants:

---

64. The Algiers Communiqué is further mentioned in the Preamble to the Baghdad Treaty: 'Considérant la volonté sincère des deux Parties, exprimée dans l'accord d'Alger en date du 6 mars 1975, de parvenir à une solution définitive et durable de tous les problèmes pendants entre les deux pays, ...'; and in the opening sentence of each of the Protocols: 'Conformément à ce qui a été décidé dans le communiqué d'Alger en date du 6 mars 1975, ...' (in the 'military/security' protocol, the sentence is somewhat differently phrased; there does not seem to be a difference in substance). Whether the Baghdad Treaty is thus really concluded 'on the basis' of the Algiers Communiqué (apart from on the basis of the Protocols – which is clear) seems debatable (*cf.* the Protocol of 17 March 1975, referred to above in the text and in note 55 and 57).

«Si le Président de la Cour Internationale de Justice est empêché ou s'il est ressortissant de l'une des Parties, la nomination des arbitres ou du surarbitre sera faite par le Vice-Président. Si celui-qui est empêché ou s'il est ressortissant de l'une des Parties, la nomination des arbitres ou du surarbitre sera faite par le membre le plus âgé de la Cour, qui n'est ressortissant d'aucune des Parties.

«Les Parties rédigeront un compromis déterminant l'objet du litige et la procédure à suivre.

«Faute de conclusion de compromis dans un délai de quinze jours à partir de la constitution du Tribunal, ou à défaut d'indications ou de précisions suffisantes dans le compromis concernant les points indiqués dans le paragraphe précédent, il sera fait application, si nécessaire, des dispositions de la Convention de la Haye du 18 October 1907 pour le règlement pacifique des conflits internationaux.

«Dans le silence du compromis ou à défaut de compromis, le Tribunal appliquera les règles de fond énumérées dans l'article 38 du Statut de la Cour Internationale de Justice.»

Le présent additif fait partie intégrante du Traité relatif à la frontière d'Etat et au Bon Voisinage entre l'Iran et l'Irak, signé le 13 Juin 1975 à Bagdad, et sera ratifié en même temps que ledit Traité.'[65]

III BOUNDARY AGREEMENTS; THE FRONTIER IN THE SHATT-AL-ARAB

This section will discuss the border agreements regarding the Shatt-al-Arab, as far as these agreements have not yet been analysed in the preceding chapter. The arrangements and conflicts in respect to navigational rights in the waterway which are linked to the agreements on the border, fall outside the limited scope of this paper.[66]

A The Treaty of Erzeroum

The agreement on the boundary in the Shatt-al-Arab, laid down in Article II of the 1847 Treaty and the subsequent quarrels about it, had to be discussed in section II.A, *supra*, because that conflict on the waterway in fact blocked the possibility for a legally definitive agreement on the remaining boundary issues. Although the immediate installation of a boundary commission, involving also Great Britain and Russia, as

65. *UNTS* (1976), p. 57 for the French text, and p. 137 for the English translation; for the 'additif', *idem*, pp. 114/5 and for the English translation, pp. 193-194. See for a short analysis of the Article and its addendum: Post, H.H.G., "Comments; with particular reference to the Gulf War", in: Soons, A.H.A. (ed.), *International Arbitration: Past and Prospects*, Dordrecht/Boston/London 1990, pp. 189-190 and 192-193. The 'additif' was signed on 26 December 1975, together with the 'Accord concernant les commissaires de Frontière', the 'Accord concernant les règles relatives à la navigation dans le Chatt-el-Arab', the 'Accord concernant la Transhumance', and the 'Accord concernant l'utilisation des cours d'eau frontaliers'. As did the Treaty of Baghdad (with Protocols and Annexes), all these instruments entered into force on 22 July 1976.

66. *Cf.* on navigational rights in the waterway, *e.g.*, Lauterpacht, *loc.cit.* (note 23), pp. 226-232, Gehrke and Kuhn, *op.cit.* (note 1), pp. 289 *et seq.*, for the period up to 1960. On the 1975 Treaty regime, *e.g.*, Momtaz, Djamchid, "Le Statut Juridique du Chatt El-Arab dans sa perspective historique", in: *Actualités Juridiques et Politique en Asie*, Paris 1988, p. 59, at pp. 62 *et seq.*

foreseen in the Articles III and IV of the Treaty, did take place, the commission's activities did not lead to a demarcation of (parts of) the Shatt-al-Arab boundary.

B   The 1911 and 1913 Protocols

The 1911 Teheran Protocol does not contain any specific reference to the Southern area of the border. However, in Article 3, the Treaty of Erzeroum is taken as the principal starting-point for the entire boundary settlement. This is, of course, also of decisive importance for the delimitation of the boundary in the Shatt-al-Arab.

The 1913 Protocol of Constantinople draws a boundary in the Shatt-al-Arab which, with a few exceptions, indeed seems to follow Article II of the Treaty of Erzeroum. It, again, provides for a border along the low water line of the waterway, on the Eastern – Iranian – bank.[67] Both the river, and all the islands in it are thus left to Turkey, however with the following exceptions: the island of Mouhalla and its two smaller islands, and the dependencies of Abadan (Khizr) Island – four islands between Chetaït and Massouiyé, and the islands opposite Mankouhi – are to be Persian.[68] The Protocol confirms the Persian possession of Mouhammara (Khorramshar), and solves the conflict – referred to above – on the location of the border around it, which arose soon after the conclusion of the Treaty of Erzeroum. It does so on the basis of a British-Turkish settlement reached in London, in 1913.[69] In this agreement the Turkish Government had already refrained from its claims to territory East of Mouhammara (Khorramshar), and had shown its satisfaction with a boundary running to the East of, and close to, that town.

The demarcation of the 1914 Delimitation Commission did not lead to great differences in respect of the principles set out in the Constantinople Protocol. In his analysis of the Commission's minutes for the Southern area, Prof. Lauterpacht only noticed a (limited) extension of the Persian sector of the Shatt-al-Arab facing the town of Muhammara (Khorramshar) as far as the middle of the river (*medium filum aquae*).[70]

C   The 1937 Treaty of Tehran

As was mentioned above, after the First World War, with increasing pressure, Iran took the position that the border in the Shatt-al-Arab should be drawn on the basis of the

---

67. Despite this arrangement, Wilson reported that: '... jurisdiction of all kinds on the Shatt (up to the point where both banks were in the possession of Turkey) was jointly shared, the *medium filum aquae* being regarded as the boundary, notwithstanding the Treaty of 1847', in: Wilson, *op.cit.* (note 44), p. 124. According to Wilson, complete control over the waterway was really exercised from Bhagdad (in fact, Basra) during the British occupation from 1918.

68. Moreover, what could be called accretions or potential accretions to Abadan Island or to the *terra firma* below Nhar Nazaïlé, also belonged to Persia (Protocol of Constantinople Article I(a)(3)).

69. See Kaikobad's detailed report on this settlement – which, as such, of course had no binding force for Persia – signed in London on 29 July 1913, *op.cit.* (note 1), at pp. 31-35. The text is reproduced in Gehrke and Kuhn, *op.cit.* (note 1), 'Dokumentenanhang', pp. 67-68 (Doc. 26).

70. Lauterpacht, *loc.cit.* (note 23), p. 213.

Thalweg. In the Iranian view, as laid down before the War, the border did not reflect the increasing practice of states to choose the *Thalweg* in the case of a navigable river.

From the point of view of international law, the *Thalweg* usually refers to the ideal shipping route from the point of navigation.[71] The increase in shipping traffic to the Iranian oil port of Abadan in particular, led to frequent and serious friction between the neighbouring states on the implementation by Iraq of its shipping and customs regulations. Although the – rather belated – recognition by Iran of the new State of Iraq made a resumption of negotiations on the Shatt-al-Arab issues possible, only provisional agreements were the result. After the serious incidents in 1933 and 1934 in the Shatt-al-Arab, the debates following the Iraqi complaint to the League of Nations centered on the boundary dispute in the waterway. To the basic Iranian point of view that there existed no valid legal agreement on the boundary in the Shatt and that, as a consequence, the *Thalweg* principle was mandatory in such a situation (see section II.B, *supra*), Iraq replied with two arguments.

In the first place, the Iraqi representative, Nuri As-Said, declared that Iraq considered the border in the Shatt-al-Arab as laid down in the Treaty of Erzeroum, to be correct and not open to interpretation. A fundamental reason for this point of view was that from 1848 to 1914 both Parties had conducted themselves in accordance with the relevant provisions of the Treaty, and not as if the Treaty prescribed a *Thalweg* boundary.[72]

Second, Nuri As-Said did not deny that the *Thalweg* principle was often applied, but he added that the principle did not express a universally binding rule which could remove the obligations arising from a treaty.

Due to the lack of an authoritative study of international practice (in particular for the post-World War II period) and of relevant international jurisprudence, the question what international legal significance – in various sensitive phases of the conflict – the *Thalweg* principle has, is still difficult to answer conclusively.[73] In the literature the view seems to prevail that there are grounds for a rule of international customary law

---

71. For a survey of various descriptions of the *Thalweg* principle, *cf.*, *e.g.*, Lauterpacht, *loc.cit.* (note 23), pp. 216 *et seq.*, or Bouchez, L.J., "The fixing of boundaries in international boundary rivers", in: *International and Comparative Law Quarterly* (1963), pp. 793-795.

72. However, in practice, apparently a kind of *modus vivendi* between Persian and Turkish officials was maintained, until the British occupation of 1918. From that time on, complete control was exercised from Basra (see, Wilson, *op.cit.* (note 44)).

73. The principle has played some role in arbitrations, but the tribunals refrained from declarations on principle. In the British Guiana-Brazil Boundary arbitration (*BFSP* (1904), p. 930) and the North Eastern Boundary arbitration (Moore's *International Arbitrations*, vol. I, p. 127), the tribunals merely applied the principle. See for a survey of relevant municipal jurisprudence: Kaikobad, *op.cit.* (note 1), pp. 79-84, and for examples of state practice, *idem*, pp. 84-85.

stating that if no relevant treaty rule is applicable, the *Thalweg* rule applies.[74] Kaikobad is even more careful, when he concludes:

> 'The *Thalweg* doctrine is applicable only in certain circumstances, and one of these circumstances, apart, of course, from incidents of express agreement between the parties, is a situation in which neither of the parties can adduce evidence in the form either of a Treaty, municipal instruments acquiescence, or otherwise, regarding the location of the line in a navigable river.'[75]

In which other circumstances the rule applies does not become clear from this text. However, on one thing Kaikobad is very clear: the *Thalweg* rule in boundary rivers '... is not an absolute principle, that is, a 'rule' to be followed whenever a navigable river separates two or more states.'[76] The opposite view, that the rule has a mandatory ('cogent') character, does not find support in the doctrine.[77]

In the early thirties, the position of Iran seems to be that the *Thalweg* principle is a rule of customary law, applicable if there is no treaty in force stipulating a different mode of delimitation (see *supra*, section II.B). Hence, preliminary to the examination of the validity of this principal view of Iran is the question whether, at the time, all preceding written agreements were no longer in force. The Iranian evidence provided in the League of Nations debate does not sufficiently appear to support the thesis that all relevant treaty regimes are non-applicable (not validly concluded, or null and void).

Later, in 1969, the Iranian position is less clear on this matter (see section II.C, *supra*). However, it seems that Iran hints at the mandatory status of the principle. As just said, there is insufficient support in international law for such a status for the *Thalweg* principle.

The 1937 Treaty of Tehran does contain some changes in the boundary in the Shatt-al-Arab. After the confirmation in its first Article of the validity of the 1913 Constantinople Protocol and of the Minutes of the meetings of the 1914 Delimitation

---

74. In his 1960 *ICLQ* contribution (*loc.cit.* (note 23), pp. 208 *et seq.*), Professor Lauterpacht is not very clear. Following his analysis of the *Thalweg* doctrine, where he refers to the attribution of the river in part to each of the riparian states, he says, without further explanation, that such a solution is '... incorporated in the relevant rule of customary international law ...' (at p. 234). Bouchez, *loc.cit.* (note 71), p. 799, takes the same viewpoint: 'Although there is no predominating principle like the freedom of the seas, it is clear from the practice of states that the *Thalweg* boundary is a generally applied principle for rivers in which navigation is an important factor, while the median line has been frequently applied to all other rivers.'

75. Kaikobad, *op.cit.* (note 1), p. 83. Why he mentions 'municipal laws' next to acquiescence, and what is meant by 'otherwise', does not become clear from the text. A few pages earlier, he says, more bluntly: 'In general terms, the principle is that, in the absence of an agreement or evidence to the contrary, wherever a navigable river divides the territories of two (or more) states, the boundary lies, or is to be drawn, along the *Thalweg* of the river' (*idem*, p. 78). The problem with all these statements, however sensible or even probable they are, is that they are not based on an adequate survey of state practice.

76. *Idem*.

77. *Cf.* Gehrke and Kuhn (*op.cit.* (note 1), p. 293): 'Die gewohnheitsrechtliche Regel, bei Grenzflüssen bilde der Talweg die Grenzlinie, ist nirgends in der völkerrechtlichen Literatur zu solchen zwingenden Normen gezählt worden' (... has nowhere in the international legal literature been included among such mandatory norms – translation HP).

Commission, Article 2 lays down a change in the Shatt-al-Arab boundary. South of Abadan, for a distance of five kilometers, the border is no longer to be the low water line on the Iranian bank, but will be the *Thalweg*. Although Article 2 seems to give a rather detailed description of this change in the border, Article 1 of the Protocol annexed to the 1937 Treaty still forsees the definitive determination by a 'commission d'experts' composed of an equal number of members from each Party. However, neither this Article 1 nor the other provisions of the Protocol were executed.[78]

In Article 2 of the Algiers 'Communiqué Commun' of March 1975, Iran and Iraq adopted quite a different basis for their common river frontiers. Whereas in the 1937 Tehran Treaty only 5 kilometers of the Shatt were delimited along the *Thalweg*, now they decided plainly to '... délimiter leurs frontières fluviales selon la ligne du *Thalweg*; ...' This decision meant that the frontier in the Shatt-al-Arab had to be completely re-demarcated.[79] A Committee was installed 'chargé de la délimitation de la frontière fluviale.' The work of this Committee was to be laid down in one of the three final Protocols which, together with the Algiers Communiqué, should provide the basis for a Treaty.[80]

D   The 1975 Treaty of Baghdad

Article 2 of the June 1975 Treaty refers, indeed, to the 'Protocole relatif à la Délimitation de la Frontière Fluviale...' for the material provisions on that subject. Article 2(1) of this Protocol says: 'La ligne frontière dans le Chatt-El-Arab suit le *Thalweg*', defined here as 'la ligne médiane du chenal principal navigable au plus bas niveau de navigabilité.'[81] Article 2(2) deals with the consequences of changes in the main navigable channel. In accordance with prevalent legal doctrine, one may say, the parties agree that in the case of changes brought about by natural causes, the frontier line shall vary with the changes in the main channel. The frontier line shall not be affected by other changes (unless the Parties agree differently).[82] Articles 2(4) and 2(5) contain more specific provisions on changes to the bed of the Shatt brought about by natural causes. If substantial changes (specified in the Article) take place, they shall *not* change the course of the frontier line.[83]

---

78. *Cf.* Gehrke and Kuhn, *op.cit.* (note 1), pp. 248 *et seq.*, particularly, p. 251 and p. 255, for unsuccessful initiatives to break this deadlock.

79. Some parts of the border are formed by non-navigable rivers. There, as is common, the border is delimited by the mid-channel (*cf.* the descriptive record of the land frontier, referred to in footnote 59).

80. *Cf. UNTS* (1986), no. 14903, pp. 121-122 (English translation at pp. 199-200).

81. The river frontier in the Shatt-al-Arab is represented by a line drawn on four hydrographic charts annexed to the Protocol (and forming an integral part thereof – see Article 1(3)). In Article 5, the Parties agree that a new survey shall be carried out once every ten years, effective from the date of signature of the Protocol.

82. *Cf.* the decision of the arbitral tribunal in the *Chamizal* case, published, *e.g.*, in: *American Journal of International Law* (1911), pp. 782 *et seq.*, at p. 785.

83. Article 2(5) is a rather elaborate arrangement on the re-direction of the waters in such a case. An interesting point in respect to the provisions in Articles 2(2) to 2(5) may be how to determine whether there is a change in the bed of the waterway or a change in the navigable channel. It may be assumed that if the change in the bed is caused by other than natural causes, the frontier line is not affected.

IV   THE CURRENT IRANIAN-IRAQI BORDER REGIME

After the preceding sections, it should be possible to be relatively brief in an assessment of the present border regime. The decisive question, after all, is whether – despite the behaviour of the Parties – the 1975 Treaty 'system' is still in force. If the 1975 agreements are no longer in force, does in that case a preceding agreement (from 1913/4, or 1937) determine the legal border – as Iraq has argued?

Although these questions are in a sense quite formidable, our attempts to answer, are facilitated greatly by the existing literature to which it is not necessary to add very much.[84] Moreover, we will focus on the arguments which the Iraqi and Iranian Governments communicated to the United Nations, and, as in the rest of this chapter, leave questions of evidence largely aside. Finally, the difficult issues arising from the application of the Law of Treaties rules on termination and denunciation of agreements will not be dealt with exhaustively.

A   Unilateral termination of the 1975 Treaty 'system'

The June 1975 Treaty has no explicit provision on its termination or denunciation. However, according to Article 56(1) of the Vienna Convention on the Law of Treaties, denunciation is nonetheless allowed, if 'a. it is established that the parties intended to admit the possibility of denunciation (...); or b. a right of denunciation (...) may be implied by the nature of the treaty.'[85] The dispute concerning the matter of the abrogation of the Baghdad Treaty *materially* seems to come down to the question of whether or not one of the rules laid down in Article 56(1) is applicable.

Already on 17 September 1980 – five days before the date that is usually taken as the beginning of the Gulf War[86] – the Government of Iraq announced that the June 1975 Treaty of Baghdad (and its Protocols) and the four additional Treaties of December 1975 were null and void. According to Iraq this was caused by '... their

84. *Cf.* Paul Tavernier's "Le conflit frontalier entre l'Irak et l'Iran et la guerre du Chatt-el-Arab", in: *ARES; Défense et Sécurité* (1981), pp. 333 *et seq.*, also his "Les accords d'Alger et de Bagdad de 1975; sont-ils encore en vigueur?", paper to be published in: *The Iranian Journal of International Affairs* (1990), xeroxed copy; furthermore: Kaikobad, *op.cit.* (note 1), pp. 93-115, and Dekker and Post, *loc.cit.* (note 51), *supra*, pp. 83-89.

85. *Cf.* Article 56(1)(A) of the 1969 Vienna Convention on the Law of Treaties. Neither Iran, although it signed the Convention on 23 May 1969, nor Iraq are Parties. However, the provisions mentioned are generally considered to be rules of international customary law. Moreover, both Iraq and Iran, although unofficially, have invoked Articles from the Convention (see, *e.g.*, in the case of Iran: *A review of the imposed war*, Tehran 1983, pp. 138 *et seq.*)

86. However, Iraq holds that the 'real' day the war began is 4 September 1980. See for an analysis of the chronology of events: P. Tavernier, "Les Problèmes de Responsabilité Internationale et la Guerre du Golfe", in: *Thesaurus Acroasium*, vol. XX (session 1989), to be published, pp. 14-15 (xeroxed version).

violation by the Government of the Islamic Republic of Iran by word and deed ...'[87] In a letter to the Secretary-General of the United Nations, dated 27 October 1980, Iraq states that as regards border agreements: '... there is no longer any border agreement between the two countries with the exception of the Protocol for the Delimitation of the Turco-Persian Frontiers signed in 1913, the views of Iran and Iraq regarding that Protocol notwithstanding.'[88]

The most important of Iran's violations, in Iraq's view, concern two of the Protocols annexed to the June 1975 Baghdad Treaty. In the first place, Iran was accused of not having fulfilled its obligations under the 'Land Frontier' Protocol by constantly delaying the implementation of measures for the return to Iraq of territory which had unjustly been occupied.[89] Second, Iran had allowed Kurd leaders and their followers to enter and, in addition, Iran had permitted them to operate within Iraq. The 'Security' Protocol was meant to prevent such infiltrations.[90] However, the Iraqi Government does not explicitly base its denunciation of the 1975 Treaty system on these (alleged) breaches.[91] According to Iraq, the Iranian activities *together* amount to a violation of Article 4 of the June 1975 Baghdad Treaty, notably of its last sentence, which reads: 'Par voie de conséquence, toute atteinte à une des composantes de ce règlement global est, de toute évidence, incompatible avec l'esprit de l'accord d'Alger.'[92] As, in the Iraqi view, this agreement and the Treaty with its Protocols and Annexes are indivisible elements, these latter instruments are also rendered 'null and void'.

In view of the rather rigorous consequences Iraq draws from the alleged violations by Iran, it is remarkable that in the text of Article 4, 'indivisibility' does not include the

87. *UN Doc.* S/14272, Annex 1. Also: 'Résolution Irakienne relative à la Résiliation de l'Accord d'Alger signe entre l'Irak et l'Iran' of the same day, which probably provides the basis to this letter (reproduced as Annex X at p. 164, in: A. Benabdallah, *La Question du Chatt el-Arab*, Montreal 1982). See the Iraqi letter dated 21 September 1980 to the Secretary-General of the United Nations (*UN Doc.* S/14191) for a statement of alleged Iranian violations. It is not immediately clear why Iraq uses the phrase 'null and void' here, a rather uncommon terminology in respect of the termination or denunciation of treaties.

88. *UN Doc.* S/14236. This viewpoint is somewhat surprising, because so far Iraq seemed always to consider the 1937 Tehran Treaty as in force and binding. However, as this Treaty confirms the validity of the 1913 Protocol (and the 1914 'minutes'), the material differences are limited to, *e.g.*, the (small) changes the 1937 Treaty stipulates – in Iran's favour! – in the boundary in the Shatt (further, see *supra*, section III.C).

89. This concerns an area of approximately 120 sq.km. at Zain al-Qos; *cf.* Amin, S.H., "The Iran-Iraq Conflict: legal implications", 31 *ICLQ* (1982), pp. 167 *et seq.*, at p. 179, or Hünseler, P., *Der Irak und sein Konflikt mit Iran* Bonn 1982, pp. 69-70. For a report on the situation on location before the 1975 agreements (with a map): see *UN Doc.* S/11291, with annex, of 20 May 1974. See, also, Tavernier, "Le conflit frontalier entre l'Irak et l'Iran et la guerre du Chatt-el-Arab", *loc.cit.* (note 84), p. 345.

90. There had been incidents of this nature between the two states since the beginning of 1980. See Amin, *loc.cit.* (note 89), pp. 167-168; also *UN Doc.* S/14020 (letter from Iraq to the Secretary-General of the United Nations).

91. In a note dated 16 November 1980 to the Embassy of the Islamic Republic of Iran at Baghdad (in *UN Doc.* S/14272, as Annex 2), Iraq accuses Iran of persistent breaches of the June 1975 Baghdad Treaty, among others, through Iran's violation of its essential elements. And, further on: 'The escalation of Iranian aggression against Iraq by the launching of an undeclared war against frontier posts, the shelling of Iraqi towns and interference in the internal affairs of Iraq is cogent proof of Iran's clear refusal to be bound by the afore-mentioned Treaty.'

92. *UNTS* (1976), p. 57 (see for the English translation: p. 137).

Algiers 'Communiqué Commun', but 'only' applies to the June 1975 Treaty, its Protocols and its Annexes. As was mentioned above, the Algiers Agreement was not given a very prominent place in this Treaty (see, *supra*, section II.D).

Kaikobad and Tavernier have rightly pointed to the fact that Article 4 of the June Baghdad Treaty – or, we may add, any of the other relevant provisions – does not state which consequences 'incompatibility with the spirit of the Algiers agreement', would have.[93] If the consequences could be as farreaching as Iraq declares, some reference thereto might be expected.

In view of the 'territorial nature' of the Baghdad Treaty, the Iraqi interpretation is not too likely either.[94] In several codifications of International Law, such treaties have obtained a specially protected status.[95] More or less on that basis, it is argued that under general international law, this status is in fact even broader (the doctrine of continuity and finality of boundaries).[96] However, a general rule regarding the finality of boundaries is probably still *de lege ferenda*. Nevertheless, considering Article 56(1)(b) of the 1969 Vienna Convention, the doctrine contributes to the view that in any event the broad Iraqi interpretation of the 'territorial' June 1975 Baghdad Treaty, must be rejected.

Apart from denying the Iraqi allegations and rejecting the consequences the Government in Baghdad draws, Iran makes quite clear that it never intended to admit the possibility of denunciation in the Treaty of Baghdad. In its first communications to the Security Council after the outbreak of hostilities, the Government in Tehran explicitly insists on the applicability of Article 6 of the Treaty.[97] In addition, Iran denies that it terminated the Treaty and emphasizes that the June 1975 Baghdad Treaty does not allow for unilateral termination. On the contrary, such termination is expressly prohibited and Iran claims that all the agreements referred to by Iraq as null and void, are still in force and binding.[98]

---

93. The essential terminology is, anyway, rather vague and obscure. Kaikobad, *op.cit.* (note 1), pp. 97-98, or Tavernier, *loc.cit.* (note 8), at p. 8. In his excellent study – conceived at the very beginning of the War – "Le conflit frontalier entre l'Irak et l'Iran et la guerre du Chatt-el-Arab", loc.cit. (note 84), at pp. 347-351, this argument is not yet presented.

94. *Cf.* Article 56(1)(b) of the 1969 Vienna Convention on the Law of Treaties, and *Yearbook of the ILC* (1966), vol. II, p. 250 for the commentary to that article (which at the time was still Article 53). The ILC commentary already singled out 'treaties fixing a territorial boundary', although Article 53 did not yet refer to the 'nature' of the treaty. This addition was inserted at the 1968 Governmental Conference in Vienna (*cf.* *UN Doc.* A/Conf.39/C.1/L.311).

95. *Cf., e.g.*, Article 62 of the 1969 Vienna Convention on the Law of Treaties, or the Articles 11 and 12 of the 1978 Vienna Convention on Succession of States in respect of Treaties.

96. Notably, Kaikobad, K.H., "Some observations on the doctrine of continuity and finality of boundaries", in: *BYIL* (1983), pp. 119 *et seq.*, but see, in particular, his careful conclusions at pp. 136-137 (also: Wyrozumska, *loc.cit.* (note 50), pp. 251-252).

97. *Cf. UN Doc.* S/14249 of 10 November 1980, and S/14274 of 26 November 1980. In the context of his interesting study mentioned in the preceding footnote, Kaikobad would be among those tempted to agree with the Iranian point of view (see, also Tavernier, "Les Accords d'Alger...", *loc.cit.* (note 84), at pp. 9 and 10).

98. *Cf. UN Doc.* S/14249; further, on this matter, Dekker and Post, *loc.cit.* (note 51), pp. 86-87.

In view of the arguments mentioned above, the justification which Iraq presented to the United Nations, for its attitude with regard to the June 1975 Baghdad Treaty, does not seem to be tenable under international law. However, other grounds for the possible termination of the Treaty can be read or seen as implied in the Iraqi letters.

The most important of them is probably the allegation that Iran committed (several) important violations of rules of the Baghdad Treaty, or better of its protocols. Whether indeed these violations occurred, is, of course, in the first place a matter of evidence. Moreover, they must have been of a (very) serious nature so as to amount to a 'material' breach, a criterium which is not too easily fulfilled.[99]

Very important, also in this respect, is the specific position of Article 6 of the Baghdad Treaty. As pointed out above this Article (and its 'additif') contains a conclusive settlement of disputes procedure. If either state begins the proceedings under Article 6, the other cannot block the procedures for the settlement of disputes laid down in the Article. In this light, the system of responses to violations of treaties as defined in Article 60 of the 1969 Vienna Convention should be seen as a *lex generalis*, from which states can deviate by specific provisions *inter se*.[100] Article 60(4) expresses this possibility in the following terms: 'The foregoing paragraphs are without prejudice to any provision in the treaty applicable in the event of a breach.'

In any case, it is noteworthy that in a letter dated 25 November 1980, the permanent UN representative of Iraq emphatically denied that Iraq *unilaterally* had terminated the Treaty.[101]

It seems, indeed, most likely, following the Iranian argument, that the Parties intended the elaborate disputes settlement clause of Article 6 of the Baghdad Treaty, precisely for the kind of disputes and violations Iraq refers to. Is Iraq perhaps even obliged under international law to settle its disputes with Iran on the basis of Article 6, to the exclusion of other means? Although it would go much too far to discuss the intricacies of an answer to this difficult legal question, it does seem to be feasible to present a strong case for such an obligation on the part of Iraq.[102]

In a letter of 25 November 1980, Iraq denies that the Article is applicable. For this viewpoint, it makes use of the argument which was discussed above: the application of Article 6 presupposes the continued existence of the Treaty through the non-violation of any of its indivisible elements.[103] In a later letter, of 10 March 1981 to the Secretary-General, Iraq repeated this argument, but added: 'Article 6, in other words, could only operate when (...) the parties disagree on the interpretation or application of

---

99. *Cf.* the discussion in Dekker and Post, *loc.cit.* (note 51), pp. 88-89 (and the references). In its Commentary to Article 60 (then still Article 57), the ILC warned specifically against termination on the basis of mere allegations of a material breach (*Yearbook of the ILC* (1966), vol. II, pp. 254-255).

100. *Cf.* Simma, *loc.cit.* (note 44), p. 82; also Sinclair, *op.cit.* (note 50), p. 188.

101. *Cf. UN Doc.* S/14272.

102. It is evident that some courses of action, like full scale military operations, are excluded for other reasons. The really complicated issue is whether other kinds of 'countermeasures' are also excluded (see the remarks in Dekker and Post, *loc.cit.* (note 51), pp. 87-88). Tavernier seems to support the view that Iraq is under an obligation to apply the regime of Article 6 (see, his "Les Accords d'Alger...", *loc.cit.* (note 84), at p. 10).

103. *Cf. UN Doc.* S/14272.

technical details thereof.'[104] This restrictive interpretation is very difficult to accept, in the first place because the text of the Treaty gives no indication for such a view. Moreover, the (public) history of the Treaty reveals no intention to attribute such a limited significance to Article 6. The care of the Parties in drawing up the clause (*e.g.* the addition of the 'Additif' of 26 December 1975) and the reference to Article 6 in three of the four 'additional' Treaties of December 1975, reinforces that conclusion.[105]

Other grounds for termination or denunciation that are not explicitly used by Iraq and might be construed from the official Iraqi communications have either been discussed above or – satisfactorily – in the literature,[106] or seem very remote, indeed, from legally acceptable grounds for termination.[107] In any case, all these potential arguments await much more elaboration.

On the basis of the available documents, the unilateral denunciation by Iraq at the time of the outbreak of hostilities in September 1980 of the Treaty of Baghdad of 13 June 1975 , cannot be seen as valid.

B   Termination of the December 1975 Agreements

It should not be assumed too readily that *all* the 1975 Iranian-Iraqi agreements (the 1975 Treaty 'system') have been terminated or are still in force. The December 1975 'additional' agreements, *e.g.*, must be analysed on their own merits, apart from the June 1975 Baghdad Treaty to which they are more or less directly linked.

From the analysis in the preceding section, the Iraqi arguments to denounce the June 1975 Treaty of Baghdad did not appear adequate and sufficient. It is even more difficult to base the termination of at least three of the four Agreements of December 1975,[108] on the official Iraqi argument for their denunciation. The 'Accord concernant les commissaires de frontière', the 'Accord concernant les règles relatives à la navigation..' and the 'Accord concernant l'utilisation des cours d'eau frontaliers', refer only in their preambulary sentences to 'the spirit of the Algiers Agreement', whereas the 'Accord concernant la transhumance' has no reference whatsoever to the March 1975 Algiers 'Communiqué Commun'.

---

104. *UN Doc.* S/14401 (emphasis added).

105. See, further, Tavernier, "Les Accords d'Alger...", *loc.cit.* (note 84), at pp. 10-11; and Post, in: Soons (ed.), *International Arbitration...*, *loc.cit.* (note 65), p. 189.

106. It is possible to argue – with Tavernier in his "Les Accords d'Alger...", *loc.cit.* (note 84), at p. 5 – that Iraq invokes the *exceptio non-adimpleti contractus*, because it alleges that Iran would have profited from the Protocol on fluvial borders, while at the same time committing violations of the other two Protocols of the June 1975 Baghdad Treaty. See on this argument when employed by Iran *against* Iraq, *supra*, section II.C (Tavernier's reference to Article 42(2) of the 1969 Vienna Convention, *idem* on page 5, however, does not seem adequate. This article is certainly not a reflection of a rule of customary law – neither is Article 65, mentioned on the same page).

107. It is, *e.g.*, difficult to see how the Iraqi appeal to its 'historical' rights on the Shatt-al-Arab could be of any legal significance here (*cf*. Kaikobad, *op.cit.* (note 1), pp. 93-94, and, in particular, his conclusion on p. 95 rejecting the legal relevance of such an argument in this case).

108. *Cf.* for these four agreements: *UNTS* (1976), vol. 1017, nos. 14904-14907.

In the meantime, two of these agreements are (probably) terminated anyhow. The Agreement concerning Transhumance was concluded for a period of five years, and is not renewable (Article 17). The Frontier Commissioners Agreement was also concluded for five years, but is renewable by tacit agreement, unless the Parties, with six months advance notice, request denunciation or review (Article 20). Whatever the actual Iraqi reason for doing so, it may be assumed that the official Iraqi argument for its denunciation can be interpreted as a valid request thereto under Article 20 of the Agreement. Unless Iran and Iraq in the meantime have decided differently, the Frontier Commissioners Agreement, like the Agreement concerning Transhumance, terminated on 22 June 1981, five years after its entry into force.

The Navigation Agreement has no provisions regarding duration or denunciation. However, due to its object and purpose, it is reasonable to conceive the Agreement as inseparably linked to the River Frontier Protocol.[109] Hence if the June 1975 Treaty (and its Protocols) should be terminated, either Party seems to have the right to terminate or suspend the operation of the Navigation Agreement on the basis of its impossibility to perform.[110] However, if the Iraqi arguments for the denunciation of the June Treaty are rejected, the Navigation Agreement should be considered as being still in force (although its operation, for the time being, is suspended).[111]

The Agreement concerning the use of Frontier Watercourses does not provide for duration or denunciation either. Moreover, its relationship to the June 1975 Baghdad Treaty is much more remote than in the case of the Navigation Agreement. Virtually all the waters the Agreement deals with were in the same territory before and after the entry into force of the June 1975 Treaty's Land Frontiers Protocol. Hence, whereas there is a possible link between the Iraqi argument and the Navigation Agreement, that line of reasoning does not hold for the termination of this latter agreement. It cannot be considered terminated on the basis of the Iraqi unilateral denunciation.

C   War and the 1975 Treaty 'system'

Hostile relations or even all-out war, do not automatically terminate all treaties in force between the parties to a conflict. However, the relevant international law is complicated, and the outcome depends in the first place on the nature of the treaty. The Agreements concluded in 1975 have no explicit provisions regarding the effects of armed conflict between the Parties, but the definitive character of the boundaries is stressed (Article 5 of the June Baghdad Treaty). Moreover, Kaikobad rightly concludes

---

109. The Navigation Agreement is based on the division of the Shatt-al-Arab according to the *Thalweg* principle, as provided by the June Treaty and Protocol. If the Treaty is terminated, this basis no longer exists (unless, *e.g.*, an agreement on a partial division of the Shatt were to replace it; in that case the Agreement may retain – part of – its object and purpose).

110. *Cf.*, the Vienna Convention on the Law of Treaties, Article 61(1), which is generally considered to be declaratory of international law (*cf. Yearbook of the ILC* (1966), vol. II, p. 256). Of course, this possibility to terminate or suspend is different from the Iraqi stance that the Agreement is rendered 'null and void'.

111. That is, as long as the Shatt-al-Arab remains obstructed for all shipping, as it was since the beginning of the Gulf War (*cf.* Article 61(1), last sentence, of the 1969 Vienna Convention).

that there seems to be general agreement in the literature '... that boundary agreements are recognized as belonging to that category of treaties which are not annulled upon the occurrence of war between two or more states.'[112]

It can be considered 'classic' international law, indeed, that such agreements are suspended in relevant respects for the duration of the War, but remain valid (until the Parties decide otherwise). Both relevant jurisprudence and – at least – relevant examples of post-World War II state practice seem to confirm this general rule. Moreover, in modern international law, there is general support for the view that even if a war is the outcome of the legitimate use of force, '... *unilateral* changes in the status of a territory are to be regarded as unlawful.'[113] Article 2(4) of the United Nations Charter which obliges member states to refrain from the threat or use of force against the territorial integrity or political independence of states, in this respect, of course, has been of decisive importance.[114]

Although war and hostile relations in general have an important impact on the factual situation at the borders of the states involved, they do not have as a consequence the abrogation of the Parties' boundary rights, included those laid down in the relevant treaties. Hence, it may be concluded that for Iraq and Iran the Baghdad Treaty of 13 June 1975, with its Protocols and Annexes, is still in force.

D   Negotiations since the 1988 cease-fire

Iran and Iraq are free to conclude new agreements regarding the subject matter covered in the 1975 Agreements. According to Article 59 of the 1969 Vienna Convention, such agreements shall be considered as terminated, if 'a. it appears from the later treaty or is otherwise established that the parties intended that the matter should be governed by that treaty; or b. the provisions of the later treaty are so far incompatible with those of the earlier one that the two treaties are not capable of being applied at the same time.'[115] It is not very likely that Iran and Iraq will go as far as the conclusion of an entirely new boundary regime. However, an agreement on certain changes in the 1975 Treaty 'system' cannot be excluded.

After the cease-fire of August 1988, negotiations in different forms between the two neighbouring states on more definitive solutions to their dispute have been undertaken. However, it was not until the Iraqi military action in Kuwait of 2 August 1990 that these negotiations seemed to gain a new momentum. In a letter dated 14 August 1990, the Iraqi Government declared that it will withdraw its 'forces opposing you along the borders'.[116] In a letter dated 23 August 1990, the Iraqi foreign minister, Tariq Aziz,

---

112. Kaikobad, *op.cit.* (note 1), p. 100 (in particular the references he gives).

113. *Idem*, p. 108.

114. It would lead much too far, here, to analyse this subject matter in any depth. Moreover, Kaikobad has already undertaken an important study of the relevant issues. We can agree with his major conclusions (*cf. idem*, pp. 99-115, especially at pp. 114-115).

115. Article 59 is generally considered in substance to reflect customary law (*cf., e.g.,* Brownlie, I., *Principles of Public International Law*, 4th ed., Oxford 1990, p. 617).

116. *UN Doc.* S/21528.

announced that the Iraqi withdrawal had, indeed, been completed in conformity with Security Council Resolution 598 (1987), *i.e.*, 'to the internationally recognized boundaries'.[117]

With regard to the border issue, Iraq in the same letter stated that it was now prepared to agree to an Iranian proposal dated 8 August 1990 'to the effect that the 1975 Accord should be used as a basis.' This may signify a willingness to accept that (some of ?) the 1975 Agreements have remained in force. The Iranian Minister of Foreign Affairs, at least, believes so. On 17 August, he responded to the Iraqi letter by stating that the President of Iraq 'declared Iraq's renewed commitment to the 1975 Treaty of State Frontier and Neighborly Relations between Iran and Iraq.'[118] However, the documents that have so far been made public still show the ambiguity characteristic of such negotiations.[119] Nonetheless, although more definitive solutions seem to await new proposals, the *de facto* return of both states within their international borders and – perhaps – even the mutual recognition of these boundaries, seems to indicate an important improvement in the neighbourly relations between the parties.

V   SUMMARY AND CONCLUSION

In the preceding pages, the legal history of the Iranian-Iraqi border disputes has been reviewed. In doing so, two more or less complete demarcations of the international boundary between the two states have been broadly described: the demarcations of 1913/1914 (including subsequent modifications) and of 1975. Which of the two defines the current location of this international boundary, is, primarily, determined by answers to questions of international law. Several of the relevant international legal issues have been discussed and, where possible, solutions to them have been suggested. The most important of these issues were brought forward within the context of attempts to terminate, or otherwise invalidate, agreements on delimitation of the international boundaries.

Both Iran and Iraq, at different moments in time and triggered off by different degrees of political crisis in their relations, have tried unilaterally to terminate their boundary agreements. We have not been able to disclose sufficient grounds to concur with either of their views at these crucial moments in the history of the mutual relations of both countries. At the most, some legal doubt regarding the question whether or not

---

117. *UN Doc.* S/21621. In the accompanying letter signed by the Iraqi Permanent Representative, the letter of Mr. Tariq Aziz is described as a letter '... concerning the completion of the Iraqi armed forces' withdrawal from Iranian territory'.

118. *UN Doc.* S/21556.

119. Notwithstanding its important concessions regarding the exchange of prisoners of war and the withdrawal of its armies, the essential paragraph 1 of the 15 August letter is rather obscurely formulated. It could be interpreted as if Iraq considers it possible to combine its 'full sovereignty over the Shatt-al-Arab' with using 'the 1975 Accord (...) as a basis', while applying 'the concept of the *Thalweg* line in respect of navigation rights between Iraq and Iran' (citations from the Iraqi letter of 30 July 1990 to which paragraph 1 refers; included as enclosure II, in *UN Doc.* S/21528).

both states were still bound to their international obligations under these agreements could be detected. On the basis of further evidence these arguments, might, perhaps, be elaborated into a valid ground for termination. However, generally speaking, that seems unlikely: the law of treaties cannot be said to give much room for the unilateral termination of a treaty, and even less so, if the treaty *in casu* is a boundary treaty.

In a material sense it often does not matter very much whether a boundary is drawn a few miles further on or not. It can matter, of course, if the territory, *e.g.*, happens to be a rich oil-field. Normally speaking, even if the territory is of great relevance (an important waterway), it is, technically, always possible to devise a regime for the area which adequately serves the needs of both parties and fulfills basic conditions of equality. The remaining problems can be left to a judicial solution or to arbitration.

In view of the rather obvious lack of success of the Iranian-Iraqi boundary agreements to bring international stability between the two neighbouring states, the question may be asked: were the Iranian-Iraqi boundary agreements perhaps inadequately drafted from an international lawyers' point of view? Probably the answer must be: on the contrary. In particular, the agreements drawn up in the 20th century can be considered as quite professional boundary settlements, and not only the ones drafted under the 'tutelage' of Western powers. This is illustrated by the early inclusion of comprehensive compromissory clauses. However, what strikes one most about these clauses is that (almost) always they were inoperative at the moments when they were most needed: in times of great tension or actual conflict. During such periods the Governments of the day did not show much inclination to try and prove the legality of their points of view by means of an appeal to these provisions. The most prominent example is, of course, provided by the disaster of the 1980-1988 Gulf War.

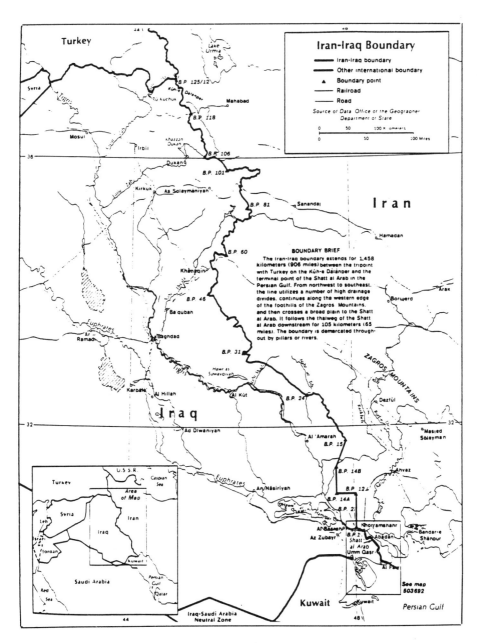

Iran-Iraq Boundary

— Iran-Iraq boundary
— Other international boundary
▲ Boundary point
— Railroad
— Road

Source of Data: Office of the Geographer
Department of State

BOUNDARY BRIEF

The Iran-Iraq boundary extends for 1,458 kilometers (906 miles) between the tripoint with Turkey on the Kūh-e Dālānpar and the terminal point of the Shatt al Arab in the Persian Gulf. From northwest to southeast, the line utilizes a number of high drainage divides, continues along the western edge of the foothills of the Zagros Mountains, and then crosses a broad plain to the Shatt al Arab. It follows the thalweg of the Shatt al Arab downstream for 105 kilometers (65 miles). The boundary is demarcated throughout by pillars or rivers.

Annex A

Source: *International Boundary Study*, no. 164 Iran-Iraq; US Department of State, Washington (USA), 1978

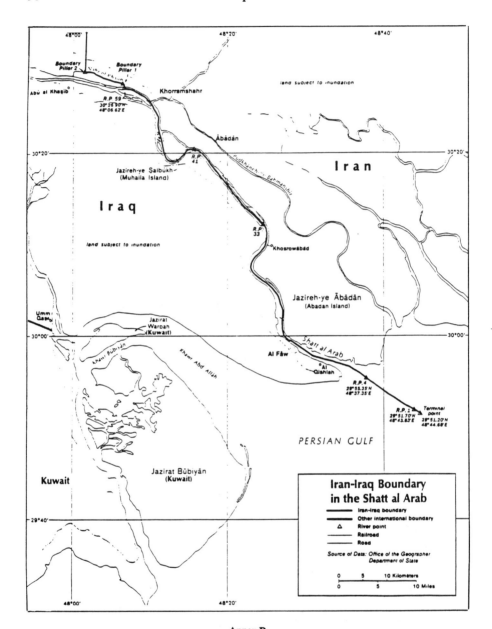

Annex B

Source: *International Boundary Study*, no. 164 Iran-Iraq; US Department of State, Washington (USA), 1978

COMMENTS

Erik Franckx[*]

In order to structure my remarks, I propose to start by making a few specific comments on the paper. Subsequently some more general ideas will be put forward on topics touched upon by Dr. Post when elaborating on the problem.

I   SPECIFIC COMMENTS

A first remark concerns the mere presentation of facts. I am fully aware that in this conflict it must prove to be an almost impossible task to present a completely neutral and objective account of the facts, which would be acceptable to both Iran and Iraq. Indeed, when reading through the history of this issue, one is left with the impression that Iran as well as Iraq have disputed the correctness of about every single element that could possibly be doubted.

On several occasions nevertheless, I had the feeling that facts deserved to be presented more carefully by Dr. Post in order not to prejudice a possible later objective legal analysis by the reader. Two examples will be mentioned to illustrate this point.

a) Article II of the Treaty of Erzeroum
When the author mentions Article II of the Treaty of Erzeroum of 1847, he immediately implies that the boundary in the Shatt-al-Arab will follow 'the low water line on the eastern – Persian – bank' (see p. 8. The same thought is also implied in section II B, on p. 24, 'it, *again* ...'). Article II(3), of the said treaty, however, simply states:

> 'The Ottoman Government formally recognizes the unrestricted sovereignty of the Persian Government over the city and port of Muhammara, the island of Khizr, the Abadan anchorage, and the land on the eastern bank – that is to say the left bank – of the Shatt-al-Arab, which are in the possession of tribes recognized as belonging to Persia (.) Further, Persian vessels shall have the right to navigate freely without let or hindrance on the Shatt-al-Arab from the mouth of the same to the point of contact of the frontiers of the two Parties.'[1]

It cannot be overlooked that this Article II does not specifically mention the division of the water area. It certainly does not mention the *low* water line.

---

* Erik Franckx, Professor in international law of the sea at the Vrije Universiteit Brussel.

1. Treaty of Erzeroum, 31 May 1947, as reprinted in Al-Izzi, K., *The Shatt-al-Arab River Dispute in Terms of Law*, Ministry of Information Baghdad 1972, p. 123. See for the (official) French text of article III, footnote 3 of this chapter and the sources mentioned there.

I.F. Dekker and H.H.G. Post, eds., The Gulf War of 1980-1988

This may seem to be a far-fetched argument, but because the Persian representative actually based himself on such a construction before the League of Nations,[2] it appears that the effect of Article II should be presented more carefully.

b) Treaty of Erzeroum: 1847 or 1848?

On page 10 the author writes: 'Article 3 of the Teheran Protocol states that the Treaty of Erzeroum will be the basis of the work of the Commission ...' Again, Article 3 refers to the 'treaty known as the Treaty of Erzer(o)um, concluded in 1847.'[3] This latter element, namely 1847, appears to be of special importance, for Iran has argued that a fundamental difference exists between the Treaty of 1847 and the one referred to as the Treaty of Erzeroum of 1848. The latter includes the crucial 'Note explicative', for a long time contested by Persia, the former not. Once more, this is an argument which has been explicitly made by one of the parties.[4]

Even though most provisions of the various conventions which are of crucial importance for this study are reproduced in the French, *i.e.*, the authoritative,[5] language, I do not find the text of the Delimitation Commission of 1914. In order to understand the chronology of boundary changes this text would appear to be of primordial importance because for the first time the *medium filum aequae* was used as a delimitation method inside the Shatt-al-Arab.[6]

The author's surprise that the 1937 Teheran Treaty was at a certain point of time no longer considered valid by Iraq (see footnote 88 of the paper of Dr. Post), may well find its logical explanation in the fact that this 1937 Treaty for the first time introduced, for a very short segment of only 7 km, the *Thalweg* principle in front of Abadan. Iraq, as a consequence, might have had good reasons to fall back on the 1913 Protocol only, and not on the 1937 Teheran Treaty, for by 1980 the abolishment of the *Thalweg* principle had become *the* central theme in the policy of Iraq. Or as stated by the Iranian Times (7 June 1990, p. 1), this element was transformed into a 'battle cry that is no more than a battle cry and meant and directed at those who shout it rather than a particular audience.' Under these circumstances, the Iraqi attitude referred to above may well be considered as a logical consequence rather than as an element which should occasion surprise.

---

2. See statement made by the representative of Persia before the 84th session of the Council of the League of Nations, fourth meeting, 15 January 1935.

3. Teheran Protocol, 21 December 1911, English translation as reprinted in Al-Izzi, K., *op.cit.* (note 1), p. 129. The (official) French text says: '... du Traité dit d'Erzeroum Conclu en 1263; ...' (See footnote 14 of this chapter and the sources mentioned there; 1263 of the Hegira corresponds with 1847.)

4. See statement made by the representative of Persia, *supra* note 2.

5. For convenience, English translations have been used by the present author. The French original apparently did not raise any interpretation problems with respect to the articles cited.

6. The French text can be found, for instance, in the so-called Iraqi 'White Book'. See *Facts Concerning the Iraqi-Iranian Frontier*, Ministry of Foreign Affairs, Baghdad 1960, p. 17, note 1.

What particularly intrigued me was the Wilson statement, referred to by many commentators, and also included by Dr. Post in his paper (see footnote 67). Because Mr. Wilson was the British representative in the Frontier Demarcation Commission in 1913-1914, his views might be very illuminating on the question.

The crux of his statement was that a *modus vivendi* had existed between Turkish and Persian authorities for a long time, namely that jurisdiction in the Shatt-al-Arab was jointly shared, the *medium filum aequae* being used as boundary, notwithstanding the Treaty of 1847. Over the years quite different opinions are to be found on this very topic in the legal literature. Al-Izzi, for instance, in his doctoral dissertation of 1971, emphatically denies that such a statement is to be found in Wilson's book of 1932, entitled *Persia*.[7] Lauterpacht, on the other hand, is of a totally different opinion.[8] In his 1960 article on the question Lauterpacht argues that, since Wilson even mentioned a detailed report drafted by himself on this very topic, this '"detailed historical report" will no doubt appear when the relevant Foreign Office archives become public' and shed some additional light on the issue.[9]

II   GENERAL COMMENTS

I completely agree with the conclusion reached by Dr. Post, when he writes that the boundary agreements, and particularly those drawn up in the 20th century, are 'quite professional boundary settlements' (section V of his paper). I would like to illustrate this particular point by means of the legal formulations used in the different treaties concerning the Shatt-al-Arab maritime boundaries over the years. It will be noted that a clear trend can be observed moving from implicit descriptions, over rudimentary formulations towards highly technical provisions.

1) If we start with the Treaty of Erzeroum of 1847, it has already been argued that this treaty did not provide much precise guidance. Iran, as a matter of fact, even refused to recognize that the treaty provided anything at all in this respect.[10]

2) The Protocol of Constantinople of 1913 mainly reaffirms the principles of the 1847 Treaty of Erzeroum but states *expressis verbis* that the Shatt-al-Arab, and all the

---

7. Al-Izzi, K., *The Shatt al-Arab Dispute*, Proefschrift ter verkrijging van het doctoraat in de Rechtsgeleerdheid, Rijksuniversiteit te Groningen 1971, p. 75. This dissertation was later published by the Ministry of Information, where the same argument can be found. See Al-Izzi, K., *op.cit.* (note 1), pp. 47-48.

8. Lauterpacht, E., "River Boundaries: Legal Aspects of the Shatt-Al-Arab Frontier", 9 *ICLQ* (1960), 208, p. 210, footnote 7.

9. *Idem.* Recently, the Archive International Group (Neuchâtel, Switzerland), in association with the International Boundaries Research Unit (University of Durham, U.K.) has published a collection in ten volumes (eight volumes of text, two volumes of maps), entitled *The Iran-Iraq Border 1840-1958*, edited by Richard Schofield. This collection, based on the British Public Record Office and the India Office Library and Records, London, covers a period during which Britain was very much involved in the evolution of this boundary.

10. See *supra* note 2 and accompanying text.

islands therein shall remain under Ottoman sovereignty.[11] Some detailed rules are already to be found in this Protocol, such as the provision that

> 'any small islands now existing or that may be formed which are connected at low water with the island of Abadan or with Persian *terra firma*'[12]

would belong to Persia. Ottoman sovereignty would, moreover, not be recognized over

> 'the parts of the Persian coast that may be tempor(a)rily covered by water at high tide or by other accidental causes. Persian jurisdiction, on its side, shall not be exercised over lands that may be temporarily or accidentally uncovered when the water is below the normal low-water level.'[13]

3) The report of the 1913-1914 Boundary Commission for the first time introduced the method of the *medium filum aequae*, be it for a rather short segment of 7 km in front of Khorramshahr.[14] This notion, which can mean different things (from the middle of the navigational channel to the middle of the *Thalweg*) was, however, not specified in the text.

4) The Treaty of Tehran of 1937, which refers back to the 1913 Constantinople Protocol as well as to the report of the 1913-1914 Boundary Commission, adds a new method to the list without, once more, clearly describing it. Indeed, Article 2 states that in front of Abadan 'the *Thalweg* of the Shatt-al-Arab' shall be used.[15] This concept, which is not very clearly defined under present-day international law, can mean, *inter alia*, the main current of the river normally used by downstream traffic or simply the line of deepest sounding, without any reference to navigation whatsoever. Notwithstanding these many possible meanings, the Treaty of Tehran simply uses the term without any further clarification.

5) Finally, the Treaty of Baghdad of 1975 should be mentioned, and more particularly its Protocol Concerning the Delimitation of the River Frontier Between Iran and Iraq.[16] As stated by Dr. Post in his paper, this agreement introduces the *Thalweg* principle as general rule to determine the frontier line in the Shatt-al-Arab.[17] This time, however, the *Thalweg* principle is accurately defined: '*i.e.*, the median line of the main navigable channel at the lowest navigable level.'[18] Moreover, a whole list of technical problems, which can occur with respect to the application of this principle in the future,

11. Protocol Relating to the Delimitation of the Turco-Persian Boundary, 4 November 1913, Article I, as reprinted in Al-Izzi, *op.cit.* (note 1), pp. 131, 137. This time the notion of 'low water' was explicitly referred to (see for the official French text, the sources mentioned in footnote 22 of this chapter).

12. *Ibidem*, Article 1(a)(3).

13. *Ibidem*, Article 1(d).

14. Text reprinted in the Iraqi 'White Book', *op.cit.* (note 6), p. 18.

15. Boundary Treaty, 4 July 1937, as reprinted in Al-Izzi, *op.cit.* (note 1), pp. 142, 143.

16. 1017 UNTS 54. The English translation of the Protocol here of importance can be found on pp. 138 *et seq.*

17. Article 2(A).

18. *Idem.*

are addressed. The frontier line will only vary with changes brought about by natural causes. Other changes will not affect the boundary unless the parties decide otherwise (Article 2(2)). However, if the eventuality of changes brought about by natural causes is accompanied by the fact that it involves a change in the national character of the territory involved, the general rule mentioned above will be reversed (no change; Article 2(4)). If a new bed is followed by the river, the water shall be normally re-directed to the 1975 bed at the expense of both parties, unless an agreement to the contrary is reached (Article 2(5)). Furthermore, a Mixed Iraqi-Iranian Commission will be established in order to solve controversies on this topic (Article 5). The application of the *Thalweg* principle, finally, also requires accurate and regular hydrographic surveys of the river in question. The convention addresses this need by providing, as a rule, for such a survey every ten years. Again, parties can agree to conduct a survey at an earlier time (Article 6).

It is clear from this brief analysis that the relative provisions of the different agreements have become more and more sophisticated. One can safely conclude, therefore, that the 1975 Baghdad Treaty represents a high-tech river boundary delimitation agreement, which beyond a shadow of doubt lives up to present day international standards. Apparently, this could not prevent the dispute from re-emerging once more after Iraq officially abrogated the 1975 Baghdad Agreement on 17 September 1980.

I would like to conclude this commentary by the following remark which, I must admit, may well be inspired by my personal interests in general maritime delimitation matters more than anything else. In a work, entitled 'Border conflicts between Iran and Iraq,' one is struck by the fact that nothing is said about the maritime delimitation outside the Shatt-al-Arab in the Persian Gulf. Because Dr. Post's paper is certainly not restricted to the Shatt-al-Arab *stricto sensu* – other, land boundary problems are discussed as well – a section on the territorial sea and other maritime delimitations in the Persian Gulf would certainly have completed the picture. As I understand it, in this region too there appears to be ample reason for further disagreement between the parties concerned.

COMMENTS

Gerard J. Tanja*

In the following pages some remarks will be made with respect to the (perceived) difference between 'delimitation' and 'demarcation'. It is the impression of this commentator that these terms and concepts have been referred to interchangeable and not always consistent in the preceding chapter.

A closely related issue concerns the use of legal terms like 'frontier', 'boundary' and/or 'border'. It is my intention to, primarily, discuss these two issues. The freedom of navigation on international rivers, more specifically on the Shatt-al-Arab will, despite the fact that it was only marginally touched upon, not be considered here.

I   'DELIMITATION', 'DETERMINATION' AND/OR 'DEMARCATION'

In international law there is at present not yet an established reference scheme which indicates as precisely as possible the legal scope and meaning of terms like delimitation, determination (of a boundary/frontier) and demarcation. It was only in 1985/1986 that Prescott, a well-known authority on maritime boundaries, observed that it was rather unfortunate that these terms apparently had been used at random in the 1982 Law of the Sea Convention (LOSC).[1] With respect to land frontriers, Verzijl makes use of the same terminology, referring to 'delimitation', 'establishment', 'fixing' or 'demarcations'.[2] Dr. Post apparently follows this path.

However, as a result of increasing state practice and recent case law in the field of international delimitations (mainly *maritime* delimitations) it may be possible to identify some emerging trends which are helpful for a better understanding of the substantive law involved. Secondly, it appears from the *travaux préparatoires* of the 1982 LOSC and the Convention itself that there are some reasons to question the observations of Prescott (and, therefore, indirectly Post and Verzijl).

First of all it is necessary to draw a distinction between *national* and *international* delimitation. In international law national delimitation relates to the process by which, on the basis of applicable international legal principles, and rules, a state unilaterally

---

* G.J. Tanja, Ministry of Foreign Affairs, The Netherlands. The views expressed are in no way attributable to the Ministry.

1. Prescott, J.R.V., *The Maritime Political Boundaries of the World*, London 1985.
2. Verzijl, J.H.W., *International Law in Historical Perspective*, Volume III, pp. 513 *et seq*. See also his references to state practice, especially on rivers as international 'boundaries'. Verzijl, however, acknowledged the difference between demarcation and delimitation. He described demarcation as an 'activity on the spot', often 'prescribed by a boundary agreement as an indispensable means of complementing the more schematic delimitation by a map line or in terms of verbal description', *Ibidem*, at pp. 526-527.

I.F. Dekker and H.H.G. Post, eds., The Gulf War of 1980-1988
© 1992, T.M.C. Asser Instituut, The Hague

decides to *legally* establish outer limites for exercising either full territorial sovereignty or functional sovereignty. Whether it concerns land territory or maritime areas, in both situations the competence to establish such an outer limit arises directly from the legal title of a state by reference to which it can validly claim full or functional sovereignty.[3]

International delimitation, however, is the process by which a line of separation is legally determined between neighbouring states in order to anticipate or prevent a clash of legal title. In the words, the legal determination of the area of validity in space of the norms of the legal order of one state *vis-à-vis* the area of validity in space of the norms of the legal order of another state (or states).[4]

It is noteworthy that already in the 1958 Conventions on the Territorial Sea/Contiguous Zone and the Continental Shelf terms like 'draw', 'establishment' (Articles 4 and 5 Territorial Sea Convention) and 'limit' (Article 1 Convention on the Continental Shelf) were only used in relation to *national* delimitation. This is further confirmed by the 1982 LOSC: Article 3 speaks of the 'right to establish' the breadth of the territoral sea, whereas the outer limits of the Exclusive Economic Zone (EEZ) and continental shelf are either 'measured' (Articles 57, 76) or 'delineated' (Article 76).

With respect to international delimitation, however, both the above-mentioned 1958 Conventions and the 1982 LOSC make consistent (and deliberate) use of the term 'delimitation' (Article 12 Convention on the Territorial Sea and Articles 74 and 83 of the 1982 LOSC) or 'determination' of a *boundary* (Article 6, Convention on the Continental Shelf).

Further proof of this deliberate use of terminology can be found in the *travaux préparatoires* of the 1982 LOSC. In the List of Subjects and Issues, which was formally approved by the Seabed Committee on 18 August 1972 and later constituted the provisional agenda for the LOS Conference, Item 6.7.2. was initially entitled '*Delineation* between adjacent and opposite states'. At the Conference, however, this was changed in 'Delimitation ... *etc.*'.[5]

---

3. In this commentary the issues relating to the meaning and difference between concepts such as functional sovereignty and (exclusive) jurisdiction (*cf.* Article 56(1)(a) and (1)(b) of the 1982 LOSC) will not be addressed, but see Kwiatkowska, B., *The 200 Mile Exclusive Economic Zone in the New Law of the Sea*, Dordrecht 1989. National delimitation law is concerned with 'apportionment'.

4. As the International Court of Justice (ICJ), states in the *Aegean Sea Continental Shelf Case* it concerns the determination of the 'exact line or lines where the extension in space of the sovereign powers and rights of Greece meets those of Turkey.' The Court noted furthermore that there is in this respect no difference between '... a land frontier or a boudary line in the continental shelf ...', *ICJ Reports* (1978), § 85, at pp. 36-37. For recent case law, see the *Award of the Arbitration Tribunal for the Determination of the Maritime Boundary between Guinea-Bissau and Senegal*, Repr. in *Annex to the Application Instituting Proceedings of the Government of the Republic of Guinea-Bissau; Case Concerning the Arbitral Award of 31 July 1989* (Guinea-Bissau v. Senegal), *ICJ Annex*, § 63, at p. 51. Note the case law cited there. See also the Dissenting Opinion of Judge Bedjaoui, *Annex*, § 22, at pp. 93-94. Bedjaoui speaks of '... a line the function of which is to separate the domain of exercise of the competences of the state from the areas under the *jurisdiction* of another state' (emphasis added). *Ibidem*. The recent *Case Concerning the Frontier Dispute* (Burkina Faso/Republic of Mali) also touched upon the concept of international delimitation, *ICJ Reports* (1986).

5. See for a discussion of the *travaux préparatoires* in this respect G.J. Tanja, *The Legal Determination of International Maritime Boundàries*, 1990, pp. 81-116.

It is the opinion of the present author, therefore, that we are witnessing an emerging trend in international law to the following effect: the term 'delimitation' should be used (or is preferred) when one refers to the process by which *international* maritime boundaries or frontiers (for the alleged difference, see *infra*) are legally determined. The nucleus of this process consists of the identification of principles and rules of applicable delimitation law; it concerns the *legal determination* of the boundary or frontier, but excludes the actual demarcation.[6]

Another interesting development in this respect can be found in the case at present before the Court on the 'Maritime *Delimitation* in the Area between Greenland and Jan Mayen' (emphasis added). Initially – and on the basis of the formulas adopted by the Parties –, the case was entitled 'Maritime *Boundary* in the Area between Greenland and Jan Mayen' (emphasis added), apparently, *inter alia*, in the belief that the word 'delimitation' more adequately described the legal process by which applicable principles and rules of delimitation law are identified in the particular situation.[7]

Demarcation (or delineation) is a physical act by which a boundary or frontier is finally drawn or constructed; it is a rather technical process based on various *methods*. I have the impression that Dr. Post is of the same opinion. These methods, however, result *idealiter* from a correct application of the principles and rules of delimitation law; the rules prescribe a method or combination of methods which relates to the actual fixing or drawing of the boundary or frontier.

At the same time states can agree to – or ask an adjudicatory body to indicate in its Judgment – the exact boundary or frontier reference points on the basis of which the boundary is actually drawn. In these circumstances, the demarcation plays only a minor role. Every demarcation or delineation must, however, unless otherwise indicated by the Parties, be agreed upon in order to become legally binding upon the Parties. States have developed various procedures in this respect.[8]

One could, therefore, also speak of the *actual* or *technical* determination of the boundary or frontier as opposed to the *legal* determination. For the reasons referred to above and in footnotes 5 and 7, this is to be preferred. There seems to be no compelling reason to differentiate in this respect between a land frontier and a maritime boundary.

With respect to the perceived difference as elaborated above, some interesting observations were made in the recent dispute between Israel and Egypt concerning the Taba Area.[9] In her Dissenting Opinion Judge Lapidoth rejected the arguments of the

---

6. Recent case law with respect to maritime delimitation shows, however, that Parties frequently ask the adjudicating body to indicate the practical method or to actually draw the boundary. In these instances the – rather strict – distinction between delimitation (identification of applicable principles and rules) and demarcation (the use of methods on the basis of the law) tends to disappear, mainly because the Tribunals and Courts involved have not yet developed an adequate concept of 'delimitation'. To a certain extent this is the consequence of the embryonic state of international (maritime) delimitation law.

7. For another explanation see the Dissenting Opinion of Bedjaoui in the Arbitral Award between Guinea-Bissau and Senegal concerning the Determination of the Maritime Boundary, *loc.cit.* (note 4), § 25, at p. 96.

8. See in this respect Verzijl, *op.cit.* (note 2), at pp. 527-530.

9. *Award of the Egypt-Israel Arbitration Tribunal in the Dispute Concerning the Taba Area*. Repr. in XXVII *ILM* (1988), pp. 1421 *et seq*.

majority of the Tribunal to the effect that '... in international law demarcation prevails over delimitation ...' once the demarcated frontier has been approved by the Parties to the conflict.

According to Lapidoth the final demarcation should always be based on an official report prepared by a demarcation commission and approved by the states concerned. She cites Jones and Rousseau where she states that, '... [t]he most important and elaborate document prepared by a demarcation commission is its final report, sometimes called the boundary protocol ...' and further that 'le résultat de la démarcation (...) est consigné dans des protocols (...) ou des procès-verbaux'[10] (see in this respect also the observations by Dr. Post at page 13 of his paper concerning the validity of the 'Carte Identique' and the Protocol of Constantinople). In his view, however, the term demarcation also comprises the instructions and guidelines for demarcation commissions. Apparently, he excludes from a 'demarcation process' the 'technical operation which should not have involved any measurements or technical expertise.'[11]

A second remark by Judge Lapidoth points to the relative weight of demarcation *vis-à-vis* delimitation. She criticizes the majority opinion that an authentic interpretation of legal title is proven once the states to the dispute have over a long period of time consented to a demarcated frontier. Judge Lapidoth bases her arguments on the view of Professor Ress who has stated that: '... [p]robably demarcation (...) only shifts the burden of evidence to the party which wants to argue that the demarcation was wrong.'[12] Elaborating further on this argument, Judge Lapidoth comes to the conclusion that:

'... the relative weight of delimitation and demarcation depends on the circumstances of each case, *i.e.*, the degree of precision and of detail in the delimitation agreement, the seriousness of the pre-delimitation survey, the degree of care with which the demarcation has been effected and reported, and of course whether it was undertaken unilaterally or bilaterally.'[13]

From the observations of Judge Lapidoth one gets the impression that she has in mind a three-fold delimitation process of which the first stages belong to the legal scene:

a) delimitation; the conclusion of a framework-treaty (or parent treaty) indicating the legal rules and principles on which the demarcation should be based. This stage also comprises the institutional arrangements necessary for the establishment of a frontier (or boundary) demarcation commission and the mandate and guidelines for such a commission;

---

10. Dissenting Opinion Judge Lapidoth, *ibidem*, § 26, at p. 1503. The issue at stake was whether the *replacement* of boundary pillars was part of an official demarcation process. Jones, S.B., *Boundary-Making: a Handbook for Statesmen, Treaty Editors and Boundary Commissions*, Washington 1945, pp. 197-299; Rousseau, Ch., *Droit International Public*, vol. 3, Paris 1977, pp. 270-271.

11. Dissenting Opinion Judge Lapidoth, *ibidem*, § 28, at p. 1503.

12. Ress, G., "The Delimitation and Demarcation of Frontiers in International Treaties and Maps", XIV *Thesaurus Acroasium* (1985), p. 431.

13. Dissenting Opinion Judge Lapidoth, *loc.cit.* (note 10), § 30, at p. 1504.

b) demarcation: the implementation of the delimitation agreement, including the official approval of the minutes of the demarcation commission, and the signing and ratification of a frontier (or boundary) protocol;

c) the real technical operations carried out by the demarcation commission including measurements, *etc.*, and the physical acts by which frontiers/boundaries are put on maps.

It seems that these observations concerning demarcation and delimitation are appropriate in the light of the difficulties and problems encountered by the Parties with respect to the legality of the various agreements involved (see the observations by Dr. Post on the historical background of the Shatt-al-Arab dispute).

With respect to the sensitive issue of the Shatt-al-Arab frontier dispute it is to be preferred, therefore, that the terminology be carefully balanced as it may have an impact on the legal conclusions one arrives at.

II   'FRONTIER', 'BOUNDARY', AND/OR 'BORDER'

A second observation relates to the use of the terms 'frontier' and 'boundary' in the paper. It seems that Dr. Post has a preference for the term 'frontier' when addressing the Shatt-al-Arab dispute, but this is, however, not always obvious from the text (for example, section III on the Frontier in the Shatt-al-Arab and section II entitled: Boundary Agreements; Land Frontiers; section IV on the Current Iranian-Iraqi Border Regime).

In 1989 the alleged legal difference came up in the Arbitral Award of 31 July 1989 concerning the Determination of the Maritime Boundary between Guinea-Bissau and Senegal. In that dispute Guinea-Bissau submitted various arguments to indicate the existence in international law of a difference in scope between an land frontier (*frontière*) and a maritime 'delimitation' or 'boundary'. The reason behind this submission was that state succession could not arise in respect of maritime boundaries, and that the principle of *uti possidetis* could not be invoked in respect of maritime boundaries. It was further argued that a frontier is a line of separation between sovereign powers and jurisdictional limits which is valid for *all* activities in one state *vis-à-vis* another state whereas a maritime boundary relates to the line separating the exercise of functional sovereignty. According to Guinea-Bissau, this had the result that a land frontier and a maritime boundary in fact establish different legal regimes.

Although the Tribunal and Judge Bedjaoui rejected some of the arguments of Guinea-Bissau – be it on different grounds –, it was not denied that the nature and character of a maritime boundary or delimitation could not be completely equated with the regime of a land frontier, as the *uti possidetis* principle for example, can only be invoked with respect to land frontiers (Bedjaoui). Although Judge Bedjaoui spoke of maritime 'frontiers', he stated quite clearly that such 'frontiers' are of a '... different nature or category', indicating that this asked '... for a difference in legal regimes'.[14]

For these reasons it is suggested that the term frontier (frontière) should be reserved for international land frontiers, as it relates to that particular legal regime only, and that the term 'boundary' should be used when we refer to (functional) maritime delimitation. It seems to the present author that to a certain extent this trend can already be observed in case where the ICJ, apart from the Gulf of Maine Case, has apparently preferred the expression 'maritime boundary' (although it is far too early to speak of an emerging rule or a rule which is still *de lege ferenda*).[15]

As the dispute under review relates to an international river separating the sovereign domain between two (or more) states, the use of the legal term 'frontier' should be preferred. Here, the line separating the respective areas of spatial validity of the legal order of the states concerned relates, in principle, to the waters of the river Shatt-al-Arab.

It is acknowledged that the suggested and alleged difference between international frontier and boundary is questionable. In the Arbitral Award between Egypt and Israel concerning the Taba Area the terms frontier and boundary were, for example, used interchangingly, although in the agreements which were at stake and the ensuing correspondence the term frontier was consistently applied.[16] The Arbitral Tribunal, however, made reference to both terms.

In the *Temple of Preah Vihear* Case the ICJ deliberately applied the term frontier with respect to territory. In one of the most important observations in this respect the ICJ observed:

'In general, when two countries establish a *frontier* between them, one of the primary objects is to achieve stability and finality. This is impossible if the line so established can, at any moment, and on the basis of a continuously available process, be called in question, and its rectification claimed, whenever any inaccurary by reference to a clause in the *parent* treaty

---

14. Dissenting Opinion Judge Bedjaoui, *loc.cit.* (note 4), § 35, at pp. 105-106. In the 1978 Convention on Succession of States in Respect of Treaties, however, Article 11 speaks of 'Boundary regimes', without indicating whether this provision also includes maritime boundaries. According to Bedjaoui this is not the case. He may find some support in Articles 12 and 15 which refer to 'territory', but nowhere mentions maritime areas or 'territories'. *Ibidem*, § 26, at pp. 96-97.

15. Doctrine is still divided though most authorities seem to prefer the term 'boundary'. See, *inter alia*, Kittichaisaree, K., *The Law of the Sea and Maritime Boundary Delimitation in South-East Asia*, 1987; Prescott, *op.cit.* (note 1); Jagota, S.P., *Maritime Boundary*, The Hague 1985; Johnston, D.M., *Theory and History of Ocean Boundary Making*, 1988; Johnston, D.M., Saunders, P., *Ocean Boundary Making: Regional Issues and Development*, 1989; Bravender-Coyle, P., "The Emerging Legal Principles and Equitable Criteria Governing the Delimitation of Maritime Boundaries Between States", 19 *ODILA* (1988). Various authors refer to maritime delimitation, thereby indicating the process described in paragraph 2, but obviously having a preference for boundary instead of frontier. See, *inter alia*, Weil, P., *The Law of Maritime Delimitation – Reflections*, 1989; Evans, M.E., *Relevant Circumstances and Maritime Delimitation*, 1989.

16. For example, in the 1926 correspondence between the Prime Minister of Egypt and the British High Commissioner in Egypt: '... toutes réserves en ce qui concerne *les frontières* de l'Egypt avec la Palestine, qui ne sauraient être en aucune façon affecteés par la délimitation des frontières palestiniennes' (emphasis added). The British answer referred to the 'frontiers as defined in the year 1906'.

is discovered. Such a process could continue indefinitely, and finality would never be reached so long as possible errors still remained to be discovered. Such a frontier, so far from being stable, would be completely precarious' (emphasis added).[17]

---

17. *ICJ Reports* (1962), at p. 34. The Court also frequently referred to the 'frontier line' and 'frontier zone'. *Idem.*

Chapter 2

'IUS AD BELLUM': LEGAL IMPLICATIONS OF THE IRAN-IRAQ WAR

Kaiyan Homi Kaikobad*

INTRODUCTION

Historically speaking, several major areas of concern have served to hamper good relations between Iran and Iraq. In the first place there is the Shia-Sunni denominational problem. While over half of Iraq's population is comprised of Shia muslims, the wealthier and more powerful Sunnis dominate the political and economic systems. A related problem is that Shi'ite holy places, *viz.* Kerbala, Najaf and Samarra, are all located in Iraq.[1] These difficulties are compounded by the fact that Iraq is by and large an Arab nation while the Iranians are an Aryan people with a distinctively non-Arab outlook and a strong Iranian/Persian language and cultural background.

In the 1970s, Iran forged a major politico-military alignment with the United States and acquired considerable international importance, a fact which may not have sat easily with Iraq. The paramount problem, however, has always been the boundary problem in the Shatt-al-Arab, the joint waters of the Tigris and Euphrates.[2] In very general terms, Iran and Iraq have had perennially conflicting claims regarding the boundary in this river. By virtue of the Baghdad Treaty of 1975, the boundary was drawn along the main navigable channel. Iraq, however, was politically unable to reconcile herself to the loss of sovereignty over the ceded half of the river and the dispute smouldered on. Following the termination of the Iranian Shah's rule and the installation of the Islamic government of Ayatollah Khomeini, the differences between the two governments magnified, and it is this relatively modern era which is characterized by a reversion to the old historical claims and accusations. Matters worsened and hostilities broke out in September 1980. During the period of the war, the Security Council passed a series of resolutions, calling upon the states to cease hostilities, withdraw their forces to the recognized international boundaries, and to refrain from aggravating the conflict. The war ended on 17 July 1988 when Iran finally accepted Security Council Resolution 598 (1987) of 20 July 1987.

---

* K.H. Kaikobad, Legal Adviser, Ministry of State for Legal Affairs, Government of Bahrain. The views expressed below do not reflect the position held by the Government of Bahrain. The author has written a more detailed study of the subject-matter of this Chapter. He would like to record a word of gratitude to his wife for her assistance in editing and finalising the text and to Mr. B. Bong for his expert advice on and gracious loan of his computer facilities.

1. U.K. Foreign Affairs Committee, House of Commons, 2nd. Report, *Current UK Policy Towards the Iran/Iraq Conflict*, 27 June 1988, HMSO, London, pp. xi-xiii.

2. See Chapter 1 of this book.

I.F. Dekker and H.H.G. Post, eds., The Gulf War of 1980-1988
© 1992, T.M.C. Asser Instituut, The Hague

Against this brief statement on the historical and political background to the war, the following analysis of the legal rights and obligations of the parties to the conflict should be understood. This analysis comprises two parts. First, some of the major legal themes and the more subtle points of law raised by the war are examined in general doctrinal terms. This is followed by an application of these principles and rules to the situations created by the actions of the states. Wherever possible and necessary, the study proceeds on the assumption that the claims made by one or both of the parties are factually correct. This affords an opportunity of investigating these claims with a view to determining their veracity in the light of the relevant principles of law. It is hoped that by so doing and by incorporating new materials, including the watershed decision of the International Court of Justice in the *Military and Paramilitary Activities against Nicaragua* Case of 27 June 1986, a more contemporary picture of certain features of *ius ad bellum* will emerge.

I   AGGRESSION AND INTERVENTION: THE UNITED NATIONS CHARTER
        AND RELATED INSTRUMENTS

A   **Brief description of the claims of the parties**

Generally speaking the claims of the two parties involve three categories of accusations on either side. First, both states claim to be victims of direct armed attack carried out by conventional means. For Iran, these attacks began on 22nd September 1980 when Iraq made a large-scale invasion of Iranian territory and executed air strikes on cities, airports and industrial installations.[3] Iraq, however, claims that on 4 September Iran shelled and bombarded various towns and border posts in Khanqin and Mandali.[4] The second legal category of accusations constitutes the sending of armed agents who conducted campaigns of bombing, terrorism and sabotage, including the poisoning of wells. Iran contended that these acts were carried out in Kurdistan, Khuzistan, Kermanshah and Ilam.[5] Iraq maintained that Iran's agents had infiltrated and committed acts of similar depravity in Baghdad, Najaf, Amarah, Basrah and Nasriyeh.[6] The third category of accusations involves the crime of assistance rendered to

3. Letter of Iranian Representative to the UN Secretary-General of 1 Oct. 1980, *UN Doc.* S/14206; Iranian Prime Minister's statement to the Security Council of 17 Oct. 1980, *UN Doc.* S/PV.2251.

4. Letter of the Iraqi Representative to the Secretary-General, enclosure: letter of the Iraqi Foreign Minister to Secretary-General of 24 Oct. 1980, *UN Doc.* S/14236; and his statement to the Security Council of 15 Oct. 1980, *UN Doc.* S/PV.2250; and *UN Doc.* S/PV.2251, *loc. cit.* (note 3). Further see letters of the Iraqi Representative to the Secretary-General of 25 Nov. 1980, *UN Doc.* S/14272, of 10 March 1981, *UN Doc.* S/14401; and of 18 July 1985, *UN Doc.* S/17347

5. See *UN Doc.* S/PV.2251, *loc.cit.* (note 3), and letter of the Iranian Foreign Minister to the Secretary-General of 23 July 1980, *UN Doc.* S/14070; and *UN Doc.* S/14206, *loc.cit.* (note 3).

6. See *UN Doc.* S/PV.2250, *loc.cit.* (note 4); and letter of the Iraqi Representative to the Secretary-General of 21 Sept. 1980, *UN Doc.* S/14191; enclosure letter of the Iraqi Foreign Minister to the Secretary-General of 21 Sept. 1980; and letter of the Iraqi Representative to the Secretary-General of 20 June 1980, *UN Doc.* S/14020.

insurgents. Iran contended that Iraq assisted counter-revolutionaries in Kurdistan, Khuzistan, Seistan and Baluchistan in order to undermine the stability of the new republic.[7] Iraq claimed that Iran had aided insurgents and fomented civil strife amongst the Kurdish people, especially the followers of the Kurdish rebel leader, Barzani.[8] Both states also claimed that the other had carried out hostile radio and newspaper campaigns calculated to cause war hysteria and civil unrest. Iran, furthermore, maintained that Iraq had expelled 40,000 Iranians of Shi'ite origins.[9] The legal implications of these accusations and counter-accusations are discussed below.

B   The duty not to use force

Article 2(4) of the Charter of the United Nations expressly prohibits the threat or use of force by Members in their international relations against the territorial integrity or political independence of any state or in any manner inconsistent with the purposes of the United Nations. It is generally recognized that Article 2(4) reflects customary international law. Over the years, the duty not to use force has been reiterated in a number of international instruments, including the 1970 Friendly Relations and Cooperation Declaration and the 1975 Helsinki Final Act.[10] The categories of direct and indirect use of force are examined below.

1   *Direct use of force*

The direct use of force includes invasion, armed attack, military occupation, bombardment, blockade and attacks on land, sea and air. These and other acts are defined in Article 3 of the 1974 Definition of Aggression[11] as acts of aggression. In the Iran-Iraq war, both states accused each other of direct aggression, namely, bombardment and shelling of towns and oil installations by heavy artillery. The following two observations may be made. First, the state which initiated the war would be in breach of Article 2(4) of the Charter and would come under Article 3(a), (b) and (d) of the Definition of Aggression. Hence once the identity of the aggressor state is conclusively established, it may be possible to charge that state with the crime of committing acts against international peace, as provided in Article 5(2) of the Definition, a crime for which international responsibility will be incurred.

Secondly, it is more than likely that both parties at different times carried out unlawful acts of armed force against each other for which they would individually be held responsible.

---

7. See *UN Doc.* S/PV.2251, *loc.cit.* (note 3).

8. *UN Doc.* S/PV.2250, *loc.cit.* (note 4); *UN Doc.* S/PV.2251, *loc.cit.* (note 3); and see *UN Doc.* S/14191, *loc.cit.* (note 6).

9. Letter of the Iranian Foreign Minister to the Secretary-General of 23 July 1980, *UN Doc.* S/14070; letter of the Iranian Representative to the Secretary-General of 28 April 1980; *UN Doc.* S/13915, and *UN Doc.* S/PV.2250, *loc.cit.* (note 4).

10. A/RES/2625(XXV) annex, 24 Oct. 1970, and 14 *ILM* (1975), p. 1292 respectively.

11. A/RES/3314(XXIX) annex, 14 Dec. 1974.

2   *Indirect use of force*

The indirect use of force includes the lending of support and assistance to insurgents, as in the supply of weapons, the fomenting of civil strife , the sending of armed bands into the territory of another state with a view to overthrowing the established administration. In legal terms, the indirect use of force may be regarded as falling into two main categories, namely (i) the indirect use of force amounting to aggression; and (ii) the indirect use of force not amounting to aggression. Category (i) has its source in Article 3(f) and (g) of the Definition of Aggression, the latter of which provides that 'The sending by or on behalf of a state of armed bands, groups, irregulars or mercenaries, which carry out acts of armed force against another state of such gravity as to amount to [invasion, bombardment and the like] or its substantial involvement therein.' Category (ii) may generally be regarded as constituting all other activities not falling under category (i) and may also generally be referred to as assistance and interference. The implications of this distinction are important. Inasmuch as category (i) constitutes aggression and can be assimilated to the notion of armed attack, the right of self-defence will be available to the state subjected to this kind of use of force, and it follows that there is no recourse to the right of self-defence for acts falling under category (ii). These matters are examined more closely in paragraph II.A and 3 of this Chapter.

The main focus of enquiry here involves an examination of the obligations and responsibilities of the parties in the context of an indirect use of force. First, both categories (i) and (ii) constitute a breach of Article 2(4) of the Charter. The duty not to use indirect force, including the duty not to render assistance to insurgents and to interfere in the internal affairs of a state has been recognized by writers[12] and is supported by state practice. Evidence of the latter category can be seen in a variety of international instruments including the 1965 Declaration on the Inadmissibility of Intervention in the Domestic Affairs of states[13] and the 1987 Declaration on the Enhancement of the Effectiveness of the Principle of Refraining from the Threat or Use of Force.[14] In the *Military and Paramilitary Activities* Case, the Court, referring to Nicaragua's claims that the United States had supported *contra* forces in terms of training, weapons and logistic support, ruled that indirect forms of support for subversive or terrorist armed activities within another state were wrongful in light of the principles of non-use of force and non-intervention.[15]

The second implication of category (i) is that the indirect use of force apart from constituting a breach of the general duty not to use force as contained in Article 2(4) of

---

12. Brownlie,I., *International Law and the Use of Force by States*, Oxford 1963, pp. 370, 373 and pp. 361-362; 278-279; Schachter, O., "General Course on Public International Law", 178 *Hague Receuil* (1982, V), pp. 160-166; Dinstein, Y., *War, Aggression and Self-Defence*, London 1988, pp. 188-190; and Jiménez de Aréchaga, E, "General Course on Public International Law: International Law in the Past Third of a Century", 159 *Hague Receuil* (1978, I), p. 93.

13. A/RES/2131(XX), 21 Dec. 1965.

14. A/RES/42/22 annex, 18 Nov. 1987. See for text, 27 *ILM* (1988), p. 1678.

15. *ICJ Reports* (1986), p. 14 at pp. 106-112; 118-119; 123-126.

the Charter, also constitutes an act of aggression against the victim state which will give rise to international responsibility. In the context of the Iran-Iraq war, the state demonstrated to have effected acts of indirect aggression will *prima facie*: (a) be in breach of Article 2(4) of the Charter; (b) to the extent that the relevant acts fall under category (i), also be responsible for acts of aggression. On a bilateral level, the state effecting the infiltration of armed bands across the frontiers will be in breach of Article 3 of the Iran-Iraq Treaty concerning the state Frontier and Neighbourly Relations concluded in Baghdad on 13 June 1975.[16] Similarly, the relevant state will also be regarded as being in breach of Articles 1,2 and 4 of the attached Protocol concerning Security on the Frontier Between Iran and Iraq relative to the Prevention of Subversive Insubordination and Rebellion.[17]

Finally, the observations made with respect to mutual acts of direct use of force in subsection 1 above apply *mutatis mutandis* to this sub-section as well; both states at different periods of time or even simultaneously may have carried out acts of *indirect* use of force amounting to aggression – category (i) – and acts not amounting to aggression – category (ii).

C   Armed intervention

The duty not to intervene arises from the duty not to use force as stipulated in Article 2(4) of the Charter, and insofar as armed intervention may be direct or indirect, it overlaps with the notions of both direct and indirect aggression and also with the concept of indirect force not amounting to aggression. It is clear that the so-called 'right' of intervention is essentially incompatible with the principle of the outlawry of war and the use of force as an instrument of national policy. Post-1945 practice, as seen in several United Nations General Assembly declarations, resolutions and other international instruments, including the 1970 Friendly Relations and Cooperation Declaration, is consistent with the express prohibition of intervention. The latter declaration stipulates, *inter alia*, that intervention cannot be justified on the basis of any ground whatever. Certain regional instruments also support the general principle of non-intervention, including the Charter of the Organization of American States, the Charter of the Organization of African Unity[18] and the 1975 Helsinki Final Act. The observations made by the International Court of Justice in the *Military and Paramilitary Activities* Case more than amply confirm that there is no 'principle' of intervention in international law.[19]

In the context of the war, the question of humanitarian intervention is relatively more important. It arises in the light of the fact that Iraq forcibly expelled about 40,000 Shia Muslims, an incident which caused great anxiety in Iran. Iranian protests showed that Iran wished to put a stop to further abuses of human rights. A right of humanitarian

---

16. 1017 *UNTS* No. 14903
17. *Idem.*
18. 46 *AJIL* (1952) (Supp.), p. 43; and 479 *UNTS* 39, respectively.
19. *ICJ Reports* (1986), pp. 106-112; 123-126.

intervention cannot be admitted, not least because the general right of intervention as such does not exist in the international system. Where a weak and controversial notion of intervention could not have survived an express prohibition contained in Article 2(4) of the Charter, the right of humanitarian intervention must in greater measure also be a notion difficult in law to accept. Writers who advocate the existence of a right of humanitarian intervention fail to observe some of the legal and logical difficulties which flow from such views. The Charter does not provide for any exceptions other than self-defence in Article 51 and enforcement action under Chapter VII, Article 42. If the right had been as 'venerable' as it has been contended to be, it should have been mentioned in the Charter, perhaps even as an 'inherent right' as was done in the case of self-defence in Article 51.

The theory of humanitarian intervention is further weakened by the highly subjective nature of the 'conditions' or 'tests' writers choose to place on the exercise of such a 'right', especially where the crucial cause for concern, namely the gross abuse of human rights, may be difficult to determine objectively. The glib reference to genocide is unfortunately an impracticable and imperfect guide in circumstances where communal clashes and sectarian violence are perennial and indeed historical problems, where the 'facts' are partial and inaccurate and the criteria employed highly controversial. If the proponents of the right of humanitarian intervention are to be believed, the intervening state would be free to frame the tests, apply them to a particular situation and then proceed to exercise such a 'right'. That state would thus become the legislator, judge and executor. Such an accumulation of powers is neither correct in principle nor acceptable as a proposition of law, not least because of the enormous potential for abuse of such powers. It follows, therefore, that if humanitarian intervention is to be regarded as a general, well-received right of states it must be shown to be based on and supported by clear and uncontroversial principles of law. If it is to be exercised the *imprimatur* of the United Nations is essential to its exercise.

The implication of these observations is that in principle the influx of refugees into the territory of a state does not invest the receiving state with the right of intervention against the sending state on any grounds. Consequently, Iran would have no right to employ force against Iraq, direct or indirect, to arrest the flow of refugees on the pretext of installing a regime having greater respect for humanitarian values.

D   Radio and newspaper war propaganda

There is general agreement on the view that the term 'force' as used in Article 2(4) of the Charter refers to military and quasi-military armed physical coercion. Clearly, therefore the carrying out of hostile radio and newspaper campaigns with the intention of creating civil strife in the affected state is not, strictly speaking, a breach of Article 2(4). Such campaigns are nevertheless contrary to the purposes laid down in Article 1(2) of the Charter which refers to the development of friendly relations among nations and the adoption of measures to strengthen universal peace. Apart from this, such campaigns are inconsistent with the duty of states to cooperate with one another in the maintenance of international peace and security as provided in the 1970 Declaration on Friendly Relations, and with the general duty of non-intervention provided both in customary international law and in numerous international and regional instruments, including the 1965 Declaration on the Inadmissibility of Intervention in the Domestic Affairs of States and the Protection of their Independence and Sovereignty.[20]

On a more specific note, state practice appears to be reflected in the 1966 International Covenant on Civil and Political Rights, which provided in Article 20(1) that 'Any advocacy of national, racial or religious hatred that constitutes incitement to discrimination, hostility or violence shall be prohibited by law.'[21] In general, it appears that the weight of instruments and the opinions of writers is in favour of regarding war propaganda or radio campaigns intended to cause civil strife in affected states as being in principle unlawful. It is true that this general principle cannot ignore the importance of the recognized freedoms of information and the expression of opinions. Nor can the potential for subjective interpretations of the rule be ignored for what may appear to be hostile propaganda and incitement to disaffection to one party may appear to be incontrovertible truths to the other. In this context, Professor Stone's cautious, philosophical approach to the matter is instructive.[22]

Nevertheless, on this view, greater weight needs to be given to the duty *not* to carry out such campaigns. The rights of freedom of speech and information enshrined in municipal law and the duty of the administration to maintain public order within the state provide clues to ways in which these two apparently conflicting principles may be reconciled on the international legal plane. Hence, by this yardstick, it would be reasonable to suggest that on the face of it there appears to be a much greater general need to maintain international peace and stability and to minimize tension and hostility between states as opposed to the need of states to inform and express opinions without regard to their consequences. This is particularly true where the states in question are potential belligerents or have had a history of hostility.

Consequently, where radio and related campaigns have the potential of breaking a fragile peace or of raising hostility to unacceptable levels, there would be some justification in requiring the offending state either to cease or reasonably restrict the operation of such hostile 'media offensives'. As Professor Röling said,

'Freedom of expression has, however, never been absolute. There has never been freedom to make propaganda for crime, and the penalty provision is no vaguer than many other such provisions.'[23]

In the context of the Iran-Iraq war, there appears to be little doubt that hostile propaganda was indeed broadcasted and that the parties had little concern for matters of principle in terms of the rights of freedom of expression and information, and more for outright provocation. This war propaganda, consistent with the pattern of behaviour adopted by the states in the matter of direct and indirect use of force, may have emerged independently from either side from time to time and may then have unreasonably

20. A/RES/2131(XX), 21 Dec. 1965.
21. Adopted by A/RES/2200A(XXI), 16 Dec. 1966.
22. Stone, J., *Legal Controls of International Conflict*, London 1954, pp. 318-323.
23. Röling, B.V.A., "International Law and the Maintenance of Peace", 4 *NYIL* (1973), p. 1, at pp. 84-85.

escalated. Given this state of affairs, the idea of placing responsibility upon either *one* of the two states for the breach of the general duty not to broadcast propaganda for wars of aggression is both unrealistic and inappropriate. It is safer in both legal and factual terms to place responsibility on both states for a mutual violation of this duty and for creating a situation which ultimately erupted in a breach of international peace.

II   THE RIGHT OF SELF-DEFENCE

A   General principles

Both Iran and Iraq have accused each other of (i) direct and indirect aggression and (ii) the fomenting of civil strife and of rendering assistance to insurgents in their respective territories. The question of self-defence in the context of (i) is discussed in section 2, while the general question regarding whether or not the right of self-defence can be pleaded in the matter of assistance and interference is examined in section 3.

1   *Preliminary remarks on the right of self-defence*

The first important observation here is that under Article 51, a state must be subjected to an armed attack before the right can be exercised by that state. In the second place, once the right has been exercised it must be justified on the basis of the relevant provisions of international law, especially the terms of Article 51. Hence, it will not be sufficient for a state to *claim* that circumstances existed which justified the adoption of measures of self-defence. It will at some point have to demonstrate by evidence that such circumstances had indeed existed, and by virtue of Article 51 these circumstances are limited to the occurrence of an armed attack upon the defending state. A similar point was upheld by the Nuremberg International Military Tribunal which observed that the question whether or not the action taken under the claim of self-defence was in fact aggressive or defensive must ultimately be subjected to investigation and adjudication if international law is to be enforced.[24]

Third, the state exercising this right will have to discharge a heavy burden of proof in order to succeed in justifying the use of armed force. This precept was effectively confirmed in the very elaborate judgment given by the International Court in the *Military and Paramilitary Activities* Case with regard to the position of the United States in the matter of measures of collective self-defence adopted by her against alleged Nicaraguan intervention in El Salvador. The fact that the Court ultimately rejected this claim demonstrates that self-defence is a right which is to be exercised with due care and is not to be lightly interpreted.

---

24. 41 *AJIL* (1947), p. 172.

2   *Self-defence and direct and indirect aggression*

The acts of aggression described in Article 3(a) to (e) of the Definition of Aggression can easily be regarded as a species of a direct use of force, and hence also as armed attack. *Prima facie*, therefore, the occurrence of any of these acts against a state would give rise to the right of self-defence under Article 51 of the Charter by the victim state. Acts, however, falling under Article 3(f) and (g) dealing with indirect force do not readily fall into the category of 'armed attack', and consequently the main question here is whether the sending of armed bands which carry out grave acts of force in the territory of a state constitutes an 'armed attack' within the meaning of Article 51 of the Charter.

In the *Military and Paramilitary Activities* Case the International Court held that it may now be considered to be agreed that an armed attack must be understood as including not merely action by regular armed forces across international borders, but also the sending of armed bands and other irregular groups which carry out grave acts of armed force. It concluded by observing that Article 3(g) of the Definition of Aggression may be taken to reflect customary international law.[25] Therefore, the state claiming self-defence must establish armed attack or its related notion of aggression, namely the commission of one or more of the acts described in Article 3 of the Definition of Aggression.

Both Iran and Iraq claim to have been victims of direct and indirect aggression and consequently both claim the right of self-defence. Three points need to be noticed here. First, as regards the initial act of self-defence carried out in response to a direct armed attack, it is the case that the matter essentially devolves into one of fact, and to this extent, the issue turns upon evidence. Secondly, as far as indirect aggression within the meaning of Article 3(g) of the Definition of Aggression is concerned, Iraq will have to demonstrate that the alleged acts carried out by Iranian armed bands in Iraq were of sufficient gravity effectively to constitute an Iranian invasion, bombardment or attack; it will not be sufficient for Iraq to give evidence involving simply a number of bombing incidents or the poisoning of water supplies and the like.

Iran, of course, relies primarily on the incidents of 22 September 1980 as the basis of its right under Article 51 and may therefore not have to rely heavily on the claim that Iraqi armed bands allegedly operated in Iran, although such activities may serve as a concurrent basis for defensive measures. If this is so the condition of sufficient gravity will be equally applicable here.

Furthermore, the burden of proving self-defence will be a heavy one because, as regards indirect aggression, once the offence under Article 3(g) is firmly established it would justify any appropriate armed response made by the victim state.

Thirdly, there is a clear probability that both states on different occasions and over a period of time may have carried out individual acts of armed provocation against the

25. *ICJ Reports* (1986), p. 103, pp. 124-125; See also the dissenting opinion of Judge Schwebel, *ibidem*, pp. 331-341. For an appraisal of the judgment, see Briggs, H.W., 'The International Court of Justice Lives up to its Name', 81 *AJIL* (1987), p. 78, at pp. 83-84.

other. This would have serious implications for both states: they may both have committed crimes against peace for which they will individually have to bear international responsibility. Although, in principle, both states may *equally* claim the right of self-defence where either of them are attacked, the assertion of such mutual claims would appear to be an unsatisfactory state of affairs. On this view, a state can hardly be heard to rely on this right where she may have herself participated in unlawful acts of armed force. It appears reasonable to suggest that a state claiming the right of self-defence must come with clean hands. In such a situation, the primary operative norm would not be Article 51 alone but also Article 2(4) and (3) of the Charter, namely the duty not to use force and the duty to settle all disputes likely to threaten the breach of peace by peaceful means.

3   *Self-defence, assistance to insurgents and the fomenting of civil strife*

Although assistance rendered by a state to insurgents operating in another state may constitute an unlawful use of force, it does not, as such, constitute either aggression or armed attack within the meaning of Article 51 and hence precludes the operation of a right of self-defence. This view was confirmed by the International Court in the *Military and Paramilitary Activities* Case. It observed that it does not 'believe that the concept of "armed attack" includes not only acts of armed bands where such acts occur on a significant scale but also assistance to rebels in the form of the provision of weapons or logistical or other support. Such assistance may be regarded as a threat or use of force, or amount to intervention in the internal or external affairs of another state.'[26]

Notwithstanding these observations, this rule is not without its difficulties. In those circumstances where both (a) the level of involvement, in terms of assistance given to insurgents by the intervening state and (b) the extent of disruption caused by such assistance and interference in the affected state are of considerable proportions and occur to a substantial degree, a state may effectively wage a proxy war against another. While the former state will clearly be in breach of Article 2(4) and, importantly, even be in a position to overthrow an existing government, it will not strictly speaking have carried out an armed attack against the affected state. As a consequence the affected state will have no remedy under Article 51, because no armed attack within the meaning of this Article may be said to have occurred. Moreover, the use of armed force in response to such assistance in the territory of the assisting state would plausibly be in breach of Article 2(4).

These difficulties may be overcome by simply assimilating the concept of assistance to insurgents and the fomenting of civil strife with the notions of aggression and armed attack, provided that (a) the assistance rendered to the insurgents by the intervening state and (b) the extent of the disturbances effected are both of considerable proportions. This is recommended on the following grounds. First, all proportionate armed counter-measures executed for defensive purposes become lawful uses of force. This

---

26. *ICJ Reports* (1986), pp. 103-104; see also *ibidem*, pp. 126-127.

protects the state from placing itself in a position of effectively committing an act of agression, an act this state would otherwise be seen to be committing if it were to carry out armed counter-measures in response to interference. Secondly, if both direct and indirect, overt and covert uses of force are all generally speaking unlawful it appears reasonable to propose that the legal significance and implications of these acts be alike. There is little factual difference, it appears, between large-scale disruption caused by activities of armed bands infiltrating into the territory of a state and similar situations created by assistance given to insurgents.

Despite these arguments one crucial difficulty cannot be ignored. If assistance and interference are assimilated to the concepts of aggression and armed attack the scope for the exercise of the right of self-defence will be greatly enhanced. The number of situations in which armed force will become a viable lawful option will markedly increase leaving the way open for a grand escalation of hostilities. At any rate, in the light of the existing law, it appears that even if the claims of Iraq are accepted at face-value, *viz.*, that Iran assisted insurgents and fomented civil strife in Iraq, the latter would still not be justified in adopting measures of self-defence, inasmuch as the *sine qua non* element, namely armed attack, would not have been satisfied. This conclusion, it must be stressed, is applicable only in those cases where Iraq has claimed to have acted in response to interference and assistance by Iran. It follows that the armed attack which Iraq initiated in response to the alleged assistance of insurgents by Iran must then be regarded in principle as being an unlawful use of force.

B   Substantive and procedural limitations

Substantive limitations on the right of self-defence are, for the purposes of this examination, those which relate to the problems of proportionality and necessity and are examined in section 1. Procedural limitations are those which are inherent in the right of self-defence by virtue of the obligations created by the United Nations Charter in Articles 51, 39 and 40. These are discussed in section 2 below.

1   *Substantive limitations*

a   Proportionality and necessity

In circumstances where the law expressly sanctions the use of force in self-defence, or to put the matter in another way, permits the use of violence by one state against another, it is reasonable that it should also prescribe certain limits to the use of such violence or force. The tests of proportionality, necessity and immediacy are these limiting conditions of self-defence and owing to the nature of the right are essential to it. They involve an obligation which requires the defending state not only to use all measures of self-defence in proportion to the armed attack but to see that they are limited to the necessity of defending the state.[27] However, proportionality is not to be equated with equality; the measures adopted to put them into effect may not necessarily be confined to the territory of the defending state, and may include large-scale strikes to repel numerous small-scale 'pin-prick' attacks.[28] In the matter of self-defence against armed bands, the International Court in the *Military and Paramilitary Activities* Case noted that the United States mining of and attacks on Nicaraguan ports, oil installations and its air and sea clashes did not satisfy the criterion of proportionality. 'Whatever uncertainty', it ruled, 'may exist as to the exact scale of the aid received by the Salvadorian armed opposition from Nicaragua, it is clear that these latter United States activities in question could not have been proportionate to that aid.'[29]

Despite certain features of uncertainty, there is a core of certainty regarding the proportionality of measures. In many straight-forward cases, there will normally be no great difficulty in determining whether or not an act is proportional to the initial attack. Apart from this, in circumstances where a defending state's response exceeds the requirements of self-defence that state will have to bear international responsibility not only for acts which do not constitute lawful defence, but also for the inevitable escalation of the conflict, on the ground that the aggressor state will, on the balance of probabilities, respond with even greater force. It is clear, therefore, that insofar as the *initial response* is crucial for the future conduct of the war, international law imposes a special duty of care upon the state exercising its right of self-defence to ensure that its response does not exceed the objectives of defence.

The difficulty, however, with the proportionality rule is that it is an extremely relative concept, dependent as it is upon a variety of factors including the nature, scale, frequency, duration and destructive potential of the armed attack, direct or indirect. A related problem is that on many occasions it may be difficult to determine the precise nature of proportional measures and to compare them with aggressive attacks, and an attempt to do so may be illustrative of a degree of artificiality. Another aspect of this artificiality is that not only may *defensive* force be used to a degree greater than the *aggressive* use of force, it may also cause wastage on a scale greater than that caused by the initial attack. This is true even where the response is essentially limited by its objectives.

These observations highlight the central point here. The criterion of proportionality effectively places a *maximum limit* on the degree of force a state may lawfully employ

---

27. See generally, Brownlie, *op.cit.* (note 12), pp. 261-64; McDougal, M./Feliciano, F.P., "Legal Regulations of Resort to International Coercion: Aggression and International Coercion in Policy Perspective", 68 *Yale Law Journal* (1958-59), p. 1057, at pp. 1132-1153, especially pp. 1150-1153; Dinstein, *op.cit.* (note 12), pp. 190-192; 216-220; Ago, R., "State Responsibility: Addendum to the 8th. Report on State Responsibility", *Yearbook ILC* (1980), vol. II, Part 1, p. 41, at pp. 69-70; Kelsen, H., *Principles of International Law*, 2nd. edition, New York 1966, pp. 81-83; Greenwood, C., "Self-Defence and the Conduct of International Armed Conflict", in: Dinstein, Y. (ed.), *International Law at a Time of Perplexity*, Dordrecht 1988, p. 273; Combacau, J., "The Exception of Self-Defence in UN Practice", in: Cassese, A. (ed.), *The Current Legal Regulation of the Use of Force*, Dordrecht 1986, p. 28.

28. Ago, *loc.cit.* (note 12), p. 69; Brownlie, *op.cit.* (note 12), p. 264; Schachter, *loc. cit.* (note 12), pp. 155-156.

29. *ICJ Reports* (1986), p. 122.

in its defence, a situation in which military responses may dwindle quickly into retaliation under the protective guise of measures of self-defence. Judge Schwebel, in his Dissenting Opinion in the *Military and Paramilitary Activities* Case, aptly illustrated this 'maximum limit' principle when he said

> 'Even if it be accepted, *arguendo*, that the current object of United States policy is to overthrow the Nicaraguan Government and this is by no means established that is not necessarily disproportionate to the obvious object of Nicaragua in supporting the Salvadorian rebels who seek [the] overthrow of the Government of El Salvador.'[30]

In view of these problems, it is submitted that a subjective approach be abandoned in favour of a relatively more useful test which, while ceasing to be a 'proportionality' test, will obviate some of the difficulties attendant with the identification of what constitutes proportionality in response to an attack. In this test, the limits of self-defence will be determined by three elements:
(a) the objectives of self-defence,
(b) the means and measures adopted by the defending state, and
(c) the consequences of the means adopted.

The objectives of self-defence are three-fold: (i) fending off current, persistent attacks; (ii) fending off and protection from further attacks which constitute an integral part of the continuum of hostilities; (iii) the restoration of the territorial *status quo*. Category (b) consists of all kinds of armed manoeuvres, including strategic and tactical measures, direct and indirect uses of force and aerial strikes. It also includes matters relative to intensity, scale and duration of such measures, and the weaponry used to carry them into effect. Category (c) refers to all kinds of adverse consequences flowing directly from category (b), *viz.* loss of life, destruction of property and wastage of resources.

Putting the proposition at its simplest, not only are all three elements to be seen restrictively and narrowly, but categories (a) and (b) are to be effected with maximum restraint. Thus, neither the objectives nor the means can be adopted or carried out liberally. Similarly, the measures of defence must be the *least possible means* the state could reasonably have adopted to secure the stated objectives. The consequences of these measures must also be minimal in terms of wastage of life, property and resources. In 1964, Britain carried out counter-measures on Harib Fort in Yemen following the latter's alleged bombardment of Saudi territory. In the Security Council, Sir Patrick Dean, the United Kingdom representative, stated that in order to minimize loss of life and danger to civilian property an isolated target was chosen. 'To destroy the fort', he said, 'with the minimum use of force was therefore a defensive measure which was proportionate to and confined to the necessities of the case.'[31]

The chief merit here is that while the proportionality test lays down a maximum proportionate limit, the minimal conditions test obliges the defending state to maintain

30. *ICJ Reports* (1986), p. 270.
31. *UN Doc.* S/PV.1106 of 2 April 1964, paragraphs 54 and 55. See also *UN Doc.* S/PV.1109 of 7 April 1964.

minimum objectives and conditions. This is compatible with both the principle of the non-use of force in the settlement of disputes between states and with the proposition that since international law abhors the use of armed force between states, even the legitimate use of force is to be viewed as restrictively as possible. Yet the minimal conditions test has its difficulties, chief of which are the problems of evaluating the notion and determining the nature of minimum measures and consequences. Since features of relativity and subjectivity are not alien to this concept either, the substitution of one set of difficulties for another is not altogether a satisfactory solution. Nevertheless, once a conflict has begun and is proving difficult to stop, one of the most pressing considerations must be to ensure that the hostilities do not escalate. Hence the rationale of placing a duty upon the defending state to use minimum as opposed to proportionate force consistent with the objectives of self-defence is not without appeal.

b   The right to continue measures of self-defence

Some writers contend that a state has the right to continue her measures of self-defence even though the aggressor state may have lost its 'appetite' for hostilities and may have called for a cessation thereof.[32] It is submitted that this view is unsatisfactory . It ignores the fact that the matter is indeed complex. Self-defence is to be seen restrictively and has to be confined to one or more of the three basic objectives. Hence, where the aggressor state indicates a willingness to end hostilities either by clear statements or necessary implication, or where the manifestations of aggression disappear, there is, subject to the following conditions, a duty to end self-defensive measures. In the *Military and Paramilitary Activities* Case, the International Court dismissed United States claims of self-defence on the ground that 'the reaction of the United States in the context of what it regarded as self-defence was continued long after the period in which any presumed armed attack by Nicaragua could reasonably be contemplated.'[33] However, the duty to cease hostilities once an aggressor state has indicated its willingness to stop must, on this view, be qualified by three exceptions. Accordingly, the defending state would *not* be obliged to cease hostilities:

a) Where the ensuing peace would be used by the aggressor not only to reinforce her capacity to wage war but also to launch fresh attacks upon the defending state. In other words, a state exercising her right of self-defence would be justified in not accepting an offer to end hostilities where there is *clear evidence* to demonstrate that the offer is not a *bona fide* one.

(b) Where a restoration of the territorial *status quo* cannot be effected. In circumstances where the aggressor state has acquired control over territory pertaining *prima facie* to the defending state, a cease-fire would tend to entrench positions of

---

32. Dinstein, *op.cit.* (note 12), p. 219; Oppenheim, L., Lauterpacht, H., *International Law. Disputes, War and Neutrality*, vol. II, 7th. edition, London 1952, p. 225; Kunz, J.L., "Individual and Collective Self-Defence in Article 51 of the Charter of the United Nations", 41 *AJIL* (1947), pp. 876-877; Ago, *loc.cit.* (note 21), pp. 54-55, 56; Greenwood, *loc.cit.* (note 12), p. 282.

33. *ICJ Reports* (1986), pp. 122-123.

control, and recovery through negotiations may prove a difficult, if not an impossible, task.

(c) Where United Nations enforcement measures under Article 42 of the Charter can be assimilated to collective self-defence. The *a priori* assumption here is that any action taken by the United Nations is by definition a lawful and just measure. It follows that any decision to continue or end hostilities will depend upon a careful assessment of all the relevant factors and not simply upon a call made by the aggressor state to end hostilities. The Security Council and relevant United Nations forces may lawfully refuse to terminate the war until all conditions are satisfied.

c   Proportionality of self-defence: Iraq and Iran

Iraq. Before the question of the proportionality of Iraq's measures is examined, two preliminary observations are to be noted. If acting in self-defence on 22 September 1980, Iraq would have to demonstrate that its measures were necessary and proportional to Iran's armed attack. Second, in order to determine whether the measures, generally considered to be large-scale military initiatives causing considerable destruction, were disproportionate reference will have to be made to the degree of force she was subjected to by: (a) the alleged shelling and bombardment of Iraqi border posts, towns and oil targets on and before 4 September 1980, and (b) the sending by Iran of armed bands across the frontier line.

As regards (a), it appears *prima facie* that the bombing and destruction of oil installations and the swift invasion of Iranian territory were on a scale greater than any of the alleged attacks carried out by Iranian forces. Apparently, therefore, Iraqi measures of self-defence were not proportionate to the armed attack and were, to the extent of their disproportionality, invalid measures. Equally, the responsibility for escalating the conflict may also fall on Iraq on the ground that her initial response was so considerably out of proportion that it resulted in Iran responding with equal vigour. Yet the matter has to be kept in perspective. Even if it is agreed that the alleged Iranian attacks were minor in comparison with those carried out by Iraqi forces, it may nevertheless be that the latter's measures were a genuine response to actual aggression carried out by Iran and were based on a *bona fide* assessment of the danger posed to the Iraqi State. It is relevant that Iran was accused by Iraq of violating Iraqi airspace at least fifty-seven times between February 1979 and May 1980; one hundred and eighty-seven violations of the border between June and September 1980 and fifteen intensive bombardment incidents between August 1979 and June 1980.[34] If, therefore, Iraq was responding to an 'accumulation of events' situation, her response could arguably be seen as a large-scale decisive blow inflicted to overcome a series of smaller attacks. Such measures, then, may not necessarily have been excessive. The fact nevertheless remains that Iraq clearly initiated an offensive along a three-hundred mile front.

Secondly, as the Iran-Iraq conflict continued and developed into full-scale war, the question of proportionality could be seen as having lost some, but not all, of its

---

34. *UN Doc.* S/PV.2250, *loc.cit.* (note 4) and *UN Doc.* S/PV.2251, *loc.cit.* (note 3).

significance, a fact which serves to highlight the weakness inherent in the criterion. At the same time, it emphasises the importance, by contrast, of the minimal conditions test, for were it to be applied to the situation at hand, Iraqi actions could easily be demonstrated as being unlawful, since they were clearly not minimal either in intensity or in scale. At any rate, the observations made in connexion with both the proportionality and minimal conditions tests have to be put into context with other important facts of the war which call into question the validity of Iraqi defensive measures. First, on many occasions during the war Iraq employed chemical warfare agents in various sectors of the front which killed or injured both civilian and military personnel.[35] Accordingly, the Iraqi Government was in breach of international humanitarian law, especially the Geneva Protocol on the Prohibition of Gases of 1925.[36] Quite apart from the criminal responsibility of the Iraqi Government regarding these breaches, the measures adopted were clearly neither proportionate nor minimum in nature, scale or intensity.

Secondly, similar considerations apply to Iraq's indiscriminate bombing of civilian and residential areas, measures prohibited under Article 51(5)(b) of the 1977 Geneva Protocol I Additional to the Geneva Conventions of 12 April 1949.[37] This provision reflects on this view customary international law on the matter, and therefore it is immaterial whether or not the treaty-regime applies to the two states.[38] It is also legally irrelevant that Iraq may have been retaliating to Iranian attacks of a similar nature. The legality or otherwise of reprisals is not relevant here because the study is confined to issues *ius ad bellum* as opposed to *ius in bello*. The doctrine of self-defence does not sanction retaliation, and retaliation which involves breaches of international humanitarian law constitutes a still graver abuse of the right of self-defence. In sum, therefore, all incidents of the use of force which were disproportionate to, or exceeded the minimum requirements of defence, especially those relative to chemical weapons, could not be classified as acts of self-defence and were hence unlawful and Iraq must bear full responsibility for them.

As regards (b), *viz.*, the alleged sending of armed bands by Iranian authorities across the international boundary, the Government of Iraq may find itself in further difficulties. Large-scale attacks on towns and prime industrial installations would appear *prima facie* to be a disproportionate use of force in the face of such indirect aggression. Even if, as Bryde observed, there is evidence of indirect aggression, the proportionality rule will not usually justify direct action against the supporting state;

35. See Specialist Reports, *UN Doc*. S/15834 of 20 June 1983, and *UN Doc*. S/16433 of 26 March 1984. Both reports confirmed that tabun and mustard gas had been used. Further, see *UN Doc*. S/17127 of 24 April 1985; *UN Doc*. S/17911 & Add. 1 of 12 March 1986; *UN Doc*. S/18852 of 8 May 1987; and *UN Doc*. S/19823 of 25 April 1988. The Specialist Report of 14 April 1988 confirmed that both sides had used chemical weapons: see 25 *UN Chronicle* (1988), No. 3, p. 40. See also *UN Doc*. S/20060 of 20 July 1988, and *UN Doc*. S/20134 of 19 August 1988.

36. 94 *LNTS* (1929), p. 65. Both states are parties. See Chapter 3, paragraph II.A of this book.

37. 16 *ILM* (1977), p. 1391. Iran signed but did not ratify; Iraq did neither. For the view of the Security Council, see S/RES/582(1986) of 24 Febr. 1986.

38. See Chapter 3, paragraph I and II of this book.

although, he added, the latter state might allow attacks on the bases of such groups on foreign territory.[39] In a similar vein, Iraq's difficulties appear to be compounded in the face of evidence of chemical warfare and the indiscriminate bombing of civilian areas. Observations made above regarding reprisals *ius in bello* are equally relevant here.

Iran. If, on the other hand, Iranian contentions of self-defence are to believed, its initial responses against Iraqi manoeuvres were, on the whole, proportional to the attack; but even here certain measures were grossly disproportionate and unnecessary. First, there were a considerable number of attacks by Iran on neutral shipping in the Persian Gulf. Such attacks constitute a violation of the rights of neutral merchantmen not carrying contraband, under Article 1 of the 1907 Hague Convention No. XIII Concerning the Rights and Duties of Neutral Powers in Naval War, a treaty regarded as being declaratory of customary international law.[40]

It is instructive that in the *Military and Paramilitary Activities* Case, Judge Schwebel, in his Dissenting Opinion, held that whereas the mining of Nicaraguan ports by the United States was a lawful measure in the course of collective self-defence, it was unlawful where these mines damaged ships of third states: the United States Government had neither notified the mining of the ports to third states, nor announced warnings of the existence of such mines. Hence, international responsibility of the United States may arise for injuries and damages sustained to third state nationals.[41]

Despite this relatively clear-cut violation of the law, there do exist certain countervailing consid rations. One of these is that maritime operational zones have not been uncommon features of wars between states in relatively recent times. Such zones were maintained by belligerents on both sides in the First and Second World Wars. Neutral shipping entering such zones did so at its own peril.[42] It follows that Iraq's measures *within*, as opposed to outside, its zone may not necessarily have been unlawful, especially in view of the great intensity of the war. Acts outside such zones are incompatible with self-defence.

Another fact detracting from her alleged measures of self-defence is that Iran also used chemical weapons against Iraq,[43] perhaps in retaliation. Not only was their use a breach of the relevant principles of humanitarian law, it was also incompatible with the right of self-defence in terms of both the proportionality and the minimal conditions criteria. Moreover, even if Iran were retaliating against Iraq's use of chemical weapons,

39. Bryde, B-O., "Self-Defence", in: Bernhardt, R., *Encyclopedia of Public International Law,* Instalment 4, Amsterdam 1982, p. 212 at p. 214.

40. See for the text 2 *AJIL* (1908) (Supp.), p. 202; Iran/Persia signed but did not ratify.

41. *ICJ Reports* (1986), pp. 379-380.

42. See generally, O'Connell, D.P., *International Law of the Sea,* vol. II, Oxford 1984, pp. 1095-1101; Oppenheim, *op.cit.* (note 32), pp. 673-684; Detter De Lupis, I., *The Law of War,* Cambridge 1987, pp. 152-153; Doswald-Beck, L., "The International Law of Naval Armed Conflicts: The Need for Reform", 7 *Italian Year Book of International Law* (1986-87), p. 251; and Jenkins, M., "Air Attacks on Neutral Shipping in the Persian Gulf: The Legality of the Iraqi Exclusive Zone and Iranian Reprisals", 8 *Boston College International and Comparative Law Review* (1985), pp. 517, *et seq.*

43. See Specialist Report of 14 Apr. 1988, *loc.cit.* (note 29); and *UN Doc.* S/20063 of 25 July 1988; *cf.* the Report of 8 May 1987, *UN Doc.* S/18852.

Iran lost sight of the fact that, although an alleged victim of aggression, it would nevertheless have to bear responsibility for such reprisals.[44] Finally, Iranian attacks on civilian targets were equally disproportionate and unnecessary and constituted invalid measures of self-defence.

d   Rejections of Security Council resolutions

This issue involves examining the legal problems created by Iran's steadfast refusal to comply with various Security Council resolutions in the period extending between September 1980 and July 1988, especially Resolution 598 (1987) of 20 July 1987. While Iraq agreed to comply with these resolutions,[45] Iran rejected them on various grounds including the claim that Iraq's original objective of ouster of the revolutionary regime had not changed.[46] It was also alleged that a fair end to the war could only be found if the Iraqi aggressor were vanquished and punished[47] and the regime removed. It is submitted that these are not valid reasons for continuing to exercise the right of self-defence. The law on this issue has been stated in section b above. Inasmuch as Iraq, the alleged aggressor, had agreed in principle to accept the resolutions, and thereby to cease hostilities and restore the territorial *status quo,* Iran was not justified, on this view, in rejecting the offer to comply with the relevant Security Council resolutions. Nor is there conclusive evidence to suggest that Iraq's offers to cease hostilities were intended to gain time for further offensives. The territorial dimension to the problem is discussed below.

2   *Procedural limitations and obligations: Articles 51, 39 and 40 of the Charter*

Two procedural limitations contained in the Charter remain to be noted. Article 51 provides that the inherent right of self-defence continues 'until the Security Council has taken measures necessary to maintain international peace and security.' While the article simply refers to 'measures necessary', the phrase has generally been interpreted to mean *effective measures*.[48] The question whether or not such measures are indeed effective is a matter to be determined by an objective, as opposed to a subjective, appreciation of all the facts and circumstances of the case.[49] In practical terms what constitutes effective measures depends not only upon the simple functional success of such measures but also on the circumstances of the conflict and the attitude of the

44. See Chapter 3, para. II.A of this book.

45. See letter of the Iraqi Representative to the Secretary-General of 29 Sept. 1980, *UN Doc.* S/14203; and see Report of the Secretary-General of 17 Oct. 1982, *UN Doc.* S/15499; and letter of the Iraqi Representative to the Secretary-General of 14 Aug. 1987, *UN Doc.* S/19045.

46. See letter of the Iranian Representative to the Secretary-General in Report of the Secretary-General to the Security Council of 26 Nov. 1986, *UN Doc.* S/18480.

47. *UN Doc.* S/PV.2251, *loc.cit.* (note 3). See Chapter 8, paragraph IV of this book.

48. Bowett, D.W., *Self-Defence in International Law*, Manchester 1958, p. 196; Kelsen, *op.cit.* (note 28), p. 795.

49. Bowett, *op.cit.* (note 48), p. 196.

belligerents. Where, for example, peace-keeping forces are in place, the defending state cannot, *in all the appropriate circumstances,* either resume or continue hostilities. Where, however, United Nations measures are in the nature of resolutions of the Security Council calling upon the belligerents to end hostilities, they may be deemed to have become effective once the aggressor state has agreed in principle to comply with the terms of the resolutions, either unilaterally or bilaterally, that is to say, where she has agreed both to the cessation of hostilities and to the withdrawal of troops. The agreement in principle by Iraq to abide by these resolutions is of some importance because if it is accepted, for the purposes of this analysis, that Iraq was indeed the aggressor, its willingness to cooperate and implement the resolutions would make them effective measures for the simple reason that the resolutions could then be seen as having had successful practical consequences. In short, these resolutions were arguably effective measures within the meaning of Article 51, and it follows therefore that Iran, as the defending state, was, on receiving notice of Iraq's agreement in principle, obliged to cease hostilities as soon as was practicable.

The Iranian Government has, of course, been concerned about Iraq's territorial claims. Its source for concern may have been the fact that although the Government in Baghdad had agreed to observe a cease-fire, it had no intention of withdrawing to the international boundary, namely the *Thalweg* of the Shatt-al-Arab established by the 1975 Treaty. Consequently, Iran could plausibly contend that Iraqi acceptance of the resolutions was in fact pretence and the resolutions were, to that extent, ineffective. There was, on the basis of this argumentation, no obligation upon Iran to cease deploying defensive measures. Iran, however, cannot be supported for refusing to comply with these resolutions. Iran could have agreed in principle to comply with the resolutions provided Iraq gave a specific commitment to restore the *status quo ante* and withdraw along the 1975 alignment. Iran could also have ceased hostilities and cooperated with a United Nations supervised withdrawal along the 1975 line. If Iraq either refused to give a specific commitment or failed to withdraw along the 1975 *Thalweg* line, Iran could have maintained its right either to continue or to resume hostilities on the grounds (a) that the Security Council resolutions had failed to become effective; and (b) that the aggression was effectively a continuing one. Article 3(a) of the Definition of Aggression defines 'any military occupation, however temporary, resulting from such invasion or attack, or any annexation by the use of force of the territory of another state or part thereof ...' as an act of aggression, which act may be equated with the notion of armed attack. In principle, therefore, this would validate the continued use of force in self-defence by Iran. The inevitable conclusion is that Iran's continued use of force became legally unacceptable and that Iran would have to bear international responsibility for refusing to comply with the relevant resolutions.

Quite apart from these considerations, Iran would still have to contend with the legal obligations arising from action taken by the Security Council under Articles 39 and 40 of the Charter. Resolution 598 (1987) was expressly passed on the bases of these articles, the latter of which provides that it may, before proceeding under Article 39, 'call upon the parties concerned to comply with such provisional measures as it deems necessary or desirable', and goes on to stipulate that the Council shall take account of failure to comply with such provisional measures. It is generally agreed that such provisional measures, which include recommendations calling upon Members to terminate hostilities and to withdraw to the international frontier are obligatory,[50] and failure so to do is unlawful.[51] This is especially so where the Security Council specifically mentions Article 40. In these circumstances, both parties were under a legal duty to accept Resolution 598 (1987) promptly, a duty Iraq discharged on 14 August 1987 by virtue of her letter of acceptance addressed to the President of the Security Council. Iran, however, failed to respond favourably to the resolution and accepted it after almost a year had elapsed on 17 July 1988. These observations reinforce the view that Iran will have to bear international responsibility for an unwarranted continuation of hostilities in general, and for those effected during the period extending between July 1987 and July 1988.

50. Goodrich, L.M./Hambro, E./Simons, A.P., *Charter of the United Nations,* 3rd edition, New York 1969, p. 306; Bowett, *op.cit.* (note 48), p. 197; De Arechaga, *loc.cit.* (note 12), pp. 120-121; Kelsen, H., "Collective Security under the Charter of the United Nations", 42 *AJIL* (1948), p. 783, at pp. 787-788.

51. Brownlie, *op.cit.* (note 12), p. 264 and Bowett, *op.cit.* (note 48), p. 197.

COMMENTS: THE USE OF FORCE AND COLLECTIVE SECURITY

Marc Weller[*]

Abstract law does not control life. It has to be analyzed in concrete terms and applied to actual or potential situations if it is to control human behaviour. This is especially true in international law, the development of which is so heavily dependent on state practice.

Perhaps in contrast to this basic truth, Dr Kaikobad has provided us with an abstract analysis of the Iran-Iraq conflict. In his impressive paper, he consciously abstains from challenging the factual allegations of the parties involved in the conflict and he assumes their respective claims to be correct, even if those are conflicting and mutually exclusive. This approach must, by necessity, lead to somewhat misleading conclusions.

I   THE USE OF FORCE

It is not disputed that Iraq launched a massive invasion of territory which had been under the effective control of the Iranian authorities until 22 September 1980. The status of that territory had been confirmed in the Treaty on International Borders and Good Neighbourly Relations of 13 June 1975.[1] An integral part of the treaty was a clause and Additional Protocol relating to the suppression of subversive penetrations in the border area.[2]

Iraq attempted to rebut the *prima facie* case of an act of aggression having taken place with reference to three principal justifications, all of which appeared to involve the right of self-defence. First, Iraq alleged a campaign of subversion having been mounted from Iran. Secondly, Iraq claimed that 'when Khomeini's subversive sabotage and terrorism through the Dawa Party had failed to achieve their aim, military actions began. (...) [T]he continuous shelling of our border towns, villages and roads became a daily routine in the conduct of the Iranian forces.'[3] Therefore, the Iraqi delegate to the United Nations Security Council asserted, 'my government was left with no choice but to direct preventative strikes against military targets in Iran. There was, to borrow from the well-known Caroline Case, a "necessity of self-

* M. Weller, Research Fellow, Research Centre for International Law, University of Cambridge, St. Catharine's College, Cambridge.

1. 14 *ILM* 1133 (1975).
2. Article 2 of the Treaty, and the Third Additional Protocol.
3. *Security Council Official Records*, 35th yr, 2251st mtg, paras. 51 *et seq.*

I.F. Dekker and H.H.G. Post, eds., The Gulf War of 1980-1988
© 1992, T.M.C. Asser Instituut, The Hague

defence, instant, overwhelming, leaving no choice of means and no moment of deliberation".[4]

These two justifications fail. If there had been a concerted campaign of sabotage and subversion, the government of Iraq would have had the option to seek the protection of the United Nations Security Council or to utilize other means of dispute settlement. In addition, the 1 million strong Iraqi army could have been deployed along the established border so as to make further infiltration impossible. And if the alleged subversive campaign had been severe enough to constitute an armed attack imputable to Iran, then a proportional response would have had to be limited to operations against the basis of these subversive bands in Iran.

The response to the alleged shelling of border areas of early September would similarly have had to be directed at, and limited to, the suppression of the artillery deployments on the Iranian side of the border after all peaceful means of achieving that result, including the involvement of the United Nations Security Council, had been exhausted. Furthermore, the response was not only disproportionate to the alleged armed attack, but it was also delayed. Even if the Caroline formula is still applicable, there was no evidence of an 'instant and overwhelming necessity, leaving no choice of means and no moment of deliberation', on 22 September 1980.

However, the fatal flaw in the Iraqi case is inherent in the third element of its purported justification for the presence of its forces on territory hitherto under the authority of Iran. The government of Iraq argued that the 1975 Boundary Treaty had been terminated through non-compliance with its terms by Iran. The alleged violations of the Treaty was two-fold. In the first place, Iraq claimed that Iran had failed to relinquish all territories that should have been transferred to it under the terms of the Treaty. Secondly, Iraq claimed that the Treaty was null and void due to the failure of Iran to implement its provisions concerning the suppression of subversive activities.

In light of this alleged automatic termination of the boundary agreement, armed action was undertaken 'in the exercise of self-defence of the purpose of restoring Iraq's sovereignty over the totality of its territory.'[5] And the totality of Iraqi territory was defined as all 'land and water territories in Shatt-al-Arab, as was the case before the Algiers agreement.'[6] In effect, therefore, Iraq openly admitted to the use of force for the vindication of territorial claims – a clear breach of Article 2(3) of the United Nations Charter, even if the territorial claims of Iraq had been justified.

Instead of providing such a fairly straightforward analysis, Dr Kaikobad complicates his own argument needlessly. It is not clear why he considers it necessary to analyze the controversial concept of humanitarian intervention in the context of the Iran-Iraq conflict. Even if the alleged expulsion of 40,000 Iranians from Iraq 'caused concern' in Iran, as he suggests, this fact could not really justify the acts of subversion allegedly committed by Iran. First of all, the individuals referred to were, by the

---

4. *Security Council Official Records*, 35th yr, 2250th mtg, para. 40.
5. *Security Council Official Records*, 35th yr, 2251st mtg, para. 60.
6. *Ibidem*, para. 59.

very nature of the act of an expulsion, no longer under the control of the Iraqi authorities. Only if the very lives of large numbers of Shia Muslims who remained in Iraq had been threatened in circumstances of an overwhelming necessity, leaving no choice of means and no moment of deliberation, then, perhaps, the concept of humanitarian intervention might have been relevant. However, no such claim has been made. And even if such a situation had prevailed in Iraq, it would be necessary to discuss the link between these individuals and Iran more closely, as there is a well known and important distinction to be made in international law between the rescue by a state of its own nationals whose lives are imperiled abroad, and an intervention on behalf of foreigners in a foreign country.

Of course, Iran did not respond to the alleged mistreatment of Shiites (or possibly Iranian nationals) with an intervention on their behalf. Its response, according to the allegations put forward by Iraq, was a campaign of 'terrorism' and subversion directed against the Iraqi authorities. There is no evidence of actual operations undertaken which would yield a tangible benefit to the minority which was allegedly mistreated in Iraq. Therefore, the discussion of humanitarian intervention appears to be unconnected with the Iran-Iraq conflict.

Dr Kaikobad's analysis of the distinct concepts of a use of force, an act of aggression, an armed attack and an intervention involving the use of force is, on the other hand, most welcome, for it provides the key to the legal evaluation of the Iran-Iraq conflict. The rapporteur has made a laudable effort to distinguish these concepts. However, one further problem arises. Dr Kaikobad finds that 'there is a clear probability that both states on different occasions and over a period of time may have carried out individual acts of armed provocation against the other.' From this he concludes that '(A)lthough, in principle, both states may *equally* claim the right of self-defence where either of them are attacked, the assertion of such mutual claims would appear to be an unsatisfactory state of affairs. On this view, a state can hardly be heard to rely on this right where it may have itself participated in unlawful acts of armed force. It appears reasonable to suggest that a state claiming the right of self-defence must come with clean hands.'

This view requires re-examination by the author. There is no evidence to be found that involvement by a state in low-grade intervention or in armed incidents would render it (legally) defenceless in case of a large-scale armed attack directed against it. Even a state which has itself launched an armed attack of significant gravity is protected in international law from counter-measures which go beyond that what is necessary to repel the attack and restore the *status quo*. A wrong perpetrated by the organs of state, serious though it may be, does not extinguish the right of that state to exist and to protect its existence within the limits set out in international law.[7]

7. Of course, if there had been a series of subversive acts and of armed incidents imputable to Iran, then Iraq might be entitled to compensation. While the Iraqi claims are not persuasive to justify the virtual invasion of Iran, they might, if well-founded, be offset to an extent against Iranian claims for compensation.

The problem of assistance rendered to groups engaged in insurgent activities abroad might also merit further attention. Dr Kaikobad appears to be arguing in favour of 'assimilating the concept of assistance to insurgents and the fomenting of civil strife with the notions of aggression and armed attack.' This interesting proposition was emphatically rejected in the negotiations which led up to most of the recent United Nations standards concerning the non-use of force and intervention, and it would have to be defended with much greater reference to actual state practice.

II   THE USE OF FORCE AND COLLECTIVE SECURITY

A   The response at the United Nations

The response to the use of force by Iraq in the United Nations Security Council – the organ charged with primary responsibility for the maintenance of international peace and security – was hesitant and muted. In its initial Resolution 479 (1980), the Security Council merely called upon the parties to refrain immediately from further use of force and settle the dispute peacefully.[8] Iran rejected that resolution, stating that the Council 'should condemn the premeditated act of aggression that has taken place, call for the immediate withdrawal of the Iraqi forces from Iranian territory and call upon Iraq to compensate Iran for damages. It should also condemn the Iraqi authorities for war crimes.'[9] Iraq, on the other hand, rejected the demand for a withdrawal as a 'precondition for a cease-fire', and argued:[10]

> 'This is contrary to resolution 479 (1980), which we have accepted and Iran has rejected, it is contrary to the elementary rules of logic and contrary to a realistic approach by the Council to settling the dispute once and for all. Indeed, it may very well be a formula for prolonging the armed conflict indefinitely.'

The Council itself treated its own resolution as somehow negotiable and the Secretary-General was charged with a good offices mission to secure the consent of the parties to the proposed resolution of the crisis.[11] In fact, the Council did respond to the views of at least one of the parties, amending the text of its resolution. In Resolution 514 (1982), which was also accepted by Iraq, the Council called for a withdrawal of forces to internationally recognized boundaries in addition to the call for a cease-fire, fulfilling one of Iran's demands.[12] In a further concession to Iran,

---

8. 1980 *Resolutions and Decisions of the Security Council*, p. 23.

9. *Security Council Official Records*, 35th yr, 2252nd mtg, para. 87.

10. *Ibidem*, para. 77.

11. Para. 4 of Resolution 479, and Presidential Statement of 5 November 1980, 1980 *Resolutions and Decisions of the Security Council*, p. 23.

12. 1982 *Resolutions and Decisions of the Security Council*, p. 19.

the Council affirmed the desirability 'of an objective examination of the causes of the war' in Resolution 540 (1983).[13]

In 1984 the good offices of the Secretary-General resulted in a partial and temporary success. He negotiated the 'truce of the cities' which was to exclude attacks on the populations centres of both parties. This measure was embraced by the Council which almost appeared content with achieving an amelioration of the conflict, leaving the modalities of its conclusion to be negotiated between Iran and Iraq.[14]

In Resolution 582 (1986) the Council deplored the initial acts which gave rise to the conflict, coming another step closer to Iranian demands. It also deplored the escalation of the conflict and repeated its call for an immediate cease-fire and withdrawal.[15] It was only in 1987 that the Council, freed from the strictures of cold war rhetoric and obstruction, was able to act more decisively. In Resolution 598 (1987) the Council determined that there existed a breach of the peace as regards the conflict between Iran and Iraq.[16] As a first step towards a negotiated settlement it *demanded* an immediate cease-fire, acting expressly under Articles 39 and 40 of the Charter. However, the cease-fire demand was apparently not deemed to be an independent injunction, but it was part of the 'integrated whole' of the resolution of the conflict envisaged in Resolution 598 (1987).[17] The cease-fire had thus been linked to the respective claims of the parties concerning a supervised withdrawal, the repatriation of prisoners of war, the inquiry into responsibility for the conflict, the question of economic reconstruction and other issues which were reflected in the terms of Resolution 598 (1987).

Upon adoption of Resolution 598 (1987) on 20 July 1987, the government of Iraq affirmed its willingness to respond positively to its terms.[18] In a letter dated 14 August 1987, Iraq welcomed the resolution formally and expressed readiness to cooperate with the Secretary-General and with the Security Council in implementing it in good faith with a view to finding a comprehensive, just, lasting and honourable settlement of the conflict with Iran. The letter continued:[19]

'On the basis of the contents of the resolution and its binding character under Chapter VII of the Charter, it is, of course, obvious that Iran's clear approval of the resolution, confirmed by you, and its clear readiness to fulfil its obligations thereunder, without any terms of conditions, in good faith and with serious intent, are essential for the corresponding obligations which rest upon us ...'

13. 1983 *Resolutions and Decisions of the Security Council*, p. 6.
14. 1984 *Resolutions and Decisions of the Security Council*, p. 11. See also 1985 *Resolutions and Decisions of the Security Council*, p. 6.
15. 1986 *Resolutions and Decisions of the Security Council*, p. 11; also Resolution 588 (1986), *ibidem*, at p. 13.
16. 1987 *Resolutions and Decisions of the Security Council*, p. 5.
17. Presidential Statement, *ibidem*, at p. 6.
18. *UN Doc*. S/PV.2750, p. 86.
19. *UN Doc*. S/19045. That communication also included certain interpretative provisions concerning the time-frame of a withdrawal and the timing of the repatriation of prisoners of war.

Iran, however, had already informed the Security Council in a communication of 11 August that is was unable to accept Resolution 598 (1987). It claimed the resolution had been formulated by the United States with the explicit intention of intervention in the Persian Gulf region, that Iran had not been consulted, and that it would in effect terminate the war in favour of an aggressor state. Iran, describing itself as the victim of Iraq, claimed to be 'the main party to determine how the war can be terminated, and no change can be effected in the course of war as long as conditions of the Islamic Republic of Iran are not met.'[20]

The government of Iran consequently rejected the legal force of Resolution 598 (1987), asserting that there was no justification to suddenly determine that a breach of the peace had taken place, years after the initial act of aggression and when the conflict appeared to be reaching a conclusion favouring Iran. Having failed to fulfil its primary responsibility for the suppression of acts of aggression, Iran argued, the Council had made matters even worse as it had now turned itself into a party to the conflict. According to the position of Iran, a true solution could only be achieved if the Council would abandon that position and identify Iraq as the aggressor state which would be liable to pay reparations.

The government of Iraq countered that Resolution 598 (1987) demanded 'unconditional compliance.' The Iranian attitude, it argued, was liable to promote a precedent '... whereby a state "may not have accepted" or "may not have rejected" a binding Security Council Resolution – without any legal basis ...'[21] Iraq therefore requested the Council to 'vigorously oppose' Iran's methods, in effect seeking the Council's protection.[22] On Christmas eve of 1987, the Council threatened to 'consider further steps to ensure compliance' with Resolution 598 (1987). But very few of its Members expressed a view on the fact that only Iraq had accepted the Resolution, even as late as July of 1988.[23]

Following upon the downing of an Iranian airliner by a US naval vessel in the Gulf, Iran, 'because of the importance it attaches to saving the lives of human beings and the establishment of justice and regional and international peace and security' agreed to cooperate in the implementation of Security Council Resolution 598 (1987). The Secretary-General declared a cease-fire as of 0300 (GMT) on 20 August 1988.[24] That action was endorsed by the Council[25] which established, in Reso-

---

20. *UN Doc.* S/19031.

21. *UN Doc.* S/19049 of 17 August 1987.

22. *UN Doc.* S/19108 of 4 September 1987.

23. The exception was the United States delegation, which drew attention to this fact when defending itself against allegations concerning the downing of an Iranian airliner in the Gulf. *UN Doc.* S/PV.2818, at pp. 54-55.

24. 1988 *Resolutions and Decisions of the Security Council*, p. 10.

25. *Ibidem*, at p. 11.

lution 619 (1988),[26] the Iran-Iraq Military Observer Group to supervise compliance. However, it took two years until the withdrawal could be effected.[27]

B   The legal effects of the Security Council Resolutions

It is, of course, tempting to claim that responsibility for the failure to settle the dispute or situation peacefully and to abstain from the use of force actually shifted during the course of the Iran-Iraq conflict. Undoubtedly, the initiation of massive hostilities by Iraq engaged international responsibility of that state. However, it was Iraq which eagerly offered compliance with the first Security Council Resolution 479 (1980). Did Iran's refusal to comply with that offer and with the other calls for a cease-fire preceeding Resolution 598 (1987) modify its legal relationship with Iraq and possibly with the international community as represented at or by the United Nations and did it engage international responsibility? Or, alternatively, did such a change in legal relationships occur when Iran failed to comply immediately with Resolution 598 (1987)?[28]

There are two kinds of obligations which Iran may have violated in refusing a cease-fire.[29] Firstly, the failure to comply with a Security Council Resolution might violate that Resolution directly, and this violation would also necessarily imply a violation of Article 25 of the Charter. Secondly, the continued use of force in the face of Security Council Resolutions might constitute a breach of the obligation to refrain from the threat or use of force and to settle disputes peacefully.[30] The function of the Resolutions of the Council in this respect would be declaratory and incidental to establishing a breach of obligations in general international law.

---

26. *Idem.*

27. The Iraqi decision to seek a definite conclusion of the conflict was apparently linked to its desire to have a free hand in its policy towards Kuwait. The relevant exchange of letters between Iraq and Iran can be found in *UN Doc.* S/21528 and *UN Doc.* S/21556 and is reprinted, together with the applicable report of the United Nations Iran-Iraq Military Observer Group, *UN Doc.* S/21803, in Lauterpacht, H., *et al.*, *The Kuwait Crisis: Basic Documents*, Cambridge 1991, pp. 64 *et seq.*

28. Either way, Iraq would of course remain responsible for the initiation and prosecution of the conflict up to the point at which responsibility shifted.

29. The issue of bilateral rights and obligations of the parties cannot be addressed within this short comment on the use of force and collective security.

30. Reliance of Article 2(3) instead of Article 2(4) in this context would avoid the problem concerning the 'territorial integrity and political independence' in case of disputed territory. However, the Council itself referred to the prohibition of the use of force in Resolution 479 (1980). Both obligations are of course established both in the United Nations Charter and subsidiary instruments and in customary international law. *E.g.*, *Case Concerning Military and Paramilitary Activities in and against Nicaragua*, *ICJ Reports* (1986), p. 14, pp. 98 *et seq.*

1   *Direct violation of Security Council Resolutions and of Article 25*
         of the Charter

Only if the relevant Security Council Resolutions created binding obligations for the
parties to the conflict could their breach have directly engaged international responsibility.[31] The power of international organizations to make binding decisions rests
upon a grant of authority from their membership. The United Nations has been
accorded such authority in general terms in Article 25. As the International Court of
Justice pointed out in the Namibia Opinion:[32]

> 'It has been contended that Article 25 of the Charter applies only to enforcement
> measures adopted under Chapter VII of the Charter. It is not possible to find in the
> Charter any support for this view. Article 25 is not confined to decisions in regard to
> enforcement action but applies to 'the decisions of the Security Council' adopted in
> accordance with the Charter. Moreover, that Article is placed, not in Chapter VII, but
> immediately after Article 24 in that part of the Charter which deals with the functions and
> powers of the Security Council. If Article 25 had reference solely to decisions of the
> Security Council concerning enforcement action under Articles 41 and 42 of the Charter,
> that is to say, if it were only such decisions which had binding effect, then Article 25
> would be superfluous, since this effect is secured by Articles 48 and 49 of the Charter.'

However, it is necessary to keep in mind the context of the Namibia Opinion. In that
case, the Security Council's demands, expressed in Resolution 276 (1970), were a
reflection of an existing legal situation which prevailed since the General Assembly
had revoked South Africa's Mandate for that territory. The Council's Resolution did
not in itself render the continued occupation of Namibia illegal, but it expressed the
fact of its illegality authoritatively on behalf of the Members of the United Nations.

From the illegality of the situation in objective law, independent of the Council's
determination, flowed certain consequences for other states, such as the obligation of
non-recognition. Again, the Council's call upon states to comply with that obligation
did not in itself create a new obligation, but merely reflected a pre-existing one.[33]
On the other hand, the fact that the Council had made an authoritative determination
of the obligations of the United Nations membership not only clarified the obligations, but strenghtened it in law. Following upon the adoption of Resolution 276
(1970), which specifically invoked Article 25, a failure to comply with the requirement of non-recognition would not only have violated an obligation in general

31. Compare Article 18 of the ILC draft on state responsibility.
32. *Opinion concerning the Legal Consequences for States of the Continued Presence of South Africa
in Namibia (South West Africa) Notwithstanding Security Council Resolution 276 (1970), ICJ Reports*
(1971), p. 14, pp. 52 *et seq.*
33. The attempt to attach binding consequences in excess to those paralleled in general international
law to the finding made by the Council in Resolution 276 (1970) did, of course, lead to great controversy.
However, that aspect of the problem was not dealt with by the Court, although it was anticipated by
Judges Petrén and Fitzmaurice. *Namibia Opinion, op.cit.* (note 32), at pp. 136, 296.

international law, but it would have similarly violated that Resolution and the United Nations Charter.[34]

a   Resolutions preceding the adoption of Resolution 598 (1987)

Of course, the Resolutions of the Council can also create original obligations. Those are not mere reflections of pre-existing obligations which have been adopted by the Council, but they are entirely of its own making and can even contravene and override legal obligations of Members, and possibly Non-members.[35] Such binding decision-making powers of the Council must be exercised in accordance with the purposes and principles of the United Nations.[36] As opposed to measures which might resemble executive decisions of the organization,[37] an active intervention by the Council in the rights or obligations of states would need to be founded on a specific source of authority. In addition, the exercise of specific powers granted to the organization in explicit terms would require compliance with the respective procedural requirements enunciated in the Charter, even if these powers are only recommendatory.[38] The authority and powers granted to the Security Council for the discharge of its duties are laid down in Chapters VI, VII, VIII and XII.[39]

In the case of the Iran-Iraq conflict, the Council was clearly dealing with an issue falling within its competence, inasmuch as the issue was relating to the maintenance of international peace and security.[40] The Council, in Resolution 479 (1980), did in fact invoke explicitly Article 24 of the Charter, which provides that the Council acts on behalf of the United Nations membership in that area of activity.

34. Compare Article 17 of the ILC's draft on state responsibility: '1. An act of a State which constitutes a breach of an international obligation is an internationally wrongful act regardless of the origin, whether customary, conventional or other, of that obligation. 2. The origin of the international obligation breached by a State does not affect the international responsibility arising from the internationally wrongful act of that State.'

35. *E.g.*, Resolution 679 (1990) instituting an air-embargo against Iraq and occupied Kuwait, in which the Council decided that: '... notwithstanding the existence of any rights or obligations conferred or imposed by any international agreement or any contract entered into or any licence or permit granted before the date of the present resolution, shall deny permission to any aircraft to take off from the territory if the aircraft would carry any cargo to or from Iraq of Kuwait other than food in humanitarian circumstances, subject to authorization by the Council or the Committee established by resolution 661 (1990) and in accordance with resolution 666 (1990), or supplies intended strictly for medical purposes or solely for UNIIMOG ...'

36. Article 24(2) of the United Nations Charter.

37. Like, for example, the apportionment of certain expenses incurred by the organization.

38. It would therefore appear difficult to base the authority to take measures other than those which reflect pre-existing obligations in the area of international peace and security on 'implied powers', or on the general rule contained in Article 25, as the Charter itself regulates that area explicitly. The *lex specialis* rule prevailes.

39. Article 24(2) United Nations Charter.

40. According to Article 24(1) of the Charter, the Council enjoys primary responsibility for the maintenance of international peace and security.

The wording 'calls upon'. In principle the call for a cease-fire in Resolution 479 (1980) could have been meant to amount to a binding injunction, for example as a provisional measure under Article 40, even if it did not involve the application of Articles 41 or 42 on enforcement measures. The wording 'calls upon' does not necessarily in itself determine whether a binding obligation was or was not intended,[41] although it is, *prima facie*, consistent with an injuction when used in the context of calls for a cease-fire.[42]

In a resolution concerning Indonesia, for example, the Council called for an immediate discontinuance of all military operations, but it only recommended that negotiations should take place in a certain political framework.[43] This distinction, which can be found in a number of other resolutions adopted in similar circumstances, would seem to make no sense, if it was not intended to signify a different legal force which was to be attributed the call for a cease-fire and the recommendation to initiate negotiations.[44]

On the other hand, it has to be admitted that the Council on occasion itself uses the stronger words 'demands' or 'orders' in connection with a cease-fire.[45] The absence of such a wording in the resolutions concerning Iran and Iraq which preceded Resolution 598 (1987) would tend to rebut a presumption in favour of a binding injunction having been issued, but practice in the Council is not consistent enough to allow a definite conclusion.

The formal requirement of Article 39. An additional difficulty arises with respect to the determination concerning a threat to the peace, a breach of the peace or an act of aggression in accordance with Article 39. In Resolution 479 (1980), the Council expressed deep concern about 'the developing situation between Iran and Iraq', and subsequently, in a more direct reference to the language of the Charter, it found that

41. In the *Namibia* Case, the Court proposed that the determination of whether or not a binding obligation had been created depended on the terms of the resolution, its *travaux preparatoires* and other relevant circumstances, *op.cit.* (note 32), at p. 53.

42. See, *e.g.*, Krökel, M., *Die Bindungswirkung von Resolutionen des Sicherheitsrates der Vereinten Nationen gegenüber Mitgliedsstaaten*, 1977, p. 137; Bowett, D.W., *United Nations Forces*, London 1964, p. 281. See also Stone, J., *Legal Controls of International Conflicts*, London 1954, p. 220: 'As to provisional measures under Article 40, it is difficult to conceive that the "call" (for instance to "cease-fire") should not impose, at any rate on Parties who are United Nations Members, the obligation to obey ...' Article 40 itself, of course, empowers the Council to 'call upon' the parties concerned to comply with such provisional measures as it deems necessary or desirable.

43. Resolution 67 (1949), 1949 *Resolutions and Decisions of the Security Council*, p. 2.

44. While in different contexts the French version uses the words 'invite', 'prie' or 'fait appel', a number of cease-fire *calls* are translated as 'demande'. But that word itself can be translated back into English in a variety of different ways, including *requests* and *demands*. E.g., Resolutions 209 (1965) and 210 (1965), 1965 *Resolutions and Decisions of the Security Council*, p. 13f. When the Council uses the word 'demands', it is translated as 'demande formellement'. *E.g.*, Resolution 214 (1965), *ibidem*, at p. 16. However, the discriminating approach is not carried through consistently, *e.g,* Resolution 91 (1951), 1951 *Resolutions and Decisions of the Security Council*, p. 1f.

45. Most recently, of course, in the context of the Kuwait crisis, *i.e.*, Resolution 660 (1990).

the situation 'gravely endangers international peace and security'.[46] This formulation, adopted in an agreed statement of the Council President, and reflected in subsequent resolutions,[47] would certainly identify the conflict as a dispute or situation the continuance of which is likely to endanger the maintenance of international peace and security in accordance with Articles 33 and 36 of the Charter, which are part of Chapter VI concerning the peaceful settlement of disputes.[48] In fact, the Council went slightly further, stating that the dispute was not only likely to endanger international peace and security, but that it did in fact endanger peace and security. Thus, the Council came tantalizingly close to a finding under Article 39, and it may well be argued that it did at least imply such a finding. However, the Council, by employing the word 'endangers' instead of 'threatens' may well have attempted to indicate that it was stopping short of an Article 39 finding.[49] In order to assess the relevance of this point, it is first necessary to investigate whether the requirement of Article 39 would be applicable to provisional measures under Article 40.

According to one view, the necessity of a finding under Article 39 stems 'from the fact that the provision [Article 40] is placed between Article 39 and the other Articles of Chapter VII dealing with "action with respect to threats to the peace ...".'[50] But the argument based on the position of the Article concerning provisional measures, which is indeed sandwiched between Article 39 and Articles 41 and 42, is not necessarily conclusive. The provision was a late addition to the Charter and its place may well have been the result of an accident of legal draftsmanship.[51] And the fact that Article 39 specifically refers to Articles 41 and 42, but not to Article 40, would tend to weaken the link between the requirement of a finding concerning

---

46. Statement by the Council President of 21 February 1983, 1983 *Resolutions and Decisions of the Security Council*, p. 6. In a Presidential Statement which was issued five days before Resolution 479 (1980) was adopted, the Council expressed deep concern that the conflict 'can prove increasingly serious and could pose a grave threat to international peace and security', 1980 *Resolutions and Decisions of the Security Council*, p. 23. It is perhaps significant that this formulation was not taken up in the Council's resolutions.

47. Resolutions 514 (1982), 522 (1982). In a Statement of 21 February 1983, the situation was deemed to be one 'which gravely endangers international peace and security', 1983 *Resolutions and Decisions of the Security Council*, p. 6. Similar formulations in Presidential Statements of 30 March 1984, 1984 *Resolutions and Decisions of the Security Council*, p. 10; 14 May 1987, 1987 *Resolutions and Decisions of the Security Council*, p. 5 and in Resolution 588 (1986).

48. Article 33 refers only to disputes the continuance of which is likely to endanger the maintenance of international peace and security, but Article 36 extends this wording to 'a situation of a like nature'.

49. On 16 January 1987 the Council stated that the risk that the conflict 'may pose a *further threat* to the security of the region has increased', 1987 *Resolutions and Decisions of the Security Council*, p. 5 (emphasis added). But apparently this was not meant to be taken to introduce a new and different finding of the Council. A few months later, and shortly before the adoption of Resolution 598 (1987), the Council returned to the formulation 'endanger'. Presidential Statement of 14 May 1987, *idem*.

50. Kelsen, H., *The Law of the United Nations*, London 1950, p. 739.

51. See USGPO, *The United Nations Conference on International Organization: Selected Documents*, New York 1946, p. 184.

threats to the peace, breaches of the peace or acts of aggression and provisional measures.

The logical progression of a formal finding, followed by provisional measures and then possibly by enforcement is also more apparent than real and furnishes no decisive argument. The strong emphasis of the Charter on preventing situations from escalating into manifest threats to the peace might indicate that provisional measures, almost by definition, have to be taken at an early state of a crisis in order to avoid armed conflict.[52] But then, again, Article 40 is indeed part of Chapter VII, which specifically addresses threats to the peace, breaches of the peace and acts of aggression, and Article 1(1) of the United Nations Charter, which outlines the purposes of the organization, refers to effective collective measures for the prevention and removal of *threats to the peace*, in addition to the suppression of acts of aggression or other breaches of the peace. The explicit linkage of collective and preventive measures, which would include provisional measures, to 'threats to the peace' would confirm the interpretation requiring a finding under Article 39 before Article 40 can come into operation.

At most, it seems, it could be said that the Charter 'does not make it clear whether the prior determination as specified in Article 39 is required.'[53] Unfortunately, practice in the Council is not fully consistent on this point either.[54] Again, the case of Indonesia furnishes a convenient example. In August of 1947, the Council noted with concern the hostilities in progress between the armed forces of the Netherlands and the Republic of Indonesia, stopping short of a formal finding of a threat to the peace. Nevertheless, it called upon the parties to cease hostilities forthwith and to settle their dispute peacefully.[55] Later that month, it reminded both Governments of this 'cease-fire *order*'.[56] This would indicate that the initial Resolution was indeed meant to be taken as a binding injunction. Still, the Council, in the same Resolution, referred to that cease-fire order as a 'recommendation'.[57]

In a number of other instances, the Council has even *demanded* cease-fires and taken other action which can only be understood to have been meant to be binding, without having made a finding under Article 39. And on occasion individual member states have viewed the failure of states to comply with such calls or

52. Cot., J.-P./Pellet, A. (ed.), *La Charte des Nations Unies*, Paris/Brussels 1985, p. 672.

53. Sonnenfeld, R., *Resolutions of the United Nations Security Council*, Dordrecht 1988, p. 92.

54. On the divergence of practice in the Council, see, *e.g.*, Goodrich, L.M./Hambro, E./Simmons, A.P., *Charter of the United Nations*, 3rd ed., New York 1969, pp. 303 *et seq.*, Cot/Pellet, *op.cit.* (note 52), pp. 647 *et seq.* Kelsen also admits that: 'There are cases where the Security Council has called upon the parties to comply with measures, such as to cease hostilities, or to achieve a truce, which could be understood only as provisional measures within the meaning of Article 40, without having previously determined the existence of a threat to, or breach of, the peace, and without expressly referring to Article 40', *op.cit.* (note 50), p. 740.

55. Resolution 27 (1947), 1947 *Resolutions and Decisions of the Security Council*, p. 6.

56. Resolution 32 (1947), 1947 *Resolutions and Decisions of the Security Council*, p. 8 (emphasis added).

57. The fact that recommendations might indirectly create binding obligations for the United Nations membership is not relevant in the context of injunctive demands.

demands for cease-fires as violations of binding obligations, although this assess-ment was often disputed by other participants in the discussions of the Council. At best, the practice of the organization in this respect can be described as one of constructive ambiguity, allowing the Council to act without committing itself to a source of authority and without defining the legal status of its pronouncements.

Not surprisingly, the most distinguished experts on the Security Council come to diverging conclusions when attempting to draw conclusions from an analysis of this pragmatic approach. For instance, Professor Higgins finds that a specific finding under Article 39 is not necessary. Instead, an implied finding would be sufficient, at least where Article 40 is concerned.[58] Sydney Bailey, on the other hand, asserts that it is now the 'conventional view that the Council can take binding decisions only under Chapter VII and after an express determination under Article 39.'[59] This view can be supported with reference to the formal findings made under Article 39 in the case of a few select cease-fire Resolutions.[60] The Resolutions in question then go on to invoke Articles 39 and 40 explicitly. Again, that extra effort would at first sight appear to be difficult to explain if it was not intended to produce legal results different from cease-fire calls adopted without such formal references having been included.[61]

However, to require a finding in accordance with Article 39 in order to bring Article 40 into play would create certain problems. It would mean that any call made by the Council, whether recommendatory or mandatory, would be covered by this requirement. After all, Article 39 specifically links both recommendations and decisions under Articles 41 and 42 to the determination concerning a threat to the peace, breach of the peace, or act of aggression, and it would be difficult to see why it should be otherwise in the case of Article 40. But this would mean that virtually almost all of the over 200 calls for a cease-fire which have been made by the Council over the years were in effect adopted in violation of the Charter, even as recommendations, because the Council has only made an Article 39 determination in a very small number of instances.

To avoid this absurd result,[62] it would be necessary to consider calls for a cease-fire as measures adopted under Chapter VI, instead of Chapter VII.[63] The cease-fire would then be viewed as being contextually linked to measures concerning the

---

58. Higgins, R., *The Development of International Law through the Political Organs of the United Nations*, London 1963, p. 263, also Cot/Pellet, *op.cit.* (note 52), p. 676, for a more recent assessment.

59. Bailey, S.D., *The Procedure of the UN Security Council*, 2nd ed., Oxford 1988, p. 241.

60. For a recent example, see Resolution 660 (1990), adopted in the context of the Kuwait crisis. For further cases see Bailey, S.D., *How Wars End*, New York/Oxford 1982, vol. I, pp. 89 *et seq.*

61. An alternative explanation is, however, offered below.

62. 'A resolution of a properly constituted organ of the United Nations which is passed in accordance with that organ's rules of procedure, and is declared by its President to have been so passed, must be presumed to have been validly adopted', *Namibia Opinion, op.cit.* (note 32), p. 22. 'When the Organizati-on takes action which warrants the assertion that it was appropriate for the fulfilment of one of the stated purposes of the United Nations, the presumption is that such action is *not ultra* vires the Organization', *Certain Expenses of the United Nations, ICJ Reports* 1962, pp. 149, 168.

63. *E.g.*, Cot/Pellet, *op.cit.* (note 52), at pp. 686 *et seq.*

peaceful settlement of disputes. And, of course, a cease-fire is in effect a pre-condition for the application of the means of dispute resolution referred to in Article 33 of the Charter.

This explanation of the course of recommendatory power covering a cease-fire would be consistent with the approach adopted by the Council in the Iran-Iraq Case. In an agreed Statement of 1983, the Members of the Council 'urgently call once again for an immediate cease-fire and an end to all military operations as well as the withdrawal of forces up to internationally recognized boundaries *with a view to seeking a peaceful settlement in accordance with the principles of the Charter.*'[64] As late as 1986, the Council adopted a Resolution which explicitly recalled that 'under the Charter, member states have conferred on the Security Council primary responsibility for the maintenance of international peace and security and to this end have agreed to accept the role of the Security Council *in the settlement of disputes.*'[65]

To consider a call for a cease-fire as a recommendatory rather than a mandatory measure, and to conceive of it as an element of peaceful dispute resolution, would appear at first sight to be inconsistent with the strong emphasis expressed throughout the United Nations Charter on the active suppression of the use of force by States. In fact, this proposition might appear somewhat cynical, considering that Resolution 479 (1980) and subsequent Resolutions were adopted with respect to a most destructive conflict which was raging at the time. But this approach does of course reflect the role to which the Council had been reduced over the decades in order to permit its functioning within the constraints placed upon it by a Cold War climate. Realizing that enforcement would not be a credible option, its Members appear to have accepted that most Council Resolutions are in effect only going to be treated as a guide-line for negotiations among the parties to a dispute or situation. And there could be no better case to demonstrate this phenomenon than the Iran-Iraq conflict. For example, in his statement following upon the adoption of Resolution 479 (1980), the Council President expressed the full support of the member states for the Secretary-General's efforts, 'so that *negotiations* for peace can proceed on an urgent basis.'[66]

The parties themselves appear to have regarded the cease-fire resolutions as part of the process of the settlement of a dispute. Iraq saw in the actions of the Council, and in particular in Resolution 479 (1980), a 'realistic approach (...) to settling the dispute once and for all.'[67] Iran evidently regarded the provisions of that and

---

64. Statement by the Council President of 21 February 1983, 1983 *Resolutions and Decisions of the Security Council*, p. 6 (emphasis added).

65. Resolution 588 (1988) (emphasis added); see also the Presidential Statement of 22 December 1986, emphasizing 'the obligation of member states to settle their disputes by peaceful means and, in this context, to cooperate with the Security Council. In this regard, the members of the Council urge the Secretary-General to continue with his efforts and call upon the parties to co-operate with him', 1986 *Resolutions and Decisions of the Security Council*, p. 13.

66. 1980 *Resolutions and Decisions of the Security Council*, p. 24 (emphasis added).

67. *Supra* note 9.

subsequent resolutions to be negotiable, and its expectations were fulfilled to an extent by the Council.

The willingness of the Council and of the parties to negotiate about the relevant Resolutions preceding Resolution 598 (1987) would of course undermine claims concerning their binding effect, even if they had been adopted as mandatory provisional measures under Article 40. It is difficult to see how Iran and Iraq could be expected to treat as a binding injunction a resolution which was viewed by the Council only as a basis for negotiations and which was subsequently modified by the Council itself in order to make it acceptable to them

In conclusion, therefore, Resolution 479 (1980) and other Resolutions which preceded Resolution 598 (1987) could have been adopted as recommendatory measures under Chapter VI. But even if the formal requirements of Article 39 do not apply to Article 40, and if those resolutions had been adopted under that provision, they could have developed no more than a recommendatory effect. Either they were intended as recommendations under Article 40 from the outset, or the Council would have been precluded by its own behaviour from claiming binding force for those resolutions, even if, theoretically, they might have amounted to mandatory injunctions. Thus, in neither case would Iran's failure to implement those Resolutions constitute a direct breach of a binding obligation.

b   Resolution 598 (1987)

The question remains whether the adoption of Resolution 598 (1987) might have had a different effect. Could Iran not reasonably expect the Council to incorporate even more of its views in further Resolutions, as it had done before? And if that was the case, why then should Iran have felt bound by Resolution 598 (1987)?

There are three possible explanations of the functions of Resolution 598 (1987), all leading to the same result with respect to its legal status. If initially the cease-fire had been adopted as a recommendation under Article 36, then the determination that there existed a breach of the peace and the explicit invocation of Articles 39 and 40 served to lift the Council's activities out of the context of Chapter VI and to transport them into the setting of mandatory measures under Chapter VII. If previous Resolutions had been adopted as recommendations under Article 40, then the change in the wording from *calling* for a cease-fire to *demanding* one would indicate that now a binding obligation was intended. And if the earlier cease-fire call had been binding all along, at least in theory, then all of these explicit changes in the wording adopted by the Council might only have had a procedural function. Notice was served upon the participants in the hostilities that the Council was not only demanding a cease-fire, but that in this instance it was also willing to enforce it by adopting further measures under Articles 41 and 42. The failure of the Council throughout the past decades to treat most of its own cease-fire calls as if they were binding obligations, even if they had been conceived in technically mandatory terms, might make such a procedure actually legally necessary.

The change in the legal status of the Resolution is evident in the pronouncements made on behalf of the Council after its adoption. Previously, the Council had appealed to the parties to implement its Resolutions, or it had urged that they adopt a constructive attitude.[68] Now, the Council left no doubt that what was expected was implementation, not negotiation.[69]

Still, the Council did not insist upon the unconditional implementation of the cease-fire in Resolution 598 (1987). The statement of the President on behalf of the Council of 24 December 1987 did threaten further steps to ensure compliance, but in effect it confirmed that the cease-fire demand was not directly applicable without its modalities having been settled.[70]

When the Secretary-General memorialized the expressed willingness of the parties to cooperate in the implementation of the cease-fire, he specifically affirmed that he had been 'assured by the two parties to the conflict that they will observe this cease-fire in the context of the full implementation of Resolution 598 (1987).'[71] This condition was repeated by the Council when approving the report of the Secretary-General. The Council President once more reiterated the determination of the membership to see the resolution 'fully implemented as an integrated whole.'[72]

By emphasizing the commitment to Resolution 598 (1987) as an 'integrated whole' the Council legitimized the demands of the parties for assurances concerning negotiations on the other elements of a settlement before instituting a cease-fire. The acceptance of the cease-fire was therefore mandatory, but not absolute. It only became an effective obligation once certain conditions had been met.

Of course, the Council would have been at liberty to certify that there was no reason to suspect that all elements of Resolution 598 (1987) would not actually be complied with. Then, Iran's refusal to institute a cease-fire would indeed have violated the Resolution from its inception. But no such determination was made and there was actually very little discussion of this issue in the Council.

However, this fact does not really assist the case of Iran. For, in its letter to the Secretary-General of 14 August 1987, Iraq committed itself unconditionally to Resolution 598 (1987) and emphasized that it was to be treated 'as an integrated and indivisible whole in respect of the contents, the time-limits and the measures for the implementation of all its paragraphs ...'[73] As of that date, there existed a clear undertaking of Iraq to withdraw fully and to comply with other obligations linked to the cease-fire. The condition for a mandatory cease-fire inherent in Resolution 598 (1987) was fulfilled. From that point onwards, Iran's failure to comply amounted to a breach of the Resolution and of the Charter of the United Nations.

---

68. Even after the adoption of Resolution 582 (1986), the Council still only issued an 'urgent appeal' for compliance; 1987 *Resolutions and Decisions of the Security Council*, p. 5.

69. Resolution 598 (1987), operative para. 9, Statement by the Council President of 24 December 1987, 1980 *Resolutions and Decisions of the Security Council*, p. 6. In the Statement of 16 March 1988, the Council Members expressed 'grave concern that resolution 598 (1987), *which has a mandatory character*, has not yet been implemented', 1988 *Resolutions and Decisions of the Security Council*, p. 9 (emphasis added).

70. 1987 *Resolutions and Decisions of the Security Council*, p. 6.

71. 1988 *Resolutions and Decisions of the Security Council*, p. 10.

72. *Ibidem*, p. 11.

73. *UN Doc.* S/19045, para. 3.

2   *The Resolutions of the Council and their relation to the possible violation of the obligations to refrain from the use of force and to settle disputes peacefully*

A breach of the obligations to refrain from the threat and use of force and to settle disputes exclusively by peaceful means would undoubtedly engage responsibility and, as Dr Kaikobad argues, it might in addition constitute an international crime. But the exercise of the right of self-defence by Iran would create a circumstance precluding wrongfulness in that context. Self-defence continues to apply while the armed attack which triggered its application continues. And in this case, as Dr Kaikobad has demonstrated, the armed attack continued as long as Iraqi troops were actively engaging in hostilities in territory previously held by Iran. However, self-defence ceases to apply once the United Nations Security Council has taken the 'measures necessary for the restoration of international peace and security.'[74] The adoption of Security Council Resolutions, which might constitute a 'measure necessary', could therefore possibly preclude the invocation of the right of self-defence. In that case, Iran's conduct following upon such an intervention by the Council would conflict with the prohibition of the use of force and, wrongfulness not being precluded, it would engage international responsibility.

It is, of course, contested whether it is the Council itself which defines what is 'necessary' in adopting, or failing to adopt, certain measures, or whether it is left to the state under attack to make that determination. But at least it is generally accepted that even if a state claims the right to make this determination for itself, its conduct may subsequently be reviewed and censured by the Security Council.[75]

Clearly, Iran, the victim of the armed attack, did not regard the measures adopted by the Council as impinging upon its right to self-defence. And up to the adoption of

74. Article 51 of the United Nations Charter. The question of whether the provision concerning 'necessary measures' is also part of customary law on self-defence can be ignored in this context. In any event the ILC draft on state responsibility would link the exercise of the right of self-defence, defined as a circumstance precluding wrongful, to the relevant United Nations Charter provision, *i.e.*, Articles 2(4) and 51.

75. Still the most convincing view in Bowett, D.W., *Self-Defence in International Law*, New York 1958, p. 196: 'Whether such positive action by the Council, or by member states pursuant to its decisions or recommendations, does in fact constitute the necessary measures must be decided on the facts of the individual situation. It may well be that in some circumstances an order to the attacking state which is obeyed so as to end the attack will be sufficient; in other circumstances nothing less than the use of armed force will suffice. On the other hand, to allow the defending state to be the sole judge of whether the Council has taken the necessary measures, opens up the possibility of unilateral action ousting collective action in matters relating to international peace and security, and this would plainly contravene the very spirit of the Charter. (...) On balance, therefore, it is suggested that the preferable view, and one which is not excluded by the Charter, is that whether the necessary measures have been taken must be determined objectively, as a question of fact, and that both the SC and the defending state are able to reach their own decisions on this. Should those decisions conflict, then the individual member admittedly runs the risk of its continued action being characterized as a "threat to the peace, breach of the peace, or act of aggression" under Art. 39, but this is only a somewhat greater hazard that it runs in any event by resorting to self-defence and would probably be undertaken in preference to annihilation by the attacking state'.

Resolution 598 (1987), the Council itself only deplored the continuation of hostilities in a general sense. In fact, the Council revised its own measures considerably to make them acceptable to the parties. It is difficult to see how, in 1980, a cease-fire in itself could have been a measure necessary, while at later stages it was a cease-fire coupled with a withdrawal, then a cease-fire, a withdrawal and an inquiry into responsibility for the conflict, *etc.* In treating its own initial pronouncements as being subject to negotiation and frequent modification, the Council in effect validated Iran's refusal to accept them as measures necessary to restore international peace and security. And initially that refusal was not only based on Iran's own subjective view. Resolution 479 (1980) did not include a withdrawal requirement and fell well short of the standard set by the Council in its own practice in the majority of similar cases.[76]

However, the legal situation changed when Iraq indicated its willingness to effect a full withdrawal. By 1982, Iran had pushed back the Iraqi forces behind its borders in most areas and was attempting to enter Iraqi territory.[77] Rejecting repeated cease-fire offers made by the government of Iraq, the Iranian authorities demanded an unconditional surrender, reparations in the order of US $ 150,000 million, agreement to the establishment of a committee to determine responsibility for the outbreak of hostilities, the repatriation of Iraqi Shiities who had been expelled from Iraq and the overthrow of the regime of President Hussein, his trial and the establishment of an Islamic Republic of Iraq.[78]

It is highly questionable whether, in general international law and under the United Nations Charter, Iran retained the right to fight for the implementation of these goals at this stage of the conflict.[79] And in a sense, the Council did offer some guidance on this point. In Resolution 522 (1982), it welcomed the fact that one of the parties (*i.e.*, Iraq) had already expressed its readiness to cooperate in the implementation of Resolution 514 (1982) and called upon the other to do likewise.[80] Could this Resolution have had a certain legal effect, although it only exerted

76. It might be possible to argue that a measure adopted by the Council could by definition not be a 'necessary' one, if even after full implementation the condition which gave rise to the application of the right of self-defence would not have been dissolved, *i.e.*, if the measure in itself could not in itself cause the removal of the attacking forces from the territory of the target state.

77. Keesing's *Contemporary Archive* 31849 (1982) reports the following developments which occurred between June and November of 1982: '(i) the Iraqi withdrawal of almost all of its troops from Iranian soil; (ii) the invasion of Iraqi territory by Iranian forces, heading in the direction of Basra; and (iii) the opening of new fronts along the border, posing a threat to Baghdad'.

78. *Ibidem*, p. 31851.

79. For an extreme and excessive argument on this point, see Dinstein, Y., *War Aggression and Self Defence*, Cambridge 1988, p. 219: 'War, if waged legitimately as a response to an armed attack, does not have to be terminated at the point when the aggressor is driven back, and it may be carried on by the defending state until final victory.' This view obviously mistakes the nature of the right of self-defence as a provisional measure limited to the immediate protection of the territorial integrity of a state.

80. Four years later, the Council once more noted that the Government of Iraq had expressed its willingness to heed the call for the immediate cessation of hostilities and stressed the urgent need for full compliance by both parties with its resolutions. 1986 *Resolutions and Decisions of the Security Council*, p. 12.

recommendatory power?[81] After all, it did record Iraq's decision to implement Resolution 514 (1982) requiring a withdrawal from Iranian territory and including a number of other provisions in line with the standard of guarantees customarily offered to the victim of an armed attack by the Council when calling for a cease-fire.

When the Council formally noted the desire of the government of Iraq to implement Resolution 514 (1982), it confirmed the existence of a certain factual situation. In general international law, the existence of such facts would trigger specific legal consequences. For, as soon as the terms of Resolution 514 (1982) were embraced in their entirety by the government of Iraq, the right of self-defence previously exercised by the government of Iran simply expired. In a sense, Resolution 514 (1982) served as a catalyst which led Iraq to memorialize clearly and unambiguously that the armed attack it had initiated would cease and would in fact be reversed by way of a withdrawal, and that a number of other conditions deemed essential by Iran and pronounced valid by the Council would be fulfilled. This undertaking was credible as it was given within the framework of the United Nations which was offering to supervise compliance. Thus, the Council certified Iraq's willingness to comply with conditions which, in objective law, would terminate the right of self-defence. Such a determination of factual circumstances implied a finding as to legal results flowing from such facts.

Obviously, this explicit determination of facts and implicit determination of law by the Council did not impose upon Iran obligations which were not already inherent in general international law. Rather like the adoption of Resolution 276 (1970) in the Namibia Case, it merely gave an authoritative assessment of an existing legal situation. And according to the rationale which underlies the finding of the ICJ in the Namibia Opinion, a finding by the Council as to factual circumstances which trigger consequences in general international law is in itself opposable to the United Nations membership.[82] This result is not affected by the failure of the Council to attach directly binding legal consequences to its finding in the case of the Iran-Iraq conflict. For, the existence of a factual situation, and the certification of its existence by the Council, cannot be dependent on whether or not the Council was willing to enforce compliance with the legal obligations which flow from it.

In addition to the lapse of the right of self-defence in general customary international law due to the absence of a continued armed attack, the unconditional acceptance of Resolution 514 (1982) also had an effect on that right as defined specifically in Article 51 of the Charter. It actually transformed Resolution 514 (1982) into a 'measure necessary' for the maintenance of international peace and security in the sense of that provision. For, even under the widest possible interpretation, an action by the Council which actually archives the removal of the circumstance which gave rise to the exercise of the right of self-defence must qualify, almost by definition, as a 'measure necessary'. And following upon Iraq's declar-

81. See section IIA.2.a above.
82. Depending on the circumstances, the authority to make such an authoritative finding would be based upon Articles 24 and 25, or on the specific provisions of Chapter VI and VII.

ation concerning compliance, the implementation of Resolution 514 (1982), which provided for the full withdrawal of Iraqi forces,[83] was in fact assured.[84] Again, it was at this point that the right to repel the armed attack against Iran through the use of force lapsed. Self-defence no longer being available as a circumstance precluding wrongfulness, Iran's international responsibility was engaged.

III   CONCLUSION

1) The invasion of Iranian territory launched by Iraq constituted a breach of the obligations to refrain from the use of force and to settle disputes peacefully. The subversive activities and armed incidents which had allegedly been caused by Iran would not constitute a circumstance precluding wrongfulness and this respect, although such actions might reduce the amount of compensation which might be due to Iran.

2) The Security Council Resolutions preceding Resolution 598 (1987) were most likely meant to be of a recommendatory nature. Even if these Resolutions were intended to create binding obligations, practice of the Council itself would bar an allegation that a failure to comply with them constituted a breach.

3) Resolution 598 (1987) created binding obligations, although the mandatory nature of the call for a cease-fire was made dependent on certain conditions. Once those conditions were fulfilled, the failure to comply amounted to a breach of the Resolution and of Article 25 of the Charter.

4) Recommendatory Resolution 514 (1982) reflected an objective legal standard concerning the expiry of the right of self-defence with respect to Iran. Resolution 522 (1982) certified acceptance of this standard by Iraq. Once the implementation of this acceptance was assured, Iran's right of self-defence lapsed. The continuance of hostilities by the government of Iran amounted to a breach of the obligations to refrain from the use of force and to settle disputes peacefully.

---

83. In that aspect the situation was different from that created by Iraq's determination to implement Resolution 479 (1980).

84. The determination of Iran itself to obstruct the implementation of a measure which had been adopted in its favour can obviously not be invoked to demonstrate that the measure was not effective.

COMMENTS

Rob Siekmann[*]

First of all, I would like to compliment Dr Kaikobad upon his balanced treatment of the ins and outs of the *ius ad bellum*, especially in relation to the Gulf War. In my commentary I will focus attention on a series of major and minor points. I will concentrate on the aspect of collective security which remains somewhat underdeveloped in Dr Kaikobad's contribution. In this connection I will also take the opportunity to make some observations on the Kuwait crisis.

I. In his contribution Dr Kaikobad gives a penetrating analysis of the concept of *humanitarian intervention*. His statement that interventionists could in fact become legislators, judges and executors is especially striking. Is this not a general defect of public international law in the field of peace and war, if not with regard to all three functions, then at least with regard to those of judge and executor? Nevertheless, as far as humanitarian intervention is concerned, there is a vacuum in international law, which could be called a dilemma in political terms. Should it be simply tolerated that human rights comprising universal norms are being systematically violated? I do not mention the examples, that all of us may readily imagine. But should they be countered by *unilateral* action? In this connection, Dr Kaikobad's remark that the imprimatur of the United Nations would be essential to exercise humanitarian intervention is quite interesting. I submit the following observation to you which is related to the Kuwait crisis.

In resolution 664 (1990) demanding that Iraq permits the immediate departure of nationals of third countries – the so-called 'guestages' in present day diplomatic parlance – the Security Council is explicitly acting under Chapter VII of the United Nations Charter. Is this merely staying true to form? All Security Council resolutions with respect to the question of Kuwait have so far been adopted under the aegis of Chapter VII. The Security Council treats all aspects (invasion, annexation, diplomatic missions, guestages, damages, requests for assistance under Article 50 of the Charter) as a whole. Or is the reference to Chapter VII of the United Nations Charter not a formality? That would imply that the Security Council in fact considers the question of the 'guestages' as a threat to international peace and security under Article 39 of the Charter. It remains true that, in principle, humanitarian intervention, or self-help, to rescue them, is not out of the question. By declaring Chapter VII to be applicable, however, the Security Council has blocked unilateral action in a similar way as the right of individual or collective self-defence may be blocked by taking measures under

* R.C.R. Siekmann, Senior research officer in the Public International Law Department, T.M.C. Asser Institute, The Hague.

I.F. Dekker and H.H.G. Post, eds., The Gulf War of 1980-1988

Chapter VII. And it should not be forgotten that humanitarian intervention for the benefit of nationals is sometimes presented as an admissible form of self-defence. In this perspective, the Security Council, by adopting resolution 664 (1990), has blocked beforehand any appeal to Article 51 of the Charter or to the existence of a right of humanitarian intervention by individual member states. In other words, action for the liberation of their nationals would be possible only on the basis of an imprimatur of the Security Council! (NB: Did Security Council resolution 678 (1990) imply an authorization at least for 'member states co-operating with the Government of Kuwait' to use all necessary means not only for the liberation of Kuwait, but also for this purpose?) Maybe this specific interpretation of resolution 664 (1990) is incorrect, which could be proved with the help of the *travaux préparatoires* of the resolution. Perhaps, the reference to Chapter VII is an automatic one within the framework of the series of resolutions on the Kuwait crisis. Of course, while interpreting resolutions of the Security Council, one should not only pay attention to the wording, but also to the circumstances of the adoption of resolutions.

II. I agree with Dr Kaikobad's remark that '*necessity*' – the right to continue measures of self-defence – does not apply to United Nations action, but I do not agree with his terminology. Dr Kaikobad speaks about the termination of war, but the United Nations do not wage war, they undertake enforcement action against a member state which has violated the Charter (Article 42 of the Charter is the formal basis for it). The *ius ad bellum* does not apply as such. Kaikobad also speaks about 'action of collective self-defence under the imprimatur or supervision of the United Nations'. The United Nations do not act on the basis of self-defence, but for the purpose of maintaining or restoring international peace and security. Therefore, the term 'enforcement action' was chosen in the Charter instead of 'war'. Article 51 rules it out: self-defence is allowed *until* the Security Council has taken the necessary measures (*cf.* the North Atlantic Treaty in Article 5: measures of collective self-defence by the Organisation shall be terminated when the Security Council has taken measures). Dr Kaikobad's terminology creates confusion.

I submit that even the action in Korea – under the imprimatur of the Security Council – was not self-defence, any more than a real United Nations action under the direct authority of the Security Council and with a United Nations Command would be self-defence. Member states acted with the authorization of the Security Council on the basis of a specific mandate. The term self-defence would suggest in this context that the principles of proportionality and necessity would be automatically applicable, which is not true. (NB: The operation against Iraq for the liberation of Kuwait resembles in many respects the Korean action, as it is based on a Security Council authorization. As far as the modalities of the operation are concerned, the 'necessary means' that may be taken under resolution 678 (1990) should, generally speaking, be interpreted in the light of the mandate to be fulfilled.)

III. On the last pages of his contribution, Dr Kaikobad deals with the meaning of Security Council resolution 598 (1987) in relation to the exercise of the right of self-defence. Dr Kaikobad obviously fails to appreciate that the cease-fire which was demanded by the Security Council is a mandatory decision, irrespective of the circumstance that the Security Council was acting under Articles 39 and 40 of the Charter. Over the years this demand was preceded by resolutions in which Iran and Iraq were merely called upon to end hostilities (for example, in resolution 582 (1986)). Moreover, in resolution 598 (1987) further steps to ensure compliance with the resolution were announced. From the legal point of view, therefore, it was not necessary for implementation of resolution 598 (1987) that it be accepted by the parties concerned, that they had to comply with it only on the basis of reciprocity. Resolution 598 (1987) is a mandatory resolution, which is also evident from the Security Council debate preceding its adoption. Moreover, resolution 598 (1987) demanded an immediate cease-fire. Parties not observing this did violate the resolution, which is a binding decision under international law taken by the organ that is invested with the primary responsibility for the maintenance of international peace and security under the United Nations Charter.

This is not altered by the fact that in practice the United Nations Secretary-General handled the resolution in a political manner. On behalf of the Security Council, he commenced negotiations with Iran and Iraq concerning the time and conditions for a cease-fire. During these negotiations other elements of resolution 598 (1987) were brought into the discussion, such as entrusting an impartial body with enquiring into the responsibility for the conflict. Finally, on 9 August 1988 (resolution 598 (1987) dates from 20 July 1987!) it was possible to send a United Nations military observer group (UNIIMOG) to the area to supervise the cease-fire and withdrawal of troops (enabling Security Council resolution 619 (1988)).

How could continued self-defence be legally qualified, if at the same time a Security Council resolution demands a cease-fire? One could argue that it looks like a reprisal. As such this continued self-defence is unlawful. As it takes place in reaction to the illegitimately continuing attacks by the other party – here Iran – it is nevertheless acceptable under international law.

IV. Finally, Dr Kaikobad gives attention to *Article 51* of the United Nations Charter in connection with the Gulf War. 'Necessary measures' is generally interpreted as 'effective measures', he says. But who shall determine what is effective? Individual member states or the Security Council itself? It is incorrect, I think, as a matter of principle, for the parties concerned to determine the effectiveness of Security Council measures which they have themselves to implement! Thus, I do not agree that the effectiveness of resolution 598 (1987) should be judged by the aggressor's reaction, as Dr Kaikobad suggests. That would be a political evaluation of the resolution, which deprives a mandatory Security Council resolution of its legal value. Such resolutions would become mere factual elements in the consideration of disputes instead of being legal directives. Effectiveness in fact is a political concept, at most a concept of legal policy.

V. I would like to finish this commentary by trying to give an answer to a theoretical, but nevertheless, I think, relevant question: what military action could the United

Nations in principle have taken, apart from resolution 598 (1987), in the several stages of the Gulf War? I take the opportunity to submit the following options.

- *Before* the war between Iran and Iraq broke out, a preventive buffer force could have been stationed between them on the basis of a Security Council resolution under Article 39 (threat to the peace). If the parties concerned would have agreed to such a force, it would have been a peace-keeping operation. Without the consent of both parties it would have been some kind of 'preventive enforcement action'. This seems to be a *contradictio in terminis* (*cf.*, the terminology used in Articles 5 and 50 of the United Nations Charter: 'preventive *or* enforcement action'!), but 'enforcement' here is meant to refer not to the actual use of military force, but to deterring the threatening state by deploying United Nations armed forces. Curiously, the only precedent for this type of action is a non-United Nations, regional operation, the so-called *Force de Sécurité de la Ligue Arabe*, which was placed between Iraq and Kuwait as a buffer force after the latter's independence (Kuwait agreed to the Force, Iraq did not). Preceding the stationing of a force of this type, military observers could have been dispatched to report on the situation. As far as I know, there is no United Nations precedent for such preventive action. Generally speaking, preventive action has proved to be the weak point of United Nations peace-keeping to date.

- *During* the Gulf War the Security Council, in principle, could have taken enforcement action against one or both parties concerned in order to establish a cease-fire. There are no precedents in United Nations history for this type of intervening action.

- Of course, *after* the war, instead of UNIIMOG, the observer mission, a peace-keeping force could have been stationed in the area as a buffer force.

- Finally, a United Nations maritime force to guarantee free navigation in the Gulf would have been somewhat of a novelty in United Nations history. The consent of the parties concerned would not have been necessary, since the maritime force would have been operating in an international area. It would have used force only in self-defence and for the protection of merchant vessels. As we know, this task was fulfilled by a multinational fleet without a unified command structure.

Part II

The *Ius in Bello*

Chapter 3

PROHIBITIONS OR RESTRICTIONS ON THE USE OF METHODS AND MEANS OF WARFARE

Frits Kalshoven[*]

INTRODUCTION

Prolonged international armed conflict invariably brings into play a wide array of methods and means by which the belligerent parties seek to obtain their goals. The Gulf War between Iran and Iraq, 1980-1988, has been no exception to this rule. Methods and means used have ranged from non-violent (though often vitriolic) rhetoric and propaganda, through all shapes of economic pressure, to attacks with a great variety of more or less sophisticated weapons of war, including chemical weapons, and directed both against military and civilian targets.

While a complete history of the Gulf War might be expected to cover all these aspects, the purpose of this chapter is far more modest. Leaving matters of grand strategy and rules relating to the use of force in inter-state relations (*ius ad bellum*) on one side, it concentrates on those rules of the law of war (*ius in bello*) embodying prohibitions or restrictions on the employment of violent methods or means of warfare. As the conduct of war at sea is dealt with elsewhere (Part III), the scope of this chapter is moreover limited to war on land, including attacks from the air on objects on land.

Paul Tavernier[1] and Eric David[2] have earlier furnished useful overviews of relevant facts and legal aspects. We have made grateful use of the data provided in their articles as well as of other public and readily available information.

The first task in hand will be to determine the rules applicable in the Gulf War. The actual conduct of the belligerent parties will then be considered in the light of these rules. Finally, we shall take a brief look at the repercussions in the outside world of some of the belligerents' modes of waging the war.

I   THE APPLICABLE LAW

Rules prohibiting or restricting the use of methods or means of warfare may be found in treaties, in customary law and, arguably, among the principles of law.

---

* F. Kalshoven, Professor of Public International and Humanitarian Law (ret.) at the University of Leyden.

1. Tavernier, P., "La guerre du Golfe: Quelques aspects de l'application du droit des conflits armés et du droit humanitaire", 30 *AFDI* (1984), pp. 43 *et seq.*
2. David, E., "La guerre du Golfe et le droit international", 23 *Rev. belge* (1987-1), pp. 153 *et seq.*

I.F. Dekker and H.H.G. Post, eds., The Gulf War of 1980-1988

Taking the relevant treaties in chronological order, it appears that:
- Iran (or Persia, as it was then named) is a party to the Hague Convention on Land Warfare with annexed Regulations of 1899;[3] it has not become a party to the revised version of 1907;[4] Iraq is party to neither version;
- Iran is, but Iraq is not, a party to the Declaration (IV, 3) Concerning Expanding Bullets, of 1899;[5] the Declaration records the agreement of the parties 'to abstain from the use of bullets which expand or flatten easily in the human body, such as bullets with a hard envelope which does not entirely cover the core or is pierced with incisions'; the bullets are commonly referred to as dum-dum bullets;
- both Iran and Iraq have ratified the Geneva Gas Protocol of 1925, which reaffirms the prohibition of 'the use in war of asphyxiating, poisonous or other gases, and of all analogous liquids materials or devices' (chemical weapons, for short); Iraq has attached a reservation providing in part that it 'shall cease to be bound by the Protocol towards any Power at enmity with him whose armed forces, or the armed forces of whose allies, do not respect the Protocol';[6]
- Iran and Iraq have joined in the adoption by consensus of Protocol I of 1977;[7] Iran has subsequently signed but not ratified the Protocol; as it has not made its intention clear not to become a party, it 'is obliged to refrain from acts which would defeat [its] object and purpose';[8]
- neither state has become a party to or a signatory of the Conventional Weapons Convention of 1980;[9]
- both Iran and Iraq are signatories but not parties to the ENMOD Convention.[10]

Although rules of customary international law are notoriously more difficult to trace, it may be safe to state that:
- the substantive rules embodied in the Hague Convention and Regulations of 1899/1907 have become part and parcel of the body of customary law; the pertinent

---

3. Convention (II) with Respect to the Laws and Customs of War on Land, with annexed Regulations; signed at The Hague, 29 July 1899; Schindler, D/Toman, J., *The Laws of Armed Conflicts*, 3rd ed., Dordrecht/Geneva 1988, p. 69; list of signatures, ratifications and accessions, p. 94.

4. Convention (IV) Respecting the Laws and Customs of War on Land, with annexed Regulations; signed at The Hague, 18 October 1907; *idem*.

5. Signed at The Hague, 29 July 1899; Persia ratified the Declaration on 4 September 1900; *ibidem*, p. 109.

6. Protocol for the Prohibition of the Use in War of Asphyxiating, Poisonous or Other Gases, and of Bacteriological Methods of Warfare, signed at Geneva, 17 June 1925; *ibidem*, p. 115; Iraqi reservation, *ibidem*, p. 123.

7. Protocol Additional to the Geneva Conventions of 12 August 1949, and Relating to the Protection of Victims of International Armed Conflicts (Protocol I), adopted at Geneva, 8 June 1977; *ibidem*, p. 621.

8. Article 18 of the Vienna Convention on the Law of Treaties, adopted on 23 May 1969.

9. Convention on Prohibitions or Restrictions on the Use of Certain Conventional Weapons Which May be Deemed to be Excessively Injurious or to Have Indiscriminate Effects, with annexed Protocols; adopted at Geneva, 10 October 1980; Schindler/Toman, *op.cit.* (note 3), p. 179.

10. Convention on the Prohibition of Military or Any Other Hostile Use of Environmental Modification Techniques, adopted by A/RES/31/72 on 10 December 1976; *ibidem*, p. 163; while Iran voted in favour of the resolution, Iraq abstained; *ibidem*, p. 169; subsequently, both states signed the Convention; *ibidem*, p. 170.

part of the Regulations is Chapter I (Means of Injuring the Enemy, Sieges, and Bombardments) of Section II (Hostilities);
- the prohibition on the use of dum-dum bullets has also long since formed part of the realm of customary law;
- a significant part of the rules on methods and means of warfare, embodied mainly though not exclusively in Section I (Methods and Means of Warfare) of Part III (Methods and Means of Warfare, Combatant and Prisoner-of-War Status) of Protocol I of 1977, is generally regarded as belonging to customary law;[11]
- these latter rules govern the use of all methods and means of warfare, whether old or new and including incendiary weapons, or delayed-action munitions such as land mines;[12]
- confirmation of the customary law character of some of the pertinent basic rules may be seen in the unanimous adoption by the General Assembly of the United Nations on 19 December 1968, of Resolution 2444(XXIII),[13] and in the adoption with no votes against by the same organ, on 9 December 1970, of Resolution 2675(XXV).[14]

Turning to principles next, we fortunately need not enter here into the perennial debate about the recognition of principles of law as a separate source of international law, since relevant normative statements that may have commenced their existence as mere principles at best, have meanwhile been incorporated in treaties in force and thereby acquired the status of conventional law. To characterize these normative statements as principles now serves merely to point to their high level of abstraction, resulting in a lesser capacity than other, more concrete rules to provide direct answers to specific questions about the legality of given methods or means of warfare. Pertinent instances include:[15]
- the statement that the right of the parties to an armed conflict to choose methods or means of warfare is not unlimited;[16]
- the prohibition on the employment of 'weapons, projectiles and material and methods of warfare of a nature to cause superfluous injury or unnecessary suffering';[17]

11. On this, see Meron, T., *Human Rights and Humanitarian Norms as Customary Law*, Oxford 1989.

12. It is suggested, in other words, that the bulk of the provisions in the Mines and Incendiary Weapons Protocols annexed to the Conventional Weapons Convention of 1980 have the status of customary law.

13. *Op.cit.* (note 3), p. 263.

14. *Ibidem*, p. 267; as mentioned on p. 268, the resolution 'was adopted by 109 votes to none, with 18 states abstaining or absent', and a note specifies that 'A roll-call did not take place.'

15. See Kalshoven, F., "The Conventional Weapons Convention: Underlying Principles", 30 *International Review of the Red Cross* (1990), pp. 510 *et seq.*

16. Hague Regulations, Article 22; A/RES/2444(XXIII); Protocol I, Article 35(1).

17. Hague Regulations, Article 23(e) (with slightly different wording); the text as quoted is in Protocol I, Article 35(2).

- the prohibition on the employment of 'methods or means of warfare which are intended, or may be expected, to cause widespread, long-term and severe damage to the natural environment';[18] and
- the principle that the belligerent parties 'shall at all times distinguish between the civilian population and combatants and between civilian objects and military objectives'.[19]

Other notions of primordial interest to our present discussion include:

- the responsibility of the state for all acts committed by persons forming part of its armed forces;[20]
- its obligation to issue orders and instructions to its armed forces in conformity with the applicable rules;[21]
- the individual criminal liability of all persons for war crimes committed by them or under their responsibility;[22] and, last but not least,
- the right and moral duty of the international community to ensure respect for the law of war.[23]

Mention should finally be made of the Martens clause, according to which (paraphrasing Article 1(2) of Protocol 1) in cases not covered by treaties applicable between the parties at war, 'civilians and combatants remain under the protection and authority of the principles of international law derived from established custom, from the principles of humanity and from the dictates of the public conscience.'[24] It should be pointed out that, in spite of occasional suggestions to the contrary, the clause does not have the effect of elevating in particular the 'principles of humanity' and 'dictates of the public conscience' to the rank of direct, independent sources of international obligation; on the other hand, they do represent important driving forces behind the law of war and its development.

18. Protocol I, Article 35(3); thus far, this recent addition to the list probably has force only as treaty law between the parties to the Protocol, whereas other belligerent parties can probably at best be said to be under a moral obligation not to employ means or methods of warfare that may cause such damage.

19. The principle is implicit in the Hague Regulations; it was expressed in slightly different terms in A/RES/2444(XXIII) and 2675(XXV); the phrase quoted in the text is from Protocol I, Article 48.

20. Hague Convention, version of 1907, Article 3; Protocol I, Article 91.

21. As already in Article 1 of the Hague Convention of 1899, unchanged in 1907; Article 80(2) of Protocol I adds the obligation to supervise the execution of the instructions.

22. Criminal liability for war crimes exists since time immemorial as a rule of customary law. See also chapter 8 of this book, especially the comment by Eric David.

23. This principle can be derived, *e.g.*, from Article 1(1) of Protocol I, providing that 'The High Contracting Parties undertake to respect and to ensure respect for this Protocol in all circumstances'; it may be seen in operation in a long series of resolutions of the United Nations General Assembly and Security Council and of International Conferences of the Red Cross calling upon belligerent parties to respect the law.

24. The clause stems from the preamble to the Hague Convention on Land Warfare of 1899, where it was introduced at the initiative of the Russian delegate to the Peace Conference, Von Martens, to discard the unsolved and at the time insoluble problem posed by armed resistance on the part of the inhabitants of occupied territory.

II   THE ACTUAL CONDUCT OF THE WAR ON LAND

In the Gulf War, as between the belligerent parties, few means of warfare were prohibited from the outset. However, all means of warfare without exception were subject to rules restricting their use. Moreover, both prohibitions and restrictions may conceivably have been subject to the operation of the principle of reciprocity or the right of reprisal.

A   Prohibited means of warfare: chemical weapons

Specifically prohibited from use were two classes of weapons: dum-dum bullets, and chemical means of warfare. Whereas dum-dum bullets do not appear to have played any significant part in the Gulf War (nor in other armed conflicts), chemical weapons did, from a fairly early stage of the war down to the bitter end.

The parties were moreover restricted in their choice of weapons by the principle prohibiting the use of means of warfare of a nature to cause unnecessary suffering. They may also have been under a moral obligation to avoid excessive ecological damage.[25] This author has not, however, come across any claim that in their conduct of war on land, either of these principles has been specifically violated.

In practical terms, therefore, we are left with chemical means of warfare as the only specific category of weapons to be considered under the present heading. There appears to be no room for doubt that in the Gulf War, Iraq has been the first, and for a long time the only belligerent to have recourse to such weapons: whether Iran reciprocated in the end is a matter of some uncertainty.[26] No matter the precise facts, too many words need not be wasted on the legal side of the matter: in the relations between Iraq and Iran, the 1925 Geneva Protocol was fully applicable, and the reported Iraqi employment of chemical weapons, whether against Iranian combatants (as it may have been in most instances) or civilians, was indubitably unlawful.

It should be pointed out that this lack of legality taints only the Iraqi use of the prohibited weapons. Under the terms of that state's reservation[27] as well as, plausibly, as a matter of customary law,[28] the first use by Iraq effectively freed Iran as the victim state of its obligation of non-use for the duration of the war. While this would strictly speaking have permitted Iran to respond by unrestrained recourse to chemical weapons, a more commendable course, and one more in conformity with the principle of proportionality, would have been to limit itself to a reprisal in kind (and respecting the

---

25. See above, note 18.
26. See hereafter, notes 74, 76.
27. On the basis of the principle of reciprocity it was open to Iran to avail itself of the Iraqi reservation.
28. Bothe, M., *Das völkerrechtliche Verbot des Einsatzes chemischer und bakteriologischer Waffen – Kritische Würdigung und Dokumentation der Rechtsgrundlagen*, Köln/Bonn 1973, pp. 70-75.

thereof) or even to no use at all (with mere propagandistic exploitation of the psychological advantage thus gained).[29]

B   Prohibited methods of warfare

In contrast with the relative paucity of prohibitions on the use of specific means of warfare, quite a few broad principles and detailed rules restrict belligerents in their choice of methods of warfare. The principles and rules have been authoritatively stated or reaffirmed in Protocol I of 1977. Important principles include:
-   the prohibition not 'to kill, injure or capture an adversary by resort to perfidy';[30]
-   the prohibition not 'to make improper use of the distinctive emblem of the red cross [or the] red crescent ...';[31]
-   the prohibition not 'to order that there shall be no survivors, to threaten an adversary therewith or to conduct hostilities on this basis';[32]
-   the prohibition not to resort to 'starvation of civilians as a method of warfare'.[33]

In common with most wars, isolated offences against either of these principles or the rules elaborating them are likely to have occurred in the Gulf War. The norms in question do not, however, appear to have been the target of systematic, government-controlled encroachment and consequently have not come to the fore in the discussions about the conduct of the belligerent parties. We may accordingly leave it at that.

1   *The principle of distinction*

This is different when it comes to the principles, reaffirmed already in 1968 by the United Nations General Assembly, 'That it is prohibited to launch attacks against the civilian population as such' and 'That distinction must be made at all times between persons taking part in the hostilities and members of the civilian population to the effect that the latter be spared as much as possible.'[34] Upon closer inspection, the principle of distinction stands out as the more fundamental notion, with the categorical prohibition not to attack the civilian population and civilian objects and the obligation when attacking military objectives to spare the civilian population as much as possible figuring as its derivatives. As noted above, Protocol I of 1977 elaborates these principles into a set of more or less precise, detailed rules which at least in part belong to customary law and to that extent were therefore applicable, alongside the fundamental principles, in the Gulf War.

---

29. For a case of such propagandistic exploitation, see the remarks of the Iranian representative in the Commission on Disarmament, quoted in Tavernier, *loc.cit.* (note 1), p. 55. See also Kalshoven, F., "Belligerent Reprisals Revisited", 21 *NYIL* (1990) p. 43.

30. Protocol I, Article 37.

31. Protocol I, Article 38.

32. Protocol I, Article 40.

33. Protocol I, Article 54.

34. A/RES/2444(XXIII), *supra* note 13.

All these principles appear to have been openly flouted by both parties. Throughout the war the civilian population and civilian objects in enemy territory have often had to suffer the effects of attacks with all available means, including missiles, and directed either deliberately against them or against military objectives but with insufficient regard for the civilian persons and objects in the vicinity. It should be pointed out that at issue here are, on the one hand, a prohibited method, *viz.*, attack against the civilian population, and on the other, restrictions on recourse to an otherwise permissible method, *viz.*, attack on military objectives. In this context the means used in the attacks, whether as payload (explosive, incendiary, chemical) or carriers (shells, bombs, land mines, ballistic or guided missiles), are largely immaterial.

Assuming for the moment that the civilian persons and objects affected were truly civilian in character, the legal state of affairs may be summarized as follows: the prohibition on deliberately making such people or objects the object of attack is straightforward and categorical – except for a possible justification as reprisals, a point to which we shall come back shortly. Attacks on military objectives, on the other hand, are permissible in principle, and it is only by the transgression of certain limits that such attacks become unlawful. The limit at issue here was expressed in broad terms in the quoted Resolution 2444 of 1968 of the United Nations General Assembly as the duty to spare the civilian population as much as possible. Protocol I of 1977 develops this precept into a set of rules relating to 'incidental loss of civilian life, injury to civilians and damage to civilian objects'.[35] The ideal is total avoidance of such loss or damage; when this proves impracticable, loss or damage should be minimized; and the outer limit is where such loss or damage would be 'excessive in relation to the concrete and direct military advantage anticipated' as a result of the attack: violation of this rule of proportionality turns the operation into an indiscriminate attack.[36]

Implicit in these rules is the assumption of the truly civilian character of the persons and objects in question. Can it be argued that in the Gulf War, the populations of the countries at war had lost that quality? In an article appearing in 1984, Geoffrey Best has forcefully reminded us of the developments in the late 19th and 20th centuries, with the increasing involvement of the populations in the economic and political processes that determine the capacity of a state to wage war.[37] These developments, which in the past already had led to the practice of 'total war', were very much in evidence in the Gulf War. At the same time, Best exhorts us to bear in mind that 'The principles of discrimination between the real civilian and the real combatant remain crucial to a morally acceptable law of war.'[38]

This is, of course, precisely the purpose of the principles and rules on protection of the civilian population against effects of hostilities, as elaborated in Protocol I of 1977 but, it should be reiterated, with their roots firmly anchored in customary law. And the authors of these principles and rules have consciously rejected all notions of 'war effort'

---

35. Protocol I, Articles 51-57; the quoted phrase is from Article 57(2)(a)(ii).
36. Protocol I, Article 51(4) and (5); Article 57(2)(a)(iii) and (b).
37. Best, G., "Civilians in Contemporary Wars, a problem in ethics, law, and fact", 35 *Air University Review* (March-April 1984), pp. 29 *et seq.*
38. *Ibidem*, p. 39.

or political inseparability of civilians and combatants, as factors to be taken into account in the elaboration of the principle of distinction. In effect, the single factor capable of temporarily depriving civilians of their protection as such is specified as 'taking a direct part in hostilities'.[39] No matter how broadly construed, this term definitely does not encompass participation in the economic war effort, let alone belonging to the same political party or adhering to the same ideology as the national leader. Our conclusion is, therefore, that for purposes of the law of war, and irrespective of the possible degree of solidarity between combatants and civilians, the non-combatant part of the populations in Iran and Iraq had retained its civilian character throughout the war.

There remains the question of the possible relevance of theories of reciprocity or reprisal for the justification of one belligerent's attacks on, or causing incidental damage to, its adversary's civilian population. A first point is that plain negative reciprocity apparently has never been claimed as a consideration justifying such attacks, and understandably so, because the factor of direct military necessity that could warrant such a construction does not apply here.[40]

But what about reprisals? While many classes of persons and objects have long been effectively protected from the impact of belligerent reprisals, with an important set of broad prohibitions dating from the Geneva Conventions of 1949,[41] the alleged right of reprisal against the civilian population or civilian objects in unoccupied enemy territory has remained a highly controversial issue even after the introduction of a series of express prohibitions on recourse to such reprisals in the section of Protocol I of 1977 devoted to the general protection of the civilian population against the effects of hostilities.[42] As these treaty prohibitions did not as such bind the parties to the Gulf War, their relations in this respect were governed by the uncertain rules of customary law.

The uncertainty of the law concerns the question whether reprisals against the enemy civilian population and civilian objects are at all permissible. Assuming for the

---

39. Protocol I, Article 51(3).

40. Negative reciprocity, *i.e.*, the right to disregard a rule because the enemy has previously done so, may be a valid argument when it comes to the employment of weapons (such as chemical weapons) of direct military significance to the progress of the military operations. It may be seen to underlie the reservations many states have attached to their acceptance of the prohibition of chemical weapons.

41. Kalshoven, F., *Belligerent Reprisals*, Leiden 1971.

42. Article 51(6): attacks against the civilian population or civilians by way of reprisals; Article 52(1): civilian objects not the object of reprisals; Article 53(c): no reprisals against protected cultural objects or places of worship; Article 54(4): no reprisals against objects indispensable to the survival of the civilian population; Article 55(2): prohibition of attacks against the natural environment by way of reprisals; Article 56(4): no reprisals against works or installations containing dangerous forces the release of which may entail severe losses among the civilian population. Recent literature on the subject includes: Hampson, F.J., "Belligerent Reprisals and the 1977 Protocols to the Geneva Conventions of 1949", 37 *ICLQ* (1988), pp. 818 *et seq.*; Greenwood, C.J., "The Twilight of the Law of Belligerent Reprisals", 20 *NYIL* (1989), pp. 35 *et seq.*; Kalshoven, *loc.cit.* (note 29).

sake of convenience that this is still the case,[43] they are then governed by the established customary rules applying to belligerent reprisals in general, *viz.*, recourse only after due warning and as a last resort, proportionality to the wrong retaliated against, termination as soon as the cause no longer obtains. An additional constraint is sometimes seen in the principle of humanity (with reprisal attacks against the civilian population being regarded as inhumane), but it is precisely here that uncertainty has prevailed ever since the matter was first brought up for discussion.[44] To this author it seems unsafe to rely on such a controversial principle.

In this situation, it is a question of fact whether in the Gulf War, a first serious encroachment on the rules for the protection of the civilian population might have been followed by a genuine reprisal. An episode related by Tavernier[45] is of interest here, suggesting as it does that Iraq in late 1983 came close to formulating what might have amounted to a threat of reprisals. By that time, however, Iraq probably had forfeited any right of reprisal if we may assume, with David, that it had been the first in 1982 to start the bombardment of enemy cities.[46] Be this as it may, it seems likely that, as on earlier occasions and notably in the Second World War, this or the other party may occasionally have used the word 'reprisal' or phraseology reminiscent of that notion, but such use was rhetorical and propagandistic rather than that it was really meant to justify their attacks against or affecting the enemy civilian population.

By way of conclusion it is submitted that the attacks carried out on either side against the civilian population and civilian objects in enemy territory violated basic precepts of the law of war applicable between the parties and could not be justified as legitimate reprisals. The attacks were, rather, acts of terror designed to bring the enemy

43. To buttress his denial of the continued legality of reprisals against the civilian population David advances the following arguments: (1) Article 60(5), of the Vienna Convention on the law of treaties excludes 'provisions relating to the protection of the human person contained in treaties of a humanitarian character, in particular (...) provisions prohibiting any form of reprisals against persons protected by such treaties' from the application of the principle that a party to a multilateral treaty specially affected by a material breach may invoke the breach 'as a ground for suspending the operation of the treaty in whole or in part in the relations between itself and the defaulting state'; (2) Article 51(6) of Protocol I prohibits reprisals against the civilian population, and (3) the statement in A/RES/2675(XXV) that civilians 'should not be the object of reprisals ...'; *op.cit.* (note 2), pp. 163-164. As against this, it should be noted that Article 60 of the Vienna Convention is applicable to treaty law and as David himself specifies, the single treaty provision relevant here, the cited paragraph of Article 51, Protocol I, was not in force between the parties; as the negotiating history of Protocol I makes abundantly clear, the paragraph cannot with any degree of certainty be said to reflect customary law, and neither can A/RES/2675(XXV) be held to have decided the issue in a manner legally binding the parties to an armed conflict. This is not to suggest that reprisals against the civilian population are something commendable: far from it, and there is a strong moral argument against them. See further Kalshoven, *op.cit.* (note 41).

44. Kalshoven, *op.cit.* (note 41), pp. 112-114, 353-361.

45. *Op.cit.* (note 1), pp. 59-60.

46. David, *loc.cit.* (note 2), pp. 161-162. There may, however, be some ground for the view that the early bombardments and shellings affecting civilian areas were not directed against the civilian population as such and, possibly, were not even clearly indiscriminate; see the report of the United Nations mission that in 1983 inspected civilian areas in Iran and Iraq which had been subject to attack, annex to S/15834.

to his knees. Even as such they failed completely, as neither party budged an inch under the impact of the attacks.

2   *Nuclear and oil facilities*

While in the foregoing the focus was on the civilian population and civilian objects in general and without differentiation as to specific targets, it remains to mention two such specific classes of target, *viz.*, nuclear and oil facilities.

Tavenier makes mention of an accusation on the part of Iran that Iraq had attacked a nuclear power station in Iranian territory.[47] Assuming this to have been the case, the question arises whether the attack was necessarily unlawful. Had Protocol I of 1977 been applicable between the parties, Article 56 would have provided the answer. Under its terms the installation was immune from attack even if it represented a military objective, provided such attack might 'cause the release of dangerous forces and consequent severe losses among the civilian population', and even then unless the power station 'provide[d] electrical power in regular, significant and direct support of military operations and if such attack [was] the only feasible way to terminate such support'. The answer was, in other words, a greatly qualified 'yes', with the final outcome depending on the facts of the case.

It should be added that the whole matter of enhanced protection of 'works and installations containing dangerous forces' was controversial from the outset and the language now found in Article 56 is very much a result of compromise. In these circumstances it appears inadmissible to treat the rules embodied in Article 56 as anything but treaty law. There is, moreover, little evidence that customary law already prohibits attacks on nuclear power stations other than in terms of the general principles for the protection of the civilian population and civilian objects. It seems therefore safe to conclude that as between the parties to the Gulf War, an attack on a nuclear power station would have been perfectly proper if there were sufficient grounds to regard the object as a military objective and the attack could be carried out without unduly severe losses among the civilian population.

From an early stage of the Diplomatic Conference on the Reaffirmation and Development of International Humanitarian Law Applicable in Armed Conflicts, 1974–1977, representatives of a number of Arab States, with Iraq among them, have done their best to make oil facilities the object of special protection. Their initiative may have been prompted more by a desire to protect their vast economic resources rather than any other value, such as civilian life or the environment. At all events, they initially, first covertly[48] and later openly,[49] attempted to bring these objects under the

---

47. *Op.cit.* (note 1), p. 45.

48. This appears to be the most plausible interpretation of the proposal of 14 Arab States to replace the word 'namely' in paragraph 1 of the draft Article (making the list of objects containing dangerous forces a limitative one) by 'such as' (which would turn it into an open-ended provision); 3 *Official Records* (or *O.R.*), p. 224: CDDH/III/76 and Add. 1, 21 March 1974; more plausible, in effect, than the official reason given by the Egyptian representative introducing the amendment, that 'the article should cover any new installations that might be produced by modern technology in the future.' 14 *O.R.*, p. 151: CDDH/III/SR./18, para. 32: Mr. El Ghonemy.

umbrella of the 'works or installations containing dangerous forces' of Article 56. Subsequently, once the idea of oil facilities as objects containing dangerous forces within the meaning of this Article had failed to gain currency,[50] they strove to achieve their purpose by introducing proposals for their separate protection.[51] Finally, when these attempts remained equally unsuccessful, the representatives withdrew their proposals.[52]

It is indeed fairly obvious that oil facilities are too much of a natural military objective in many situations, and had proved so in the past, to make the idea of their special protection widely acceptable. It is just one of those ironies of history that the Gulf War, with one of the belligerent parties having been among the most directly interested protagonists of such protection, should have been the first major war since the adoption of Protocol I to see the proposed principle summarily brushed aside.[53] Be this as it may, the episode can lead to no other conclusion than that as between the belligerent parties, oil facilities were not specially protected from attack.[54]

3   *Attitudes of the parties*

The above overview of the actual conduct of the war shows a high degree of disrespect for relevant parts of the law, demonstrated at the highest political and military levels. Throughout the war, Iraq persisted in its employment of chemical weapons, and both belligerents frequently and openly disregarded the principles and rules for the protection

49. Oil facilities were openly proposed for protection in the competent working group of Committee III in the course of the 2nd (1975) session; 15 *O.R.*, p. 352: CDDH/III/264/Rev. 1, Report to Committee III on the work of the Working Group submitted by the Rapporteur.

50. As noted in the report of the Rapporteur (*supra* note 48): 'it was agreed that these [*i.e.*, oil rigs, petroleum storage facilities, and oil refineries] were not objects containing dangerous forces within the meaning of this article ...'

51. The report goes on to say 'that, if these objects are to be given any special protection by the Protocol, it should be done by another article, perhaps by a special article for that purpose. The Rapporteur has agreed to consult further with interested representatives on this question.'

52. Significantly, already the report of Committee III on its work during the 1975 session, which repeats *verbatim* the greater part of the reports of the Working Group, no longer contains the language quoted in the previous notes; CDDH/III/215/Rev. 1, pp. 282-284. However, it does record the adoption by consensus of the article on 14 March 1975; p. 284. After the vote, the Egyptian delegate repeated his expectation 'that questions concerning petroleum refineries and related installations would be covered in a separate article'; 14 O.R., p. 299: CDDH/III/SR. 31, para. 56: Mr. El Ghonemy. The report of Committee III on the work at the 4th (1977) session, CDDH/407/Rev. 1, para. 12, records the ultimate failure: '... a proposal concerning "General principles for the protection of oil and of installations for its extraction, storage, transport and refining" (CDDH/III/GT/62/Rev. 1) was withdrawn by its sponsors.'

53. Interestingly, Iranian authorities in Abadan at one stage explicitly took the view that an oil refinery complex near the city, which had been under Iraqi attack, 'was not a civilian area and could be considered an economic installation of military significance and, therefore, a legitimate target'; as stated in the report of the United Nations mission that in 1983 inspected civilian areas in Iran and Iraq which had been subject to attack, *UN Doc.* S/15834, annex para. 42.

54. Another matter is whether attacks on such installations may become unlawful as against third parties when they entail unacceptable environmental pollution; on this see David, *loc.cit.* (note 2), pp. 164-166.

of the civilian population against the effects of hostilities. The fact that Iran did not in turn make massive use of chemical weapons may have had as much to do with practical capabilities as with a sense of moral obligation.

Yet it is of interest to quote here from a report of the United Nations Secretary-General on a visit he had paid to Iran and Iraq in April 1985. In the course of his visit he had made a double attempt: to induce both parties to agree to a cease-fire as well as, in the meantime, to respect the applicable law of war. On the latter point, the position of Iran was that 'the application of specific conventions and protocols cannot be conditional upon a cease-fire: they have been adopted precisely to mitigate the effects of the war.' However, Iraq took the position that 'any specific measures to mitigate the effects of war must be clearly linked to a comprehensive cease-fire within a timetable; otherwise they would have the effect of prolonging the war.'[55]

One can only comment that Iran's position was of course entirely correct; and if Iraq was really serious in what it told the Secretary-General, it had completely missed the point of the law of war. One wonders moreover how in 1985, after five years of ruthless warfare, Iraq could still believe that its gross and systematic violations of the law were effectively shortening the war: to the interested onlooker, nothing of the kind appears to have been the case.[56]

III   REPERCUSSIONS IN THE OUTSIDE WORLD

To say that the Gulf War has entailed strong repercussions in the outside world is to force an open door. Much of this had of course to do with the vast economic and other interests involved: the procurement of oil, the arms trade, *etc*. As for public opinion and the media, there was however also a good deal of protest against certain unlawful modes of conducting the war by either belligerent. It would be of interest to know whether condemnation of these practices was general, perhaps even world-wide, or merely restricted, say, to the Western world. For want of such information, I can only say that at least in the Netherlands, both the use of chemical weapons and the indiscriminate attacks affecting the civilian population were generally condemned, with perhaps the stronger focus on chemical weapens.

For the states that did not take an active part in the war, an obvious main concern was to maintain, and be seen to maintain, a neutral posture, especially when it came to defending their rights and notably the crucially important freedom of navigation in the face of both belligerents' military operations. But they too were concerned with the issues arising out of the employment of chemical weapons and the attacks on civilian targets, and from time to time exerted such influence as they had to bring the belligerents to respect their obligations under the law of war. In this respect, it seems safe to regard at least the right of states to attempt to induce in belligerent parties a

---

55. *UN Doc*. S/17097, 12 April 1985, paras. 8, 9.
56. See also Kalshoven, F., *Constraints on the Waging of War*, Geneva 1987, pp. 2-3.

greater respect of the law of war, whether customary or conventional, as of general applicability.[57]

A   Protecting Powers

'The present Convention shall be applied with the co-operation and under the scrutiny of the Protecting Powers whose duty it is to safeguard the interests of the Parties to the conflict.' Thus reads the opening sentence of Article 8 common to Geneva Conventions I-III, and Article 9 of Convention IV, of 1949. Ever since its adoption, rare exceptions apart, the phrase has remained the expression of a pious wish rather than a living reality; neither has the reinforcement of the system of Protecting Powers in Article 5 of Protocol I of 1977 thus far been able to modify the state of affairs. In the Gulf War of 1980-1988, in line with this regrettable trend, Protecting Powers were not appointed by the belligerents.

Even had it been otherwise, the impact of the activities of Protecting Powers on the events discussed in the present paper might have been limited at best. The idea of a significant role for Protecting Powers in the 'supervision and implementation'[58] of the law of war was devised especially in the context of the part of the law properly called the 'law of Geneva' and dealing with the treatment of war victims in the hands of the enemy. Significantly, while the supervisory function of Protecting Powers blossomed in the First World War and was for the first time incorporated in the Prisoners of War Convention of 1929,[59] the international legislators of the period did not consider entering a similar provision in the Geneva Gas Protocol of 1925.

True, the broad language of Article 5 of Protocol I of 1977 suggests an expansion of the role of Protecting Powers to encompass the Hague-type rules in the Protocol as well,[60] and these include the rules relating to means and methods of warfare. However, to implement this in practice would imply a significant departure from the original idea of a Protecting Power which (in addition to its normal diplomatic function of safeguarding the interests of belligerent party A in its relations with party B) assumes, at the behest of A and with the agreement of B, the supervision of the treatment of nationals of A in the hands of B. To supervise, say, the implementation of the rules relating to the protection of the civilian population from the effects of military operations, or those prohibiting the use of a specific (class of) weapon, would require for the Protecting Power, reversing its traditional role, also to perform supervisory

---

57. That states are entitled to react to belligerent parties' violations of the law of war is expressed in so many words in Article 1 common to the Geneva Conventions of 1949 (and of course, in its form as treaty law directly applicable only to those Conventions), as part of the undertaking of the contracting states 'to respect and to ensure respect for the present Convention in all circumstances.' Article 1(1) of Protocol I of 1977 reiterates the same formula.

58. To use the terms of Article 5 of Protocol I.

59. Articles 86, 87; *op.cit.* (note 3), p. 359.

60. The opening phrase of Article 5 reads: 'It is the duty of the Parties to a conflict from the beginning of that conflict to secure the supervision and implementation of the Convention *and of this Protocol* by the application of the system of Protecting Powers, ...' (emphasis added).

activities on behalf of B, as the potential victim of violations of the rules on the part of A. This would in turn require, not only the need to bring into the field an entirely different type of inspector, but a more perfectly neutral stance than a Protecting Power would normally be expected to maintain: a sort of Swiss neutrality, so to speak.

B   The International Committee of the Red Cross

This brings to mind the institution that from its creation in the 1860s has done its utmost to maintain such a 'Swiss' neutrality and in all armed conflicts to extend its supervisory functions to both sides to the conflict: *i.e.*, the International Committee of the Red Cross (or ICRC).[61] As far as relevant here, this is recognized in two ways in treaty law: by indicating the ICRC as a natural substitute at least for the humanitarian functions of Protecting Powers,[62] and by recognizing its independent right of humanitarian initiative.[63] While these functions and this right of initiative primarily envisage the protection of war victims in the classical Geneva sense (in the main, the wounded and sick, prisoners of war, and civilians in occupied territory), the ICRC has long also been concerned with the fate of human beings suffering the direct impact of hostilities. Thus, ever since the First World War it has raised its voice against the use of chemical weapons and the bombardment of civilians.

In the Gulf War too, the ICRC from an early stage has continued to remind the parties of their obligations not to attack the civilian population and in attacking military objectives to spare it as much as possible. Shedding its habitual discretion it repeatedly made its concerns public, calling on the parties to the conflict to terminate their violations of the fundamental principles involved and asking the international community to support these appeals.[64] In the same vein, though initially somewhat more hesitantly, it publicly exposed the use of chemical weapons.[65]

The immediate effect of its remonstrations on the belligerents' conduct of the war may have been slight, although of course each belligerent was invariably willing to assure the ICRC of its intention to respect the law and at one time even asked the ICRC to send delegates to visit the civilian victims of its enemy's acts of indiscriminate violence.[66] More important may have been the indirect effects, through the mobilisation of public opinion, third states and the United Nations.

---

61. See Kalshoven, F., "Impartiality and Neutrality in Humanitarian Law and Practice", 30 *International Review of the Red Cross* (1990), pp. 516-535, in particular pp. 527-531.

62. Article 10(3), common to Geneva Conventions I-III; Article 11(3) of Convention IV; Article 5(4) of Protocol I of 1977.

63. Article 9 common to Conventions I-III, Article 10 of Convention IV; Article 81(1) of Protocol I.

64. Public appeals of this order are recorded in each of the ICRC's annual reports for the years 1983-1988.

65. As related in the annual report for 1984, a first veiled condemnation (of 'products prohibited by the law of war') was made public on 7 March 1984. The report for 1987 relates that after a special United Nations mission had reported on the use of chemical weapons, the ICRC in May of that year had officially informed the belligerents of its concern in this regard.

66. Report for 1987.

C   The United Nations

While the Security Council from the outset was concerned with the war between Iran and Iraq, its prime focus throughout the war obviously was on the termination of hostilities and the restoration of peace and security in the region. This also determined the main thrust of the mandate of the Secretary-General in his many activities relating to the war. Yet, in the course of time, both United Nations organs became involved in efforts to bring the belligerents to an attitude of respect for the law of war as long as the fighting lasted. As far as the issues dealt with in this chapter are concerned, the effect of military operations on the civilian population chronologically was the first to require their attention, soon to be accompanied and in some measure overshadowed by the employment of chemical weapons.

1   *The principle of distinction*

On 31 October 1983 the Security Council for the first time officially expressed its concern at the 'heavy losses of civilian lives and extensive damage caused to cities, property and economic infrastructures' as a result of the war, and it called 'for the immediate cessation of all military operations against civilian targets, including city and residential areas.'[67] It did this on the basis, *inter alia*, of a report of the Secretary-General dated 20 June 1983 on a mission he had dispatched to both countries at war to inspect civilian areas that had suffered the effects of military operations.[68]

The mission had toured war zones in Iran and Iraq in May 1983 and visited a number of cities and villages located in the border area, which had suffered greater or lesser damage as a result of the impact of bombs, missiles or artillery shells. Its report provides excellent insight into the functions of a fact-finding mission in a war zone, the skills required of its members and the difficulties it may expect to encounter. Striking features are the systematic, detailed description of relevant facts such as losses and damage suffered or the presence of objects in the vicinity that might be regarded as military objectives, and the carefully phrased, balanced conclusions drawn on the basis of the facts so established. Significantly, the mission neither accused any party of having carried out attacks in violation of the law, whether against the civilian population as such or indiscriminately against military objectives and civilian objects, nor did it attempt to justify any attacks on military or legal grounds. Had it done so, it would surely have overstepped the limits of its terms of reference as well as, more importantly, of its possibilities in the circumstances.

In subsequent phases of the war, both parties resorted to deliberate attacks on civilian targets in the enemy hinterland to a far greater degree than in the comparatively mild opening phase of the war. Both the Security Council[69] and the President speaking

---

67. S/RES/540(1983) of 31 October 1983.
68. *UN Doc.* S/15834.
69. S/RES/582(1986) of 24 February 1986; S/RES/598(1987) of 20 July 1987.

on behalf of its members[70] more than once condemned recourse to such methods and called upon the parties to put an end to it.

Particularly vigorous efforts to the latter effect were made by the Secretary-General, who from an early stage attempted to bring about a sort of cease-fire, or moratorium, by which the belligerents would agree to desist from deliberate attacking purely civilian targets. On 14 June 1984 he was able to report to the Security Council that the belligerents had given such undertakings effective from 12 June. Noting that each of the parties 'had made independent requests for arrangements to verify compliance with the undertakings', he set up two teams, each consisting of three officers drawn from the United Nations Truce Supervision Organization and one official of the Secretariat, and with the mandate to inspect specific allegations of violations of the undertakings and report to him.[71] On 29 June, in a letter to both parties, he noted with satisfaction that they were 'implementing in good faith their undertakings to refrain from military attacks on purely civilian areas.'[72] Even so, the belligerents soon resumed their attacks with increased intensity, leading the Secretary-General to express his dismay 'that the moratorium on attacks on purely civilian areas has not been respected.'[73]

2   *Chemical weapons*

A similar, rather disappointing story must be told about the exertions of United Nations organs to make the belligerents refrain from the use of chemical weapons. From 1984 onwards the President of the Security Council,[74] and since 1987 the Council itself,[75] have frequently reminded the belligerents of the need to abide strictly by the provisions of the Gas Protocol of 1925. The President in particular has not hesitated to do so in terms that were ever more directly addressed to Iraq. All of these statements and resolutions were based on the findings of specialists dispatched by the Secretary-General to investigate allegations (mostly by Iran) that chemical weapons had been used.

70. *UN Doc.* S/17004, 5 March 1985, expressing alarm over reports that the parties were 'attacking or preparing to attack civilian areas'; *UN Doc.* S/17036, 15 March 1985, expressing concern 'over the scale of the renewed hostilities'; *UN Doc.* S/18538, 22 December 1986; *UN Doc.* S/19626, 16 March 1988.

71. *UN Doc.* S/16627. The members of the Security Council soon agreed with the proposed measures (*UN Doc.* S/16628) and the system became effective as from 15 June 1984.

72. *UN Doc.* S/16663.

73. *UN Doc.* S/17097, 12 April 1985: report on his visit to Iran and Iraq, para. 2.

74. *Un Doc.* S/16454, 30 March 1984; *UN Doc.* S/17130, 25 April 1985, specifying that chemical weapons had been used 'against Iranian soldiers'; *UN Doc.* S/17932, 21 March 1986, repeating in so many words the conclusion of experts 'that chemical weapons on many occasions have been used by Iraqi forces against Iranian forces'; *UN Doc.* S/18863, 14 May 1987, adding to the previous statement 'that civilians in Iran also have been injured by chemical weapons' and, using a significantly different phraseology, 'that Iraqi military personnel have sustained injuries from chemical agents.'

75. S/RES/598(1987) of 20 July 1987, referring cautiously to 'the use of chemical weapons contrary to obligations under the 1925 Geneva Protocol'; S/RES/612(1988) of 9 May 1988, expressing the Council's expectation that 'both sides [would] refrain from the future use of chemical weapons'; S/RES/620(1988) of 26 August 1988 (!).

The first mission was sent in March 1984, and the last one in mid-August 1988.[76] Again, their reports represent important sources of information on the task of fact-finding missions in countries at war and the obstacles they are apt to encounter. Unfortunately, however, none of this was enough to bring about a change in the Iraqi mode of conducting the war. In the end, even the specialists were losing faith. As they noted in their report of 6 May 1987:

'We all firmly believe that, at the specialist level, we have done all we can to identify the types of chemicals and chemical weapons being used in the Iran-Iraq conflict. If, in the future, a further mission is requested, then we will of course all be ready to respond. However, we now feel that technically there is little more that we can do that is likely to assist the United Nations in its efforts to prevent the use of chemical weapons in the present conflict. In our view, only concerted efforts at the political level can be effective in ensuring that all the signatories of the Geneva Protocol of 1925 abide by their obligations. Otherwise, if the Protocol is irreparably weakened after 60 years of general international respect, this may lead, in the future, to the world facing the spectre of the threat of biological weapons.'

In transmitting the specialists' report to the Security Council, the Secretary-General underscored their concern and he urged 'the parties concerned and all Governments to direct their full attention to the implications of the present report.' On 25 July 1988, once again transmitting a report of the specialists, he added that:

'In stressing once more the necessity for restraint and compliance with universally recognized rules of international law, and bearing in mind the ongoing efforts being pursued in the Conference on Disarmament towards a multilateral convention on the complete and effective prohibition of the development, production and stockpiling of chemical weapons and on their destruction, the Secretary-General considers it important that all concerned focus their attention to the need to end a continuous and vicious circle of development and use of those weapons.'

In the 1970s, when important parts of the law of war came up for revision, one crucial problem was how to improve the enforcement of the law. Of all the ideas put forward,

---

76. *UN Doc.* S/16433, 26 March 1984; *UN Doc.* S/17127 and Add. 1, 17 April 1985; *UN Doc.* S/17911 and Add. 1, 12 March 1986, containing testimony even of Iraqi military personnel on the use of chemical weapons by their own forces; *UN Doc.* S/18852, 8 May 1987, investigating also Iraqi allegations of Iranian use and concluding on this score that 'Iraqi forces [had] been affected by mustard gas and a pulmonary irritant, possibly phosgene' but adding that 'in the absence of conclusive evidence of the weapons used, it could not be determined how the injuries were caused' (leaving open, in other words, which side the chemical agents had come from); *UN Doc.* S/19823, 25 April 1988; *UN Doc.* S/20060, 20 July 1988, making the point that in view of the rapid disappearance of certain volatile gases it might 'be necessary to review existing machinery for verification by United Nations teams of the use of chemical weapons in order to ensure the timely presence of experts at the site of alleged attacks'; *UN Doc.* S/20063, 25 July 1988; *UN Doc.* S/20134, 19 August 1988.

few were retained, and then for the most part in greatly watered-down fashion.[77] Two aspects are of particular interest here. One is that attempts to introduce the United Nations in a supervisory capacity were unsuccessful: the only provision in Protocol I reminiscent of these attempts is Article 89, laying down the undertaking of the contracting states in 'situations of serious violations of the Conventions or of this Protocol (...) to act, jointly or individually, in co-operation with the United Nations and in conformity with the United Nations Charter.' The other is the introduction in Article 90 of an independent International Fact-Finding Commission, to be established when twenty contracting states have agreed to accept its comptence as outlined in the Article.

The experience of the Gulf War highlights the importance of fact-finding in the field. True, it did not noticeably change the practices of the belligerents. Yet, it did provide a solid basis for the endeavours of the international community to put a stop to their reprehensible conduct. When in due time the International Fact-Finding Commission of Article 90 is established, it will do well to study closely the reports of the various missions on their visits to the area.

The Gulf War also has highlighted the potentialities of a United Nations Secretary--General dedicated to the cause of humanitarian principles. His 'overriding constitutional responsibility under the Charter' was from the outset, and remained throughout, 'to seek an end to the conflict.' However, until that goal was achieved, he considered himself 'also legally obliged under recognized international humanitarian rules to try to mitigate its effects, in areas such as attacks on civilian population centres, use of chemical weapons, treatment of prisoners of war and safety of navigation and civil aviation.'[78] Little does it matter that his sense of legal obligation finds no basis in the conventional law of war: what counts is that his persistent efforts have contributed greatly to enhancing general understanding and respect for the law of war.

There remains, of course, a sense of deep frustration that all the efforts to bring the belligerent parties to respect their clear legal obligations under the law of war ultimately remained without success. This shows, on the one hand, the tremendous difficulty in including a really determined leadership to change its modes of conducting a war; and, on the other, the urgent need to continue the dissemination of knowledge and understanding of the principles of the humanitarian law of war.

77. The relevant provisions in Protocol I of 1977 include: Article 5 on the appointment of Protecting Powers or substitutes; Article 6 on the recruitment and training of qualified personnel; Article 7 on meetings of the contracting states 'to consider general problems concerning the application of the Conventions and of the Protocol'; Article 81(1), on facilities for the ICRC; Article 89 on cooperation among the contracting states in the event of serious violations; and Article 90 on the establishment and facultative functioning of an International Fact-Finding Commission.

78. *UN Doc.* S/17097, 12 April 1985: report of the Secretary-General on his visit to Iran and Iraq, para. 7.

COMMENTS: METHODS OR MEANS OF WARFARE, BELLIGERENT REPRISALS, AND THE PRINCIPLE OF PROPORTIONALITY

Rainer Lagoni*

Professor Kalshoven has confined his very fine and very scholarly paper on the Gulf War to the measures and means of warfare on land. As my own research related mainly to the naval aspects of that armed conflict, I will address two questions of a general legal nature, rather than dwelling on particular events. I have to confess, however, that both questions lay at the fringe of Professor Kalshoven's topic. The first is, whether or not the principle of proportionality could limit the use of methods or means of warfare and the second asks, whether this principle could also limit belligerent reprisals.

Writing here, of course, in my personal capacity, I consider the questions from an academic point of view, although they are in no way of an academic nature. To limit the choice of measures and means of warfare is essential for the concept of the limited war, and to avoid its escalation resulting from belligerent reprisals is crucial to it. Therefore, both questions are of the greatest practical relevance for the limitation of armed conflicts in our time.

I   LEGAL LIMITS TO THE CHOICE OF METHODS OR MEANS OF WARFARE

'Means of warfare' are, according to a general definition, man-made objects with destructive effect, whereas the term 'methods of warfare' refers to the way in which the means of warfare are used in a given strategic or tactical situation. There is no doubt that the right of the parties to an armed conflict to choose methods or means of warfare is not unlimited. This principle has been restated for the Parties in Article 35(1) of the Additional Protocol I of 1977. There is also no doubt that the belligerents are limited in their choice of methods or means by principles and rules of international law. Accordingly, a belligerent may choose only such methods or means of warfare, that are not prohibited by a convention binding upon it, by customary international law or by the general principles of law recognized by civilized nations.

An international agreement may contain very specific prohibitions concerning the choice of methods or means of warfare. An example is the 1925 Geneva Protocol for the Prohibition of the Use in War of Asphyxiating, Poisonous or Other Gases, and of Bacteriological Methods of Warfare. However, such conventional prohibitions frequently give rise to questions of interpretation and application. A case in point was the attitude of Iraq during the Gulf War. When acceding to it in 1931, Iraq had

---

* R. Lagoni, Professor of International Law at the University of Hamburg.

I.F. Dekker and H.H.G. Post, eds., The Gulf War of 1980-1988
© 1992, T.M.C. Asser Instituut, The Hague

formulated a reservation to the 1925 Geneva Protocol, according to which it is not bound by the said Protocol as regards states which have neither signed nor ratified it or acceded to it. Therefore, it was not bound by the 1925 Protocol with respect to Iran, which had not signed it nor became a party to it.

Yet, this does not mean that Iraq was free to use poisonous gas against Iran during the Gulf War. Although it was not bound by the conventional prohibition to use poisonous gas as a means of warfare *vis à vis* Iran, the corresponding prohibition of customary international law nevertheless applied, because the case remained under the protection and authority of customary international law, which prohibits this means of warfare.

This was already recognized in the famous De Martens Clause, which has found its way into the Preamble of the Hague Convention No. IV of 1907 on the Laws and Customs of War on Land as well as into Article 1(2) of Protocol I. In the same line the International Court of Justice made the following observation in its Judgment on the Merits concerning *Military and Paramilitary Activities in and against Nicaragua*:

> 'But in addition, even if a treaty norm and a customary norm relevant to the present dispute were to have exactly the same content, this would not be a reason for the Court to take the view that the operation of the treaty process must necessarily deprive the customary norm of its separate applicability. Nor can the multilateral treaty reservation be interpreted as meaning that, once applicable to a given dispute, it would exclude the application of any rule of customary international law the content of which was the same as, or analogous to, that of the treaty-law rule which had caused the reservation to become effective.'[1]

No doubt, most international lawyers would agree with Professor Kalshoven that it is 'notoriously difficult to trace a rule of customary law'. And one can add that it is particularly difficult to determine why belligerents do not use certain methods or means of warfare. Are they behaving so for legal reasons – which means: because they consider themselves to be bound by the law to do so – or simply for reasons of military or political convenience? Nevertheless, during the last two decades the situation has been improved to a certain extent, by developments in the doctrine of customary law. The International Court of Justice held in 1969 in the *North Sea Continental Shelf* Cases that rules of customary law can develop in a considerably short time from international agreements, if those states, which are mostly affected by the new rule, act in conformity with it in their practice.[2] This development can also proceed from an agreement which has not entered into force. Several customary rules concerning the methods or means of warfare have been codified in Protocol I while others may have developed into customary law since 1977. Therefore one can share Professor Kalshoven's view that a significant part of the rules on methods and means of warfare embodied in Part III of this Protocol embody customary law.

In spite of this development of customary rules, the law of warfare remains in many areas underdeveloped and full of loopholes. In the absence of specific rules, general

1. *ICJ Reports* 1986, p. 14 at p. 94, para. 175.
2. *ICJ Reports* 1969, p. 3 at p. 41.

principles of international law are of some significance for the interpretation, application and completion of the rules of warfare. While there seems to be consensus about the necessity of applying general principles of international law in the modern law of warfare, the nature and content of these principles are nevertheless, very controversial.

The term 'principles of international law', as it is used in Article 1(2) of Protocol I and in the following sections, means legal principles of an abstract nature, which are part of the body of customary international law. Concerning the sources of international law they are neither 'general principles of law recognized by civilized nations' mentioned in Article 38(1)(c) of the Statute of the International Court of Justice. Nor are they moral or political principles, which may constitute strong driving forces for the development of the law of warfare. Unlike a specific rule, a general principle of customary international law normally cannot be applied directly to a given situation. Because of its abstract nature, it has to be applied in connection with the interpretation or application of specific rules of warfare. Yet, this in no way affects their importance for the limitation of the use of methods or means of warfare.

II   THE PRINCIPLE OF PROPORTIONALITY

Professor Kalshoven has mentioned several general principles in his paper without presenting, however, an exclusive list. In addition, I suggest that the principle of proportionality may also form an important limit to the choice of methods or means of warfare. In the law of warfare this principle means that the use of methods or means to achieve a certain military advantage shall be necessary, adequate and proportional in relation to that advantage. To employ means of warfare for no military advantage at all is unnecessary and accordingly contrary to the principle of proportionality. To give an example from another armed conflict: it was not necessary for the Argentine air force to bomb the crude-oil tanker 'Hercules' during the Falklands/Malvinas conflict in June 1982 some 500 nautical miles from the Falklands on the high seas, because this attack on a ship flying the Liberian flag and owned by an American shipping company produced no military advantage at all. Under normal circumstances, destroying a civil object is not necessary to achieve any military advantage. And, finally, it would not be proportional to cause a severe humanitarian or environmental damage in order to achieve a comparatively small military advantage. The principle of proportionality requires a cautious balance between the anticipated military advantage and the foreseeable detrimental effects on other values recognized by the law.

The principle of proportionality is embodied in Article 23(e) and (g) of the Annex to the Hague Convention No. IV of 1907. In addition, it is contained in several provisions of the 1977 Protocol I: Article 35, the first article of the section on methods and means of warfare, prohibits in paragraph 2 the employment of weapons, projectiles and material and methods of warfare of a nature to cause 'superfluous' injury or 'unnecessary' suffering. This means injury that is not proportional and suffering that is not necessary to achieve a specific military advantage. The principle of proportionality finds clear expression also in Article 51(5)(b) of Protocol I, according to which an attack is prohibited, if the loss of civilian life, injury to civilians, damage to civilian objects, or a combination thereof 'would be excessive in relation to the concrete and direct military advantage anticipated'. The obligation 'to take all reasonable precautions to avoid losses of civilian lives and damages to civilian objects', which is embodied in Article 57(4) of Protocol I, is not only a consequence of the principle of distinction (Article 48), it forms also a specification of the principle of proportionality.

No expert on the law of warfare and humanitarian law would ignore this principle, if it is contained in the rules mentioned. Most experts do agree that the law of warfare is open – and has always been open – to general principles of customary law. Nevertheless, they are not prepared to recognize the principle of proportionality as a general principle which applies in the realm of warfare, because they are concerned that this principle would affect the consistency and force of the existing body of humanitarian law. Whether or not there are sufficient reasons for this concern will be shown below. In any event, as it is contained in several specific rules of this law, one can conclude that the principle forms a part of the whole corpus of the modern law of warfare and humanitarian law.

III   QUESTIONS OF ITS APPLICATION

Because of its nature as a general principle of customary law, the principle of proportionality may apply only in the absence of specific rules, if the circumstances of a given situation warrant this. Accordingly, the existence of sufficiently specific rules for the actual combat normally leaves no room for its application in a tactical situation. However, taking strategic decisions on the use of certain methods or means of warfare generally warrants an application of the principle. 'Strategic' in this sense would be the choice of a particular method of warfare or of means which have a considerable impact on the conduct or the outcome of the armed conflict concerned. Whether or not a decision is of a strategic nature depends therefore upon the particular circumstances of a given conflict, as some examples for such strategic decisions show: the beginning of warfare at sea during an ongoing war on land (or *vice versa*), the decision to attack merchant ships on sight, the decision to use nuclear weapons or to deploy any other means which would escalate the armed conflict in a similar way.

The application of the principle of proportionality on strategic decisions is, however, not only *de facto* necessary for the reasons mentioned. It is also required by the law itself as a consequence of the legal impact of the Charter of the United Nations on the law of warfare. And, by the way, it should be mentioned here that it is exactly this impact which turns the traditional law of warfare into a modern law of armed conflict.

As the Charter is not suspended during any armed conflict – including a war in the formal sense – the legal relationship between the belligerents themselves as well as the relationship between any belligerent and the Security Council is subject to the principles and rules of the United Nations Charter. While there is no doubt about this, the subsequent question, whether or not the Charter has any impact on the law of warfare, is, however, very controversial. Many legal experts consider the traditional law of warfare (the *ius in bello*), on the one hand, and those principles and rules of the United Nations Charter, which prohibit the use of armed force (the *ius contra bellum*), on the other hand, as two separate bodies of law. In their view these distinct bodies of law are neither connected with each other nor even related to each other, because they govern separate legal questions and, besides that, besides that, they serve different legal purposes.

Unlike this traditionalist view a more timely way of considering this issue rests on the fact that the United Nations Charter prohibits the use of armed force and determines also the particular situations in which force is still permissible in present-day international relations. These situations are:

- individual or collective self-defence (Article 51);
- regional enforcement actions authorized by the Security Council (Article 53(1);
- action taken by the Security Council (under Article 42);
- formerly also action against an 'enemy state' under Article 53(1) and Article 107). However, most international lawyers rightly consider the enemy-state clauses as now obsolete.

Outside these specific situation, armed force may no longer be used by states in their international relations. Accordingly, there are no international armed conflicts – independent of whether or not they are wars in a formal sense – outside the scope of application of the Charter of the United Nations.

Its conclusive enumeration of situations, in which the use of armed force is still permissible today, means that the United Nations Charter covers the whole area of the regulation of the use of force in international relations, as the International Court of Justice rightly observed in the Merits of the Nicaragua Case.[3] Nevertheless, it directly affects the way in which armed force may be used in international relations, because in the situation of self-defence, to take the most important example, armed force may only be used under the conditions and within the specific restrictions which international law provides for the exercise of this right. Accordingly, the law of warfare cannot grant a greater freedom to take armed measures than the parties to an armed conflict have under the Charter itself. Or, to put it in other words: any measure which is prohibited under the Charter is also prohibited in the law of warfare. This may also be seen in the analogous case regulated in Article 103 of the Charter. Moreover, these common legal restrictions concerning the modalities of the use of armed force, which are imposed by the Charter, form the 'missing link' between the law of the Charter and the law of warfare. Recalling the latin phrases and adding another one, one can say that the *ius contra bellum* of the Charter transformed the traditional *ius in bello* into a modern *ius ad defensionem*. This transformation is mainly effective on the strategic level of an armed conflict.

For the case of self-defence, which has been the most frequent reason for the use of armed force in international relations since the end of the Second World War, the United Nations Charter itself, however, does not expressly spell out the specific legal

---

3. *ICJ Reports* 1986, p. 94, para. 176.

restrictions. Instead, it refers to customary law embodying them, as the Court observed in the Merits of the Nicaragua Case.

> 'On one essential point, this treaty itself refers to pre-existing customary international law; this reference to customary law is contained in the actual text of Article 51, which mentions the "inherent right" (in the French text the "droit naturel") of individual or collective self-defence, which "nothing in the present Charter shall impair" and which applies in the event of an armed attack. The Court therefore finds that Article 51 of the Charter is only meaningful on the basis that there is a "natural" or "inherent" right of self-defence, and it is hard to see how this can be other than of a customary nature, even if its present content has been confirmed and influenced by the Charter. Moreover the Charter, having itself recognized the existence of this right, does not go on to regulate directly all aspects of its content.'[4]

Turning to the specific restrictions on the use of armed force in self-defence, the Court went on:

> 'For example, it does not contain any specific rule whereby self-defence would warrant only measures which are proportional to the armed attack and necessary to respond to it, a rule well established in customary international law.'[5]

The reason for the mentioned customary rule that only measures are warranted which are proportional to the armed attack and necessary to respond to it resides in the concept and the purpose of self-defence itself. Self-defence under Article 51 of the United Nations Charter does not simply mean to bring the enemy to its knees, but primarily the right to defend oneself against an illegal threat or use of force in international relations. Accordingly, by exercising the inherent right of self-defence, a state may not use armed force simply to win the war but only to restore and preserve its territorial integrity or political independence as it was before the first strike. This limitation to use armed force only for the purpose of restoration and preservation of the *status quo ante* affects also the choice of methods or means of warfare, as will be seen below.

It shall only briefly be mentioned here that these restrictions apply not only to a state, which refers to self-defence as a justification for using armed force – as in fact nearly all states have done in their international relations since 1945 – but also to an aggressor state, because the latter cannot be privileged under the law.

IV   THE EFFECT OF THE PRINCIPLE

Generally stated, the effect of the principle of proportionality on the choice of methods or means of warfare is that no such methods or means may be used which are not necessary for the purpose of self-defence, as that is recognized by the United Nations Charter, or which are not proportional in relation to this purpose. However, this would

4. *Idem.*
5. *Idem.*

not exclude the use of any particular weapon of any kind, except for weapons which are prohibited by the rules of warfare, as, for example, poisonous gas is. Accordingly, even nuclear weapons could be employed, if this is necessary and proportional to the legally-recognized purpose of self-defence.

Turning to some examples from the Gulf War, the limiting effect of the principle of proportionality on the choice of methods or means of warfare is dependent upon the strategic situation of the armed conflict concerned. The so-called 'tanker war' launched by Iraq from 1983 in order to cut off Iranian oil exports was no longer proportional in relation to the objectives of self-defence, at least at the moment when it became obvious that the oil exports of Iran could neither effectively be interrupted nor any longer seriously be impeded. However, if Iran were to have closed the Strait of Hormuz, which it occasionally threatened to do during the Gulf War, that measure would not only have violated the territorial integrity of Oman and certain international rules concerning the passage through straits, it would also have been an illegal violation of the principle of proportionality, because this could in no way affect the war-sustaining efforts of Iraq, which received its supply via Jordan and Saudi Arabia. Or, to mention a final example, balancing the comparatively small military advantage of the Iraqi attacks on 7 Iranian off-shore production platforms in the Novruz Oilfield in March 1983 against the widespread, long-term and severe oil pollution which these attacks caused to the marine environment of the whole Gulf, these methods were unproportional and accordingly illegal within the meaning of Article 35(3), 55(1) and 56(1) of Protocol I of 1977. The situation was different, however, when US naval forces bombed the Rostam and Rakash platforms on 19 October 1987, which served Iranian forces as a military basis.

V   BELLIGERENT REPRISALS

Finally, turning to the question of belligerent reprisals, I will be comparatively brief on this topic, because Professor Kalshoven is an outstanding legal expert on it. Nevertheless, as belligerent reprisals are often used by the parties to an armed conflict to brush away existing legal limits to the choice of methods or means of warfare thus making the reprisals issue of great practical importance, I will address one single point. This point again is related to the principle of proportionality.

A reprisal is by definition a countermeasure against a violation of international law which in itself would be illegal if it were not employed in order to compel the law-breaking party to obey the law. In short, it is an illegal means turned legal, because it serves a legal end. In international law in general the principle of proportionality is again an inherent element of the reprisal, because reprisals 'altogether out of proportion with the act which prompted them' are illegal, as was held in the *Naulilaa* Arbitration of 1928.[6] Nevertheless, states were often reluctant to apply the principle of proportionality to belligerent reprisals, whereas scholars of international law generally

---

6. *Reports of International Arbitral Awards*, vol. II, pp. 1011, 1026, 1028.

advocate its application advocating, however, a more or less strict proportionality between the illegal act and the countermeasure.

The issue I would like to raise is, whether Iran has been freed 'for the rest of the war' from the legal restriction on using chemical weapons after Iraq used gas in the Gulf War. It seems to me that in the absence of a positive rule prohibiting its violation by way of reprisal – and there are indeed several 'reprisal-safe' rules in Additional Protocol I, such as Articles 20, 51(6), 53(c), 54(4), 55(2), 56(4), which may well be of a customary nature – the principle of proportionality would not exclude the use of gas as a reprisal during the time of the actual employment of gas by the enemy. But it would hardly be proportional to proceed with the use of gas after the enemy has ceased to use this prohibited means of warfare. The belligerent reprisal means a tit-for-tat against breaking the law in order to preserve the law; it does not entitle any belligerent to open *Pandora's* box for the rest of the war.

CONCLUSION

The principle of proportionality forms an integral part of the modern law of warfare. In the situation of self-defence it effectively limits the choice of methods or means of warfare as well as the scope and duration of a belligerent reprisal. Therefore, it does not negatively affect humanitarian law as it is contained in the Protocols of 1977. On the contrary, it strengthens this body of law.

COMMENTS

Gert-Jan van Hegelsom[*]

INTRODUCTION

This commentator is in general agreement with the views presented by Professor Kalshoven. These comments will highlight a number of aspects, raise certain points which might be controversial and try to ascertain whether the suggestions by Professor Kalshoven will lead to improvements in respect for the law of war. The comments will generally follow the line of argument by Professor Kalshoven. In addition, this paper will address a point raised by Professor Lagoni.

Whether the law of armed conflict will actually be respected by belligerents in a given situation depends on a number of factors. Obviously, knowledge of the law is a prerequisite: it is not quite clear whether, save for some political arguments which have been used in the public debate, either Iraq or Iran have made any particular effort to disseminate knowledge of the law of war among the armed forces or at the political decision-making level. Secondly, technical and operational capabilities can play an important role: the absence of adequate communications can severely limit the influence of commanders on the actual behaviour of their troops in the midst of battle. It would seem that this issue did not give rise to any specific difficulties during the Iran-Iraq conflict. Perhaps the most important factor regarding respect for the law is the political will of a party to the conflict to exercise such control over the behaviour of its armed forces that the law is actually taken into consideration during operations. It is submitted that this political will has been totally absent from the very beginning through to the end of the war. Operations have not been conducted on the basis of the law of armed conflict as Western countries know it. Whether law played a role in the war at all is left to more qualified commentators, specifically those who view the conflict from the point of view of Islamic law. In the absence of an indication that the standards of the law of armed conflict were considered applicable, it remains a question of fact whether the law was violated in specific instances. In the light of these comments little is to be added to Professor Kalshoven's analysis, except perhaps to deplore that, for instance, during the campaigns of random targeting of cities international concern was not as strong as one might have wished.

---

* G-J.F. van Hegelsom, Directorate of Legal Affairs, Netherlands Ministry of Defense. The opinions expressed in the comments are not in any way attributable to the Ministry of Defense.

I.F. Dekker and H.H.G. Post, eds., The Gulf War of 1980-1988

I   KALSHOVEN'S ANALYSIS

A   **The actual conduct of the war**

1   *Prohibited means of warfare*

Professor Kalshoven assumes that the reciprocity reservation with regard to the
chemical weapons Protocol can plausibly be called upon by non-reserving states as a
matter of customary law. It is submitted that the exact extent of such a customary norm
is uncertain: can states which did not reserve the right to second-use invoke the
reservation when confronted with a belligerent who did not ratify the 1925 Protocol?
What is the position of states which have knowingly decided not to make the
reservation? What is the position of states which have withdrawn the 'second use'
reservation?[1] In the light of the ongoing negotiations in the Committee on Disarmament regarding a comprehensive ban on chemical weapons, certain countries are
contemplating lifting of this reservation. It could be argued that these states will forfeit
their right to invoke the reservation in order to justify second use of chemical weapons
and therefore could justify such use solely under the doctrine of reprisal.

    Only few means of warfare have been banned: it is difficult to ascertain whether,
given the general principles, a means is or should be prohibited in a specific situation.
It is obvious that any means of warfare can be used unlawfully. In general, however,
means of warfare are inherently discriminate either because of the fact that they can be
set to a certain objective or because of the fact that they are individually triggered. The
identification of the legitimate military objective is the key to respect for the law of war.
The question of respect then revolves around the question whether political and military
decision-makers want to apply 'precautions in attack'.[2]

2   *Prohibited methods of warfare*

If one shares the proposition of Professor Kalshoven that the principle of distinction is
a fundamental principle of the law of armed conflict which can be applied directly to
the use of means of warfare by belligerents, no debate should arise as to the validity of
Kalshoven's thesis that the principle of distinction and the prohibition of attacks against
the civilian population have been violated on a routine basis by the belligerents. Bearing
in mind, however, that an effective protection of the civilian population has only been
achieved in the 1977 Additional Protocol I, one might question the relative simplicity
of that conclusion.

    In his exposé on the matter, Professor Kalshoven, on the basis of the duty to spare
the civilian population as much as possible,[3] relies heavily on the rules in Additional

---

1. *E.g.* Schindler, D., and Toman, J., *The Laws of Armed Conflict*, 2nd. edition, Alphen a/d Rijn 1988, p.
121.
    2. *Cf.* Article 57 of Protocol I additional to the Geneva Conventions of 12 August 1949.
    3. *Cf.* A/RES/2444(XXIII) of 19 December 1968.

Protocol I: avoidance of incidental loss of life among the civilian population or damage to civilian objects, the duty to minimize or stop an attack if the loss or damage is found to be excessive in relation to the concrete and direct military advantage expected. One might wonder whether these are rules which are already firmly anchored in customary law. Professor Kalshoven asserts that the civilian population has not (even temporarily) been deprived of its civilian character as 'it did not participate directly in hostilities'. Again, Additional Protocol I language is used to determine the obligations of the parties to the conflict. Attributing such an absolute character to the principle of distinction, it has gradually become a tool for the condemnation of the use of military force in general: the bomb that went astray and hit the French embassy during the US raid on Lybia, the downing of Iran Air flight 655 by the USS Vincennes. Methods of warfare, however, should be assessed in the context of all relevant general principles: are the 'precautions in attack' respected? Is the military objective to be achieved proportional to the danger of collateral damage to be expected?

It is submitted that Professor Kalshoven's conclusions, in view of their absolute character and their exclusive reliance on legal obligations based on Additional Protocol I, go too far. Unlawful attacks on civilians and civilian objects occur on a daily basis all around the world. Without justifying them in any way, it would seem too early to condemn these solely on the basis of the customary law value of the relevant Additional Protocol I provisions. While one may easily agree that civilians may not individually be attacked, the extensive reliance by armed forces on civilian logistic support is bound to cloud the issue even further in the future. It would seem that a more effective assessment should be carried out on the basis of the principle of proportionality. Also, practical circumstances which are not necessarily within the control of the armed forces of belligerents will continue to hamper strict adherence to the rules of Additional Protocol I.

It is clear, however, that in the Iran-Iraq war the long-range attacks were meant solely to terrorise the civilian population and should on those grounds be considered fundamental violations of the applicable law. Logically then, this analysis does not lead to a different conclusion than Professor Kalshoven's.

Professor Kalshoven would seem to contradict himself in the consideration of attacks on nuclear and oil facilities. If one were to accept his earlier proposition that the 'environmental' prohibition of Article 35(3) of Additional Protocol I has become a customary norm, systematic attacks against nuclear and oil facilities should be assessed in the light of that customary norm. At this stage, however, his assessment of the conduct of the belligerents, with which I am in total agreement, is conducted on the basis of positive law. Attacks on nuclear facilities *a fortiori* can be expected to cause widespread, long-term and severe damage to the natural environment; the negotiations on a radiological weapons convention within the framework of the Conference on Disarmament have addressed the enhancement of the protection of nuclear facilities as laid down in Additional Protocol I. To some countries, the regulation of the conse-quences of the use of a radiological weapon and of the consequences of an attack on a nuclear facility in one and the same legally binding instrument would seem appropriate. Others would prefer to stick with a more conservative approach and treat these issues separately. Environmental considerations would seem to be in the forefront of the thoughts of those who consider the protection of nuclear facilities in Article 56 of Additional Protocol I insufficient.

The fact that the principle of proportionality is not discussed in the paper, save in the paragraphs with regard to nuclear and oil facilities, should be noted; even there it is only alluded to in passing. No evidence has been found that that principle has been grossly violated during the conflict, although arguably an assessment of the attacks on civilian objects could have been conducted if parties, *e.g.*, were to have alleged that the civilian objects concerned were essential for the war-fighting capabilities of the opponent. Perhaps Professor Kalshoven thought such an approach to be superfluous as he reached his conclusions on the basis of the sole fact that the civilian population was not deprived of its truly civilian character.

B   Repercussions in the outside world

This commentator finds himself in complete agreement with the submission that a system of 'protecting powers' will not be able to function effectively even if Additional Protocol I is ratified on a worldwide basis. Although assistance by the International Committee of the Red Cross (ICRC) to belligerents might seem an attractive option, it appears that their activities are only welcomed by belligerents in a number of specific instances: when belligerents themselves are not in a position to perform effectively a number of the responsibilities under the Geneva Conventions, when they consider ICRC involvement useful for propaganda purposes or when they want to further acceptance of the legitimacy of their cause. Criticism by the ICRC, whether openly or privately, routinely leads to eviction of ICRC delegates or the curtailing of their activities. Acceptance of the ICRC's role in an armed conflict is therefore highly contingent upon, again, the political will of the belligerents.

The dispatch of fact-finding missions to the belligerents might very well prove a dead end: their practical influence on the conduct of belligerents in war is limited. From the outset the ratification process with regard to Additional Protocol I showed a marked resentment of states to accept the competence of the fact-finding Commission on the basis of Article 90 of that Protocol.[4]

In the light of recent developments, only the increasing role played by the United Nations should be considered a promising sign. Whether this improved position will also have noticeable effects with regard to respect for *ius in bello* as opposed to *ius ad bellum* remains to be seen. Unfortunately, actions by outside actors normally have very little effect on the actual conduct of belligerents.

The optimism of Professor Kalshoven with regard to outside pressure on belligerents to stand by their obligations under the law of armed conflict is therefore not shared.

---

4. The 20th declaration (required by the Protocol for activation of the relevant provisions) has only recently been made, 12 years after the opening of the Protocol for ratification or accession. Presently only one fifth of the parties to Additional Protocol I accept the competence of the Commission.

II   THE COMMENTS BY PROFESSOR R. LAGONI

Although discussion of the principle of proportionalty within the context of the prohibited means and methods of warfare would seem to be justified, the views presented by Professor Lagoni[5] on the issue are not shared by this author. For a number of years, a school of thought has been developing which argues that it is not only the principle of proportionality as laid down in the *ius in bello* that should be considered applicable to belligerent behaviour, but also the principles of proportionality and necessity as expressed in Article 51 of the United Nations Charter. This school[6] asserts that belligerents are limited in their freedom of operation throughout the conflict by the requirements of necessity and proportionality as implied by that provision. Belligerents should in that view limit their actions on both the tactical and strategic level to those which are strictly necessary in order to defend themselves: for instance, belligerents would not be at liberty to extend the conflict in a geographical sense.

The opponents of this view maintain that, while the requirements of necessity and proportionality of Article 51 are applicable to the initial attack, as soon as an armed conflict has developed, belligerent behaviour is governed by *ius in bello* rules only.

Discussion of the subject has already clearly shown that the 'Article 51' argument is untenable at the tactical level: it might be necessary to exert a disproportionate degree of force locally in order to gain strategic advantage; one might wish to deny the use of areas to an enemy, *etc.*

If, subsequently, one tries to determine the exact implications of those limitations, other relevant questions immediately come to mind. Single, isolated belligerent acts might force an adversary to disperse his forces: it might therefore be very appropriate to engage in combat in a geographical area which has not until that moment been the theatre of hostilities. Would this be unlawful? The 'Article 51 school' would certainly maintain that such is the case. The, by now, standard example given is that, during the Falklands conflict, a British warship meets an Argentinian freighter carrying war supplies off the coast of Japan: necessity and proportionality would not permit engagement of that ship. The Argentinian freighter would only constitute a legitimate target if and when it sails in South Atlantic waters.

The 'Article 51' school interprets political self-restraint in past conflicts as constituting state practice relevant for the development of customary law. It is the position of this commentator that this approach should be rejected.[7]

---

5. See, *inter alia*, Lagoni, R., "Schiffahrtfreiheit im Golfkrieg", in: *Festschrift für Wolfgang Zeidler*, Fürst W., Herzog, R., Umbach, D.C. (eds), Berlin 1987.

6. Among its supporters one also finds Prof. N. Ronzitti (University of Pisa) in, for instance, "The Law of Naval Warfare", Alphen a/d Rijn 1988 and Professor Chr. Greenwood (Magdalen College, Cambridge) in "Self-Defense and the Conduct of International Armed Conflict", in: Dinstein, Y. (ed.), *International Law at a Time of Perplexity*, Dordrecht 1989.

7. This specific question will be addressed in detail in the on-going Round Tables of Experts on Humanitarian Law applicable at sea to be held at Bergen, Norway in September 1991.

CONCLUSION

In any armed conflict, violations of the law will occur. In the Iran-Iraq war, the blatant disregard of a number of fundamental rules has been a major concern. The indifference of the world at large, however, should be considered even more distressing.

Chapter 4

COMBATANTS AND NON-COMBATANTS

Paul Tavernier[*]

INTRODUCTION

The distinction between combatants and non-combatants is at the heart of the law of armed conflicts, *i.e.*, the law of war (law of The Hague) and humanitarian law (law of Geneva). As noted by Jean Pictet, however, the principle of this distinction has taken a long time to be established:

> 'For centuries, we have considered that the war opposed not only states and their armies, but also people; therefore, the civilians were left to the victors' goodwill, who, if they let them alive, sent them to hard labour, sacked their goods and treated them in contempt of the most basic rights.'[1]

The development of the law has thus consisted in clearly separating those who take part in combat and those who remain extraneous to it. This process has been very slow and has taken several centuries in European countries, but it is not unknown in Islamic countries. As pointed out by Hamed Sultan, former professor of public law at the University of Cairo, 'according to the Islamic humanitarian concept, it is a duty to distinguish between two categories of persons in cases of armed conflict whatever its nature: combatants and non-combatants. Hostilities are permitted only between combatants. This is a basic binding rule of the Islamic system (...) Islamic jurists unanimously recognize the obligation to distinguish between combatants and non-combatants.'[2] Such a convergence is comforting, but, in practice, the distinction between combatants and non-combatants still raises many problems. The discussions which resulted in the adoption of Protocol I of 1977, provided ample proof of such problems. Protocol I took into account new combat methods of guerrillas and national liberation wars, which make it much more difficult to draw a distinction between combatants and non-combatants.[3]

---

* P. Tavernier, Professor at the University of Rouen (France), Head of CREDHO, (Centre de Recherche et d'Etudes sur les Droits de l'Homme et le droit humanitaire).

1. Pictet, J., *Development and principles of international humanitarian law*, Dordrecht-Geneva 1985.

2. Sultan, H., "The Islamic Concept", in: *International Dimensions of Humanitarian Law*, Paris-Dordrecht 1988, p. 37.

3. It is well known that Protocol I, Article 1, has integrated national liberation wars in international armed conflicts.

I.F. Dekker and H.H.G. Post, eds., The Gulf War of 1980-1988

Moreover, the evolution of modern wars, which often take the form of total war, also leads to elimination of the line between those who participate in combat and those who do not. The Gulf War, which opposed Iraq and Iran for nearly eight years, assumes in many respects the characteristics of a total war. Does this mean, as Maurice Torrelli asserts, that this war 'relève de la logique de la guerre qui nie le droit humanitaire et qui accuse l'impuissance de la communauté internationale'?[4] Such a pessimistic conclusion seems exaggerated. Of course, the application of the rules of the law of Geneva, or of the law of the Hague, which establish the distinction between combatants and non-combatants, has encountered difficulties in the Iran-Iraq war; but the belligerents did not object to these rules *per se*. On the contrary, they have invoked them in order to accuse the other party of their violation, without questioning, however, whether they themselves always respected these principles.

It is, therefore, interesting to examine the conduct of the two states during this conflict, which resulted in many victims, both civilian and military,[5] and to compare that conduct with the existing rules of international law. Such an examination will allow us to see that certain deficiencies remain in the international law of armed conflicts, but that more often than not that rule of law nevertheless exists. It is not possible, within the limited scope of this study, to scrutinize all the bearings of the law of armed conflicts which refer to the distinction between combatants and non-combatants: they are too numerous and Professor Kalshoven has touched on some of them in his contribution on prohibited means of warfare. Therefore, we shall limit our study to two matters which are directly in our field, and which have raised many questions during the Gulf War: status and treatment of the prisoners of war and the issue of child-soldiers.

I   PRISONERS OF WAR

The evolution of humanitarian law has enabled more and more people to benefit from the status of prisoner of war so that all combatants are now included. Only non-combatants, who are subject to other protective clauses, spies and mercenaries are excluded from this status (Protocol I, 1977, Articles 46 and 47).[6] The Gulf War has shown that some problems remain in practice.

In that conflict, the fate of prisoners of war aroused world public opinion and the international community.[7] The International Committee of the Red Cross (ICRC)

---

4. Torrelli, M., "La guerre du Golfe et le droit humanitaire", Report to the CEDSI seminar, Grenoble, December 7-8, 1989, on *Les enseignements militaires, politiques, juridiques et économiques de la guerre du Golfe.*

5. The estimates in connection with the Gulf War's victims vary substantially and are sometimes whimsical: from hundreds of thousands of victims to several millions. It would, accordingly, be most useful to have a serious and reliable study on that point.

6. Lapidoth, R., "Qui a droit au statut de prisonnier de guerre?", 82 *RGDIP* (1978), pp. 170 *et seq.*

7. Tavernier, P., "La guerre du Golfe: Quelques aspects de l'application du droit des conflits armés et du droit humanitaire", 30 *AFDI* (1984), pp. 61 *et seq.*

encountered many difficulties in achieving the mission which the IVth Geneva Convention of 1979 entrusted to it. Yet, as soon as the conflict began, the ICRC intervened, as much in Iran as in Iraq. It visited prisoner of war camps and facilitated prisoners' exchanges. This meritorious action encountered many obstacles which led it to resort twice to an unusual device: the call in May 1983, then in February 1984, to the community of states party to the Geneva Conventions of 1949, asking them to do their utmost to enforce humanitarian law in the conflict between Iran and Iraq.[8]

As the Red Cross action was at risk of being crippled, the United Nations has, in a way, taken the baton from the ICRC. The United Nations Secretary-General, despite limited powers, in 1985 and in 1988 has succeeded in carrying out an interesting action, securing the two parties' agreement for sending missions in order to scrutinize the situation of the prisoners of war.[9] The two missions' reports are a most valuable source of information, which complete the materials already available in the ICRC's publications. Nevertheless, the United Nations Security Council has not expressed its opinion on the basis of those reports, though it expressed concern about some aspects of the prisoners of war question, indirectly or more directly. In Resolution 540, adopted on 31 October 1983, the Council 'condemns all violations of international humanitarian law, in particular, the provisions of the Geneva Conventions of 1949 in all their aspects' (§ 2), but it does not specifically mention the prisoner of war problem. On the other hand, in Resolution 582, adopted on 24 February 1986, the Council 'urges that a comprehensive exchange of prisoners of war be completed within a short period after the cessation of hostilities in co-operation with the International Committee of the Red Cross' (§ 4); and in Resolution 598, adopted on 20 July 1987, which the two parties ultimately accepted, and that led one year later to the cease fire, the Council 'urges that prisoners of war be released and repatriated without delay after the cessation of active hostilities in accordance with the IIIrd Geneva Convention of 12 August 1949.'[10] This latest provision furthermore gave rise to different interpretations between Iran, Iraq and the ICRC.[11] Finally, the repatriation of prisoners of war began only in August 1990, after the spectacular reversal of the Iraqi position towards Iran, following the invasion of Kuwait by Baghdad's troops. More than 70,000 prisoners, according to the ICRC's

8. Sandoz, Y., "Appel du CICR dans le cadre du conflit entre l'Irak et l'Iran", 29 *AFDI* (1983), pp. 161 *et seq.*

9. S/16962 on 22 February 1985 and S/20147 on 24 August 1988, reports of the missions sent by the Secretary-General.

10. See Tavernier, P., "La résolution 598 du 20 juillet 1987 et le rôle du Conseil de sécurité dans la guerre entre l'Irak et l'Iran", 1988/2, A/RES, pp. 209 *et seq.* Tavernier, P., "Le caractère obligatoire de la résolution 598 (1987) du Conseil de sécurité relative à la guerre du Golfe", 1 *European Journal of International Law* (1990), pp. 278 *et seq.* See also Decaux, E., "La résolution 598 (1987) du Conseil de sécurité et les efforts de paix des Nations Unies entre l'Iran et l'Irak", 34 *AFDI* (1988), pp. 62 *et seq.*

11. See letters from Iraq: *UN Doc.* S/20478 (22/2/1989); *UN Doc.* S/20597 (18/4/1989); *UN Doc.* S/20754 (27/7/1989); *UN Doc.* S/20814 (28/4/1989); *UN Doc.* S/20892 (10/10/1989); *UN Doc.* S/20913 (23/10/1989); *UN Doc.* S/21092 (18/1/1990); *UN Doc.* S/21097 (22/1/1990). Letters from Iran: *UN Doc.* S/20798 (18/8/1989); *UN Doc.* S/21104 (24/1/1990). On this subject, see Sahovic, M., "La question de la libération des prisonniers de guerre entre l'Irak et L'Iran", 35 *AFDI* (1989), pp. 159 *et seq.*

data, were able to come back to their country.[12] The Red Cross said that its agents had recorded the prisoners' identity and that it had made sure of their willingness to return to their country. It added that, among the repatriated prisoners, were equal numbers of captives who had not been visited by the ICRC during their captivity in Iran or in Iraq, and that its agents had recorded them on this occasion.

Indeed, among the very numerous questions of fact and questions of law raised during the conflict between Iran and Iraq by the issue of the prisoners of war, many are linked to their treatment, which has not always been in accordance with the IIIrd Geneva Convention's provisions. There were also problems about the status of prisoners of war: these matters are the only ones relevant here because they bring up the question of the distinction between combatants and non-combatants. Three kinds of problems have raised particular difficulties: the case of the interned civilians in Iraq; the *bassijis* and *pasdarans*' status, and the case of the non-Iraqi prisoners in Iran. However, one preliminary point must be dealth with: the question of the prisoners' registration.

## A	The duty to register prisoners

As appears from the document of the Red Cross (ICRC) and from the documents of the United Nations, especially the two reports of 1985 and 1988, the two parties have not registered the totality of detainees, contrary to the duties imposed under the 1949 Geneva Conventions, in force for Iran and Iraq.[13] Furthermore, the two governments mutually accused each other of keeping prisoners in secret camps, and invoked considerations based on the ideas of reciprocity and reprisals to justify their conduct. The report of the UN's mission of 1988 fairly points out that these considerations, aimed at delaying the registration, should not interfere in the framework of humanitarian questions.[14] In addition, Article 13 of the IIIrd Geneva Convention prohibits reprisals against prisoners of war.

## B	The case of the interned civilians in Iraq

The law of armed conflicts distinguishes two hypotheses: the case of combatants fallen into the enemy's power, who must be considered as prisoners of war (Article 4, IIIrd Geneva Convention); and the case of civilians who may possibly be interned (Article 79, IVth Convention, referring to the Articles 41-43, 68 and 78). Iran accused Iraq of

---

12. *Bulletin du CICR*, 177, October 1990. According to Iran a quarter of the Iranian prisoners who were repatriated after the cease-fire were civilians whose captivity in Iraq in itself constituted a violation of international law (*UN Doc*. S/20529, 17 March 1989).

13. Iran signed the four Geneva Conventions on 8 December 1949 and ratified them on 20 February 1957 and Iraq acceded to them on 14 February 1956.

14. *UN Doc*. S/20147, §§ 104-105 and 129. The Iranian authorities gave to the 1985 mission a record of 20,000 names of non-registered, or disappeared persons, many of whom would be kept in secret camps; a previous record of 110,000 names had already been given to the Human Rights Commission, for inquiry, two years before (Report, § 77). As for Iraq, it accused Iran of not having registered 15,000 Iraqi prisoners, of whom more than 1,500 were officers but the UN's mission was not able to check these allegations (§§ 194 to 201, 1985 report).

having breached these provisions, and also Article 49 of the IVth Convention which prohibits 'individual or mass forcible transfers, as well as deportations of protected persons from occupied territory to the territory of the occupying power or that of any other country, occupied or not.'[15] According to Tehran at the beginning of the conflict, the Baghdad's government deported almost 75,000 persons into Iraq.[16] The ICRC recognized, in the memorandum appended to the call of 7 May 1983, that 'tens of thousands of Iranian civilians, native of frontier regions of Khuzistan and Kurdistan, living in areas fallen under the Iraqi armed forces' control, have been deported into the Republic of Iraq's territory, in violation of the IVth Convention' and it added: 'the ICRC's agents have approached these populations only partly and incompletely.'

Iraq did not deny these facts, but it stated that it considered these Iranian citizens to be civilian refugees and not deported prisoners or interned people. Iraq accepted that they could benefit from the IVth Geneva Convention's provisions.[17] In 1985 the UN's mission gives data on a camp of 25,000 civilians originating from Arab countries from the Khuzistan region (report §§ 84-92). In 1988, the mission is more accurate (§§ 109-116), Iraq having recognized the existence of three camps regrouping 25,000 people of Irano-Kurd, 30,000 of Irano-arab and 300 of Iranian origin.

Moreover, Iran complained about Iranian civilians interned in prisoner of war camps. The ICRC, in its 1983 memorandum asserted the reality of these allegations about more than a thousand civilians among whom were elderly people and women. Iraq, in its own justification, argued that these people had been captured when they were actively participating in the hostilities, and carrying arms.[18] As for the UN's mission, in 1985, it considered 'it established beyond reasonable doubt that there are in Iraqi POW camps a number of inmates who should not properly be there' (§ 97 of the report).

Iran has also complained about the violation of Protocol I of 1977 with regard to the detention of members of the 'Red Crescent': doctors, assistants and other classes of personnel, those people not having been authorized to come into contact with Red Cross members nor with their own families.[19] It is true that Protocol I, Article 15, provides for protection of medical and religious civilian personnel, but, according to the ICRC's commentary 'no special provision is provided if members of the civilian medical personnel fall into the adversary party's hands (except in the case of the occupation of territories).'[20] For the ICRC, such persons should anyway be protected according to the IVth Convention. However, it must be pointed out that Protocol I is not in force between Iran and Iraq, since Iran only signed it but did not ratify it. However, the report of the mission sent by the Secretary-General in January 1985, is based on the First

---

15. Article 49 was also invoked in the context of Arab territories occupied by Israel, and the Security Council had many opportunities to recall Israel's duties on this point.

16. *UN Doc.* S/17299.

17. *UN Doc.* S/16978, 16996 and 17397.

18. *UN Doc.* S/17435.

19. *UN Doc.* S/16962, §§ 101-108 and Appendix I. See also *UN Doc.* S/16998 (4 March 1985).

20. *Commentaire des Protocoles additonnels du 8 juin 1977 aux Conventions de Genève du 12 août 1949*, CICR, Genève 1986, p. 190.

Convention relating to the wounded and sick, and which in Articles 24 and 26 provides, in any circumstances, for the respect of the personnel of the national Societies of the Red Cross and of other voluntary aid societies. If such people fall into the enemy's hands, they may be retained only in case of necessity due to the prisoners' state of health and number (Article 28), but otherwise they must be repatriated (Articles 30 and 31).

It is true that Iraq responded to the Secretary-General's mission that the doctors and assistants retained should be considered as military personnel, since they belonged to the regular army, or, even if they were civilians, they belonged to the voluntary forces. However, according to the first Convention, Article 28, medical and equivalent personnel who are retained are not considered as prisoners of war, even if they enjoy the advantages provided by the IIIrd Convention (see also Article 33, IIIrd Convention).

The Iranian authorities raised another particular case, that of Mr. Tondguyan, oil minister, and that of his collaborators, all captured by the Iraqi Forces. They could not be approached by the mission sent by the Secretary-General.[21]

The case of the Iranian civilians considered by Iraq as prisoners of war shows how difficult it is to draw a definite line between combatants and non-combatants,[22] in particular because Baghdad claimed that some of those people had participated in fighting alongside Iran's regular forces: that raised the question of the *pasdarans'* and *bassijis'* status.

C   The *pasdarans* and *bassijis*

Though there is no agreement on the status of some people, considered as civilians by Iran, and as combatants by Iraq, the two countries seem to agree to recognize the *pasdarans* (Islamic Revolutionary Guards) and the *bassijis* (members of the Volunteer Mass Army) as combatants and, therefore, to afford them prisoner of war status, when they are in the enemy's hands. Iran blames Iraq, not for having alloted to them that status, but for treating them as it does: Iran affirms that atrocities have been made committed against those two groups, especially mutilations and executions.[23] The Iranian authorities complained to the mission sent by the Secretary-General particularly about the mass execution of prisoners belonging to the Islamic Revolutionary Guards, in compliance with orders from the Iraqi military authorities. Iraq denied the existence of such orders and such massacres, and the Secretary-General's mission was not able to confirm it.[24] What is clear from the position of the two belligerents is that combat-ant status must be granted as much to the *pasdarans* as to the *bassijis*. Iran calls upon

---

21. *UN Doc.* S/16962, §§ 98-100. See also *UN Doc.* S/20762, 31 July 1989 (letter from Iran). Mr. Tondguyan's case has recently be evoked. See Le Monde, 24 October 1990. Though Iran affirms that there is evidence that he is still alive and kept in a secret jail in Iraq, Baghdad authorities say that he died during his detention. The ICRC has, moreover, received his death certificate.

22. According to Iran, Iraq released about 600 prisoners between 1980 and 1985, 400 of whom were civilians: *UN Doc.* S/18895 (4 June 1987) and *UN Doc.* S/20012 (13 July 1988).

23. *A review of the imposed war*, Ministry of Foreign Affairs of Iran, 1983, p. 66.

24. *UN Doc.* S/16962, §§ 72-76.

Article 45 of Protocol I, though it never ratified the Protocol.[25] As for Iraq, it admits that 'as part of the war efforts displayed by Iran, many people had participated in the fighting, beside the regular forces, particularly the Revolutionary Guards and other volunteers.'[26]

Indeed we may recall that humanitarian law leads to extending the combatant definition with regard to prisoner of war status. The 1907 Regulations provide that 'the armed forces of the belligerent parties may consist of combatants and non-combatants' (Article 3) but it adds immediately that 'in the case of capture by the enemy, both have a right to be treated as prisoners of war.'[27] The IIIrd Geneva Convention of 1949 gives an extensive meaning to people enjoying the condition of prisoner of war (Article 4) and it refers particularly to the 'Members of other militias and members of other volunteer corps', beside the 'Members of the armed forces'. As for Protocol I of 1977, it goes on extending the definition of the combatant (Articles 43, 44 and 45). Any member of the armed forces of a Party to a conflict is a combatant (Article 43(2)), forsaking the distinction drawn by the 1907 Regulations. Moreover, 'Any combatant, as defined in Article 43, who falls into the power of an adverse Party shall be a prisoner of war' (Article 44(1)) and Article 45, invoked by Iran, provides for a presumption in favour of the condition of the prisoner of war for anyone who takes part in the hostilities.

However, it does not seem useful to refer to Protocol I which does not bind Iran and Iraq whereas the Geneva Conventions of 1949 are in force *vis à vis* these two countries and they apply without any doubt to the *pasdarans* and *bassijis*. Moreover the conduct of the two belligerent is corroborated by the position adopted by some third states. For example, according to Ronzitti, that was how the United States '... ont traité les marins de l'Iran Ajr, attaqués au moment où ils étaient en train de mouiller des mines, comme des prisonniers de guerre.'[28]

However, it remains true that Iraq seems to adopt a more comprehensive definition of combatant than Iran since it considers as combatants people that Tehran sees, not without reason, as civilians. On the other hand, as will be submitted in the next section, the exclusion of some people from combatant status by the Iranian authorities is questionable.

---

25. *A review of the imposed war*, Ministry of Foreign Affairs of Iran, 1983.

26. *UN Doc.* S/16962, § 94.

27. The 1907 Regulations is appended to the IVth Convention signed at The Hague, respecting the law and customs of war on land. Persia signed it on 18 October 1907, but did not ratify it.

28. Ronzitti, N., "La guerre du Golfe, le déminage et la circulation des navires", 33 *AFDI* (1987), pp. 659 *et seq.* The author fairly points out that 'La distinction entre combattants réguliers et combattants irréguliers a peu de place dans le théâtre maritime où l'accent est posé plutôt sur la nature du navire' (*Idem*). Now, if the United States called the Iran *Ajr* a warship (*UN Doc.* S/19149), Iran affirmed it was a merchant ship (*UN Doc.* S/19153 and *UN Doc.* S/19161).

D   The case of the non-Iraqi prisoners in Iran

The missions sent by the UN Secretary-General in 1985 and 1988, reported the presence of about two hundred non-Iraqi prisoners in the Camp of Davoudieh, in Iran.[29] Most of them originated from Egypt, Lebanon, Somalia, and Sudan, but also from Algeria, Djibouti, the United Arab Emirates, Ethiopia, Jordan, Libya, Morocco, Mauritania, Nigeria, Syria and Tunisia, all in all 17 countries, essentially Arab. These prisoners were captured in 1983 and 1984. Some declared themselves to be civilians (fishermen, or employees of the Iraqi National Oil Society), but most of them declared themselves to be volunteer soldiers of the Iraqi popular army. In 1985 the ICRC did not see any of them and in 1988 the Geneva-based institution was still not able to register most of them.

From a legal perspective, we must distinguish the case of civilians and the case of volunteers who must be treated as combatants. For the mission sent by the Secretary-General in 1985, 'there is no doubt (...) that civilians of non-belligerent nationality should be returned to their country of origin.'[30] It is true that the IVth Geneva Convention of 1949 contains provisions about aliens in the territory of a party to the conflict. These provisions provide that protected persons have the right to leave the territory (Articles 35-36), but they do not prohibit their internment (Article 41). The nationals of non-belligerent countries are not protected by the IVth Convention as long as the state of which they are nationals has normal diplomatic representation in the state in whose hands they are (Article 4).

As for volunteers, they should be considered as combatants. For that reason they should enjoy prisoner of war status. However, Iran denies them this status, arguing that they are mercenaries and calling particularly upon Article 47 of Protocol I. Apart from the fact that Tehran has not ratified the Protocol, it is questionable whether the definition of mercenary given in Article 47(2), applies to them. Some conditions required under a), b) and f) seem to have been met. However, the conditions required under c), d) and e) do not seem to be met to the extent that, according to the report of the UN's mission in 1985, 'these soldiers do not seem to have acted from a desire for private gain, nor, they assured us, had they, in any case, been promised material compensation substantially in excess of that promised or paid to other Iraqi combatants; or they were residents of Iraq or territories formerly controlled by it; or they were in any case members of the Iraqi army.'[31]

The mercenary definition in Protocol I, Article 47, was restated in 1989, in the International Convention against the recruitment, use, financing and training of mercenaries[32] of which Article 1(1), repeats the six conditions provided in 1977,

---

29. *UN Doc.* S/16962, §§ 263-267 and S/20147, § 65.

30. *UN Doc.* S/16962, § 266.

31. *UN Doc.* S/16962, § 267. On the questions raised by the mercenary definition, see Tercinet, J., "Les mercenaires et le droit international", 23 *AFDI* (1977), pp. 269 *et seq.* David, E., *Mercenaires et volontaires internationaux en droit des gens*, Bruxelles 1978, p. 459.

32. A/RES/44/34 on 4 December 1989, adopted without vote.

except the one on direct participation in hostilities.[33] Anyway, Article 16 of the new Convention specifies that it 'shall be applied without prejudice to (...) b) the law of armed conflict and international humanitarian law, including the provisions relating to the status of combatant or of prisoner of war.'

Whatever legal qualification may be given to the non-Iraqi prisoners in Iran, it remains true that, in practice, the Tehran authorities treated them as prisoners of war and that some of them have been released.[34]

From all the cases here examined (civilians kept in Iran, *pasdarans* and *bassijis*, non-Iraqi prisoners in Iran) and from other cases pointed out in the reports of the two missions sent by the Secretary-General in 1985 and 1988, for example such as personnel captured by irregular forces and kept on the territory of the other party (for instance the Iranians who would be kept by the Liberation Army of Khalq Moudjahidin-,[35] it is clear that the distinction between combatants and non-combatants, theoretically simple, is not easy to apply in practice. Certainly, there is no basic problem with the legal rules, but there is often a problem in legally interpreting the facts: what is already a question of law and what is merely a matter of fact. In those conditions the legal standard works quite badly. The difficulties are even worse when the legal rule is vague, or incomplete, as is the case of child-soldiers.

II   THE QUESTION OF THE RECRUITMENT OF CHILD-SOLDIERS

For many years the destiny of children in armed conflicts has rightly aroused the concern of the international community. Public opinion has been alerted, the ICRC has conducted a vigourous campaign, assisted by several non-governmental organizations (NGO's) and lawyers have looked into the question.[36] Although, generally, the child enjoys special protection as a civilian, non-combatant, it was unfortunately often been the case, particularly and increasingly, since World War II, that children were used as

---

33. According to the commentary of the additional Protocols of 8 June 1977, published by the ICRC (Geneva 1986, p. 589), that condition excluded from the mercenary definition, alien military advisers and experts, as far as they do not actively take part in the hostilities.

34. *UN Doc.* S/20147, § 65; S/2078 (15/1/1990).

35. *UN Doc.* S/20147, § 139. We should also point out the case of children prisoners who reached their majority when still in detention (*UN Doc.* S/20832, 6 September 1989, letter from Iraq) and the case of Iranian prisoners captured after the cease-fire, to the number of 700 who should not be regarded as prisoners of war, according to Iran: *UN Doc.* S/20179, 20187, 20531, 20631, 20764, 20798, 20809, 21104. See also *UN Doc.* S/20814, letter from Iraq (28 August 1989). Moreover, Iran as from 1985 proposed an exchange of prisoners, making a distinction between categories of prisoners: *UN Doc.* S/16992 (1 March 1985), *UN Doc.* S/19044 (14 August 1987) and *UN Doc.* S/20012 (13 July 1988).

36. Plattner, D., "Protection of children in international humanitarian law", 240 *International Review of the Red Cross*, May-June 1984, pp. 140 *et seq.* Singer, S., "The protection of children during armed conflict situations", *IRRC*, May-June 1986, pp. 133 *et seq.* Dutli, M.T., "Captured Child Combatants", 278 *IRRC*, September-October 1990, pp. 421 *et seq.* Elahi, M., "The rights of the child under the Islamic law: prohibition of the child soldier", 19 *Columbia Human Rights Law Review* (1988-2), pp. 259 *et seq.*

combatants.[37] In that case, they will at least enjoy prisoner of war status if they are captured. Thus the distinction between combatants and non-combatants is particularly critical where children are concerned.

The question of children taking part in the Gulf War battles is certainly one of the most painful which was raised during this conflict. As early as 1983, the ICRC ascertained that many Iranian children had been killed when they were participating in the fighting.[38] Iraq took these findings for itself and it said that Iran 'sends children to the battle front and uses them to blow the mines.'[39] The presence of children as prisoners of war in Iraqi camps has moreover been ascertained by the missions sent by the UN's Secretary-General.[40] On this occasion, Iraq pointed out that it had created special schools for the child prisoners of war, which goes beyond its duties under the IIIrd Geneva Convention.[41] The UN's Commission on Human Rights adopted a resolution, on 12 March 1984, by which it asked Iran to 'cease immediately the use of children in the armed forces of the Islamic Republic of Iran, especially in time of war.'[42] It 'further invites the appropriate international organizations to offer all possible aid for the welfare of the children at present prisoners of war in Iraq, especially as regards their education and their physical and mental health, or, alternatively, to assist those children who so desire to settle in another Islamic country until such time as their return to the Islamic Republic of Iran becomes feasible.'

Although the problem of the child-soldiers essentially concerns the recruitment of children by the Islamic Republic, we must point out that in this respect Iraq's conduct is not beyond reproach, either. Iran published a record of 199 Iraqi teenager prisoners of war, aged from thirteen to fifteen, or older, at the time of their capture, that is to say between 1982 and 1984.[43]

The two belligerents do not disagree on the status to be afforded to the child who participates in hostilities, and they accord prisoner of war status when captured. Nevertheless, the right to recruit children and to enlist them raises problems. Does the distinction between combatants and non-combatants still has a meaning when it applies to children? Do not all children belong to the non-combatants category? From a moral perspective the answer raises no doubts. According to the ICRC, the facts mentioned and recorded in 1983, if they were proved, would go against 'an universal moral rule of paramount importance.'[44] However, in a legal perspective, the answer is more doubtful, since the law of armed conflict and humanitarian law are 'realistic' laws, which means that they broadly take the facts and reality into consideration.

---

37. According to Howard Mann, "International law and the child-soldier", 36 *ICLQ* (1987), p. 33, half a million children aged under fifteen have been killed in action during the last two decades.

38. ICRC, *Activity Report*, 1983, p. 59.

39. *UN Doc.* S/16438, 27 March 1984, Iraq's letter.

40. *UN Doc.* S/16962, §§ 129 and 130; S/20147, § 97.

41. *UN Doc.* S/16996, 4 March 1985, Iraq's letter.

42. Resolution 1984/39.

43. A/40/872-S/17622 on 11 November 1985. This document gives the rank of the teenagers in question, their names, their places of birth, the date and the place of their capture. It points out the case of some mercenaries who were children, originating from Lebanon or Egypt (nos. 21 and 76).

44. ICRC, *Activity Report*, 1983, p. 59.

This reality proves that child-soldiers exist, not only in the Gulf War, but also in many conflicts, particularly in Africa. Therefore, it is useful to scrutinize the state of the positive law and the new rules recently passed on the recruitment of child-soldiers.[45] This study unfortunately leads us to acknowledge that Protocol I, whose applicability to the conflict between Iran and Iraq is dubious to say the least, reveals gross lacunae. As for the Convention on the Rights of the Child, adopted in 1989, it remains very ambiguous on such questions.

A   The lacunae of Protocol I of 1977

Two questions must be considered concerning the Protocol I of 1977: on the one hand, is the text enforceable in respect of Iran and Iraq? On the other hand, to what extent does it prohibit the Tehran authorities (or the Baghdad authorities) to recruit child-soldiers?

1   *The legal status of Protocol I towards the two belligerents*

Apparently the answer to the first question is simple. Only Protocol I is at issue since it refers to international conflicts, which certainly includes the Gulf War. On the other hand, Protocol II, which also contains provisions related to children in armed conflicts, might not be called upon since it is applicable to non-international conflicts. However, although Protocol I came into force on 7 December 1978, it does not bind Iran and Iraq. Iraq did not sign or ratify it, and Iran only signed it (on 12 December 1977).

However, we may argue that Protocol I only repeats and sanctions, in a contractual text, rules which are already agreed between states and, therefore, would bind them without them having to follow the formal procedures for enforcement of treaties. However, as we shall see, if there is a consensus, it is based on a compromise and does not absolutely prohibit the recruitment and use of child-soldiers.

Such an argument is as valid for Iran as for Iraq, which is not the case for another argument put forward by Eric David, an argument which only concerns Iran. This author points out that Article 18 of the Vienna Convention on the law of treaties provides for a duty of good faith from the state which has signed a treaty: 'A state is obliged to refrain from acts which would defeat the object and purpose of a treaty when: a) it has signed the treaty (...) until it shall have made its intention clear not to become a party to the treaty; ...' Of course, Iraq cannot really call upon this provision since it has not itself signed Protocol I of 1977. The duty of good faith, which should eventually bind Iran, may find additional support in the conduct adopted by that country.

Indeed, the government of Teheran has often called upon the provisions of Protocol I for its own benefit, as is shown by many documents which it has sent to the United

---

45. On that point, see David, E., "La guerre du Golfe et le droit international", *Rev. belge* (1987), pp. 166 *et seq.*; Mann, *loc.cit.* (note 37), pp. 32 *et seq.*; Tavenier, *loc.cit.* (note 7), pp. 57 *et seq.*

Nations.[46] Therefore, we may ask whether Iran does not consider that Protocol I may be invoked against itself, since it seems to admit that the provisions of the Protocol are applicable in its relations with Iraq. Anyway, and whatever may be the answers given to these questions, it seems that Protocol I does not prescribe over-burdensome duties on states concerning the use of children during conflict.

2   *The content of Protocol I*

The ICRC has been concerned about the protection of children as victims of armed conflicts for many years. As early as 1918, it contemplated the creation of an organization to deal specifically with this question. It resulted in the creation of the 'Union Internationale de secours à l'enfance' and in the drawing up, in 1939, of a draft Convention for the protection of children in case of war; the draft was not adopted due to the beginning of hostilities. The IVth Geneva Convention of 1949 has protective provisions for the benefit of children. However, Article 16 which provides the principles of protection for particularly vulnerable people (wounded, sick, infirm, expectant mothers), fails to mention children. This 'strange lacuna of the IVth Convention', according to Mann,[47] has only been filled in 1977 with Article 77 of Protocol I. This provision has the additional advantage of ruling on the question of the recruitment of children and of their participation in the hostilities. That question had been obscured until then, though it had been raised during World War II because of the use of children in the army of the Third Reich, and also by the partisans and the resistance against Nazism. As Mann said, these cases were then considered as aberrations that ought not to detract from the established principles.

In this light, Article 77(2) Protocol I of 1977, is undoubtedly a step forward since it addresses for the first time the question of child-soldiers, taking into account the reality of the child combatant and not only the reality of the child, civilian victim of the conflict. According to this provision 'The Parties to the conflict shall take all feasible measures in order that children who have not attained the age of fifteen years do not take a direct part in hostilities and, in particular, they shall refrain from recruiting them into their armed forces. In recruiting among those persons who have attained the age of fifteen years but who have not attained the age of eighteen years, the Parties to the conflict shall endeavour to give priority to those who are oldest.' However, the impact of those provisions remains very limited: it is even more restricted than most commentators, including the ICRC in its commentary of Protocols, published in 1986, may point out. It is enough for us to refer to the *travaux préparatoires* and to the text itself.

The history of the elaboration of Article 77(2) has already been set out elsewhere in detail.[48] Here, it will only partly be recalled. First, it must be pointed out that the

---

46. See also the book published by the Ministry of Foreign Affairs of Iran, February 1983: *A review of the imposed war*.

47. Mann, *loc.cit.* (note 37), p. 34.

48. See Mann, *loc.cit.* (note 37), pp. 32 *et seq*. See also our study: Tavernier, *loc.cit.* (note 7).

text of Article 77 stems from a proposition of the ICRC, which was far more vigorous: 'The parties to the conflict shall take all necessary measures in order that children aged under fifteen years shall not take any part in hostilities and in particular they shall refrain from recruiting them in their armed forces or accepting their voluntary enrolment.' This text would have wholly prohibited both the recruiting and the voluntary enrolment of children aged under fifteen. Compared with the text finally adopted it has been watered-down on basic points. Article 77 addresses the recruitment, but no longer the voluntary enrolment, which is not prohibited; on the other hand, it refers to the direct participation in hostilities, which, *a contrario*, allows indirect participation; finally and above all, 'all feasible measures' took the place of 'all necessary measures'. This expression is also found in other provisions of Protocol I (Articles 57 and 58). According to the ICRC's commentary it aims at conciliating between the prescriptions of humanitarian law and military necessities. Moreover it is the sign of a compromise between opposite theses. As shown by the debates in the diplomatic conference, and particularly in Commission III[49] there was no real consensus, rather real dissent, between states on the question of the use of children as combatants. The shadow of national liberation wars and of resistance always hung over the discussions. We can better measure how far the original draft of the ICRC stands from the text of Protocol I when it is compared with the similar provision of Protocol II related to non-international armed conflicts. This second Protocol underwent many vicissitudes before it was adopted. With regard to child-soldiers, the result is quite surprising since the text ultimately adopted in Article 4(3)(c) is particularly rigorous: 'children who have not attained the age of fifteen years shall neither be recruited in the armed forces or groups nor allowed to take part in hostilities.' The prohibition of recruitment and participating in hostilities even voluntarily, is absolute, but no reason was given to explain the changes in the drafting which occurred at the last moment.[50]

In these conditions, it is difficult to say, as some commentators do, and, as the Report of Commission III seems to put it, that Article 77 of Protocol I contains an absolute prohibition of recruiting children who have not attained the age of fifteen.[51] In fact, the text of that provision does not impose much restraint. Mann criticizes one author's opinion, according to which Article 77 'only tends to prohibit the recruitment of children under fifteen into the armed forces in so far as possible.'[52] He thinks that 'this interpretation appears to be based on a misconstruction of the article brought about by incorporating the modifying phrase "all feasible measures" into the second half of the sentence. Such a construction is grammatically unnecessary and incorrect.' In our judgment, Mann's opinion may be justified towards the English drafting of the Protocol, but not towards the French one. Indeed the structure of the sentence is not the same in the two drafts: while the sentence of the English text contains two propositions coordinated by the conjunction 'and', the structure of the French text consists of one

49. Tavernier, *loc.cit.* (note 7).
50. Mann, *loc.cit.* (note 37), p. 43.
51. Mann, *loc.cit.* (note 37).
52. Pastré-Burros, S., "The protection of children in armed conflicts", 46 *Int. Child Welf. Rev.* (1980), pp. 33 *et seq.*

principal proposition and one subordinate proposition, marked by the mode of the verb (participle): 'notamment en s'abstenant ...' Therefore, the restriction included in the expression 'all feasible measures' fully extends to the whole sentence. As Article 102 of Protocol I provides that both the English and French texts are authentic, besides the Arab, Chinese, Spanish and Russian texts, they must be interpreted in order to avoid divergences between them. The doubts raised by the reading of the English text may disappear if we refer to the French text which fairly shows the hesitations of the authors and the inconsistencies they could not overcome.

If we need further argument, it is found in the debates which took place during the elaboration of the Convention on the Rights of the Child. Therefore we may conclude in respect of positive law – and whatever may be our moral judgment – that no legal rule absolutely prohibits states from recruiting child-soldiers aged under fifteen and, *a fortiori*, from enrolling volunteers. Article 77, Protocol I, imposed on contracting states only an obligation of means and not an obligation of result. The conduct of Iran may not, in these conditions, be considered as contrary to international law.

Of course, the lawyer may regret the lacunae of law, but he has the duty not to close his eyes and not to ignore the limits and the defects of the rule. He even has the duty to point them out in order eventually to bring about their correction. Unfortunately the study of the new rules adopted in the Convention of the Rights of the Child does not lead to optimism in that regard.

B   The ambiguities of the Convention on the Rights of the Child

On 20 November 1989, the General Assembly adopted without vote the Convention on the Rights of the Child, which had been under consideration since 1978. Article 38 of the Convention (former Article 20 of the tentative draft) was one of the most debated provisions: it concerns the situation during armed conflicts. That provision, which did not appear in the first draft submitted by Poland, had been introduced in 1985 on the proposal of Finland, the Netherlands and Sweden, supported by Belgium, Peru and Senegal. It repeated a proposal included in the draft of the non-governmental organizations in 1984.[53] Iran also made a proposal related to the protection of child victims of armed conflicts (in particular, victims of the bombardment of cities and the use of chemical weapons), but it did not mention the problem of child-soldiers. In 1986, Iran submitted a new provision, thereafter withdrawn, which expressly dealt with the recruitment and the participation of children in hostilities.

A draft of Article 20 was finally adopted in 1986. Paragraph 2 of Article 20 held: 'States parties to the present Convention shall take all feasible measures to ensure that no child takes a direct part in hostilities and they shall refrain in particular from recruiting any child who has not attained the age of fifteen years into their armed

---

53. For a good presentation of the history of the debates on Article 20, now Article 38, see Krill, F., "La convention des Nations Unies relative aux droits de l'enfant et sa protection dans les conflits armés", 4 *Memesker og Rettigheter* (1986). See also Turpin, D., "L'enfant dans tous ses droits", *Les Petites Affiches*, 10 January 1990, pp. 17 *et seq.*

forces.' This drafting, originating partly from Protocol I of 1977, was very much criticized by the ICRC and by the NGO's because of the great uncertainties it raised. The first part of the sentence does not protect children any better than the two 1977 Protocols: it repeats the expression 'all feasible measures'; it only mentions direct participation in hostilities; it does not exclude the participation of volunteers. As for the second part of the sentence, related to the enrolment and recruitment of children, it is less complete than Article 77 of Protocol I which specifically considers the case of children aged between fifteen and eighteen.[54]

There are some changes in the final text of Article 38 compared with the former Article 20. In addition to reiterating duties resulting from humanitarian international law, (in § 1) Article 38 contains two distinct paragraphs related to child-soldiers:

'2. States parties shall take all feasible measures to ensure that persons who have not attained the age of fifteen years do not take a direct part in hostilities.

3. States parties shall refrain from recruiting any person who has not attained the age of fifteen years into their armed forces. In recruiting among those persons who have attained the age of fifteen years but who have not attained the age of eighteen years, states parties shall endeavour to give priority to those who are oldest.'

These provisions are very close to the rules contained in Article 77 of Protocol I and they do not fill the lacunae mentioned above, in particular because of the use of the expression 'all feasible measures' and of the reference to taking direct part in hostilities, which does not prohibit indirect participation (investigations and transmission of military information, carriage of arms and munitions, provisioning, *etc.*). On the other hand, in clearly separating the question of enrolment and the question of participation in hostilities, the 1989 Convention improves the provisions of the 1977 Protocol. However, although the drafting is more vigorous, it does not exclude the participation of volunteers. Moreover, the 1989 Convention does not distinguish between international conflicts and non-international conflicts, which may raise some difficulties in so far as the two 1977 Protocols contain different rules. This is to say that the lacunae of positive law, or *lex lata*, represented by the 1977 Protocols, have not been filled by the emerging law, or *lex ferenda*, contained in the 1989 Convention.[55] Finally, the legal rule remains rather soft. It does not set formal prohibitions, but standards to follow or conduct to observe, because it must take into account the *de facto* situation (some children are actually used as soldiers in armed conflicts) but also military necessities, that is to say, the needs of the defence of the state, of the mother country, of the people (liberation wars), even of religion ...

54. Moreover, paragraph 3 of Article 20 does not mention the rule according to which it is prohibited to attack civilians, *a fortiori* children, which is an application of the distinction between the civilian population and combatants. On that point, the ICRC did not get satisfaction, as paragraph 4 of the Article 38 of the Convention reprints simply the text of 1986.

55. The Convention on the Rights of the Child has been in force since 2 September 1990 and must now be regarded as positive law.

CONCLUSION

The experience of the Gulf War, once more, incites the lawyer to modesty over what is the basic distinction between for humanitarian law and the law of armed conflicts, *i.e.,* the distinction between combatants and non-combatants. That distinction squares with moral needs which are difficult to set aside; but law must also take into account other considerations and it is often defective. Therefore, it is the lawyer's duty to denounce the lacunae of the rule or the failure of its operation, even if the evolution of the techniques of modern war makes it more and more difficult to separate civilians from people who take an active part in the fighting, that is to say, combatants from non-combatants. From that perspective, the problems of prisoners of war or of child-soldiers which we have examined, cannot be separated from the problems raised by the bombardment of urban areas or by resort to chemical weapons. They all are linked to a principle which should be ranged among the mandatory principles, or even those of *ius cogens*.

COMMENTS

Louise Doswald-Beck and Maria Teresa Dutli[*]

We would like to comment in particular on the section of Mr Tavernier's paper dealing with *The question of the recruitment of child-soldiers.*

Although the participation of children in hostilities is not absolutely prohibited, the 1977 Additional Protocols have made significant progress by banning the recruitment of persons below the age of fifteen (Protocol I, Article 77, paragraph 2 and Protocol II, Article 4, paragraph 3). These treaties are not binding on states which have not yet ratified them, but today there are already 103 states party to Protocol I and 93 to Protocol II. Moreover, the provisions of the Protocols relating to children have never been disputed, and some states even regard them as being part of customary law. Indications that the age-limit of fifteen years belongs to customary law can be seen in the position of the representative of the United States State Department, during a discussion organized by the American Society of International Law, who saw 'Article 77, paragraph 1 as already part of customary international law and Article 77, paragraphs 2, 3 and 4 as supportable for inclusion in customary law through state practice.'[1]

We cannot agree with the author's view that there exists a lacuna in the Fourth Geneva Convention regarding the protection of children because they are not specifically mentioned in Article 16, entitled 'Wounded and sick. General Protection'. The fact that they are in a special category is in our view self-evident in that there are no less than seventeen provisions of the Fourth Geneva Convention which provide special protection for children in view of their particular vulnerability.

As mentioned above, Article 77, paragraph 2, of 1977 Additional Protocol I sets the minimum age of fifteen for children participating in hostilities. This provision contains an extremely important obligation, requiring states parties not to recruit children under fifteen years of age into armed forces. The English text – 'they shall refrain from recruiting them into their armed forces ...' is more explicit than the French which says

---

* L. Doswald-Beck and M.T. Dutli, Legal Division of the International Committee of the Red Cross. These comments are the sole reponsibility of the authors, and do not necessarily reflect the opinion of the International Committee of the Red Cross.

1. Matheson, M.J., "The United States position on the relation of customary international law of the 1977 Protocols additional to the 1949 Geneva Conventions", *The American University Journal of International Law and Policy*, pp. 419 *et seq.*; also Krill, F., "The protection of Children in Armed Conflicts", in: *The Relationship between International Humanitarian Law and the UN Convention on the Rights of the Child* [First International Interdisciplinary Study-group on Ideologies of Children's Rights], to be published by M. Nijhoff, Dordrecht; and Elahi, M., "The Rights of the Child under Islamic Law: Prohibition of the Child Soldier", *Columbia Human Rights Law Review* (1988).

I.F. Dekker and H.H.G. Post, eds., The Gulf War of 1980-1988
© 1992, T.M.C. Asser Instituut, The Hague

'... notamment en s'abstenant ...' ('... in particular by refraining ...'). Moreover, in English, the word *recruitment* covers all kinds of enrolment into the army, whereas *recrutement* in French corresponds only to *conscription* in English. Nevertheless, states parties must refrain from compulsory or voluntary enrolment of children under fifteen years of age into their armed forces. Misinterpretations can arise from the fact that the Additional Protocols are published in several authentic languages, but as the deliberations took place in English, the English version should be used for purposes of interpretation.

As Mr Tavernier points out, the wording 'the parties to the conflict shall take all feasible measures' is less mandatory than that proposed by the ICRC, which had suggested that the parties should 'take all necessary measures'. The wording 'all feasible measures' which refers only to the first part of the sentence concerned, was inserted by the governments which negotiated this Article to avoid entering into an absolute obligation with regard to voluntary participation because states cannot prevent the unofficial participation of children in hostilities in all cases.[2]

The equivalent to the above-mentioned Article 77 of Additional Protocol I is Article 4, paragraph 3(c), of Additional Protocol II, which is certainly more rigorous as it contains an absolute prohibition on the participation – whether direct of indirect – of children in hostilities. This difference is certainly due to simplification and lack of attention rather than to a real intention to make a distinction.

We do not feel that in separating the question of enrolment from the question of participation in hostilities, the 1989 Convention on the Rights of the Child improves on the existing provisions of international humanitarian law. Article 38 of the Convention is certainly weaker than the provisions already contained in Article 4, paragraph 3(c), of Additional Protocol II. The ICRC closely followed the negotiation of the 1989 Convention on the Rights of the Child and it would have been interesting in this context to refer also to the ICRC's statements during the working group meetings in which it expounded its position on the subject.

2. See also Dutli, M.T., "Captured Child Combatants", *International Review of the Red Cross* (September-October 1990).

COMMENTS

George H. Aldrich*

The distinction between combatants and non-combatants is an important principle of international humanitarian law – one that is obviously related to the protections accorded by the law to non-combatants. The purpose of the distinction is the protection of non-combatants, most of whom will be civilians. If a soldier cannot tell the difference between an enemy combatant and civilian non-combatant, he is likely to shoot first and ask questions later. Similarly, if civilians are commonly made the object of attack, it becomes more difficult to keep them from taking a direct part in hostilities. These are, I believe, the psychological realities on which the principle of distinction is based.

It is difficult to discuss this issue without addressing Geneva Protocol I of 1977, because it deals directly with the questions of who is a combatant and what protections from the effects of hostilities are to be accorded civilians in unoccupied territory – questions barely addressed by the 1949 Geneva Conventions. This is so despite the fact that the Protocol was clearly not applicable *per se* in the Gulf War. The fact that at least one of the two parties to that war – Iran – has invoked Protocol I, despite its not yet having ratified it, underlines this point and may suggest that the Protocol does, to a considerable extent, represent a codification of customary international law. I believe that it does.

With respect to the registration, treatment, and repatriation of prisoners of war, as Professor Tavernier has shown, the record of the Gulf War is a record of general noncompliance with the law. To the best of my knowledge, neither state tried to justify its mistreatment of prisoners on the ground of reprisal (which would have been difficult in any event in view of Article 13 of the Third Geneva Convention), but rather acted as if the legal regime established by that Convention was either irrelevant or subordinate to dictates of reciprocity. Moreover, strictly humanitarian proposals by the ICRC, for example, proposals for the repatriation during the conflict of seriously sick and wounded prisoners were largely either ignored or rejected. In their treatment of prisoners of war, the two states committed war crimes on a vast scale. The vexing question here is why. While Professor Tavernier has shed light on this question, I suggest that definitive answers require information that neither party has yet revealed. One can only hope that, in time, sufficient information will become available to permit a fuller analysis of the reasons why prisoners of war fared so poorly during the Gulf War.

* G.H. Aldrich, Professor of Humanitarian Law, University of Leyden (The Netherlands), Judge in the Iran-United States Claims Tribunal.

I.F. Dekker and H.H.G. Post, eds., The Gulf War of 1980-1988
© 1992, T.M.C. Asser Instituut, The Hague

With respect to children soldiers, the Gulf War also represents a sad example. It is difficult to believe that either belligerent suffered such severe shortages of manpower as to necessitate the use in combat of children under fifteen years of age, but available reports suggest, as Professor Tavernier points out, that both sides did so and that on the Iranian side, in particular, a great many children were sent into combat.

With respect to the law applicable to the use of children in combat, I would like to make a few comments about the relevant provisions of Geneva Protocols I and II. As the rapporteur of the Conference Committee that produced these provisions, I am familiar with their negotiating history, and I differ to some extent with Professor Tavernier's views.

First, while the text of Article 77(2) of Protocol I was indeed the result of a compromise among divergent views, I could not agree with Professor Tavernier's view that it is ambiguous. It states unequivocally that parties 'shall refrain' from recruiting children under the age of fifteen into their armed forces. The Committee Report to the Conference Plenary in 1977 described this as a 'flat ban', and that is what it is. No person under fifteen years of age may be recruited, that is, permitted to join the armed forces.

In this connection, the fact that the phrase from the original ICRC draft relating to 'voluntary enrolment' in armed forces was not used in the final text should not be understood to mean that children may lawfully become members of the armed forces, as that would violate the flat ban on their recruitment. If a party may not 'recruit' someone in its armed forces, then it may not 'enroll' him in those armed forces. I should note that, in this respect, I believe the ICRC *Commentary* (paras. 3184 and 3185) is mistaken in its interpretation of the reference in the Conference Committee Report to the difficulty of prohibiting the 'voluntary participation' of children in direct hostilities. That reference recognized that parties may not be able, in all circumstances, to prevent such participation, which is why they are obligated only to take 'all feasible measures' to prevent it, but is was not intended to authorize the enrollment of children in the armed forces, which it is always feasible for parties to prohibit.

The Conference used the phrase 'all feasible measures' because it did not think it reasonable to hold a state responsible for a violation of the Protocol if it took all feasible (that is, all practicably possible) measures but they failed to prevent some eager children from taking a direct part in hostilities.

Further, the Conference did not find it generally acceptable to prohibit children from taking an 'indirect part' in hostilities – a term that would be very difficult to define. For example, during the Second World War, when I, as a child of twelve, collected scrap metal for reprocessing into weapons, was I participating indirectly in hostilities? What about spotting and reporting enemy aircraft or carrying messages?

Insofar as the French text of Article 77 is concerned, I am scarcely in a position to argue with Professor Tavernier about its plain meaning, although I would have thought it possible to understand a complete ban on recruitment as an example of an obligatory 'feasible measure'. To the extent one looks to the negotiating history as an aid to interpretation, I would point out that all of the redrafting was done in English by the Rapporteur.

With respect to the differences in the comparable texts of Protocols I and II, I would note that the texts were identical through the Main Committee and Drafting Committee stages of the Conference. The different text that became Article 4(3)(c) of Protocol II was presented at the last moment by Judge Hussain of Pakistan as part of a drastically reduced Protocol II and without any explanation of the change in this provision. It will be recalled that Judge Hussain made his initiative in the Plenary in order to save Protocol II from likely rejection by the many developing nations that believed the draft Protocol went much too far, particularly in according international status to rebellious or separatist groups. His proposed amendments were accepted by the Conference in its final Plenary sessions out of recognition that a broadly acceptable Protocol of limited scope was preferable to no Protocol at all or one accepted by only a few countries. I don't know if anyone noticed the change in the text on children combatants; certainly no one commented on it. In all probability, the revision was designed by Judge Hussain simply to avoid any reference to 'Parties to the conflict', a phrase he excised from all articles of Protocol II in order to eliminate any suggestion that a rebellious party was being recognized as having rights under the Treaty.

In conclusion, I would urge all who address the question of interpretation of Article 77 of Protocol I to eschew narrow interpretations of a text that goes very far to protect children from direct involvement in combat. Such interpretations may, quite unnecessarily, tempt states to use children in ways contrary to the intent of that Article.

Part III

Armed Conflict at Sea
and Neutrality

Chapter 5

TARGETING THEORY IN THE LAW OF ARMED CONFLICT AT SEA: THE MERCHANT VESSEL AS MILITARY OBJECTIVE IN THE TANKER WAR

Francis V. Russo, Jr.[*]

I INTRODUCTION

A Asymmetry of law and practice[1]

Commentators, diplomats, and jurists can today no more escape the legal impact of changing naval capabilities than were past military strategists able to ignore the impact of maneuver warfare, the repeating rifle, and the ironclad in their time. Such impact – whether legal or military – is inevitable: as disregard of technological and tactical developments became for the commander a prescription for failure in battle, so too has it been for the jurist. The failure of the traditional law of naval warfare to keep pace with contemporary modalities of force projection has been aptly described as the 'asymmetry' between the law and the practice of naval armed conflict. The tanker war was yet another example of that asymmetry.

Adaptability and flexibility are essential characteristics of an effective contemporary law of naval armed conflict. Laws of war that cannot accommodate or be adapted to the rapidly changing technological and tactical dimensions of modern armed conflict will be among the first battlefield casualties. Commanders and policymakers will, beyond certain threshold or 'baseline standards',[2] inevitably demand the necessary legal flexibility to meet these shifting dimensions. Traditional rules intended to regulate armed conflict at sea, therefore, must be interpreted and applied in light of modern

* F.V. Russo, Jr., Lieutenant Commander, Judge Advocate General's Corps, U.S. Navy; Academic Director, Naval Justice School, Newport, Rhode Island, USA. The opinions expressed in this paper are solely those of the author and do not purport to promulgate or express the views of the Naval Justice School, U.S. Naval War College, Judge Advocate General of the Navy, the Department of the Navy, or any other Agency or Department of the United States. A working draft of this paper was first presented at The Hague on 23 November 1990, before the colloquium on the Gulf War in International Legal Perspective. The commentary of Drs. Fleck and Gill provided at that time, see their written comments following this article, as well as the many spirited inquiries by colloquium participants, are gratefully acknowledged.

1. Grunawalt, R.J., "Visit and Search", Proceedings of the 82nd Annual meeting of the American Society of International Law, 21 April 1988, (publication forthcoming). A copy of the original comments is on file with the author.

2. *Idem*. This notion was developed during seminars conducted by Professor Grunawalt, in the fall of 1987, at the U.S. Naval War College. The author was a participant in those seminars, which generally examined the law of naval operations.

I.F. Dekker and H.H.G. Post, eds., The Gulf War of 1980-1988
© 1992, T.M.C. Asser Instituut, The Hague

naval capabilities and practices – the 'targeting reality' of contemporary naval conflict.[3] To do otherwise will condemn the law to obsolescence and eviscerate its humanitarian role, erecting a legal Maginot Line.

Professors McDougal and Feliciano warn about the dangers of an inflexible application of traditional laws of war to emerging developments in naval technology:

> 'To appraise the lawfulness of the newer modalities designed to meet new conditions of warfare, in terms of the requirements projected in traditional law for an older modality developed under very different conditions, is to impose an impossible rigidity upon the process of customary development and largely to doom such appraisal to irrelevance.'[4]

Accordingly, one recent commentator has called for a 'crude congruence of law and practice' in naval warfare;[5] another, in reference to U.S. policy on targeting enemy merchant vessels, for the need to 'bridge the gap between conventional law and practice'.[6]

B   Toward congruence of law and practice

This congruence cannot be achieved by a mere restatement of existing conventional law. Forged by a gradual process of state claims and counterclaims, it requires instead a critical reappraisal of its basic structure and focus in view of the *actual* conduct of naval operations. Such reappraisal must begin with an examination, heretofore largely absent from the field, of the theory underlying the law of naval targeting. This paper undertakes that examination, against a backdrop of the tanker war. It describes a

3. Robertson, H.B., Jr., "U.S. Policy on Targeting Enemy Merchant Shipping: Bridging the Gap between Conventional Law and State Practice", in: *Targeting Enemy Merchant Shipping*, U.S. Naval War College, International Law Studies, vol. 65 (publication forthcoming). This paper was presented at a symposium examining the 1936 London Submarine Protocol held at the U.S. Naval War College, 1-3 February 1990 [hereinafter Targeting Symposium]. Copies of all symposium reports and commentaries, the schedule of events, and list of participants are on file with the author. The symposium proceedings will be published as part of the U.S. Naval War College's acclaimed "Blue Book" series in international law. Also see at the same symposium VADM J. Service, USN (Ret.), "Targeting Realities: Platforms, Weapons Systems and Capabilities", and the accompanying commentary of VADM Doyle, USN (Ret.).

4. McDougal, M., Feliciano, F., *Law and Minimum World Public Order*, New Haven/London 1961, p. 479 quoted in Harlow, B.A., "The Law of Neutrality at Sea for the 80's and Beyond", note 22. This paper was prepared for the Hawaii Regional Meeting of the ASIL *Humanitarianism and Armed Conflict*, 16-18 February 1983. A copy of the paper is on file with the author.

5. Fenrick, W.J., "Military Objectives in the Law of Naval Warfare" (1989), p. 64. This paper served as the introductory report for a meeting of the Round Table of Experts on *International Humanitarian Law Applicable to Armed Conflicts at Sea* held in Bochum, FRG, November 1989 [hereinafter Bochum Round Table] (publication forthcoming). A copy of the report is on file with the author. Fenrick presents the most effective argument to date, from an historical and policy perspective, for functional-based treatment of merchant vessels in the law of naval warfare.

6. See Robertson, *loc.cit.* (note 3).

functional or objective legal theory of naval targeting[7] that accepts as a constant the impact of changing technology, tactics, and force capabilities upon the development and implementation of laws of naval warfare.

As an examination of law at the level of theory, this paper does not purport to ascertain the juridical limits of the existing conventional and customary law of naval warfare. It describes instead the current *direction* of that law and offers some *predictions* about its likely *future* content, consistent with the legal theory postulated and state practice.

C   Preliminary assessments

As developed throughout this paper, targeting theory in the law of naval armed conflict serves also as the analytical framework for appraisal of belligerent attacks against enemy maritime trade generally and, in particular, Iraqi targeting practices in the tanker war. Within this context, two preliminary assessments are made:[8]

1. The legitimacy of an expanded belligerent right, under certain circumstances, to attack third country maritime trade with an enemy which effectively and substantially contributes to that enemy's war-fighting/-sustaining, or military, capability; and, as a corollary of this assessment,
2. the legitimacy of a firm, baseline standard of protected status for genuine *commercial* maritime trade, which does not in any case *directly* enhance belligerent military capability, between countries not party to the hostilities. Shipments of military armament, *destined* ultimately for delivery to a belligerent, consequently do *not* enjoy protected status under this standard.

Both assessments implicitly reject a restrictive application of the traditional doctrine of contraband. The first assessment rests upon the further determination that putative distinctions among merchant vessels, based upon their neutral or belligerent status, are of minimal value in assessing the effectiveness and legitimacy of naval targeting rules. Whether designated neutral or belligerent, each vessel is accorded the same treatment: a *functional* targeting standard applied equally, *regardless of classification*. Additionally, the right to attack under this formulation exists only 'under certain circumstances'. These circumstances underscore the importance of humanitarian considerations in the law of armed conflict and relate to a belligerent requirement to first *attempt* to conduct

---

7. The genesis of this theory is W.T. Mallison's functional appraisal of the merchant vessel as military objective in *Studies in the Law of Naval Warfare: Submarines in General and Limited Wars*, U.S. Naval War College, International Law Studies, vol. 58 (1968). The author is deeply indebted to the ground-breaking work of Professor Mallison in this area. An initial effort by the author to apply this functional approach in a contemporary context is presented in Russo, F.V., "Neutrality at Sea in Transition: State Practice in the Gulf War as Emerging International Customary Law", 19 *Ocean Development and International Law* (1988), pp. 381-399. The author has also relied upon the contemporaneous work of others who are studying emerging developments in the law of naval warfare. Much of this work, unfortunately, is not yet in publication.

8. See Russo, *loc.cit.* (note 7), p. 382; and notes 56 and 61 *infra* and accompanying text.

visit and search or use visual identification targeting procedures (or other highly reliable means of target verification, including the use of electronically enhanced imagery) where 'feasible'. What is meant by feasible is: (1) the naval capability necessary to minimize civilian casualties exists, *i.e.*, surface combatants and military aircraft appropriate for the purpose are available; (2) it can be accomplished without undue risk to the security of those forces; and (3) it can be accomplished without undue compromise of the legitimate mission assigned to those forces. The extent to which a belligerent is able to exercise complete naval and air superiority over the combat environment will largely determine the feasibility of factors (2) and (3).[9] Subsurface forces are deliberately excluded from compliance with factor (1), since the stated requirements are inherently incompatible with the operational characteristics of those forces. The prior verification or visual identification of enemy maritime commercial trade attacked by air, where feasible, however, is specifically accepted as a required targeting procedure. This requirement parallels the humanitarian mandate to attempt visit and search, where feasible, prior to surface-based attack and approximates Article 57(2) of Additional Protocol I to the Geneva Conventions of 1949.

II   ISSUE AND APPROACH

From a naval context, the attacks upon merchant vessels were the dominant feature of the war between Iran and Iraq.[10] The loss of life and destruction occasioned by these attacks were substantial. Mine, air-, surface-, and ground-launched rocket and missile attacks by Iran on third country merchant vessels, inbound and outbound from Gulf States not party to the hostilities, were, and continue to be, widely condemned by the international community for their 'indiscriminate' and political nature.

Although these attacks, usually accomplished at close range by elements of the Revolutionary Guard, were specifically directed against third country tankers, they were based solely upon the perceived *political* – not military – value of those vessels. The Irani tanker attacks were indiscriminate, therefore, in the sense that they were conducted without regard to *any possible* military value of the objects intended for attack. Nor would the attack of such genuine third country merchant vessels, engaged at the time in intra-neutral trade, be justified on a theory of reprisal. This appraisal of

9. See note 51 *infra* and accompanying text. Compare Hegelsom, G.J.F., "Methods and Means of Combat in Naval Warfare" (1990), pp. 61-65. This paper served as the introductory report for a meeting of the Round Table of Experts on *International Humanitarian Law Applicable to Armed Conflict at Sea* held in Toulon, France, 19-23 October 1990 [hereinafter Toulon Round Table] (publication forthcoming) (analysis based on requirements of Article 57(2) of Protocol I). A copy of this report is on file with the author.

10. For an outline of the significant events surrounding the tanker war, see generally Russo, *loc.cit.* (note 7); Robertson, *loc.cit.* (note 3); Fenrick, *loc.cit.* (note 5); Grunawalt, *loc.cit.* (note 1); Peace, D., "Major Maritime Events in the Persian Gulf War" (1988); and Roach, J.A., "Missiles on Target: The Law of Targeting and the Tanker War" (1988). The Peace and Roach papers were presented before *Proceedings of the 82nd Annual Meeting of the American Society of International Law*, 21 April 1988 (publication forthcoming). Copies of these papers are on file with the author. Commander Peace provides an excellent discussion of the robust exercise of the right of self-defense by neutral U.S. forces during the Iran-Iraq War.

Irani tanker attacks, however, is not without exception: merchant vessels carrying military armament and associated support equipment intended for transshipment to Iraq. These vessels were military objects and, under some circumstances, liable to attack.

As distinguished from the rather definitive and collective negative appraisal of Irani attacks on merchant vessels, the Iraqi attacks on third country merchant vessels have not been generally condemned although their definitive appraisal remains largely incomplete. Illustrative of the ambiguous response of the international community to the Iraqi attacks were United Nations Security Council Resolutions 540 (1983), 552 (1984), and 582 (1986). While specifically condemning most of the Irani attacks, these resolutions are silent as to the Iraqi attacks.[11] The political and moral irony in this position, in light of Iraqi actions since 2 August 1990, is readily apparent. That further objective appraisal of Iraqi tanker attacks during the 1980-1988 Iran-Iraq War should for that reason be eschewed, however, is rejected. Likewise, questions about whether Iraq was the 'aggressor' with respect to *initiation* of hostilities, as some studies indicate,[12] must also be separated from appraisal of Iraqi tanker attacks *during* hostilities.[13] The former is a question for *ius ad bellum*, while the latter remains within the realm of *ius in bello*.

The few determinations made to date that the Iraqi attacks were legitimate have been premised on the problematic assessment that almost all of the third country tankers attacked had acquired enemy character because they were under Irani control, orders, employment, or charter. Practitioner-scholar, Captain J. Ashley Roach of the U.S. Navy, offers a clear statement of this position:

'Is there a different appraisal of Iraqi attacks on Iranian flag tankers than of Iraqi attacks on tankers flying national flags of other countries moving Iranian oil? Perhaps that question can be answered by inquiring whether Iran can reasonably expect to put her oil export capability, upon which she depends to continue the war against Iraq, beyond the lawful reach of Iraqi interdiction, by the simple expedient of using neutral flag shipping? I submit the answer to both questions is no. Neutral ships acquire the character of an enemy merchant vessel, *inter alia*, by operating under enemy control, orders, charter, employment, or direction. Such appears to be the case here.'[14]

This view, relying exclusively upon the doctrine of acquired enemy character, is unnecessarily *restrictive* in its approach to the concept of military objective. It leaves unanswered an important question: What is the legal status of merchant vessels which, under traditional rules, have neither formally acquired enemy character nor been

---

11. Russo, *loc.cit.* (note 7), pp. 395-396.

12. See, for example, Dekker, I.F., *infra* chapter 8 of this book.

13. Compare Henkin, L., Commentary, "Conference Report on the Gulf War", 19 *Ocean Development and International Law* (1988), pp. 309-310.

14. Roach, *loc.cit.* (note 10). Also see Peace, *loc.cit.* (note 10); and Fenrick, W.J., "The Law of War at Sea Today: A Perspective from Canada", 3 *Canadian Forces JAG Journal* (1989), p. 1. With regard to Canada's own Draft Manual, Fenrick comments that its treatment of merchant vessels 'may be too restrictive as it does not include neutral merchant ships incorporated in the belligerent war effort as military objectives'. *Idem.*

incorporated into the belligerent fleet as naval auxiliaries, but nonetheless are engaged in belligerent trade (*e.g.*, oil export, in the case of Iran) which effectively and substantially contributes to the overall military capability of that belligerent? The appraisal of Iraqi attacks as reflected above is *also* incomplete, since it fails to include a discussion of important questions about Iraqi means and methods *in conjunction with* those raised concerning military objective.

The doctrine of acquired enemy character is one of *exception* and very limited scope in the law of naval warfare. It must also be distinguished from its even more conservative legal cousin, the concept of naval auxiliary. Under this extremely narrow concept, a ship is regarded not merely as an enemy merchant vessel but as part of an enemy's *military* fleet. Whether a ship is or has become a naval auxiliary is based on two alternative factors: (1) it operates under the exclusive control or ownership of the military; or (2) it operates in *direct* support of military operations. That the second factor is equivalent to the requirements in Article 51(3) of Additional Protocol I regarding the loss of protected civilian status illustrates its exceptional nature.

Although grounded in traditional and customary law, both of these concepts provide only a partial answer to the legitimate treatment of third country and enemy flag merchant vessels during an armed conflict. Within the context of a functional targeting theory, for example, both possess only limited rulemaking value; each embraces no more than a very small portion of the set of objects of legitimate attack identified by a functional or objective targeting criterion. As one author has appropriately noted, there remains a 'very broad intermediate group of vessels'[15] between warships/naval auxiliaries and those enjoying special humanitarian protection, which lack a well-defined legal status. Whether attacks upon vessels within this intermediate category are legitimate and, if so, under what circumstances, is unsettled in light of the practices of modern naval conflicts. A functional or objective legal theory of naval targeting offers a workable, alternative approach to those questions *as well as* a basis for appraisal of the Iraqi means and methods of attack on third country shipping, which had neither become *de facto* naval auxiliaries nor strictly acquired enemy character. In short, the theory here detailed looks beyond the traditional law of naval warfare.

III   BACKGROUND

A   Legal doctrine and armed conflict

Deliberate, open, sustained, and coordinated armed hostilities at sea are regulated by the law of armed conflict. From an operational viewpoint, the doctrine of self-defence is inadequate for this purpose. A *ius ad bellum* notion of necessary and proportional self-defence, strictly and exclusively applied in war, would constrain military commanders to a fixed and reactive posture: their ability to conduct broad-based military operations all but arrested; the tactical and strategic advantage perpetually

---

15. Fenrick, *loc.cit.* (note 14), p. 20.

yielded to the enemy. This is an untenable military situation and invites the proliferation of enemy sanctuaries (otherwise legitimate military objects placed 'off limits' or beyond military reach). It also undermines a basic tenet of the operational art: that the swift pursuit and destruction of those objects of military value to the enemy secures battlefield victory. Only the law of armed conflict provides a corpus of legal controls and framework by which to regulate the violent, relentless combat operations presaged by this strategy.[16]

In the same manner that no precise demarcation exists between forceful measures of proportional response, armed attack, open and sustained military operations or armed conflict, and war, there is a degree of overlap between the doctrines of self-defence and the law of armed conflict. So, while the law of armed conflict determines the parameters for the *actual conduct* of military operations, the doctrine of self-defence establishes the *immediate and continuing justification* for the use of such force. As a matter of U.S. Government policy, for example, compliance with the law of armed conflict is required *wherever* U.S. military force is employed. Figure 1, on page 160, is a schematic outline of the relationship between law and hostilities along a continuum of escalating state and extra-state tension, conflict, and response.[17]

The peacetime law of the sea does not alter the complementary relationship between these two legal doctrines. Articles 88 and 301 of the 1982 United Nations Convention on the Law of the Sea (LOS Convention) reiterate the applicability of the doctrine of self-defence where a military commander or state must resort to force at sea, but do not otherwise diminish the authority of the law of armed conflict over naval hostilities.[18]

16. For an opposing view, compare Greenwood, C., "Self-Defense and the Conduct of International Armed Conflict", in: Dinstein, Y. (ed.), *International Law at a Time of Perplexity*, Dordrecht/Boston/Londen 1989, p. 274. Also compare Ronzitti, N., "The Right of Self-Defense and the Law of Naval Warfare", 14 *Syracuse J. Int'l L. & Com.* (1988), pp. 571-596 (especially comments at pp. 582-586) and "The Crises in the Law of Naval Warfare" (introductory essay), in Ronzitti, N. (ed.), *The Law of Naval Warfare*, Dordrecht/Boston/Londen 1988, pp. 1-51. Also see the commentary of T. Gill accompanying this paper. In accord Grunawalt, *loc.cit.* (note 1); and Fenrick, *loc.cit.* (note 14), p. 20 (full range of belligerent rights available in an international armed conflict).

17. Adopted from Figure SF5-1 in *Annotated Supplement to the Commander's Handbook on the Law of Naval Operations*, NWP 9 (Rev. A)/FMFM 1-10 [hereinafter *Commander's Handbook*], Washington D.C. 1989, § 5.1 note 3.

18. Compare Lowe, A.V., "The Commander's Handbook on the Law of Naval Operations and the Contemporary Law of the Sea", in: Robertson, H.B., Jr. (ed.), *The Law of Naval Operations*, U.S. Naval War College, International Law Studies, vol. 64, Washinton 1990 (publication forthcoming). A copy of this article is on file with the author. Also compare Henkin, L., "Use of Force: Law and U.S. Policy", in: Henkin, L./Hoffman, S./Kirkpatrick, J.J./Gerson, A./Rogers, W.D./Scheffer, D.J., *Right v. Might: International Law and the Use of Force*, New York/London 1989, pp. 37-70. The current author rejects the general applicability of the doctrine of self-defence to the *conduct* of naval warfare. Accordingly, discussion of the narrow view of self-defence reflected in the *Nicaragua Case* is considered unnecessary. See, *e.g.*, Sofaer, A., "International Law & the Use of Force", *Nat'l Interest* (Fall 1988), at pp. 54-57; and "Terrorism, the Law, and the National Defense", 126 *Military Law Review* (1989), pp. 89-124. Other works examining these issues include Mendelson, M.H., "The *Nicaragua Case* and Customary International Law", 26 *Coexistence* (1989), pp. 85-99; Schachter, O., "Self-Defence and the Rule of Law", 83 *AJIL* (1989), pp. 259-277; and, on the misunderstood *political* role of the ICJ, Reisman, W.M., "International Politics and International Law-Making – reflections on the so-called Politicization of the International Court", in: Heere, W.P. (ed.), *International Law and Its Sources*, 1988, pp. 77-92.

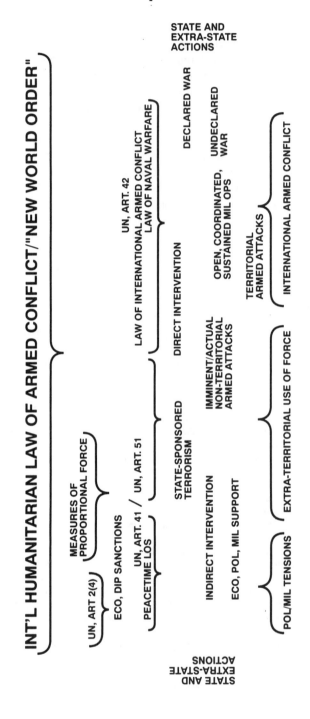

Figure 1

These articles merely underscore that ocean areas beyond the sovereign authority of coastal states are not, by virtue of their stateless nature, a lawless domain in times of armed conflict. Article 87 of the LOS Convention also appears to support this conclusion. Belligerent military operations which interfere with the peacetime navigational rights of neutral states (*e.g.*, nonsuspendable transit passage) are properly assessed in terms of compliance with necessity and proportionality in the law of armed conflict.[19]

The regulatory preeminence of the law of armed conflict in this regard will persist regardless of authoritative, definitive, and effective action by the Security Council under Articles 41 and 42 of the United Nations Charter. Such actions, where they arise, may be indicative of an emerging international legal order. This new order may ultimately establish a mechanism for formally authorized, collective state action against designated aggressor-states. It will not, however, supplant or significantly alter the law of naval armed conflict with respect to the conduct of that war, except perhaps as to certain warfare methods (*e.g.*, traditional blockade). Nor will actions taken under Articles 41 and 42 diminish the right of individual and collective self-defence against armed aggression under Article 51, *until those actions actually restore* international peace and security, or effectively provide for a victim-state's defense and the protection of its citizens.

Increasingly, however, state action under Article 51 is likely to become an option truly of last resort, proceeding only when all reasonable efforts at securing or maintaining authoritative and effective United Nations sanctions under Articles 41 and 42 have clearly been unproductive. Although the responsibility of the Security Council to act under Article 24 in this situation is primary, it is *not exclusive*. The penultimate check against probable (and until most recently, all but certain) institutional complacency and paralysis of the Security Council is individual and collective state action under Article 51. Thus, regardless of Council actions under Articles 41 and 42, the inherent right of individual and collective self-defence enshrined in Article 51 is never completely extinguished. The preeminence of state sovereignty, coupled with the Security Council's historical lack of political cohesiveness, justifies this result. What this emerging international legal order augers is an *alternative* authoritative basis for

---

19. See, *e.g.*, Harlow, *loc.cit.* (note 4). For several U.S. views of the navigational rights of third country states, see generally Grunawalt, R.J., "United States Policy on International Straits", 18 *Ocean Development and International Law* (1987), pp. 445-457; Clove, R.I., "Submarine Navigation in International Straits: A Legal Perspective", 39 *Naval Law Review* (1990), pp. 103-116; Rose, S.A., "Naval Activity in the EEZ – Troubled Waters Ahead?", 39 *Naval Law Review* (1990), pp. 67-92; and the comments submitted by H.B. Robertson, Jr., in response to van Hegelsom's Toulon Round Table report, *loc.cit.* (note 9). Compare Lowe, A.V., "The Impact of the Law of the Sea on Naval Warfare", 14 *Syracuse J. Int'l L. & Com.* (1988), pp. 657-698 as well as his article in Robertson (ed.), *op.cit.* (note 18). Rejected by the present author is the notion that belligerent naval operations must be confined to enemy territorial waters.

international measures short of armed conflict, established *alongside* a continuing right of individual and collective self-defence.[20]

B   The 1936 London Protocol and the interpretive process

From the international legal perspective, the tanker war has prompted further reexamination of the London Protocol and the discursive search for alternative criteria by which to determine legitimate objects of attack.[21] While productive to a point, this analysis, with few exceptions, has not squarely addressed the significant extent to which military technology, naval tactics, operational capability, and the tendency toward complete integration of merchant vessels into an enemy's overall military effort have dictated the actual practice of naval armed conflict and, in turn, influenced the law. This is due as much to the inherent and well-documented limitations of the London Protocol as to its generally ambiguous reception, application, and enforcement by the international community. Under the most narrow contemporary formulation, the constraints of the London Protocol are seen as applying 'only in those circumstances in which the enemy merchant vessel is totally defenseless and its destruction without warning offers no clear military advantage to the attacker'.[22] It might also be added that these circumstances include that the enemy merchant vessel is, at the time, operating in an area over which the attacker enjoys air and naval superiority. In virtually any other situation, compliance with the London Protocol is not operationally feasible.

One commentator succinctly described the situation surrounding the London Protocol with the wry observation that, depending on whether you ask a 'revisionist' or 'literalist', the Protocol is either superfluous or irrelevant.[23] In any case, although still formally recognized as a valid legal document by signatory states including the United States, the Protocol is of only the most limited practical effect.

In the revisionist view, the term 'merchant vessel' is very narrowly construed as embracing only those vessels 'not participating in hostilities'. Professor W. Thomas Mallison, Jr., the leading proponent of this construction, regards any such meaningful participation by a merchant vessel as disqualification for protected status:

'The juridical criteria to determine whether [an enemy] merchant vessel is participating in the war or hostilities in a way which results in losing the "immunities of a merchant vessel"

---

20. An excellent discussion of the contemporary application of these mandates is found in Grunawalt, R.J., "The Maritime Dimension of Operation Desert Shield", *Proceedings of the American Society of International Law*, Chicago 1990 (publication forthcoming). A copy of the original comments are on file with the author.

21. The papers and commentaries presented at the Targeting Symposium, *op.cit.* (note 3), represent the most comprehensive contemporary examination of the legal status of the 1936 London Submarine Protocol today. This matter was also considered at the Bochum Round Table, *op.cit.* (note 5). The many divergent approaches expressed by Targeting Symposium participants dramatized, for this author, the urgent need for a theoretical examination of targeting considerations affecting the treatment of merchant vessels during armed conflict at sea.

22. Robertson, *loc.cit.* (note 3).

23. Comments of Professor Robertson at the Targeting Symposium, *loc.cit.* (note 3).

should be determined by the fact of such participation and not by the particular method of participation.'[24]

The contrasting literalist view, which flows from important considerations concerning platform effectiveness and security arising from the inapposite relationship between the nature of the submarine and the practice of visit and search, is captured by D.P. O'Connell:

> 'The truth is that the requirements of the London Protocol are to be observed only in the situation where the submarine can act with minimal risk on the surface. Since that situation is now an ideal hardly ever in practice to be realized, one is compelled to draw (...) the conclusion that submarine operations in time of war are today governed by no legal text, and that no more than lip service is being paid in naval documents to the London Protocol.'[25]

The logic reflected in each of these views is incomplete and depends on the other for explanation; in fact, the two are complementary. For one, only genuine merchant vessels not participating in or furthering hostilities may justifiably demand and expect submarines to accord them protected status. For the other, where required to interdict third country maritime trade that substantially contributes to the military capability of an enemy, belligerent submarine forces may justifiably demand to operate without forsaking their security or mission effectiveness. In short, as detailed below in the legal theory of naval targeting, Mallison's *functional standard* (participation in hostilities) satisfies O'Connell's *operational concern* (submarine ineffectiveness and vulnerability on the surface). Expressed as a postulate of that theory, targeting criteria must be tested for their capacity to balance important operational *and* humanitarian considerations. Included among these considerations is whether a targeting criterion permits the effective use of an otherwise legitimate weapon or weapons platform (*e.g.*, the submarine, aircraft, mine, and guided missile). In Professor Julius Stone's view, this is critical to the rulemaking value of a proffered targeting standard:

> 'The immediate task is to regulate the future of naval warfare in which submarines and aircraft will join in the attack on enemy commerce; for it is regrettably clear that no rule purporting to exclude them from this role, however well grounded in humanity, will be brooked.'[26]

Complicating the confused situation surrounding the London Protocol has been a persistent, misplaced, and almost exclusive reliance in conventional law upon a hierarchy of superordinate, *a priori* legal norms as the preferred point of reference.[27]

---

24. Mallison, *op.cit.* (note 7), p. 120.

25. O'Connell, D.P., "International Law and Contemporary Naval Operations", 44 *BYIL* (1970), p. 18 at p. 52.

26. Stone, J., *Legal Controls of International Conflict*, 2nd ed., London 1959, p. 606.

27. In developing this appraisal, the author has borrowed from H. Kelsen, "On the Theory of Legal Interpretation", and S. L. Paulsen, "Kelsen on Legal Interpretation", 10 *Legal Studies* (1990), pp. 127-135 and pp. 136-152, respectively. Also see Russo, *loc.cit.* (note 7), at pp. 381-382; and, on the evolutionary

The oftentimes pivotal role played by normative distinctions in the law of naval warfare, such as belligerent/neutral, absolute/conditional contraband, naval auxiliary/merchant vessel, or aggressor/victim, is illustrative. In essence, these terms are immutable classifications turned into targeting determinants. This classical normative frame of reference, by its nature, has all but stymied the realistic and concrete interpretation of the law of naval warfare demanded by a constantly evolving combat environment. With respect to the traditional law of neutrality at sea, for example, over-dependence upon this classical or literalist approach has often led to the cynical view that either no law exists or that virtually everyone has violated it. Compared to the progressive dialectic of the customary lawmaking process, such a system of laws is antithetical to the interpretive process. It compels a literal application of rules of law, the effect of which, in the case of armed conflict, is to render those rules of law useless for the reality they were intended to regulate. Exceptions to this proposition are those several, over-arching principles of the law of armed conflict, discussed below, that act as minimum humanitarian controls for naval targeting practices.

IV   THEORY OVERVIEW

A   Basic considerations in targeting theory

As formulated and presented here, targeting theory in the law of naval armed conflict is premised upon four fundamental considerations. These considerations serve two purposes: they define the outer limits within which objects of legitimate attack may generally be identified; and they establish the requirements which, in any given situation, further circumscribe the set of generally identified objects of legitimate attack. With only some very limited exceptions noted below, each follow-on consideration represents a *fully inclusive* subset of the set of generally defined objects of legitimate attack. Figure 2, on page 165, illustrates what may be termed a principle of limitation in the law of naval warfare, by which each successive basic consideration or definitional requirement narrows the set of generally identified objects of legitimate attack.

1   *Functional targeting criterion*

The legal exposure or immunity of a merchant vessel to attack is based upon the function performed by that vessel (what it does) in relationship to the overall conflict, *i.e.*, function as the primary indicator of military value. The military value of a merchant vessel is, in turn, judged by the degree to which it effectively and substantially contributes to the war-fighting/-sustaining, or military, capability of a belligerent. In this

---

nature of the law of neutrality in naval warfare, Tucker, R.W., *The Law of War and Neutrality at Sea*, U.S. Naval War College, International Law Studies, vol. 50, Washington 1955.

PRINCIPLE OF LIMITATION

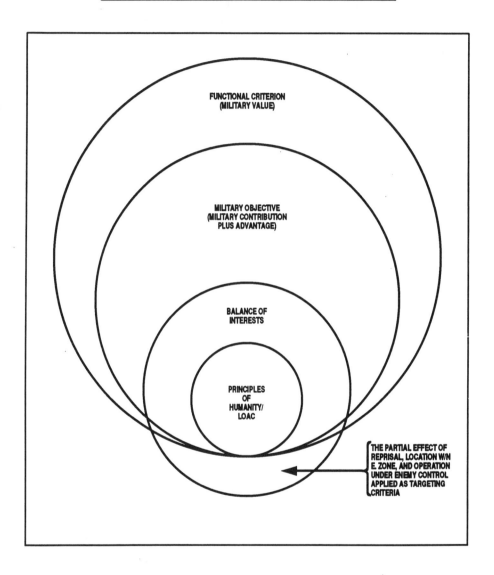

Figure 2

regard, it is specifically contemplated that commercial maritime trade, which substantially contributes to belligerent military capability, will be encompassed within the set of objects of possible legitimate attack defined by a functional targeting criterion. Commander W.J. Fenrick, Director of International Law, Canadian Department of National Defence, frames this issue by the question: 'Is there a valid legal reason why neutral merchant ships should be immune from attack when they are employed on tasks functionally indistinguishable from those where enemy merchant vessels are subject to attack?'[28]

Professor Mallison anticipated this question in 1966. Extending the same juridical criteria (participation in hostilities) to neutral merchant vessels found applicable to enemy merchantman, he offered the following *theoretical* assessment of nonconforming neutral merchant vessels given the constraints of the London Protocol:

> 'It has been documented that the Protocol does not protect enemy merchant ships which are participating in the war or hostilities. There is no reason in experience or logic why the Protocol should be interpreted as protecting neutral merchant ships which are engaged in the same functional activities that result in lack of protection for an enemy merchant ship.'[29]

The notion of function as a principal indicator of military value is pivotal in targeting theory. It is the definitional criterion for the set of all possible objects of legitimate attack, except objects of reprisals. In this connection, the set of objects it describes is coextensive with the set of objects identified by the first prong of the standard of military objective (substantial contribution to military capability) discussed below. As such, maritime commercial trade which substantially contributes to the military capability of a belligerent is also embraced within the broadly defined first prong of military objective. The significance of a functional targeting criterion is fully developed with a multiple attribute analytical model.[30] This model, which adopts a positivist approach to targeting assessment, represents a fundamental departure from the categorical jurisprudence underlying much of the conventional law pertaining to naval targeting. In contrast to the rigid legalism endemic to that approach, the model presented here assesses the *relative* rulemaking value of various naval targeting criteria. It does so by explicitly focusing upon the *comparative* ability of those proffered criteria to satisfy key operational and humanitarian considerations in naval armed conflict. The views of Mallison and O'Connell concerning the London Protocol, examined above, furnished a limited example of the necessary *evaluative link* between a proffered targeting criterion (participation in hostilities) and pertinent operational considerations (incompatibility of submarine effectiveness and security with visit and search). Figure 4, below, depicts the multiple attribute model constructed to assess targeting criteria generally, and merchant vessels in particular.

---

28. Fenrick, *loc.cit.* (note 5), p. 63.

29. Mallison, *op.cit.* (note 7), pp. 129-130.

30. The concept is borrowed from the field of defense analysis and was suggested by Major Steve Day, U.S. Marine Corps, of the Oceans Law and Policy Department, Center for Naval Warfare Studies, U.S. Naval War College.

Within this analytical framework, selected forms of maritime commerce, regardless of a carrier's flag, are specifically evaluated as objects of definite military value in the *overall* conduct of an armed conflict. This assessment comports with 'a modern trend in the law of naval warfare, wherein targeting of an enemy's economic base is the *sine qua non* of a successful campaign.'[31] This targeting trend extends, without limitation, to *all* enemy seaborne trade of substantial military importance. The numerous failed efforts among Arab States to secure protected status for oil fields during the negotiating phase for Additional Protocol I[32] suggested a growing recognition of this trend, at least as concerns belligerent capacity to trade in oil. The tanker war is further evidence of that trend.

In this regard, several commentators have concluded that it was the 'integration' of belligerent merchant vessels into the military 'effort' of the enemy (*i.e.*, the exercise of military *control* in furtherance of its war aims) that historically deprived those vessels of their immunity from attack.[33] This description, however, is an unfortunate one in a targeting context. It suggests several divergent targeting standards for merchant vessels. The confusion and difficulty surround the terms 'integration' and 'effort'. If what is meant by 'integration' is the exercise of strict and pervasive military or state control over shipping, it is unnecessarily restrictive; if what is meant by 'effort' is almost any shipping that may in some way sustain the military enterprise and enemy will to fight, however indirectly or remotely, it is dangerously expansive. Such notions, without further definition or description, are misleading and inadequate targeting guides for civilian merchant vessels. A more appropriate description of the merchant vessel's historical loss of immunity is one that focuses on the *function* that such vessels actually perform, *in addition to* their level of possible integration into the overall war effort. As related above, the principal indicator of military value for an object is whether, under the circumstances, it effectively and substantially contributes to the war-fighting/-sustaining, or military, capability of a belligerent. The integration of merchant vessels into the war effort is merely one measure of the level of contribution those vessels make to belligerent military capability. Military capability in this sense *may*, but does not necessarily, equate to a *formal* integration of those objects into the war effort. Accordingly, the functional standard of 'substantial contribution to military capability' is the basis adopted for the two primary targeting criteria listed in the analytical model described below. Put simply, the economic activities or functions of a belligerent that substantially enhance its military capability are of strategic significance and thereby represent, to an enemy, objects of distinct military value.[34]

---

31. Grunawalt, R.J., "The Rights of Belligerents and Neutrals", in: "Conference Report on the Gulf War", 19 *Ocean Development and International Law* (1988), p. 306. For a discussion of this question from the Japanese viewpoint see Mayama, A., "The Law of Neutrality and Economic Warfare at Sea", presented at the annual meeting of the Japanese Association of World Law (April 1988). A copy of the paper is on file with the author.

32. See Kalshoven, F., *supra* chapter 3 in this book, at notes 51-53 and accompanying text.

33. Robertson, *loc.cit.* (note 3), citing Tucker, *op.cit.* (note 27), pp. 68-69. Also see Mallison, *op.cit.* (note 7).

34. See, *e.g.*, Grunawalt, *loc.cit.* (note 31), p. 308; also *infra* note 51.

2   *Standard of military objective*

The relative importance of a merchant vessel's function to the overall conflict and its status as a possible legitimate target are assessed against the standard of military objective, defined generally and by example. As examined below, this standard consists of two prongs, one of flexibility (substantial contribution to enemy war-fighting/-sustaining, or military, capability) and one of limitation (definite military advantage to the attacker). The first prong, as noted above, is the equivalent of a functional targeting criterion. This is appropriate since, as Commander Fenrick observes, 'The key test to determine whether or not a merchant ship is a legitimate military objective should be a functional test: What is it doing and to what extent is it either directly participating in hostilities or contributing to the enemy war effort?'[35] Expressly embraced by this functional test are those economic activities of a belligerent which effectively and substantially contribute to its military capability. The second prong is equivalent to the threshold operational consideration, 'permits attacks on the full spectrum of objects of definite military value', used to assess targeting criteria in the analytical model described below.

These two prongs are similar, but not identical, to the definition of military objective at Article 52(2) of Additional Protocol I.[36] The applicability of that definition, however, without modification to the unique aspects of the law of armed conflict at sea, is rejected. The ongoing debate over whether the narrowly drawn language of Article 52(2) extends to economic objects of military value dictates this position. Any standard of military objective in a naval context must allow for the possibility that, under certain circumstances, maritime trade will be a legitimate object of attack. So long as the interpretation of Article 52(2) remains ambiguous on this point, it is of dubious legitimacy and rulemaking value in the law of armed conflict at sea.[37] All of the

35. Fenrick, *loc.cit.* (note 5), p. 72.

36. See *Commander's Handbook, op.cit.* (note 17), § 8.1.1 at note 9. Interestingly, and without explanation, the *Commander's Handbook* appears to *accept*, in principle, the applicability of Article 52(2) of Additional Protocol I to naval warfare. The Bochum Round Table, *loc.cit.* (note 5), clearly takes this position. The present author categorically rejects that view. Also see Fenrick, *loc.cit.* (note 14), p. 21. 'Simple transposition of this definition [Article 52(2)] to a naval warfare context would be inappropriate'. *Ibidem.* Parts III and IV of Additional Protocol I do not comprise a modern law of naval warfare or restatement of the customary law of armed conflict at sea. The full scope of *interests* concerning the law of *naval* warfare were simply not the focus or in issue in the drafting of Additional Protocol I. No amount of exegesis now of its language can alter that fact. In accord see Levie, H., "Means and Methods of Combat at Sea", 14 *Syracuse J. Int'l L. & Com.* (1988), pp. 728-730; compare Fenrick, *loc.cit.* (note 5), pp. 42-48. Also see Bothe, M., "1977 Geneva Protocol I (commentary)", in: Ronzitti, N. (ed.), *op.cit.* (note 16), p. 762. 'Thus, ship to ship, ship to air or air to ship attacks are not covered by [Part IV section 1 of] Protocol I, unless and to the extent that (...) there is collateral civilian damage on land. The definition of civilian objects contained in Article 52 does not apply to such attacks.' *Idem.*

37. See Meyrowitz, H., "Le Protocole additionnel I aux conventions de Geneve de 1949 et le droit de la guerre maritime", *Revue Generale de Droit International Public* (1985), pp. 254-255 cited in: Van Hegelsom, *loc.cit.* (note 9), p. 10 (economic warfare is an integral aspect of armed conflict at sea of which the law must adequately take account). For opposing views see Van Hegelsom, *idem*; the commentary of D. Fleck accompanying this paper as well as his paper, "The 1936 London Protocol in Today's Perspective", Targeting

possible relationships between these two prongs are depicted with Venn diagrams at Figure 3, on page 170. Only diagram 'C' properly reflects the relationship between the two prongs.

The underlying rationale for this conclusion may briefly be summarized. Diagram A is rejected because it erroneously suggests that prongs 1 and 2 are mutually exclusive; diagram B (which best depicts the way in which Article 52(2) is currently interpreted) is rejected because it mistakenly suggests that each prong is fully inclusive of the other; diagram D is rejected because it reverses the correct relationship between the two prongs, improperly reflecting 'contribution to military capability' as the prong of limitation. Diagram E contemplates a notion of military objective that is utterly implausible in practice; namely, that some object, the destruction of which would constitute a definite military advantage, would *not* also be an object that substantially contributes to military capability.[38]

Professor Robertson has recently urged adoption of a standard of military objective in cases of naval bombardment in lieu of the Hague IX rules. These rules have failed because they artificially place enemy resources of military importance, located in an unfortified or undefended area, beyond the reach of naval forces. The Hague IX rules establish a targeting criterion that is conditioned on whether an area is open to occupation, rather than the possible overall military importance of that area or selected parts of it. This misplaced emphasis of the Hague IX rules thwarts the effectiveness of otherwise legitimate long-range naval gunfire and, thereby, undermines force security and mission accomplishment, as well as tactical flexibility. Hague IX also fails to onserve humanitarian values. Professor Robertson explains:

'An additional factor indicating the lack of current viability of Article 1 of Hague IX is that by implication, by prohibiting the bombardment of undefended towns it authorizes the indiscriminate bombardment of defended towns – that is, the whole town, not just military objectives within the town. Such a norm, however, is inconsistent with the basic principle that noncombatants should not be the object of direct attacks.'[39]

The ease with which this logic is applied to the third country ship that has acquired enemy character is equally revealing. These are merchant vessels which operate under enemy state, but not necessarily military control and direction. This excludes the ship, such as a troop carrier or logistical support vessel, that is a de facto naval auxiliary

---

Symposium, *loc.cit.* (note 3); and "Draft Results of the First Meeting of the Madrid Plan of Action", [hereinafter Bochum Draft Results], Bochum Round Table, *loc.cit.* (note 5). In his oral comments at the Targeting Symposium, *idem*, F. Kalshoven stated bluntly that the Article 52(2) definition of military objective *discards* the standard of 'contribution to war effort' in favor of 'contribution to military action'. Professor Kalshoven concludes from this that third country merchantmen providing belligerents with contraband, other than military materials, may not be attacked. In another context, however, Professor Kalshoven has also opined that 'the Diplomatic Conference [on the Protocols Additional to the 1949 Geneva Conventions] carefully avoided, in particular, the matter of naval warfare.' Quoted in: Levie, *loc.cit.* (note 36).

38. This insight was furnished by Professor Grunawalt upon studying Figure 3.

39. Robertson, H.B., Jr., "Bombardment by Naval Forces (Commentary)", in: Ronzitti, N. (ed.), *op.cit.* (note 16), p. 165.

Chapter 5

MILITARY OBJECTIVE

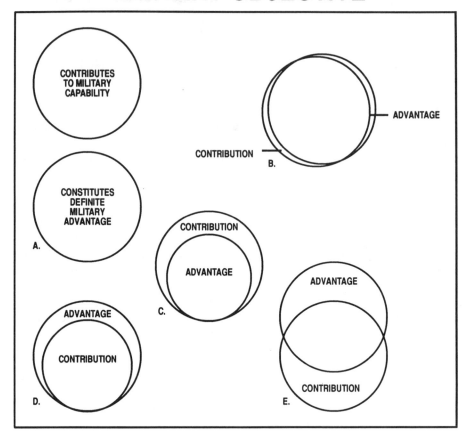

Figure 3

because it operates in direct support of enemy military operations. Except for this excluded category of ships, merchant vessels may become legitimate objects of attack under traditional law due precisely to the exercise of enemy control over them, regardless of any particular military function performed by them. Hague IX similarly authorizes bombardment of the fortified town precisely because of the military control in that situation. The legal exposure of both of these objects to attack, therefore, is determined by the shared targeting criterion or attribute of being under military control. This targeting criterion, however, is based on the problematic assumption that an object under enemy control – whether vessel or town – *necessarily* makes an effective and substantial contribution to military capability, *i.e.*, performs a valuable military function. This assumption invites chaos. Some objects of little military value may nonetheless be targeted merely because the condition of being under enemy control is satisfied. Conversely, a vessel not under enemy control or unfortified geographic area is *exempt* from attack solely for that reason, even if performing an important military function.

As a targeting criterion, then, the condition of being under enemy control is both too broad and too narrow: too broad because it permits attacks on objects lacking in military importance; too narrow because it excludes from its reach objects which in fact make a substantial military contribution. This absurd situation is not only incompatible with the actual practice of naval warfare but with the basic tenets of that law as well. Accordingly, in the analytical model (Figure 4) used below to assess the various targeting criteria applied to merchant vessels, the condition of being under enemy control (the doctrine of acquired enemy character) is evaluated as only *partially* satisfying important operational and humanitarian considerations.

Similarly, Hague IX has been rejected in practice because it fails to satisfy adequately several operational and humanitarian considerations that are essential to the legitimacy of any targeting rule; namely, the rule fosters: (1) attack on the full spectrum of objects of definite military value; (2) effective use of otherwise legitimate weapons; (3) tactical flexibility; (4) mission accomplishment; as well as (5) preservation of humanitarian values and target discrimination. Each of these considerations is listed at Figure 4. The degree to which a targeting criterion is able to satisfy these, as well as other, important operational and humanitarian considerations will determine the rulemaking value and legitimacy of that criterion in the law of naval targeting. This proposition is at the very heart of the functional or objective legal theory of naval targeting.

3   *Balance of neutral and belligerent interests*

Whether a particular function or activity satisfies the requirements of 'military objective' is further determined within the context of a balance of interests and equities between parties to the conflict and others.[40] Inherent in the law of armed conflict at sea

---

40. Concerning the special role of the law of neutrality in this regard, see Grunawalt, *loc.cit.* (note 31), p. 305 and *loc.cit.* (note 1). Also Tucker, *op.cit.* (note 27) and Russo, *loc.cit.* (note 7), pp. 384-385.

is an unrelenting tension between the interests of maritime neutrals and belligerents. Professor Rousseau provides the classic articulation of this tension:

> 'The history of maritime war is that of a continual struggle between belligerent states and neutral Powers: the first, trying to break off all economic communications between their adversaries and the rest of the world; the second, claiming the liberty to maintain their commercial relations with all states – belligerents included – in spite of hostilities.'[41]

Whether the law of naval warfare achieves an equitable balance between these fundamental, competing interests will ultimately determine the success or failure of the law itself. Laws of naval warfare which lack an evident balance of neutral and belligerent interests will be of little practical consequence or rulemaking value. Considerations relating to this balance may *further limit* the set of objects otherwise subject to legitimate attack, as those objects are generally defined by a functional targeting criterion.

The efficacy of any system of laws rests upon the legitimacy accorded that system by those whose conduct it is intended to regulate. In the law of armed conflict, this legitimacy in turn arises directly from how well a state perceives that its interests, as prospective neutral or belligerent, have been accommodated. These interests, at least in part, are also influenced by varying state perceptions about the normative content in the law of armed conflict. Acceptability of the rules and normative standards of conduct implicit in the law will be judged against a fundamental standard of respective belligerent and neutral self-interest. At any common point of 'agreement' among states, these basic interests define accepted 'baseline' or minimal normative legal requirements.

This conclusion is reflective of the overall importance for balance between neutral and belligerent interests in the law of naval warfare. Fundamental to the integrity of that balance is a baseline normative standard of protected status for *intra*-neutral/nonbelligerent maritime commerce. It is against such a standard that Irani attacks on genuine neutral merchantmen, engaged at the time in otherwise protected commercial trade with nonbelligerent Gulf States, are ultimately assessed as illegitimate. Any rule authorizing a contrary result would create an imbalance of interests and equities unacceptable to maritime and coastal state neutrals. As discussed above, such a resulting imbalance would dramatically increase the level of unpredictability in the law, throwing into question the underlying legal structure itself.

Third country merchant vessels which delivered weapons and other military-related equipment to nonbelligerent Gulf State ports for transshipment to Iraq present a different situation.[42] No sound reason in law, experience, logic, or equity exists why a merchant vessel laden with military armament, destined ultimately for a belligerent,

---

41. Rousseau, Ch., *Droit International Public*, Paris 1953, pp. 700-701, Washington 1963, quoted in: Whiteman, *Digest of International Law*, vol. 10, p. 792.

42. Russo, *loc.cit.* (note 7), p. 392 (Iraqi 'enforcement measures' of Gulf Coast neutral state obligations warranted); compare Grunawalt, *loc.cit.* (note 11) (insufficient connection between transshipped commercial goods and the Iraqi war effort to justify Irani attack).

should enjoy the same special immunity of genuine merchantmen engaged in intraneutral trade. Although of a 'neutral'-flag vessel, such cargo possesses indisputable military value. It may protract or escalate the conflict as well as cause human suffering and destruction beyond that which otherwise might have occurred. A classical notion of the common law tradition applies: equity (special treatment or exception) is available only to those who have first done equity; the petitioner seeking redress and protection must come forward with 'clean hands'. Seen in these rudimentary terms, third country merchant vessels are unable to shield themselves from the *responsibility* or risk associated with belligerent military trade that makes an obvious and substantial contribution to its war-fighting/-sustaining capability. This same logic applies with equal force to third country tankers that carried Irani oil for export or between Irani oil transfer facilities.

Several targeting situations achieve a crude balance of neutral and belligerent interests, but fall *outside* the set of objects of legitimate attack generally defined by a functional targeting criterion. This occurs because of the implied – although unacceptable – trade-off made between humanitarian values and neutral or belligerent interests in some targeting criteria. The doctrine of reprisal,[43] location within a war/exclusion zone,[44] and exercise of state control over shipping are perhaps the most dramatic examples of this. For this reason, the subset of objects identified by the requirement for a balance of neutral/belligerent interests is not completely embraced within the sets of objects defined by the other considerations. This is reflected by the intersecting Venn diagram at the bottom of Figure 2.

Achieving the desired accommodation of state interests in the naval context requires recognition by belligerents that the scope and degree of its interference with neutral commerce is circumscribed and, by neutrals, that certain forms of maritime commerce are subject to varying degrees of legitimate belligerent interference. Two mechanisms – visit and search (and the related doctrine of contraband) and close-in blockade – have traditionally been employed to effect the reciprocal duties of maritime belligerents and neutrals. As examined below in connection with Iraqi means and methods, however, neither was a viable tactical option against the Irani oil trade.

Both mechanisms are *belligerent* methods by which to monitor or disrupt the flow of maritime commerce to an enemy. Implicit in each, as noted above concerning the functional criterion, is the common-sense realization that economic activity which enhances or substantially contributes to an enemy's war-fighting capability is a military objective of definite value. While historically recognized as a belligerent means by which to reach this valuable military objective, these mechanisms were also designed to serve as enforcement and warning devices to *minimize* belligerent interference with,

---

43. See generally, for example, Greenwood, C., "The Twilight of the Law of Belligerent Reprisals", 20 *NYIL* (1989), pp. 35-69 (continuing vitality as a doctrine of international law doubtful); an opposing view is Seymour, P.A., "The Legitimacy of Peacetime Reprisal as a Tool Against State-Sponsored Terrorism", 39 *Naval Law Review* (1990), pp. 221-240, p. 224 (legitimate response to state-sponsored terrorism).

44. Russo, *loc.cit.* (note 7), pp. 391-392; compare W.J. Fenrick, "The Exclusion Zone Device in the Law of Naval Warfare", 24 *CYIL* (1986), vol. 24, pp. 91-126. Also see Levie, *loc.cit.* (note 36), at pp. 736-738 and 746 (comment).

and destruction of, neutral commerce. Imbedded in those portions of the traditional law of naval warfare affecting neutral maritime commerce, then, are humanitarian *as well as* operational considerations. *Both* considerations are critical to achieving an effective balance of neutral and belligerent interests. The 'prohibitive and permissive' nature of the law of naval warfare suggested by these dual considerations is illuminated by Richard Baxter in reference to blockade:

> 'For the purposes of an economic blockade having an impact on neutrals, it is assumed that the belligerent would resort to the use of violence against neutrals if such conduct were necessary in order to overcome the enemy. The law thus protects those neutrals by keeping coercion within the permissible limits established.'[45]

The permissive or violent nature of blockade deserves special comment. This *historical* aspect of blockade is frequently overlooked by modern commentators when assessing attacks on seaborne commerce; yet, it is precisely from this historical aspect of blockade that the traditional legitimacy of naval economic warfare, within certain well-defined and accepted limits, flows. Belligerent as well as neutral states have long recognized and accepted the destructive and coercive effects of blockade, even as applied to nonconforming third country merchant vessels. Belligerent maritime trade is today no less immune from these coercive effects, either as a result of blockade or some other *alternative* contemporary naval tactic – such as a discriminate, long-range surface-, subsurface-, or air-launched missile attack – designed to achieve the legitimate destruction of enemy economic relations of substantial military importance.

The issue of balance in contemporary practice is enormous. The economic activity of a belligerent vital to its war-fighting/-sustaining effort, almost without qualification, is an object of substantial military importance. This historic axiom remains true today. The belligerent mechanisms traditionally directed against such economic objects – visit and search and blockade – are now, however, largely ineffective, except in the extraordinary circumstance where a belligerent enjoys both air and naval superiority. Developments in military technology have provided belligerents with an array of platforms and weapons increasingly more lethal, sophisticated, and efficient than predecessor versions. Significant among these are high-performance jet aircraft, integrated air defense systems, and long-range missiles with over-the-horizon and beyond-visual-range remote guidance targeting systems. These new systems are shield and sword, enhancing both defensive and striking force capabilities, for belligerent forces. The increased accuracy and range of modern 'smart' or precision-guided missiles, coupled with the enhanced detection capability – even at significant 'stand-off' distances – of sophisticated electronic tracking systems, render visit and search or blockade tactically unsound for most naval commanders today. At the same time, they

---

45. Baxter, R.R., "The Definition of War", 16 *Rev. Egypt de Droit Int.* (1960), p. 10, quoted in Fenrick, *loc.cit.* (note 14), p. 20.

also increase the tactical options available to those commanders to interdict and target enemy commerce of military value.[46]

Professor Richard J. Grunawalt of the U.S. Naval War College addresses the 'pressure' that technology has placed on the traditional law of neutrality, where the accommodation of competing interests is crucial:

> 'What this technological explosion has done with respect to the law of neutrality is to put a great deal of pressure on the two principle mechanisms wherein belligerents can interdict the flow of contraband in neutral bottoms. With respect to the first, that of visit and search, it is very difficult to envision an effective visit and search conducted by aircraft or by submarine. The concept just doesn't lend itself to that kind of situation. A belligerent lacking surface capability but possessing air or subsurface superiority is going to seek to interdict the flow of contraband of its enemy. The law is going to have to accommodate the balance. In an age of high-performance aircraft and guided missiles, the second traditional mechanism, that of the close-in blockade maintained by surface ships, may also be impossible to maintain.'[47]

It is futile in such situations to tell the commander that effective tactical options are unavailable, because they fail to comport with the approved mechanisms of traditional law. It is similarly futile to suggest that the economic activity of substantial military importance to an enemy is 'off limits', since traditional surface operations to interdict it are no longer tactically sound. In neither instance is the commander likely to listen or disregard the tactically oriented 'decision matrix' by which he will guide the operations of his force.[48] In the end, targeting standards for merchant vessels which do not accommodate the tactical requirements of today's commander will fail to achieve either acceptance or legitimacy. In recognition of this, included among the considerations in the analytical model used below to assess targeting criteria is the degree to which they permit tactical flexibility and the effective use of otherwise legitimate weapons, *i.e.*, the ability of a commander to employ those means and methods against a military object most appropriate to the operational situation. It must be remembered, however, that the *overall* rulemaking value of proffered targeting criteria will *also* depend upon the degree to which those criteria satisfy *humanitarian* considerations.[49]

The narrowly defined or circumscribed war/exclusion zone is an example of an emerging device in the law of naval armed conflict that attempts to balance traditional humanitarian (neutral) considerations against contemporary operational (belligerent) considerations. As a criterion for the targeting of merchant vessels, this device *fails* to

---

46. See Robertson, H.B. Jr., "New Technologies and Armed Conflicts at Sea", 14 *Syracuse J. Int'l L. & Com.* (1988), pp. 698-725; Service, J. VADM USN (Ret.), *loc.cit.* (note 3) (including commentary by VADM Doyle); and Levie, *loc.cit.* (note 36).

47. Grunawalt, *loc.cit.* (note 19), p. 307.

48. Service, *loc.cit.* (note 3). Compare Figure 4 of the text, *infra*. VADM Service properly acknowledges, however, that no U.S. military commander 'would reject, out of hand, any ostensible requirement of international law when structuring his forces and tactics'. *Idem*.

49. Service, *idem*.

satisfy important humanitarian considerations because it neither conserves values, shortens the conflict, nor promotes target discrimination.

4   *Principles of the law of armed conflict*

The right of a belligerent to use force against an enemy is not unlimited. The law of armed conflict embraces five general principles of a humanitarian nature. Collectively, these principles constitute minimum controls over the authority of a belligerent to otherwise attack enemy targets. In targeting theory, they also represent a final limitation upon the set of generally identified objects of legitimate attack. These principles are:

a   The principle of distinction or discrimination

Only combatants and legitimate military objectives may be attacked. Civilians, noncombatants, and protected objects may not be deliberately or directly targeted. In the maritime context, this extends to protected naval vessels such as hospital ships, cartel ships, and small coastal fishing craft used for their intended purposes. At all times, noncombatants and civilian objects must be distinguished from combatants and legitimate military objectives. This principle, restated as a requirement for target discrimination, is one of two key humanitarian considerations used in the analytical model below to assess the rulemaking value of various targeting criteria. It is satisfied by the establishment of operationally sound procedures for target verification. Compliance with these procedures, where feasible, helps to ensure that only those objects the destruction of which, under the circumstances, constitute a definite military advantage are actually attacked.

b   The principle of necessity

Force, not otherwise forbidden by the principle of discrimination, may only be used as required to achieve legitimate military objectives. These objectives may be either narrowly or broadly defined, depending on the nature and scope of the armed conflict. Where broadly defined, in the absence of authoritative and effective international action, they are properly decided at the governmental level. This principle debunks the commonly held notion that, given so-called 'unique' circumstances of combat, absolutely any militarily expedient or convenient force is justified. The permissible scope and duration of military operations may not exceed what is required in light of the legitimate military objectives of the particular combat engagement and conflict as a whole. Given such objectives, however, the principle of necessity *favors and encourages* a use of military force that is overwhelming, lethal, swift, *and* efficient – in short, that *comports* with the principles of warfare. Further, in a large scale or protracted military campaign (war), these objectives are far broader in reach (extending, *at a minimum*, to the destruction of the enemy's 'offensive' military capability) than the restrictive grounds (defend/deter against the threat of imminent or actual armed attack) authorized as an exercise of peacetime self-defence under Article 51 of the United Nations Charter.

c   The principle of proportionality

The resulting injury, death, and destruction to noncombatants and civilian objects from the use of otherwise legitimate force may not be disproportionate to the value of the military objective against which force is directed. Implicit in this principle is the recognition that, in the course of a legitimate use of force, noncombatants and civilian objects inevitably will suffer injury, death, and destruction. The concept of collateral damage and incidental injury is an alternative statement of this principle.

d   The principle of humanity

The infliction of civilian suffering and destruction that is not otherwise authorized (by the principle of proportionality) *and* beyond what in fact is operationally required (unavoidable) to achieve a legitimate military objective is prohibited. This principle imposes an affirmative obligation to undertake measures, reasonable under the circumstances, to *minimize* collateral damage and incidental injury. It requires that the collateral damage and incidental injury permitted by the principle of proportionality be kept to the *absolute minimum possible* in light of available military capabilities, *but without* undue risk to force security and mission accomplishment. Pursuant to this principle, prior to attacking certain types of nonconforming merchant vessels (those engaged in enemy trade of substantial military importance), belligerent naval forces with the capability to do so, and presented with circumstances which make it both operationally feasible and tactically sound, must first (if surface) attempt visit and search or (if air) make every *reasonable* effort to verify *and then divert* the vessel.[50] In short, because of the generally civilian character of these merchant vessels, unlike other military objects during armed conflict, they become subject to attack only as a *last resort.* This principle, like that of necessity, will influence the operational planning process, decisions about tactics, weapon selection, and weapon-release criteria. Coupled with the principles of necessity and proportionality, it is restated as a requirement to preserve humanitarian values and shorten the conflict (through the effective *and* efficient use of military force). This requirement constitutes the other key humanitarian consideration used to assess a proffered targeting criterion.

e   The principle of honorable conduct

The misuse of protected symbols and objects (such as the Red Cross/Red Crescent), as well as medical facilities, religious shrines, and historical/cultural landmarks, is forbidden. Under no circumstances may these protected symbols and objects deliberately be employed to shield, camouflage, or disguise legitimate military objects.

---

50. See, *e.g.*, *Commander's Handbook, op.cit.* (note 17), § 8.4 (providing for the possibility of surrender to military aircraft). In recognition of the impact of technology on the customary law of naval warfare, the *Commander's Handbook* properly identifies targeting rules for enemy merchant vessels based on the operational characteristics and limitations of the targeting platform; *i.e.*, whether surface, air, or subsurface.

Regrettably, this has been a favorite practice among militarily inferior powers who use it, sometimes effectively, to secure a propaganda, tactical, or strategic advantage. Such conduct constitutes a grave breach of the international humanitarian law of armed conflict *by the perpetrator*. Shielded objects which are otherwise legitimate military objectives, however, remain so *and may lawfully be attacked* consistent with basic targeting considerations and principles of the law of armed conflict.

B   The principle of limitation in targeting theory

Each of the four basic considerations described above must be taken into account in determining whether an object generally, or, in the instant case, merchant vessels, may legitimately be attacked. It is not enough merely to conclude that a given object is performing a function of substantial military value and is thereby subject to attack as a military objective; conclusions are further required that the operative targeting rule reflects a balance of neutral and belligerent interests and that the attack, considered as a whole, conforms to humanitarian principles in the law of armed conflict. With the exception of objects subjected to attack under the doctrine of reprisal, application of a functional targeting criterion defines the set of all possible objects of legitimate attack. Each of the other basic considerations detailed limits this broadly defined set. These other considerations impose additional targeting requirements, each of which generally identifies a fully *inclusive subset* of objects of legitimate attack. These subsets of objects are embraced within the larger set of all possible objects of legitimate attack, broadly defined by application of a functional targeting criterion. The restrictive and definitional nature of these basic considerations, as well as the relationship among them, discloses in targeting theory what may be termed a principle of limitation. This principle of limitation is depicted by the diagram in Figure 2, above.

The principle of limitation also compensates for a possible serious deficiency in functional targeting theory. Functional targeting theory, unlike the superordinate, normative hierarchy of classical targeting theory, lacks the high degree of structure inherent in the latter approach. This relative lack of structure results in a corresponding lack of predictability at the level of application. The high degree of legal predictability associated with classical targeting theory also brings with it a significant disadvantage: normative rigidity or inflexibility. At the crux of the failure of traditional law in contemporary practice, however, is its inflexible response to rapidly changing modalities of warfare. The goal, then, is to identify a legal structure that *assures* predictability at *some* level, but otherwise preserves flexibility. A functional targeting theory achieves this with the principle of limitation. That principle defines what may be termed minimum, baseline standards of conduct and protections in the law of armed conflict. At this baseline or normative level, therefore, predictability and structure are preserved; beyond such baseline standards, but within the *practical* considerations of a functional targeting theory, flexibility is dominant.

V   ASSESSING THE RULEMAKING VALUE OF TARGETING CRITERIA

To accommodate or balance their respective interests, neutrals and belligerents have long sought to achieve workable mechanisms that alternatively legitimize, as circumstances warrant, the destruction *or* protected status of maritime commerce. Targeting standards or criteria for merchant vessels must likewise be assessed for how well they balance these competing objectives. A multiple attribute analytical model that evaluates targeting criteria based on the degree to which each satisfies significant operational and humanitarian considerations is used for this purpose.

A   **Analytical model**

1   *Composition*

Figure 4, on page 180, presents an assessment of thirteen targeting criteria for merchant vessels that directly links the rulemaking value of each listed criterion to eight operational and humanitarian considerations. Considerations 1 through 5 are operational in nature; 6 and 7 of a humanitarian nature; and 8, the penultimate consideration, refers to the required balance of competing interests and considerations. These eight considerations are also reflective of those factors used by states, in their role as individual decisionmakers, to appraise virtually any affirmative third state targeting claim in the customary lawmaking process. Each criterion is explicitly compared and evaluated for its relative rulemaking value. The relative rulemaking value of the criteria examined, in turn, is based on the comparative effectiveness of each to 'substantially' or 'partially' or 'minimally' satisfy the stated considerations.

The thirteen listed targeting criteria are derived from several sources. Some relate to traditional legal concepts and requirements (criterion 9, 10, and 12 are examples of these). A number are derived from the targeting standards, state practices, legal actions, and commentaries relating to the 1936 London Protocol (criterion 2, 3, 4, 7, and 10 fall into this category). Still others relate to possible emerging customary law (such as criterion 8, location within an exclusion zone). At least three (criterion 8, 9, and 10) do not so much constitute targeting *standards* as they do *methods* of naval warfare. Several (criterion 2, 6, 8, and 11), finally, suggest more about a vessel's *status* than any particular unprotected function. While some of these criteria may be *combined* in practice to form a single targeting standard, all but one are evaluated on an independent basis here. Where criteria are combined, the resulting targeting standard may also be evaluated in light of the analytical targeting model described. Combined targeting criteria will typically receive a higher overall rating of effectiveness than those judged separately. If combined, for example, criterion 2 (armed) and 11 (enemy flag vessel) would produce a somewhat improved evaluation of effectiveness than is now reflected at Figure 4 for either standard alone. Criterion 5 is an example of a combined targeting standard.

Criterion 1 and 5, which are comprehensive targeting criteria, warrant special comment. Criterion 1 is a restatement of the functional targeting criterion that identifies

ASSESSMENT OF TARGETING CRITERIA
FOR MERCHANT VESSELS

TARGETING CRITERION/LIMITATION \ OPERATIONAL/HUMANITARIAN CONSIDERATION	1. PERMITS ATTACK ON FULL SPECTRUM OF OBJECTS OF DEFINITE MILITARY VALUE (MIL. OBJ.)	2. PERMITS EFFECTIVE USE OF LEGITIMATE WEAPONS	3. PERMITS TACTICAL FLEXIBILITY/CHOICE OF MEANS/METHODS	4. PRESERVES FORCE SECURITY	5. PERMITS MISSION ACCOMPLISHMENT	6. PRESERVES HUM. VALUES/SHORTENS CONFLICT	7. FOSTERS TARGET DISCRIMINATION (OBJECTIVE-BASED)	8. ACHIEVES/BALANCE OF INTERESTS
1. MAKES SUBST. CONTRIB. TO MIL. CAPABILITY (FUNCTION PERFORMED)	+	+	+	+	+	0	0	0
2. ARMED (NONINTERNAL DEFENSE)	0	0	0	0	0	+	+	0
3. INTEGRATED INTO INTEL NETWORK	0	0	0	0	0	0	0	0
4. ACTS UNDER MIL. ORDER/DIRECTLY SUPPORTS MIL OPS, E.G., TROOP/SUPPLY SHIP (DE FACTO AUX.)	0	0	0	0	0	+	+	0
5. "INTEGRATED INTO WAR EFFORT"/CONTRIB. TO MIL. CAP. AND V&S/VID NOT "FEASIBLE"	+	+	+	+	+	+	+	+
6. ACTS UNDER ENEMY CONTROL (AQUIRES ENEMY CHARACTER)	0	0	0	0	0	−	−	−
7. OPERATES UNDER ENEMY CONVOY	0	0	0	0	0	0	0	0
8. LOCATED W/N EXCLUSION ZONE	0	0	0	0	0	−	−	−
9. BREACHES BLOCKADE AND REFUSES TO STOP	−	−	−	−	−	0	+	0
10. RESISTS VISIT AND SEARCH/REFUSES TO STOP	−	−	−	−	−	0	+	0
11. POSSESSES FORMAL ENEMY STATUS (FLAG VESSEL)	0	0	0	0	0	−	−	−
12. FORMALLY DESIGNATED ENEMY AUXILIARY	0	0	0	0	0	+	+	0
13. REPRISAL	−	−	−	−	−	−	−	−

KEY:
'+': CRITERION SUBSTANTIALLY SATISFIES CONSIDERATION
'0': CRITERION PARTIALLY SATISFIES CONSIDERATION
'-': CRITERION MINIMALLY SATISFIES CONSIDERATION

Figure 4

the set of all possible objects of legitimate attack. It is equivalent to the first prong of the standard of military objective which, as presented above, is a sufficiently broad understanding of Article 52(2) of Additional Protocol I to account for the unique characteristics of armed conflict at sea. Criterion 5 is a *refinement* of criterion 1, with the additional constraint to undertake visit and search/visual identification (*i.e.*, target verification) where 'feasible'. The abbreviation 'VID' (in criterion 5) denotes the further requirement to verify (target) identity, whether visually or through other highly reliable means. This criterion is adapted from the U.S. Navy's general targeting standard for surface-based attacks on enemy merchant vessels detailed in *The Commander's Handbook on the Law of Naval Operations*.[51]

2   Approach

The analytical model depicted at Figure 4 is inherently imprecise and is not intended to produce a definitive or authoritative appraisal of any given criterion. Indeed, such a result would be contrary to the interpretive nature of the underlying theory. At this preliminary stage, the analytical *approach* reflected by the model is of *more* significance than the individual assessments drawn from it. That approach is decidedly *not* an inquiry into 'right' and 'wrong', but rather an attempt to *identify* the characteristics of an effective targeting rule. Figure 4 is also, therefore, not a legal checklist or substitute for the exercise of critical judgment.

---

51. *Commander's Handbook, op.cit.* (note 17), § 8.2.2.2 at note 52. Compliance with the 1936 London Protocol is required unless this 'would, under the circumstances of the specific encounter, subject the surface warship to imminent danger or would otherwise preclude mission accomplishment'. *Ibidem.* See also note 9 and 50 *supra* and the accompanying text. In essence, this criterion represents the first formal, affirmative state claim of a functional targeting standard for *all enemy* merchant vessels. As a balanced but realistic *alternative* to the doctrine of military or naval auxiliary, it is a vast improvement over conventional targeting rules. In this author's view, however, it remains deficient because it is unduly *restrictive*. This same functional standard is only *indirectly* applied to neutral or third country merchant vessels engaged in *like* nonconforming practices. The doctrine of acquired enemy character is relied upon to make this indirect link; yet, as shown here, that doctrine is *also* too limited when evaluated against the operational, as well as humanitarian, considerations of a pure functional targeting theory. Compare Robertson, *op.cit.* (note 3); and Mallison, *op.cit.* (note 7), p. 123 (neither directly provides for attacks upon nonconforming 'neutral' merchant vessels). Fenrick, however, explicitly urges the adoption of this targeting standard for neutral *and* enemy merchant vessels. *Loc.cit.* (note 5), pp. 62-63 and 72-73. The criterion is also *misleading*. Text at notes 33 and 34 *supra*. Its use of the term 'integration', for example, suggests a much *narrower* definition of military objective than is otherwise required to satisfy a functional targeting standard. These deficiencies notwithstanding, the targeting standards established in the *Commander's Handbook* will have significant impact in defining the law of naval warfare. Other examples of combined targeting criteria for merchant vessels include the Bochum Draft Results, *loc.cit.* (note 37), §§ D and E; and those of the Canadian, Australian, and French naval forces detailed in Fenrick, *loc.cit.* (note 5), pp. 55-59. Of considerable significance is the fact that *all* of these manuals and the Bochum Draft Results, like the *Commander's Handbook*, establish targeting standards for merchant vessels which incorporate important aspects of a functional targeting theory. On the important role played by military manuals in the customary lawmaking process, see Reisman & Lietzue, "Moving International Law from Theory to Practice: The Role of Military Manuals in Effectuating the Law of Armed Conflict", in: Robertson (ed.), *op.cit.* (note 18).

Its use suggests that the legitimacy or rulemaking value of a proffered targeting standard is, ultimately, a *function* of the degree to which the given standard satisfies *all* of the operational and humanitarian considerations essential to an effective balance of competing neutral and belligerent interests. This functional analysis of targeting rules represents a fundamental departure from the *strictly* normative-based evaluative process of the traditional law of naval warfare. It is of little consequence at this juncture, therefore, that individual observers may differ on their respective assessments about how well a particular criterion satisfies the stated considerations. That an analytical or functional approach is taken up at all, regardless of the preliminary result, constitutes an important philosophical milestone with profound implications for the emerging law of armed conflict at sea.

3   *Limitations*

Several limitations, principally flowing from the lack of precision in measuring the comparative importance among the listed operational and humanitarian considerations, surround the analytical model adopted.

a   No weighting of individual considerations

Individual considerations are all of equal weight. Thus, consideration 1 'counts' as much as any other consideration. In addition, although there are five operational considerations to only two humanitarian considerations, both groups of considerations *equally influence* the ultimate rulemaking value of a given targeting criterion. Within each of these groups, however, two considerations (1 and 6) 'control' or embrace the evaluations assigned to the other considerations in their respective groups.

b   No ranking of equivalent targeting criteria

Several groupings of the listed targeting criteria (*e.g.*, criterion 3, 4, 7, and 12; as well as 9 and 10; and 2, 6, 8, and 11) are evaluated 'equally' on Figure 4. This occurs, since only three general evaluative standards are used to describe the degree to which a criterion satisfies the listed considerations. The lack of intermediate evaluative categories prevents a more precise discrimination among similarly evaluated targeting criteria.

c   Reliance upon subjective interpretive or evaluative standards

Each criterion is evaluated for the degree to which it either 'substantially' ('+') or 'partially' ('o') or 'minimally' ('-') satisfies the considerations listed. These standards are inherently subjective in nature. To minimize this subjective component, an established interpretation for each was adopted and then applied uniformly to all criteria and considerations. These established interpretive standards or 'rules' are discussed in the section below.

4   *Interpretive standards*

a   Operational considerations

Consideration 1 is the point of reference for all other operational considerations. Consideration 1, as the equivalent of the definition of military objective and the set of all possible objects of legitimate attack under a functional targeting theory, is the 'lead' operational consideration. Thus, a '+', or 'o', or '-' assigned to consideration 1 will result in the same respective evaluation for all of the other operational considerations. This interpretive standard or rule is simply stated as:

> '*Rule*: the degree to which a targeting criterion satisfies considerations 2, 3, 4, and 5 is *equal* to the degree to which it satisfies consideration 1.'

Some of the targeting criteria implicitly establish *multiple* targeting conditions which artificially *restrict* the set of objects otherwise subject to legitimate attack. These criteria are evaluated as 'minimally' ('-') satisfying operational considerations. Breaching blockade as a targeting criterion, for example, requires: proper declaration of an imminent blockade, its establishment, the surface capability necessary to effectively enforce that blockade, and its breach – coupled with a refusal to stop by the noncomplying vessel – all of which are *conditions precedent* to attack upon that vessel. Observance of all of these conditions would permit the targeting of only a small portion of those merchant vessels comprising the entire set of legitimate military targets. Criteria which limit the set of objects of legitimate attack to the *single* targeting condition described by a given targeting criterion are only slightly better. Such targeting standards, like criterion 11 (enemy flag vessel), are evaluated as 'partially' ('o') satisfying the listed operational considerations. Thus, only criterion 1 and 5, which are *comprehensive* functional targeting standards, 'substantially' ('+') satisfy consideration 1 and the other operational considerations.

b   Humanitarian considerations

Similar interpretive rules are established to assess the degree to which the stated criterion either substantially, partially, or minimally satisfies humanitarian considerations. As the 'lead' humanitarian consideration, for example, consideration 6 embraces consideration 7.

> '*Rule*: the degree to which a criterion is evaluated as satisfying consideration 6 may be *no greater* than the degree to which it is evaluated as satisfying consideration 7.'

The degree to which consideration 7 ('fosters target discrimination') is satisfied is based on whether: (1) protected objects are excluded from possible attack; (2) the distinction between protected and unprotected vessels rests upon discernible or objectively based standards and factors (whether these factors are determined at the on-scene or governmental level); *and* (3) visit and search or highly reliable means of target verification, if operationally feasible and not incompatible with the characteristics of the target vessel (as, for example, it would be if integrated into the enemy's intelligence network), are required prior to attack. The question of degree to which consideration 6 ('preserves humanitarian (normative) values/shortens conflict') is satisfied is determined *in part* by: (1) the appraisal assigned to consideration 7, per the stated rule; *plus* (2) the degree to which use of the criterion will likely curtail or prolong the conflict; and (3) whether the criterion complies with recognized baseline, or minimum normative, standards in the law of armed conflict at sea. The degree to which various targeting criteria 'shorten the conflict' is the 'bridge' between operational and humanitarian considerations. Evaluation of this aspect of consideration 7 depends mainly upon how well consideration 1 is satisfied. Satisfaction of consideration 1, coupled with satisfaction of consideration 7, hastens war-termination and, thus, minimizes human suffering and destruction.[52] Criterion 5, which incorporates minimal humanitarian safeguards is, therefore, superior to criterion 1 (the other comprehensive functional targeting standard) in satisfying considerations 6 and 7.

c   Balance of interests

The degree to which a targeting criterion achieves a balance of interests, *i.e.*, satisfies consideration 8, is a function of the evaluative assessments assigned to considerations 1 and 6.

> '*Rule*: the degree to which a targeting criterion satisfies consideration 8 may be *no greater* than the degree to which it satisfies *either* consideration 1 or 6.'

B   **Appraisal**

Application of the foregoing interpretive standards indicates that criterion 5 is the 'best' targeting criterion. This criterion achieves the most effective balance of both operational and humanitarian considerations and, therefore, has the greatest potential for rulemaking value in the law of naval armed conflict. It is 'deficient' only to the extent that it fails to foster target discrimination that is based on *strictly* objective factors. The determination that a merchant vessel is 'integrated into the war effort' or 'substantially contributes' to enemy military capability is a matter *beyond* the ability and authority of most on-scene commanders to make; these questions must be resolved

---

52. Sections IV.A.4.b and d; and V.A.4.a *supra* pertain. It is for this reason that criterion 9 (breaches blockade) and 10 (resists visit and search) 'partially' satisfy consideration 6, although each 'substantially' satisfies consideration 7. These criteria, because of their multiple targeting conditions, limit the loss of protected status to all but a very small portion of the set of merchant vessels otherwise subject to legitimate attack in a functional targeting theory. The likelihood of a protracted conflict, therefore, is increased. The 'fourth objective' of VADM Service's 'decision matrix' for the commander is pertinent: '... Interdiction of enemy *economic* resupply efforts [is] a viable means of shortening the conflict and minimizing damage on both sides.' Service, *loc.cit.* (note 3) (emphasis added).

at the governmental level and necessarily involve issues of policy and judgment.[53] In the end, however, examination of these issues should yield a set of discernible factors or standards appropriate to the combat environment and conflict as a whole. Where such standards are not forthcoming, a corresponding evaluation of the targeting criterion that is less satisfactory must result. In contrast to criterion 5, the rulemaking value of criterion 2 (armed), 6/11 (operating under state control), 8 (location within an exclusive zone), and 13 (reprisal) are relatively limited, since each only 'minimally' satisfies the humanitarian considerations.

VI   IRAQI TANKER ATTACKS AND MILITARY OBJECTIVE

The threshold issue raised by the Iraqi tanker attacks is whether, under the circumstances of the Iran-Iraq war, *enemy* oil tankers were legitimate objects of attack. A follow-on issue is whether *third country* tankers, which were *similarly* integrated into the Irani oil export system, *also* represented legitimate objects of attack. Figure 5, on page 186, provides a rough depiction of Irani and Iraqi attacks on shipping during the tanker war.[54]

A   General description of vessels attacked[55]

Iraq targeted merchant vessels performing one of two principal functions. Both functions were performed by oil tankers; one group of tankers was engaged strictly in the export of oil from Iran. This is significant, since the revenues that Iran earned from oil exports fueled virtually every aspect of its war with Iraq. For export of its oil, Iran depended almost exclusively upon third country Persian Gulf tanker trade. These third country export tankers traveled to or from the Irani oil terminal at Kharg Island or the oil transfer facilities at Sirri, Lavan, or Larak Islands.

Another group of tankers targeted by Iraq was carrying oil from the Kharg Island oil terminal in the northern part of the Gulf to the oil transfer facilities at Sirri, Lavan, or Larak Islands in the south. These third country *and* Irani-flag *shuttle* tankers were not engaged in oil export per se, but did facilitate that trade. Operating under Irani charter, they moved oil from Kharg Island, where the risk of Iraqi attack was greatest, to the oil transfer facilities near the Strait of Hormuz, where it was more difficult for Iraq to strike. Some of these shuttle tankers also sailed under convoy of regular Irani naval

---

53. See Robertson, *loc.cit.* (note 3) (similar assessment of the *Commander's Handbook* general targeting rule for nonconforming enemy merchant vessels, *op.cit.* (note 51) and accompanying text). Also see Fenrick, *loc.cit.* (note 14), p. 21, concerning the Canadian draft rules on targeting merchant vessels. He calls for the development of 'standards of reasonableness' (*idem*) and useable 'word descriptions' like criterion 5. Written comments presented at the Targeting Symposium, *op.cit.* (note 3).

54. Figure 5 is adapted from "Battle Lines in the Gulf: What Tankers Are Up Against", *The New York Times* (14 August 1988), p. A9.

55. Also see *supra* note 10 concerning attacks on shipping.

ATTACKS ON SHIPPING IN THE TANKER WAR

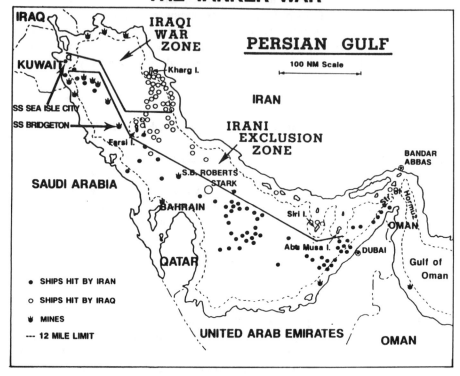

FIGURE 5. SOURCE: COPYRIGHT © THE NEW YORK TIMES COMPANY.

Figure 5

forces. By these measures, Iran minimized the amount of tanker traffic required to enter the Iraqi-proclaimed 'prohibited war exclusion zone' around Kharg Island.

B   Assessment as military objective

Such economic functions are embraced within the set of legitimate military objectives and, as outlined above, include the economic relations of a belligerent which substantially contribute to its war-fighting/-sustaining, or military, capability. The historical tension between the belligerent state goal to disrupt or destroy enemy economic relations and the neutral state interest to strictly limit such interference underscore considerations relating to the balance of those interests. Quite apart from theory, neutral and belligerent states have always *recognized and accepted*, in law and in practice, that *certain* belligerent economic activities possess definite military value.

Common to all of the tankers attacked by Iraq, because of their function as oil carriers, was their integration into the Irani oil export system – in the sense of making an effective contribution toward sustaining that system. This system was at the very foundation of Iran's national economy and was essential to maintaining its military capability. For all practical purposes, then, *any* tanker that supported the Irani oil export system, regardless of its character in the traditional sense, was treated by Iraq as a contraband-carrying 'enemy' merchant vessel. From the Iraqi viewpoint, this amounted to a comprehensive functional targeting criterion embracing the set of all possible objects of legitimate attack.

Captain Roach explains the treatment of these vessels as legitimate military *objects* in terms of a functional targeting standard:

> 'Iran finances almost all of its war effort from the sale of its oil. Iran thus sustains its war effort almost solely through the export of its oil. Under these circumstances, particularly in light of the long duration of this war, (...) Iraq is within its legal rights to attack this vital source of Iran's war-sustaining economy. (...) The tankers docking at Kharg can reasonably be assumed to be taking on Iranian oil for export, and such ships and their war-sustaining cargoes are legitimate objects of attack. Further, the ships carrying Iranian crude oil, whether by shuttle from Kharg to Lavan, Sirri or Larak [Island], or from Iranian terminals destined for overseas ports, are legitimate objects of attack by Iraqi forces.'[56]

---

56. Roach, *loc.cit.* (note 10). In accord Russo, *loc.cit.* (note 7), p. 389; Fenrick, *loc.cit.* (note 14), p. 21. 'One might suggest that the unconvoyed neutral tankers which transported the oil essential to the Iranian oil economy and were attacked by Iraq constituted legitimate military objectives.' *Idem.* Also Fenrick, *loc.cit.* (note 5), p. 63 (conclusion premised upon standard of 'incorporation into the war effort') and his written comments presented to the Targeting Symposium, *op.cit.* (note 3); and Peace, *loc.cit.* (note 10). Opposing this view are Bothe, this publication (*exports* of Irani oil not 'contraband' and only subject to interdiction as authorized by U.N. Security Council: 'Neutral tankers cannot be military objectives'); Kalshoven, oral comments at Targeting Symposium, *op.cit.* (note 3) (neutral *export* tankers are not military objectives); and C. Greenwood (direct third country export trade with belligerents protected), colloquium remarks. But see note 61 *infra*.

Now left to examine, within the framework of the analytical model and functional targeting theory described above, are the specific Iraqi tactics and targeting criteria (means and methods) employed against Iran's oil trade.

C   Tactical options and choice of weapons platform (means)

During periods of protracted armed conflict, disruption and termination of an enemy's vital economic relations are recognized as objects of substantial military value. This was no less the case in the war between Iran and Iraq as concerned their oil export trade. Issues may remain as to the scope, degree, and manner of permissible interference with this trade, but not with the *right* itself to interfere. As seen above, the traditional law of naval warfare sanctions a range of belligerent mechanisms – means and methods – specifically intended to secure that right. The issue raised concerning these accepted mechanisms in the context of the tanker war is whether, under the prevailing circumstances, they were viable tactical options for Iraq, *i.e.*, operationally feasible.

Within the context of a functional targeting theory, these 'accepted' mechanisms are treated as proffered targeting criteria (criterion 9 and 10). As such, their comparative rulemaking value is partly judged by how well each satisfies important operational considerations. Included among these evaluative considerations is whether, in applying the proffered criterion, the *full* spectrum of objects of definite military value are subject to attack (consideration 1).

Objects of definite military value, including the economic relations of an enemy which effectively and substantially contribute to its military capability, consequently take *precedence* over the mechanisms traditionally authorized to reach those objects. For that reason, an otherwise legitimate military objective is not 'off limits' and immune from attack because, under the circumstances, none of the accepted means and methods are operationally feasible. A legitimate military objective, in short, remains so *regardless* of the ability of traditional or established mechanisms to accomplish it. Where such established means and methods or other targeting standards under consideration are inadequate, these must give way – not the object of military value. Tactical flexibility, therefore, is an important operational consideration in the analytical model developed to assess the rulemaking value of proffered targeting criteria. As previously noted, however, this is not merely a case of the ends justifying the means. The rulemaking value *and* legitimacy of any proffered targeting criterion ultimately depend on the degree to which that criterion satisfies operational *as well as* humanitarian considerations. A targeting standard that satisfies one set of considerations at the expense of the other is rejected under the analytical legal theory of naval targeting presented here. Indeed, targeting criteria which *contravene* recognized normative or baseline standards – *regardless* of even the very high degree to which they may satisfy operational considerations – are judged to only *minimally* satisfy humanitarian considerations and, therefore, also *fail* to achieve a balance of neutral/belligerent interests.

Iraq lacked either a surface or subsurface capability. That Iraq chose to disrupt Iran's oil export system by conducting air strikes against Irani-flag and third country oil tankers supporting that system, therefore, was no accident. Doing so was Iraq's most effective means of attack against Iran's economic base and only viable tactical option to that end. As Iraq lacked a credible surface capability, traditional mechanisms to thwart maritime belligerent trade – blockade, visit and search, contraband lists – afforded Iraq no operational relief. Were Iraq to have adhered strictly to these traditional mandates, a vital aspect of Iran's oil export system would effectively have been beyond Iraqi reach. Its reward for such legal traditionalism would have been to watch helplessly as third country and Irani-flag tankers openly engaged in enemy trade of definite military value, free from the risk of belligerent interference of even the slightest degree. Under these circumstances, Iraq's use of its air force as *the means* by which to attack military objectives associated with the Irani oil export system was justified.[57]

In 1956, Professor Julius Stone accurately predicted how states which were not naval powers, like Iraq, would react to the operational predicament created for them by the constraints of the London Protocol. Reflecting upon the implications of that reaction for the law of naval warfare, he wrote:

> '[I]t is also quite idle for Powers whose naval supremacy in surface craft enables them to pursue the aim of annihilating the enemy's seaborne commerce without 'sink at sight' warfare, to expect that states which cannot aspire to such supremacy will refrain from seeking to annihilate that commerce by such naval means available to them as submarines, aircraft and mines. To refuse to face this will save neither life nor ship in any future war; and it will also forestall the growth of real rules for the mitigation of suffering under modern conditions.'[58]

It is on this score as well that recent attempts to formulate a comprehensive doctrinal statement concerning the treatment of merchant vessels during armed conflict fall short.[59] The outcome of these efforts is a proposal that reaffirms, *without exception*, a belligerent requirement to comply with the terms of the London Protocol before targeting enemy or third country merchant vessels transporting 'contraband' other than 'military materials'. While not explicitly excluding such contraband-laden merchant vessels from the definition of military objective,[60] this proposal nonetheless effectively puts these vessels beyond the reach of *every* belligerent state not capable of securing air and naval superiority during armed conflict. In this way, it perpetuates the illusory

---

57. See Van Hegelsom, *loc.cit.* (note 9), p. 55 (no separate legal constraints required for the conduct of air operations in the law of naval warfare); and Russo, *loc.cit.* (note 7), pp. 391-392.

58. Stone, *op.cit.* (note 26), pp. 606-607. In accord Lowe, *loc.cit.* (note 18), p. 49 (unpublished comments); and Service, *loc.cit.* (note 3). 'If I were to go to war today (...), I would recommend to my superiors tactics that would be inherently at odds with the London Protocol. Not insignificantly, however, (...) those tactics would be consonant with the original purpose of the Protocol – to minimize the effects of war.' *Idem.*

59. See Bochum Draft Results, *loc.cit.* (note 37), §§ A, D, and E.

60. But see Kalshoven, *loc.cit.* (note 37) and accompanying text. Noteworthy in this regard is that the Bochum Draft Results accept, without modification or special understanding, the Article 52(2) (of Additional Protocol I) definition of military objective. *Ibidem*, § A.

distinction between merchant vessels admittedly 'carrying contraband' and those which 'make an effective contribution to military action'. It further acts to limit the effectiveness of otherwise legitimate means of naval warfare (subsurface and air forces). The proposal also purports to differentiate between *equally* nonconforming enemy and neutral merchant vessels. It extends to nonconforming neutral merchant vessels the benefit of strict targeting standards denied to similarly nonconforming enemy merchant vessels.[61] Such recent formulations are fundamentally *regressive* in approach, ignoring the lessons of past wars, the full spectrum of belligerent interests during naval warfare, the economic aspect of the doctrine of military objective, and the transformation in military technology over the last half century. Although indicative of a strong humanitarian impulse, a doctrine of this sort regrettably offers little promise of widespread acceptance or adherence.[62]

D   Target identification and weapons-release criteria (method)[63]

Iraqi tanker attacks were carried out with shore-based F-1 Mirage aircraft which served as launching platforms for the Iraqi weapon of choice against tankers, the air-to-surface Exocet missile. When searching for targets at the southern edge of the Gulf near the Strait of Hormuz, Iraqi aircraft operated at the outer limits of their effective range. On such missions, Iraqi aircraft were also required to account for limited, but credible, Irani naval air defenses based at naval port and military air facilities near Bandar Abbas. These factors made it unfeasible for Iraqi aircraft operating in the southern Gulf to loiter or take efforts to verify the identity of prospective targets. It appears, however, that similar operational limitations did not prevail in the northern Gulf around Kharg Island.

Iraq intended to attack all merchant vessels directly or indirectly engaged in activity that furthered the export of Irani oil. This included tankers carrying oil for shuttle or export, and applied regardless of their status as Irani-flag vessels or the degree of

---

61. See Roach, written comments on Van Hegelsom introductory report to the Toulon Round Table, *loc.cit.* (note 9). The Bochum Draft Results appear designed to all but assure *protected status* for nonconforming, third country merchant vessels engaged in virtually any *direct belligerent* commercial trade, whether import *or* export, that substantially contributes to enemy military capability. This is a startling conclusion given the shift in the balance of neutral/belligerent interests occasioned by modern developments in military technology. See text following notes 41 and 42 *supra*. When assessed against the analytical model at Figure 4 (see criterion 7), therefore, the Bochum targeting standard of 'effective contribution to military action (*e.g.*, carrying military materials)' is judged as no better than *partially* satisfying key operational and humanitarian considerations. The author also rejects the distinction made by some commentators between third country maritime import versus export trade with belligerents. Where such trade – import or export – has the same functional effect in sustaining a belligerent's military capability, this distinction is unjustified. It must also be remembered that *either* form of trade would be subject to attack for breach of a traditional blockade. See note 56 *supra*. Although the distinction between import and export trade is not supported on *functional* grounds, it is entirely conceivable for third country states to place a value of such significance on its maritime imports that the protection of this trade, from whatever source, rises to the level of a *normative* baseline standard the obervance of which is then *essential* to a balance of neutral/belligerent interests.
62. Compare Fenrick, *loc.cit.* (note 5), pp. 72-73, who recommended a more expansive targeting approach to merchant vessels than what was finally included in the Bochum Draft Results, *loc.cit.* (note 37).
63. *Supra* note 10.

control exercised over them by Iran. Iraq identified merchant vessels as probable 'enemy' tankers and, therefore, targets, based on the application of two controlling presumptions. Each of these presumptions was tied to location within the Irani or Iraqi exclusion zones.[64]

Most Iraqi tanker attacks occurred within its 'prohibited war zones' along the far northern coast of Iran and around Kharg Island. With respect to the latter, the Iraqi Government warned that 'it will attack all vessels appearing within [that] zone' and, further, that 'all tankers docking at Kharg Island regardless of nationality are targets for the Iraqi air force'.[65] Iraq, in effect, sought to deny complete access to Kharg Island; it regarded third country vessels found there as the equivalent of a traditional blockade runner subject to immediate attack.

Other tankers were attacked by Iraq while operating between Kharg Island in the northern Gulf and the oil transfer facilities to the south at Sirri, Larak, and Lavan Islands. These vessels traveled along the Irani coast on a north-to-south track, within Irani territorial waters. A smaller number of tankers, loaded and in ballast, were attacked while traveling to or from the oil terminal at Kharg Island or the oil transfer facilities in the south. In the main, these other vessels were hit outside the Iraqi-declared war zones, but *inside* Irani-declared zones.

As a peculiar irony of the tanker war, Iran's exclusion zones provided Iraq with one of its most convenient and easily determined targeting indicators. Iran established 'guidelines for navigational safety' which required ships not destined for Irani ports to remain outside most of the eastern side of the Gulf. Iran sought in this way to exercise at least some limited control over the eastern portion of the Gulf. Location of a vessel inside this navigational safety or exclusion zone, therefore, readily translated for Iraq into the *presumption* that such vessels were supporting Iran's oil export system and, thereby, constituted appropriate enemy targets. Iran also declared a war zone encompassing its coastal waters that was of similar utility for Iraq.

As a consequence of these presumptions, Iran's targeting criterion for merchant vessels was largely *locational* in nature. Merchant vessels located inside the exclusion zones of either Iran or Iraq were targeted on that basis alone. As a targeting criterion, this only 'minimally' satisfies the humanitarian considerations reflected at Figure 4. By definition, it neither fosters nor requires target discrimination, because it fails to exclude the possibility of attacks upon protected objects; tends to *protract* rather than curtail the conflict; and, for like reasons, fails to conserve humanitarian values or achieve an effective balance of interests.[66]

64. Russo, *loc.cit.* (note 7), pp. 389-392; Roach, *loc.cit.* (note 10); and Goldie, L.F.E., "Armed Conflicts at Sea and Low Intensity Operations", 14 *Syracuse J. Int'l L. & Com.* (1988), pp. 625-628 (identifies use of these zones as 'logistical raiding strategies').

65. DMAHTC, Washington, D.C., 221600Z SEP 85, Subj: Special Warning No. 67 (Rebroadcast of Special Warning No. 67, 201235Z SEP 85).

66. Under a functional targeting theory, any legitimacy accorded the use of an exclusion zone during naval armed conflict must flow from the extent to which it serves as a *reliable indicator* of the military value of the merchant, or other, vessel operating within that zone. The military value of a vessel in this context is primarily a question of the *function performed* by the vessel in relation to the conflict, *not* where it happens to be located when targeted. Compare Fenrick, *loc.cit.* (note 44). Even in the case where an exclusion zone is a

The inability of Iraqi aircraft to loiter in the southern Gulf, when coupled with the use of a locational targeting criterion, led predictably to Iraqi weapons-release standards which did not require Iraqi aircraft to do everything feasible to visually, or through other highly reliable means, verify target identification (VID) prior to firing. Instead, Iraqi aircraft released missiles on surface contacts beyond visual range (BVR), using the location of those contacts as the principal *indicator* of their presumed 'enemy' or nonconforming character. Considering the operational constraints which *sometimes* confronted Iraq, this was a legitimate tactic (method of attack/target verification) in certain, very *limited* circumstances. It is unclear, however, why Iraq persisted in BVR targeting practices where VID standards appear to have been operationally feasible *and* appropriate, particularly given the nonmilitary character of the intended targets. In such instances, humanitarian considerations were only 'partially' or 'minimally' satisfied.

On several occasions, the use of BVR weapons-release criteria resulted in tragic targeting errors, the most significant of which was the death of thirty-seven officers and men aboard USS *Stark*.[67] That events of this kind can happen, however, is not sufficient reason to establish an inflexible rule proscribing BVR and electronically enhanced means of targeting. The legitimacy of particular targeting standards and weapons-release criteria cannot in every case or entirely be determined based on the sometimes errant results of those criteria when applied. Even carefully drawn weapons-release criteria, as well as presumptions of hostile, enemy, or nonconforming character, can produce unexpected and tragic results. This is an inherent consequence of armed conflict that is closely linked to the concept of collateral damage and incidental injury. Combat targeting does not occur in a controlled environment. The fog of war and friction of combat invariably complicates target prosecution, regardless of preset and redundant weapons-release requirements.

Consistent with considerations in targeting theory for the conservation of humanitarian values and the balance of neutral/belligerent interests, such 'complications' of war and the untoward results they often bring compel adoption of VID targeting procedures wherever operationally feasible. This parallels the requirement that surface combatants, where operationally feasible for them to do so, comply with the constraints of the London Protocol. It is on this count that serious concerns must be raised about the Iraqi targeting methods. At no point apparently, even in relatively benign operational environments, did Iraqi aircraft attempt to institute target verification procedures or to divert targeted merchant vessels prior to weapons release. For military aircraft, this is the rough equivalent of initiating a surface attack on nonconforming third country merchant vessels without first attempting visit and search, regardless of the feasibility for doing so.

---

reliable indicator of military value, however, the attacker is obliged, if feasible, to adopt humanitarian safeguards designed to minimize civilian damage and injury. This clearly was not the case with Iraq.

67. Regarding the issues of target identification raised by this event, see generally Peace and Roach, *loc.cit.* (note 10); Russo, *loc.cit.* (note 7), p. 392; and generally Van Hegelsom, *loc.cit.* (note 9). Fenrick, *loc.cit.* (note 14), p. 22 addresses the problem in terms of a 'technological imbalance (...) between the ability to kill at long range and the ability to identify who is being killed.'

E   CONCLUSION

The law of armed conflict at sea rests on the *mutual* accommodation of neutral inviolability *and* the belligerent *prerogative* to adopt means necessary to stop an enemy's economic relations. As economic activity which effectively and substantially contributed to its overall war-fighting/-sustaining effort, Iran's oil export system and the third country oil tankers supporting it were legitimate military objectives. Any belligerent may properly adopt those means and methods which, under the circumstances, are most effective against military objectives – like enemy commerce of substantial military importance – and not otherwise violative of the principles of the law of armed conflict (under a functional targeting theory, the principle of limitation). Consistent with this proposition, as well as the other operational considerations of a functional targeting theory, the Iraqi use of its air force to attack Iran's seaborne oil export system was a legitimate *means* for that purpose. The principle of limitation in functional targeting theory also dictates, however, that naval combatants and military aircraft do everything feasible, in light of the operational environment, to conduct visit and search, verify the identity of its intended targets, and minimize civilian destruction. To the extent that Iraq failed to observe these requirements, opting instead for the convenience of an *unqualified* locational targeting strategy, its naval targeting methods were clearly unlawful under traditional standards and likewise invalid when judged against the operational and humanitarian considerations of a functional or analytical targeting theory.[68]

68. *Special acknowledgement.* I did not arrive at this point on my effort alone. Many friends and associates helped along the way. By their insight and skill, they enlivened my words and thoughts. I am particularly grateful for the assistance of Ms. Claire Smith (composition and editing); Ms. Lynn Wilson (graphics); Major Scott Thomas USMC (editing); and Captains Marion 'Spike' Bowman and Harvey Dalton, JAGC, USN (substantive review).

COMMENTS

Dieter Fleck[*]

Assessment of a complex topic can always benefit from a divergence of opinions, which certainly is a good tradition in transatlantic cooperation. I shall confine myself here to some general comments on Commander Russo's excellent contribution,[1] perhaps over-emphasizing areas of possible dispute. Let me also underline that if we differ in arguments and details, our common goal can be identified very easily: it is the strengthening of the rule of law in enhanced international cooperation.

I   STATE PRACTICE

To start off with a contrasting argument, I believe that the Gulf War does not provide convincing arguments for developing new law. This is certainly true for the *law of armed conflict at sea*, particularly considering the fact that from the beginning of the conflict almost everything that was available from the Iraqi navy was blocked by Iran in the Shatt-al-Arab.

In my opinion, the main open questions of the international law of armed conflict at sea are the definition of merchant vessels, a code of practice for mine warfare, consensus on the rules for submarine warfare, the formulation of regulations for zones of protection, the introduction of advanced technical means of identification for medical craft, and the development of rules for sea rescue and the protection of the environment.

These questions have been addressed in an interesting variety of recent academic contributions. They are regulated in military manuals of the United States[2] and other nations,[3] and they are being developed by the *International Institute of Humanitarian*

---

* D. Fleck, Director, International Legal Affairs, Federal Ministry of Defence, Bonn. The views expressed in this contribution are those of the author and do not necessarily reflect either the policy or the opinion of the German Government.

1. Russo, R.V., Chapter 5 of this book.

2. NWP 9 (Rev. A)/FMFM 1-10, *Annotated Supplement To The Commander's Handbook On The Law Of Naval Operations*, Washington, D.C. 1989.

3. Particular efforts are presently under way for the preparation of new German military manuals on humanitarian law: *Zentrale Dienstvorschrift* 15 [*Joint Services Manual* 15] – ZDv 15 – (neu) *Humanitäres Völkerrecht in bewaffneten Konflikten* [*International Humanitarian Law in Armed Conflicts*, under preparation]: ZDv 15/1 – *Grundsätze* [*Principles*] –; ZDv 15/2 – *Handbuch* [*Handbook*] –; ZDv 15/3 – *Textsammlung* [*Collection of Instruments*] –; ZDv 15/4 – *Sammlung von Fällen mit Lösungen* [*Collection of Cases and Solutions*] –. The *Handbook* will be the first complete and concise modern reader on the subject to be published in German. Chapter 10 deals with the law of armed conflict at sea and Chapter 11 with the law of neutrality. Based on an English translation of the draft handbook, allies and friends willing to support this project will be invited for consultations, the results of which will be incorporated into the final text.

I.F. Dekker and H.H.G. Post, eds., The Gulf War of 1980-1988
© 1992, T.M.C. Asser Instituut, The Hague

Law in San Remo as part of its excellent project on international humanitarian law as applicable to armed conflicts at sea, undertaken in cooperation with an increasing number of government experts.[4]

Today there already exists a broad international consensus that merchant vessels, even those of neutral and other states not parties to the conflict, can qualify as military objectives and may thus be attacked, and that, for practical purposes, one of the most important legal conditions for such qualification is that they make an effective contribution to military action (*e.g.*, by carrying military materials). In this regard I would endorse the proposition that the legitimacy of a rule is ultimately and inescapably a function of the degree to which it satisfies *all* of the operational and humanitarian considerations essential to a balance of competing neutral and belligerent interests. But in contrast to Commander Russo's statement, I believe that this can hardly be considered a fundamental change of attitude in the law of naval warfare. Rather, such acceptance seems to me inherent in all rules and principles of the law of armed conflict, applicable in any theatre.

Commander Russo may rightly take this criticism as support for the necessity and validity of his functional approach. But he might also wish to reconsider why, after all, he rejected the applicability, in the naval theatre, of the classical customary definition of military objectives as reaffirmed in Article 52, paragraph 2 of Additional Protocol I. This critical distance towards Additional Protocol I may turn out to be counterproductive also with regard to the problems rightly mentioned by Commander Russo concerning the applicability of Hague Convention N° IX, an international instrument which in fact has largely been replaced today by rules and principles restated in Additional Protocol I.

I like to suggest that the firm 'baseline standard' of protected status for commercial maritime trade advocated so convincingly by Commander Russo should not be confined to the trade between countries not party to the hostilities. The debate on the complex issue of trading with the enemy was never closed as a result of illegal state practice in the past, and I would strongly disagree with attitudes of resignation that suggest letting this debate be closed under the impression of particular state practice in the Gulf. While I agree with the major results presented by Commander Russo, I do not consider his underlying arguments to be evolutionary in nature. Rather, they demonstrate the increasing influence of traditional principles of humanitarian law, such as the prohibition of indiscriminate attacks, the prohibition of unnecessary suffering, and the prohibition of perfidy, also for the law of armed conflict at sea.

As far as the *law of armed conflict on land and in the air* is concerned the Gulf War does provide examples of grave breaches rather than of state practice designed to develop existing law: chemical weapons were used; children were sent into battle, were detained and tortured; the Kurdish minority in Iraq was made the victim of military

---

4. *International Institute of Humanitarian Law*, Results of the First Meeting of the Madrid Plan of Action held in Bochum, Germany, November 1989.

attacks by their own Government; more than one hundred thousand prisoners of war on either side were held hostage before 1989; foreign civilians were taken hostage, in particular those working in the interest of Iraq's economic relations. No legal expert can be expected to consider such flagrant violations as valid material for the shaping of new law.

The *law of neutrality*, however, might have been affected, if Commander Russo is correct in arguing that Iranian and Iraqi conduct in pursuing the tanker war, the resolutions of the United Nations Security Council in response to the Iranian and Iraqi attacks against neutral state flag merchants, and in particular the actions and policies of the United States in the Gulf have revealed trends of development in customary law with respect to neutral shipping.[5] The law of neutrality may also have been influenced by codes of conduct issued by shipping organizations, such as the General Council of British Shipping or INTERTANKO.[6] But neutral states are still not bound to prevent their nationals from supplying one of the parties to the conflict with war material, as explicitly stated in Article 7 of Hague Convention N° XIII. Rather, they have to avoid the application of different standards in their arms export control policies.

II   FUTURE DEVELOPMENTS

Looking at possible developments of the law, I submit to being realistic and to following a not too sophisticated approach. If the conduct of the belligerents in the Gulf War had any impact on the present state of the law and its future development, this would put us back centuries. As a matter of principle, I consider this to be relevant not only for the law of warfare at sea, on land and in the air, but also for the law of neutrality. This is undoubtedly true for indiscriminate attacks against neutral merchant ships. Nevertheless, the problems imposed should be solved by means of today's international cooperation. As expressed in Article 89 of Protocol I Additional to the Geneva Conventions, a text that is not binding treaty law for the parties to the Gulf conflict, but which certainly reflects a universal *opinio juris* in humanitarian law today: 'In situations of serious violations of the Conventions or of this Protocol, the High Contracting Parties undertake to act, jointly or individually, in co-operation with the United Nations and in conformity with the United Nations Charter.'

Such action is dependent on the parties' willingness and ability to communicate with one another, in order to exchange and reconcile controversial arguments. I submit that such an attitude is fundamental not only for actual conflict settlement, but also for convincing retrospective assessment. The law of armed conflict is a weak law. At times

---

5. Russo, Francis V., Jr., "Neutrality at Sea in Transition: State Practice in the Gulf War as Emerging International Customary Law", 9 *Ocean Development and International Law* (1988), pp. 381-399.

6. General Council of British Shipping (ed.), *Iran/Iraq War. The Situation in the Gulf, Guidance Notes for Shipping*, London February 1988; International Association of Independent Tanker Owners (INTERTAN-KO) (ed.), *Iran/Iraq Conflict 1984/1988. The Tanker War – No End?*, 3rd Ed., Oslo June 1988; see also monthly *Safety Circular Letters* issued by INTERTANKO during the Iran/Iraq Conflict.

large parts of it have been left in abeyance by legislators, while other parts have fallen into oblivion as instruments of policy making. A broad and open-minded exchange of opinion on the guiding powers of law-enforcement is required here as part of an inter-cultural discussion with a longterm perspective. There may be different views in other parts of the world on law enforcing powers as they exist in the opinions of Western scholars and policy-makers as guiding arguments for adherence to humanitarian rules despite their weaknesses: observance of the principle of reciprocity; maintenance of troop discipline; consideration of public opinion; use of diplomatic instruments; reciprocal interest in the services of protecting powers; readiness to accept an International Fact-Finding Commission; fear of reprisals; fear of payment of compensation; penal or disciplinary action; and appeal to the conscience of the individual. The international community should make strong efforts to reach consensus on the practical and political assessment of such law-enforcing powers and make appropriate use of them as part of their efforts for effective crisis management.

III   LESSONS FROM THE GULF WAR

The willingness and ability to enter into such a dialogue includes steadfast decisiveness to take firm responsive action. If there is one legal lesson to be learned from the Gulf War, it came when the Commander of the French naval forces, on the occasion of an incident between the Corvette Dupleix and Iranian gunboats in the Strait of Hormuz on 20 January 1988, publicly and successfully explained French rules of engagement, saying that his warships would fire on Iranian gunboats that refused to break off an attack on neutral merchant ships when French vessels came to the rescue.[7] I would like to see many more governments making such outspoken statements in announcing proportional and necessary action in the exercise of their obligation under common Article 1 of the Geneva Conventions to ensure respect for international humanitarian law in all circumstances.

The inter-cultural dialogue required to enhance and develop legal consensus must comprise strong efforts towards peaceful settlement and efforts enabling authoritative action under Articles 41 and 42 of the United Nations Charter where attempts at peaceful settlement remain unsuccessful. I agree with Commander Russo's statement that individual or collective self-defence under Article 51 should become an option truly of last resort, proceeding only when efforts at securing or monitoring authoritative United Nations action under Chapter VII have clearly been unproductive. It is my conviction that consensus in questions of implementing the law in peacetime as well as in times of armed conflicts could effectively contribute to crisis management, and hence should be pursued at all levels of conflict development.

A dialogue of such dimensions would also help towards an understanding of the relativity of present issues. It would be aimed at the development of peaceful solutions and legal regulations of universal acceptance. At the same time it might help all sides

---

7. *International Herald Tribune*, 21 January 1988, pp. 1 and 6.

to rediscover important roots of our own cultures. There is no valid alternative to cooperation even in on-going conflicts.

COMMENTS

Terry D. Gill*

My comments will be directed towards two broad areas which are addressed in Commander Russo's contribution to this book, the relationship between the law of armed conflict and the law of self-defence, and the relationship between the law of armed conflict and the collective use of force by or with the authorization of the Security Council acting under Chapter VII of the United Nations Charter.

The starting premise in my view, and in this I am in broad agreement with Commander Russo and some others here, is that the law of (naval) armed conflict and the law of self-defence are at the same time interrelated, compatible and distinct.[1] They have a parallel function which is closely related, but separate. The assessment of the legality of a particular recourse to and exercise of armed force is subject to *both* sets of criteria, each of which have their own distinct areas of applicability. Commander Russo states this in his paper in the following terms, 'while the law of armed conflict determines the parameters for the *actual conduct* of military operations, the doctrine of self-defence establishes the *immediate and continuing justification* for the use of such force.'[2]

Article 51 of the Charter relates to the justifiability of the use of force in response to a prior or imminent armed attack. The law of self-defence remains relevant after force has been resorted to in determining whether the force is employed in conformity with the criteria governing the use of force in self-defence during the course of the conflict. If the *overall* response to the attack depending on its scale, duration and effects, is carried out in conformity with the proportionality and necessity criteria underlying Article 51, the response seen as a whole, is justifiable in terms of the law of self-defence. This does not mean that every (individual) operation which forms part of a legitimate recourse to self-defence will also be justifiable in terms of the law of armed conflict (*e.g.*, the bombardment of Dresden in 1945). An operation which violates the law of armed conflict does not become justifiable because it was undertaken within the context of a legitimate recourse to force under the law of self-defence.[3]

---

* T.D. Gill, Lecturer, Public International Law, University of Utrecht.

1. See, *e.g.*, *Annotated Supplement To The Commander's Handbook On The Law of Naval Operations*, NWP 9 (Rev. A)/FMFM 1-10, para. 5.1. See also Draper, G.I.A.D., "The Development of International Humanitarian Law" in *International Humanitarian Law* (UNESCO 1988), pp. 67 *et seq.*

2. Russo, F.V. Jr., Chapter 5 of this book, p. 159. See also Greenwood, C.J., "Self-Defence and the Conduct of International Armed Conflict" in Y. Dinstein (ed.) *International Law at a Time of Perplexity*, Dordrecht/Boston/Londen 1989, pp. 273 *et seq.*

3. This of course is a principle of the law of armed conflict which can be traced back to Grotius, see *De Jure Belli Ac Pacis Libri Tres* (English translation: The Law of War and Peace, Book Three, Chapter IV, para. 18) in Kelsey, F.W. (ed.), *The Classics of International Law*, Oxford 1925, at pp. 653-656.

I.F. Dekker and H.H.G. Post, eds., The Gulf War of 1980-1988
© 1992, T.M.C. Asser Instituut, The Hague

If the proper sphere of application of the law of self-defence is in determining the legality of the response, that of the law of armed conflict is in regulating the actual conduct of hostilities. The law of armed conflict, at least parts of it, such as the basic principles of distinction between combatants and non-combatants, of necessity, operational proportionality, humanity and honorable conduct[4] become operative as soon as hostilities commence and remains so until hostilities cease; whether this comes about by mutual agreement, by authoritative directive of the international community acting under Chapter VII of the Charter, or by the incapacity of one of the parties to continue belligerent operations. While it is obvious that much of the law of armed conflict would not be relevant to incidental hostilities, there are no reasons of either a legal or a policy nature to exclude the applicability of at least the basic principles of the law of armed conflict from *any* military operations (except law enforcement operations where other standards normally apply) however limited these might be in character. The principles and rules governing who and what may be targeted, avoidance of collateral damage and incidental injury, the humanitarian treatment of civilians and persons *hors de combat*, and avoidance of harm to non-belligerent interests are as applicable to a platoon of soldiers involved in a border clash or a single warship or aircraft responding to an incidental attack as they are to large scale sustained operations. The law of self-defence does not provide a basis for the detailed conduct of operations at any level of conflict. As Commander Russo points out,[5] the consequence of not applying the relevant portions of the law of armed conflict to all belligerent operations would be that incidental and 'low intensity'[6] operations would be in many cases be subject to less exacting legal standards than full scale sustained operations, a result which I submit would be patently absurd. Obviously, as a conflict became more protracted or intensive in scale, more of the law of armed conflict would become relevant, but this should not and does not diminish the relevance and applicability of the law of armed conflict to all interstate belligerent operations, regardless of their scale, duration or intensity.

Another distinction between the law of self-defence and the law of armed conflict is that self-defence can by its nature only legitimately apply to *one* party to a conflict – there is no 'self-defence' 'against self-defence',[7] although in some cases it may not be (initially) clear which side is acting in self-defence and in some (rare) cases it may never become clear. But self-defence implies that there has been an unlawful prior attack or imminent and unequivocal threat of attack and can only be exercised by one side. If an action ostensibly taken in self-defence violates the criteria contained in

4. Russo, *loc.cit.* (note 2), pp. 176-178. See also the *British Manual of Military Law*, Part III, HMSO (1956) at pp. 1-2.

5. Russo, *loc.cit.* (note 2) at pp. 158-159.

6. For a clear exposition of one theory of 'low intensity operations' as being synonomous with illegal recourse to force and violations of the law of armed conflict see Goldie, L.F.E., "Low Intensity Conflict at Sea", in: 14 *Syracuse Journal of International Law and Commerce* (1988), pp. 597 *et seq.* 'Low Intensity' is used here, however, to denote operations in which hostilities occur at a level lower than a conventional battle, regardless if they are are legal or illegal in character.

7. Dinstein, Y., *War, Aggression and Self-Defence*, Cambridge 1988, p. 168 citing the *Ministries* Case (Nuremberg 1949), U.S.A. v. Von Weizsaecker et al., 14 *Trials of War Criminals before the Nuremberg Military Tribunals under Control Council Law No. 10* ('Green Series'), pp. 314, 329.

the law of self-defence as a result of manifest disproportionality or lack of necessity, it ceases to be lawful and may be countered by an act of self-defence. This is not self-defence against self-defence, it is self-defence against an act of aggression, but only *one* side can be lawfully acting in self-defence at any given moment. However, the law of armed conflict is at all times applicable to *both* sides in a conflict, regardless of the legality or lack thereof of the initial or continued recourse to force. Just as the law of armed conflict governs the legality of the conduct of operations of the state(s) acting in self-defence, so does it equally govern the conduct of operations of the side which has unlawfully resorted to force.[8] The consequence of not maintaining the distinction between the *ius ad bellum* of the law of self-defence and the *ius in bello* of the modern law of armed conflict would be no different under the Charter than it was when recourse to force was subject to fewer or no legal restraints. It would stimulate an even greater destruction and indiscriminate violence than already occurs during hostilities. The 'aggressor' would have no reason to observe any restraints in its conduct of operations resulting, in all probability, in a corresponding lack of restraint and indiscriminate use of force on the part of the 'defender'. The principle of distinction between the two branches of law and its applicability to both sides was recognized in both the *Nuremberg*[9] and *Nicaragua*[10] judgments and is the course that has been followed by the Security Council in its condemnation of Iraq for both illegally using force against Kuwait and for violating basic rules and principles of the law of armed conflict.[11]

In sum, both spheres of law exist side by side throughout a conflict, but have distinct applications and are subject to distinct criteria even if they do overlap in the determination of the overall legality of the use of force. The law of self-defence is relevant in determining whether force has been resorted to in accordance with the United Nations Charter and whether the actions undertaken in self-defence, taken as a whole, meet the necessity and proportionality criteria which underlie Article 51 and are an integral part of the contemporary *ius ad bellum*, and while the Charter applies to all parties to a conflict, it is clear that only one side in a particular conflict can be acting in self-defence. The law of armed conflict is relevant to the actual conduct of operations and

8. This is the inverse of the principle that the law of armed conflict governs the conduct of operations of the belligerent which has a right to resort to armed force, see notes 1 and 3 *supra*. There is no reason to assume that operations which were undertaken in contravention of the United Nations Charter would necessarily have to be violative of the law of armed conflict. An 'aggressor' state could conceivably carry out all or part of its operations in conformity with the law of armed conflict just as a 'defender' state can equally violate or comply with the law of armed conflict as numerous historical examples attest.

9. Judgment of the International Military Tribunal (1946) Nuremberg, 1 October 1946, HMSO, *Cmd.* 6964 (1946), p. 3, in which the distinction between 'Crimes Against Peace' (Unlawful Recourse to Force) and 'War Crimes' (violations of the Laws and Customs of War) was laid down.

10. *Military and Paramilitary Activities in and against Nicaragua*, 27 June 1986, *ICJ Reports* 1986, p. 14, paras 215-220, pp. 112-115 in which the Court assessed the content of the applicable rules of humanitarian law (separately from those dealing with the law of self-defence in paras 187-200 at pp. 98-105) and the responsibility of the United States for violations of humanitarian law as distinct from violations of the law relating to the use of force (in para. 226 at pp. 117 *et seq*).

11. In Security Council Resolution 660 (1990) of 2 August 1990, Iraq was condemned for its illegal use of force, while in Resolution 666 (1990) of 13 September 1990 the Council reaffirmed that the relevant rules of the law of armed conflict were binding upon Iraq.

determines whether both sides have conducted their operations in accordance with the basic customary principles of the law of armed conflict which are set out in clear terms by Commander Russo elsewhere in his chapter,[12] and with the other rules governing the conduct of operations contained in the contemporary *ius in bello*. For a given recourse to and use of force to be legal in the broadest sense, it must conform to the rules and principles contained in *both* branches of the law which govern the use of force.[13]

The fact that both areas or branches of the law become operative as soon as force is resorted to and remain applicable throughout the conflict does not, however, signify in my view that adherence to the doctrine of self-defence condemns the 'defending' party to 'a fixed and reactive posture', or that the ability of operational commanders to conduct broad-based offensive operations (in the context of a defense against armed attack) is arrested as Commander Russo mistakenly states.[14]

Once an armed attack occurs (or there is an unequivocal threat of imminent attack) the right of self-defence becomes operative. If an attack consists of an isolated 'one-off' incident or short series of incidents of a limited scale, duration and intensity – then the overall response will have to be in conformity with what is necessary to halt the attack and, if necessary, prevent further attacks. A series of 'low-intensity' attacks carried out over a period of time designed to pressure the target state to alter its policy or submit to the will of the attacker would justify a single larger scale defensive response,[15] but could not normally provide grounds for conducting protracted high intensity operations. However, if a state carries out a large scale armed attack by land, sea or air forces (or any combination thereof), the defending state(s) is (are) obviously justified in carrying out protracted, high intensity and coordinated operations designed to thwart the attack and overcome the military forces and, war-fighting capacity of the attacker. Self-defence is neither restricted to the defender's territory nor does it preclude 'offensive' operations.

Just as an armed attack can take any number of forms and be carried out at various levels of intensity, so can and must self-defence be tailored to what is necessary and proportionate to halt and overcome the attack. If an armed attack can consist of one incident or a whole series of interrelated mutually sustaining actions, so likewise can action carried out in self-defence. Once again, the doctrine of self-defence determines the *overall* legality of an operation or sustained series of operations – it does *not* have to be invoked to justify each individual operation within the context of an overall defensive response.[16]

---

12. See Russo, *loc.cit.* (note 2), pp. 176-178.

13. See Greenwood, *loc.cit.* (note 2), p. 275.

14. Russo, *loc.cit* (note 2), p. 159.

15. See R. Ago (special rapporteur) in *Yearbook of the International Law Commission* 1980, Volume II, part One, at pp. 69-70.

16. Notwithstanding the practice of the United Kingdom to the contrary in the 1982 Falklands/Malvinas War. In that conflict, the U.K. invoked Article 51 on a number of separate occasions as a justification for its operations directed at expelling the Argentinian forces from the islands. There is, however, no evidence that the U.K. Government did so because it felt it was under a legal obligation to justify each segment of its overall response. See 36 *United Nations Yearbook* 1982, pp. 1320-1347.

In this respect, self-defence *is* relevant to the conduct of operations, but only in the sense that the overall scale, intensity and duration of defensive operations must conform to the necessity and proportionality criteria underlying Article 51 of the Charter.

These criteria provide that the defensive operations must roughly conform in scale, intensity and duration to the scale intensity and duration of the attack, they do not provide a detailed guide for the conduct of operations. However, I do not see this as being a strict division between strategy and tactics. Whether the proportionality and necessity criteria underlying Article 51 will apply at the strategic or tactical level of operations will depend in large measure upon a number of factors – not least of which will be the scale and effects of the attack and the permissible scale and objects of the defense. For example, if an attack took the form of a 'one-off' attack against a warship or aircraft, the concept of proportionality contained in the law of armed conflict and that in the law of self-defence would virtually merge and the relevant level of operations would be tactical.[17] Likewise, while it is clear that the principles of humanity and proportionality contained in the law of armed conflict are primarily relevant to the tactical level of operations, this is not to say that they are exclusively so as Commander Russo states in his paper.[18] Especially in a protracted conflict, the concept of collateral damage and incidental injury is relevant in assessing strategic options, just as it is in determining the legality of the employment of force at the tactical level.[19]

A final point should be made in the context of the current revival of collective security actions under Chapter VII of the United Nations Charter and Commander Russo's comments with regard to the relationship between such action and the law of armed conflict. I am in essential agreement with Commander Russo's statements regarding that relationship as well as the relationship between collective action under Chapter VII of the Charter and self-defence under Article 51 of the Charter.[20] The respective spheres of applicability of Chapter VII and the law of armed conflict is closely analogous to the relationship between the law of self-defence and the law of armed conflict. Once the Security Council determines that a threat to or breach of the peace has occurred and invokes Chapter VII of the Charter, either by instituting collective armed action under Articles 41-42, or by authorizing member states acting individually or collectively to utilize armed force, then the law of armed conflict will govern the actual conduct of operations of the United Nations' or member state(s)'

---

17. See Dinstein, *loc.cit.* (note 7), pp. 201-202.

18. Russo, *loc.cit.* (note 2), p. 189.

19. The decision to conduct a strategic bombing offensive involving the use of area bombardment of populated areas and the employment of a strategy of unrestricted submarine warfare by both sides in World War II are examples of 'strategic' level operations which were almost certainly violative of law of armed conflict, although in both cases no specific assessment of illegality was handed down by the International Military Tribunal. Aerial bombardment was largely omitted from the charges of war crimes at Nuremburg because of Anglo-American practice, while Admiral Dönitz was not found guilty of illegal conduct in his conduct of unrestricted submarine warfare because of U.S. practice in the war against Japan. See Tusa, A. and J., *The Nuremberg Trial*, New York 1983. See also Waltzer, M., *Just and Unjust Wars*, Harmondsworth 1977, especially pp. 255-263.

20. Russo, *loc.cit.* (note 2), pp. 161-162.

forces, while the relevant resolutions of the Council will determine, in conformity with the Charter, what the overall objectives and scope of such action will be. The only significant difference would be that the Security Council action under Chapter VII would normally preclude a state from adopting a position of neutrality – although a position of *non-belligerency* would be permissible, unless the Council authoritatively determined otherwise. In any case, there can be no doubt that collective enforcement action or action authorized by the Security Council under Chapter VII of the Charter is as subject to the rules and principles of the law of armed conflict as any other belligerent operations by member states, whether they are acting in conformity with the law of the Charter, or are acting contrary to the rules governing the use of force.

The collective security provisions of Chapter VII of the Charter are another branch of the *ius ad bellum* which have a parallel and complementary relationship with the law of self-defence and to which the foregoing observations concerning the relationship between the *ius ad bellum* and the *ius in bello* apply *mutatis mutandis*.[21]

---

21. See, *e.g.*, the Resolution adopted by the Institute of International Law at its Zagreb Session, 3 September 1971, "Conditions of Application of Humanitarian Rules of Armed Conflict to Hostilities in Which United Nations Forces May Be Engaged" and the Resolution adopted by the Institute of International Law at its Wiesbaden Session, 13 August 1975, "Conditions of Application of Rules, Other Than Humanitarian Rules, Of Armed Conflict To Hostilities in Which United Nations Forces May Be Engaged", reproduced in Schindler, D./Toman, J., *The Laws of Armed Conflict*, Alphen a/d Rijn 1988, at pp. 903 *et seq.*

Chapter 6

NEUTRALITY AT SEA

Michael Bothe*

I   THE STATUS OF THE CONFLICT AND THE PARTIES

A   Neutrality as a valid legal concept

Neutrality is a well-established traditional legal concept. It provides for a balance of interest between the belligerents on the one hand, and those not participating in the war on the other.[1] The neutrals may not tip the balance of the war by supporting one of the belligerents (duty of impartiality), but on the other hand, they must not be affected by the war.[2] In order to make sure that neutral shipping is not used to support the war effort, the belligerents have a certain right of control in regard of this shipping.[3] The reasonableness of this fundamental balance of interest has not been shaken by modern developments. It is still a conceptually valid restraint on violence, to distinguish clearly between those participating in an armed conflict and those who do not.

   Certainly, the law of the United Nations has affected the traditional law of neutrality. But it does not render neutrality legally impossible. Under the Charter, there is a right of collective self-defense, but no automatic duty to assist the victim. Such duty only exists where there is a binding Security Council resolution to that effect. If there is such a decision, then the traditional law of neutrality is indeed modified. But if there is none, it remains unchanged. The power of the Security Council to adopt such decisions modifying the traditional law of neutrality remained a dead letter for more than 40 years. It was effectively reanimated during the last Gulf conflict, but even in that context, neutrality seems to retain a certain practical significance.[4]

B   The status of the conflict

Under traditional international law, the law of neutrality applied in case of war. Then, a question arose whether a certain use of armed force did or did not constitute a war.

---

* M. Bothe, Professor of International Law, J.W. Goethe-University, Juridicum, Frankfurt.

   1. Dinstein, Y., "Neutrality in Sea Warfare", in: Bernhard (ed.), *Encyclopedia of Public International Law* (EPIL), Inst. 4, Amsterdam *etc.* 1982, p. 19.
   2. Bindschedler, R., "Neutrality, Concept and General Rules", in: Bernhard, *EPIL* 4, *op.cit.* (note 1), p. 10.
   3. Dinstein, *loc.cit.* (note 1), pp. 24 *et seq.*
   4. Thus, Iran declared itself to be neutral and to observe certain neutral obligations, *i.e.* to retain soldiers and aircraft which happen to get on its territory during the whole duration of the conflict.

I.F. Dekker and H.H.G. Post, eds., The Gulf War of 1980-1988

There are quite a number of instances where one or both parties to a conflict wanted to avoid the conflict being designated as a war in the legal sense.[5] The reason for this quite often was a desire to avoid certain legal or political restraints on violence which would have applied or were supposed to apply, if it were indeed a war.

This is the reason why, in order to make this kind of strategy legally impossible, the notion of 'war' has been replaced by others, for instance by the 'use of force' in the United Nations Charter (in contradistinction to the use of the term 'war' in the League of Nations Covenant) and by the term 'armed conflict' under the Geneva Conventions for the protection of 'war' victims. It is somewhat controversial whether the same development has taken place in relation to the notion of neutrality.[6] Where there is actually large scale fighting, the reason for applying the law of neutrality exists. Thus, at least *de lege ferenda* it should be the existence of an armed conflict, not that of a war which triggers the application of the law of neutrality. In the past, however, there were instances where states denied the application of certain rules of the law of neutrality because they considered that no formal state of war existed. That argument provided the basis for denying the right of visit and search to a party to the conflict.[7] In this light it is no surprise that the shipping community maintained there was no war triggering the application of the law of neutrality.[8]

During the first Gulf War, Iran and Iraq did not seem to have declared very clearly what was, according to their view, the status of the conflict. Third states seem to have acquiesced in the exercise of the right of visit and search,[9] for which two explanations are possible: either they may have considered the conflict as being a war, or they may have considered an armed conflict as being enough to trigger the right of visit and search even in the absence of a formal state of war.

It is submitted that the practice during the Iran-Iraq war confirms the trend to substitute the notion of war by the notion of armed conflict in order to determine the field of application of what used to be called the 'law of war', including the law of neutrality.

C   The status of 'third' states

The question whether there exists an intermediate status between belligerency and neutrality is a major subject of dispute. In a number of conflicts in the past, states without formally joining a war, have supported parties thereto to an extent which was incompatible with traditional obligations of neutrality. This political attitude was called to be something different in law, a status of 'non-belligerency'. Also in relation to the

---

5. Meng, W., "War", in: *EPIL* 4, p. 285.

6. *Contra*: Bindschedler, *loc.cit.* (note 2), p. 10; unclear: Ipsen, K., *Völkerrecht*, München 1990, p. 998.

7. Ronzitti, N., "Introductory: The Crisis of the Traditional Law Regulating Armed Conflicts at Sea and the Need for its Revision", in: Ronzitti, N. (ed.), *The Law of Naval Warfare*, Alphen a/d Rijn 1988, pp. 7 *et seq*.

8. See, House of Commons, *Third Special Report from the Defence Committee* (Session 1986-87), The Protection of British Merchant Shipping in the Persian Gulf, London 1987, p. 77.

9. Ronzitti, *loc.cit.* (note 7), p. 8.

armed conflict between Iran and Iraq, a number of states supported one of the parties, most of them Iraq, in a way which was not compatible with the traditional law of neutrality, whereas only Iran and Iraq were clearly parties to the conflict. It has to be asked whether this was indeed a case of that intermediate status of non-belligerency.

The practice during this and other wars really is not sufficient for proving that a new state of non-belligerency has emerged as a concept of law. It would be all to easy to avoid duties of neutrality by just declaring a different status. Unneutral support for a belligerent party has been and still is a violation of the law of neutrality. It gives rise to a right of reprisal for the belligerent which is affected by this violation. Nowadays, this right of reprisal, is subject to the law of the United Nations, meaning that it is limited by the prohibition of the use of force. Thus, a violation of the law of neutrality (short of an armed attack) does not give rise to measures against the neutral which constitute a use of force. While thus the support given by certain Arab States to Iraq probably was a violation of neutrality and thus triggered a right of reprisal for Iran, these reprisals could not include a use of force against those states. Whether an attack against their merchant ships constitutes such use of force, however, is a question which will be examined below.

II   MILITARY ACTIONS BY NEUTRALS AGAINST BELLIGERENTS

A   Neutrality as a justification for the use of force?

Under traditional international law, there is a duty of the neutral state to defend its neutrality.[10] The reason for this is that a neutral state is obliged to prevent its territory from being used as a basis for attacks against one of the belligerents. The prohibition of the use of force, being a peremptory norm of international law, has certainly superseded traditional law of neutrality to the extent that it might have justified resort to military force by the neutral. The rule that military force may not be used except in case of collective or individual self-defense applies today. This means that military action of a neutral against the belligerent is legal only if the neutral acts in self-defense or on the basis of a binding decision of the United Nations Security Council. Again, if certain military action taken by neutrals against the belligerents are justified by prior acts of one of the belligerents, one has to ask whether these acts constituted an armed attack within the meaning of Article 51 of the Charter.

B   The neutral states' right to use military force

The right of neutral states to use military force was an important issue during the Iran-Iraq war. The major question concerned the protection of neutral shipping in the Gulf

---

10. Bindschedler, *loc.cit.* (note 1), pp. 13 *et seq.*

through the presence of neutral warships.[11] Where a warship simply escorts ships flying its flag to and from a neutral port, this does not constitute a use of force – at least not unless additional measures of coercion are used by the warship. Whether escorting constitutes an 'innocent passage' to which the warship is entitled under the relevant rules of the law of the sea is another question. Even if it does not, it is not an 'armed attack'.

A different matter is the problem whether and to what extent warships may use their fire power in order to protect merchant ships flying the same flag. They may, of course, shoot in self-defence. Whether there is a situation of self-defence, must be determined for each individual incident. As between the parties to a conflict, there is – so to say – a general situation of self-defence between the aggressor and the victim. Thus, the individual acts of violence cannot and must not be evaluated under the *ius contra bellum*. But the relationship between a party to the conflict and a third state is, in principle, a peaceful one. Thus, each incident of violence has to be evaluated on its own merits under the *ius contra bellum*. Even in a situation of tension which existed in the Gulf area, there is no general permission to use force. The case of the attack by an Iraqi aircraft against the USS Stark may clarify the point.[12] If Iraq and the United States were at war at the relevant time (which they really were not), the USA could have attacked the approaching aircraft because it clearly was a military aircraft. But in times of peace, this attack by the ship against the aircraft was permissible only if the aircraft attacked the ship. It must be admitted that respect of this rule puts the commander of the ship in an awkward position, and this was well shown by this case.

The attack against an Iranian civilian aircraft from the USS Vincennes was based upon the correct assumption that the warship could defend itself by a counterattack against an attacking aircraft. This shooting down of the aircraft was, however, the consequence of an incorrect evaluation of the situation by the responsible officer. The responsible officer, in a situation like this, has to exercise all possible care for two reasons. The use of force is only legal in case of an attack. He thus has to make sure whether a plane which is approaching the ship, even if it is a military one, can be reasonably assumed to be attacking. But there is the additional point that the right of self-defense could not go beyond what is permissible under the law of war. Under the law of war, all reasonable care has to be taken in order to make sure that the object to be attacked is not a civilian one. This rule certainly cannot apply with the same strictness in the case of aerial warfare over the sea as it does in land warfare. But as a general principle, this applies to all theatres of war.

C   The use of force against non-belligerents

While it is clear that there is a right of counterattack where the warship itself is the object of an attack, the question has to be asked whether and to what extent military

---

11. A Report to the Congress on Security Arrangements in the Persian Gulf, U.S. Secretary of Defense, 26 *ILM* (1987), pp. 1433, 1452 *et seq.*

12. On that incident, see the report in 26 *ILM* (1987), p. 1422.

measures against merchant ships trigger a right of self-defence of the flag state – and thus justify an action involving the use of fire power by a warship in the area. This is somewhat problematic. The right of visit and search, which is still valid, as already mentioned, implies also a permission to use reasonable force where the merchant ship in question refuses to comply with a request to visit it made by an approaching warship. If this kind of force constituted an 'armed attack' within the meaning of Article 51 of the United Nations Charter, it would mean that it had become illegal to stop a commercial ship in order to exercise the right of visit and search. Practice seems to show quite clearly that the development of positive law, as reflected by state behaviour, has not taken this step.

But what if force is used against a merchant ship which is unrelated to, or inappropriate for, the exercise of a right of visit and search (or other purposes legal under the laws of war, such as the enforcement of a blockade)? It is submitted that this is still not an armed attack against the state, although it is clearly illegal. In that sense, it may be equated with acts of violence against foreign nationals abroad.

However, the individual merchant ship (like nationals abroad) cannot be equated with the state itself and that the attack against it must not be seen as an armed attack against the flag state. This would be a logical explanation for the right to enforce the right to visit and search. It is also confirmed by a formulation in the United Nations Definition of Aggression[13] which gives as an example of aggression the attack against the 'marine fleet' of a state but not that against an individual ship.

This somewhat restrictive interpretation of the term 'use of force' or 'armed attack' in the context of naval warfare does not mean that a state must leave its commercial shipping unprotected. Warships of the flagstate are of course free to move in and place themselves in a position which would make an attack on a merchant ship also an attack on a warship. Then, of course, the warship may fight back if the attack is launched nevertheless.

It is not illegal, under the rules established by the International Court of Justice in the *Corfu Channel* Case,[14] to place oneself into a situation of self-defence and then exercise this right. What is thus permitted, in the cases under review, is a somewhat limited right of militarily protecting a state's commercial shipping. It would be illegal to fire at the attacking ship or aircraft from a distance or any retaliatory action against the attacking state at places other than that of the actual attack.

13. A/RES/3314(XXIX), Annex of 14 December 1974.
14. *ICJ Report 1949*, p. 3 (in particular at pp. 30 *et seq.*)

III   MILITARY ACTION BY BELLIGERENTS AGAINST NEUTRAL SHIPPING

A   The right of visit and search

It has already been pointed out that indeed there exists a right of visit and search. This includes a right to use force necessary in order to make a merchant ship comply with a request for visit. Practice in the Gulf war indeed seems to confirm this right.

B   The right of convoy

Under traditional law of neutrality, it was to a certain extent disputed whether the right of visit and search also existed in relation to a 'convoy',[15] that is to say a group of merchant ships travelling under the protection of neutral warships. It is submitted that uniting a number of merchant ships under the protection of a warship would make the whole unit a piece of the state itself. The convoy is thus to be assimilated to state territory as far as possible objects of armed attacks are concerned. An attack against the convoy would be an attack against the state and trigger the right of self-defense. Thus, belligerent states are not entitled to enforce a right of visit and search against a convoy. This seems to be a plausible explanation of certain elements of state practice which could be observed in the Gulf, where this technique of assembling ships under the protection of warships was used indeed.[16] As far as one knows, neither belligerent tried to enforce a right of visit against those groups.

C   Blockades and special zones

Blockade is a traditional means of naval warfare which probably still is a valid concept, although its limitations are to be debated. The notion of blockade only had a limited role in the Iran-Iraq conflict. As far as access to Iraq's ports is concerned, it was blocked anyway early during the conflict by Iranian bombing and there was no commercial traffic to and from Iraqi ports during the whole war. As to a blockade against Iranian ports, there are reports that Iraq declared a blockade around the island of Kharg in 1984. But this is probably only a revised version of an earlier declaration, namely that of a prohibited war zone.

Both states, as a matter of fact, declared exclusion zones very early in the conflict, Iraq an area in the north of the Persian Gulf, starting south of the oil terminal of Kharg, Iran a large area in front of its shores. The Iranian zone never had a major significance during the conflict. On the other hand, Iraq tried at least until the end of 1984 to enforce its exclusion zone by attacking neutral tankers in the Kharg island area. One cannot say that this was accepted in practice. Attacks against neutral shipping in the Gulf were

---

15. Stödter, R., "Convoy", in: *EPIL* 3, Amsterdam 1982, pp. 128 *et seq.*
16. See 26 *ILM* (1987), p. 1458.

seriously condemned by the Security Council and by many nations.[17] This applies also to those attacks occurring in the Iraqi exclusion zone. The practice in the Gulf War can thus not be alleged as being an accepted application of the very controversial notion of exclusion zones.

D   Oil, tankers and the war effort

As there were many attacks on neutral tankers during the Gulf War, several arguments must be discussed (and discarded) which could legitimize them.

Oil is a very special and important liquid. Oil destined to a belligerent port is contraband, because it is essential for fueling the war vehicles of a belligerent. In this case, oil is war material. Oil leaving a belligerent port is not contraband. Contraband is defined as material destined to a belligerent. The fact that the revenue derived from the sale of oil is important for the war effort of a belligerent does not mean that the oil becomes contraband.

For a similar reason, neutral tankers cannot be military objectives. Their significance for the war effort of the belligerent is only indirect and their contribution to this effort too remote. The idea that also a neutral tanker carrying oil bought from a belligerent is so to say incorporated into that belligerent's war effort,[18] really widens the concept of legitimate military objectives beyond acceptable limits. The practice of states during the Gulf conflict clearly rejected that idea.

17. Fenrick, W.J., "The Exclusion Zone Device in the Law of Naval Warfare", 24 *CanYBIL* (1986), p. 91, at pp. 117 *et seq.*
18. Ronzitti, *loc.cit.* (note 7), p. 41; Fenrick, *loc.cit.* (note 17), p. 120.

COMMENTS

Christopher Greenwood[*]

While I agree with much of Professor Bothe's excellent contribution, there are two points on which I must take issue with him. I also like to add some remarks in regard to another matter.

I   APPLICATION OF THE LAW OF NEUTRALITY IN THE ABSENCE OF A STATE OF WAR

Professor Bothe asserts that the law of neutrality applies in any international armed conflict, irrespective of whether that conflict is characterised as war in the formal sense. In view of the difficulties inherent in determining whether or not a state of war exists in a particular case, this position has considerable appeal and has been adopted by the United States in its *Naval Commander's Handbook*.[1]

Nevertheless, state practice is far from consistent on this point.[2] Although there have been numerous armed conflicts since 1945, there have been remarkably few cases in which a state, whether a party to a conflict or not, has invoked the law of neutrality. In the Iran-Iraq conflict (which the parties seem to have regarded as a war in the formal sense[3]), the United Kingdom took care (at least in its later pronouncements) to stress that it was 'impartial in the conflict between Iran and Iraq' rather than proclaiming itself neutral in a war between those two states.[4] Moreover, some states have expressly denied that the law of neutrality applied in its entirety in the absence of a state of war. During its 1965 conflict with Pakistan, the Government of India stated that prize court action was illegal in the absence of a state of war.[5] Some of the states which made facilities available to the United Kingdom during the Falklands conflict appear to have done so on the understanding that those facilities would have to be withdrawn if a state of war came into existence. There is also considerable support in the literature for the

[*] C.J. Greenwood, Fellow of Magdalene College, Cambridge; Lecturer in Law, University of Cambridge.
1. US Department of the Navy, *Commander's Handbook on the Law of Naval Operations* (NWP 9 (Rev A), 1989), para. 7.1.

2. See Greenwood, C.J., "The Concept of War in Modern International Law", 36 *ICLQ* (1987), p. 283 at pp. 297-301.

3. *Loc.cit.* (note 2), p. 293.

4. See, *e.g.*, the statement of 29 October 1985, *House of Commons Debates*, vol. 84, col. 450, reprinted in 56 *BYIL* (1985), p. 534.

5. McNair and Watts, *Legal Effects of War*, 4th ed., Cambridge 1966, p. 547.

I.F. Dekker and H.H.G. Post, eds., The Gulf War of 1980-1988
© 1992, T.M.C. Asser Instituut, The Hague

view that the application of the law of neutrality – and, in particular, the technical concept of prize law – is dependent upon the existence of a technical state of war.[6]

Differences over whether the law of neutrality applies in the absence of a state of war and whether a state of war existed between Iran and Iraq led to uncertainty about the legal standards to be applied in the Gulf conflict. This uncertainty was criticised by the International Chamber of Shipping in a memorandum submitted to the United Nations, in which it commented that 'the lack of clarity of the position in international law has served to protect [Iran and Iraq] from the full force of international criticism' for their attacks on merchant shipping.[7] Professor Bothe's approach would help to reduce that uncertainty and probably reflects the direction in which international law is moving. It thus deserves support as a statement *de lege ferenda* but a note of caution is needed in considering whether it represents the existing law.

II   ATTACKS ON NEUTRAL MERCHANT SHIPS

I cannot agree with Professor Bothe's thesis that the use of force by a belligerent against an individual merchant ship – as opposed to a warship or a convoy – is not an armed attack giving rise to a right of self-defence on the part of the flag state. In support of his reasoning on this point, Professor Bothe relies on the text of Article 3 of the Definition of Aggression, which refers to an attack upon the 'marine fleet' as an act of aggression. Professor Bothe argues that the reference to the marine *fleet* means that an attack upon a single ship should not be treated as an armed attack for the purposes of Article 51 of the Charter. There are three reasons for rejecting this approach.

First, even if one accepts that the reference to a 'fleet' in Article 3 of the Definition was intended to exclude attacks upon individual ships and that the concept of 'aggression' in the Definition should be equated with that of 'armed attack' in Article 51 of the Charter (and both points are open to argument), Article 6 of the Definition expressly provided that

'Nothing in this Definition shall be construed as in any way enlarging or diminishing the scope of the Charter, including its provisions concerning cases in which the use of force is lawful.'

The question whether an attack upon a merchant ship can constitute an armed attack upon the flag state for the purposes of Article 51 must therefore be answered by interpreting Article 51 in the light of the relevant practice, of which the Definition is only a part. There is no indication that Article 51, which does no more than preserve a

6. See, *e.g.*, Castren, E., *The Present Law of War and Neutrality*, Helsinki 1954, pp. 34-35, Tucker, R., *The Law of War and Neutrality at Sea*, Washington 1957, pp. 199-200, and Schindler, D., "State of War, Belligerency, Armed Conflict", in: Cassese, A. (ed.), *The New Humanitarian Law of Armed Conflict*, Naples 1979, p. 3 at p. 5.

7. Reprinted in *Third Special report* of the House of Commons Defence Committee, HC 409, 1986-1987, p. 77; paras. 10 and 11 of this memorandum are particularly interesting.

right described as 'inherent', was intended to deprive states of the right to use force to protect their merchant ships when those vessels were the victims of unlawful attacks by the forces of other states.

Secondly, state practice since 1945 strongly suggests that international law does treat an unlawful attack upon a merchant ship as an act to which the flag state may respond by force if the presence of its warships or aircraft in the vicinity of the attack give it the means of going to the assistance of the vessel under attack. The US position is summarized in the US *Naval Commander's Handbook*, which states that

> 'International law, embodied in the doctrines of self-defence and protection of nationals, provides authority for the use of proportionate force by US warships and military aircraft when necessary for the protection of US flag vessels and aircraft, US citizens (whether embarked in US or foreign flag vessels), and their property against *unlawful* violence in and over international waters.'[8]

While this statement may go too far in its reference to the defence of property, it seems to have reflected the views of the numerous neutral states which deployed naval forces to the Gulf during the Iran-Iraq conflict. The rules of engagement of United Kingdom,[9] as well as United States,[10] forces seem to have been based on the assumption that it was lawful to use force to protect their merchant ships from unlawful attacks by either of the belligerents. Although the context is different, the same assumption is evident in the US response to the Cambodian seizure of the *Mayaguez*[11] and in the report of the Commission of Inquiry in the *Red Crusader* Case.[12]

Finally, if Professor Bothe's theory is taken to its logical conclusion, then a neutral warship which witnessed an illegal attack upon a merchant ship flying the same flag would be violating international law if it opened fire upon the attacking plane or vessel. Since the attacker would presumably be a warship or military aircraft, this violation would itself amount to aggression under Article 3 of the Definition. The warship might lawfully interpose itself between the attacker and the merchant ship but that will not always be possible and, in those circumstances, Professor Bothe's theory means that the only lawful course of action would be for the warship to do nothing beyond providing humanitarian assistance. Yet it defies belief that any state would be willing to give such instructions to its naval commanders. Common sense dictates that where a merchant ship is the object of an unlawful attack, a warship flying the same flag may protect it and that protection may take the form of returning fire against the attacker when necessary. While I would justify such action as an exercise of the right of self-defence

---

8. *Op.cit.* (note 1), para. 3.11.1.

9. For discussion, see Gray, C., "The British Position with Regard to the Gulf Conflict", 37 *ICLQ* (1988), p. 420.

10. 26 *ILM* (1987), pp. 1454 *et seq.* The United States later amended the Rules of Engagement to permit US warships to use force in defence of non-US merchant ships; *Department of State Bulletin*, July 1988, p. 61. For a discussion of this change, see Lowe, A.V., "Self-Defence at Sea", in: Butler, W.E. (ed.), *The Non-Use of Force in International Law*, Dordrecht 1989, p. 185.

11. McDowell, E.C., 1975 *Digest of US Practice in International Law*, pp. 777-783.

12. 35 *ILR* 485.

recognized by Article 51 of the Charter, it is open to argument that the justification lies in a separate right of states to protect their nationals against unlawful attacks upon the high seas.

III THE EFFECT OF THE UNITED NATIONS CHARTER ON THE LAW OF NEUTRALITY

I agree with Professor Bothe's assertion that '... the relationship between a party to the conflict and a third state is, in principle, a peaceful one. Thus, each incident of violence has to be evaluated in its own merits under the *ius contra bellum*.' It is inherent in the concept of self-defence that a state which is the victim of an armed attack may use only such force as is necessary for its defence. Once it goes beyond that, its use of force is no longer justified under Article 51 of the United Nations Charter, even if it has complied with the law of armed conflict.[13] Thus the degree of force which may lawfully be employed by a victim of aggression is proportionate to the threat posed to it: the greater the threat, the greater the degree of force which may be employed in response.

If a state's right to use force against its adversary is limited by the principles of proportionality and necessity, its right to use force against the shipping of 'neutral' states must similarly be limited. That approach is evident in the statement made by the United Kingdom Government following the Iranian interception of the British merchant ship *Barber Perseus* in 1986:

'... under Article 51 of the United Nations Charter a state such as Iran, actively engaged in an armed conflict, is entitled in exercise of its inherent right to self-defence, to stop and search a foreign merchant ship on the high seas if there is reasonable ground for suspecting that the ship is taking arms to the other side for use in the conflict ...'[14]

The Netherlands has taken a similar view in the context of attacks on neutral shipping in the Gulf.[15] It would be incompatible with the whole approach to the use of force in the United Nations Charter to hold that merely because a state had become involved in an armed conflict it was automatically entitled to take the full range of measures permitted by the law of neutrality against the shipping of states not party to that conflict, even though such measures might be quite unnecessary for its defence. The limitation of measures against neutral shipping to those which are necessary for the defence of the state which takes them is all the more important if the law of neutrality is to be

---

13. See Greenwood, C.J., "Self-Defence and the Conduct of International Armed Conflict", in: Dinstein, Y. (ed.), *International law at a Time of Perplexity*, Dordrecht 1989, p. 273.

14. Statement by the Minister of State, Foreign and Commonwealth Office, 28 January 1986, *House of Commons Debates*, vol. 90, col. 426; reprinted in 57 *BYIL* (1986) p. 583.

15. Statement by the Permanent Representative to the Security Council, 1 June 1984, *UN Doc.* S/PV.2546 at p. 13. See also O'Connell, D.P., *The Law of the Sea*, vol II, Oxford 1984, pp. 1141 *et seq.* Gioia and Ronzitti evaluate the Dutch position as slightly different, see Chapter 7 of this book.

applicable in any international armed conflict. The concept of armed conflict is generally given a very wide interpretation: Pictet's commentary on the Geneva Conventions states that 'any difference arising between two states and leading to the intervention of armed forces is an armed conflict' for the purposes of the Geneva Conventions.[16] If the same definition is to be applied for the purposes of the law of neutrality, then a comparatively minor clash between two states could lead to either of them taking very extensive measures against the shipping of third states.

The law of neutrality is also very heavily qualified by the provisions of the United Nations Charter in those conflicts in which the Security Council takes action. That is most obvious in cases where the Security Council takes measures under Chapter VII of the Charter authorizing the use of force against an aggressor. Here, there is no scope for the law of neutrality to apply since all members of the United Nations are obliged to carry out the decisions of the Security Council.[17] In the recent case of Kuwait, Security Council Resolution 678 (1990) has authorized the use of force by states co-operating with the Government of Kuwait. While that resolution does not require states to participate in the use of force against Iraq, a non-participating state cannot rely upon the law of neutrality in the event of hostilities. Even where the Council's action is limited to the adoption of resolutions calling upon the parties to a conflict not to interfere with neutral shipping – such as Resolution 540 (1983) adopted during the Iran-Iraq conflict – it is arguable that the provisions of the resolution have to be taken into account in applying the law of neutrality.

16. *Commentary on the First Geneva Convention*, Geneva 1951, p. 32.

17. UN Charter, Articles 2(5) and 25. See also the resolution adopted by the Institut de droit international at Wiesbaden in 1975, Article 4 of which provides that: 'Whenever United Nations forces are engaged in hostilities, Member States of the Organization may not take advantage of the general rules of the law of neutrality in order to evade obligations laid upon them in pursuance of a decision of the Security Council acting in accordance with the Charter ...' Reprinted in Schindler, D., and Toman, J., *The Laws of Armed Conflicts*, 3rd ed., Leyden 1988, p. 907.

COMMENTS

Adriaan Bos[*]

There is a saying that lawyers like generals are always dealing with the problems of a preceding war. My doubts about the rightness of that saying are very much put to the test by this academic venture.

I would like to comment firstly on the dichotomy referred to by Professor Bothe, the dichotomy of neutrality and belligerency and in particular on the question whether under aegis of the United Nations Charter neutrality has remained a valid legal concept.

It was Hugo Grotius who argued that there is no neutrality in case of a 'bellum iniustum'. One may think that this rule got momentum since the establishment of the United Nations. In principle members of the United Nations are integrated into a system of collective security and they are not supposed to remain neutral in armed conflicts between parties one of whom has acted contrary to applicable rules of international law.

I would not go so far as to state, as Schwarzenberger once did, that in the practice of the United Nations, the opportunities of practising neutrality under the traditional law are as large as the loopholes for resort to aggression, but nevertheless the post war history shows clearly a continued need for rules of neutrality. One may even ask whether that is still more true for the rules of neutrality in sea warfare compared to those of land warfare. This may be explained by the characteristics of the sea open to all nations for the purpose of communication and commerce. Restrictions to navigation are per definition felt by a great number of states. The first important incentives for the development of rules of neutrality date from the 13th and 14th century in relation to overseas trade.

It is also true that only in the Kuwait crisis the Security Council became able to fulfill its functions provided for in the Charter. But also in the war between Iran and Iraq the possibility has been discussed of a United Nations Peacekeeping force in the Gulf to protect the freedom of navigation and commerce *erga omnes* in the international waters of the Gulf.

I recall the suggestions made by two well-known American lawyers, Vance and Richardson, of reflagging non-military vessels in the Gulf. Firstly, according to their proposal, a Security Council resolution should authorize seafaring United Nations peacekeepers to place a United Nations flag on vessels entering the Gulf that asked a United Nations guarantee of safe passage and that submitted to United Nations inspection to ensure that no contraband was on board. Once under a United Nations flag, oil tankers and other peaceful vessels desiring an escort, could request an unarmed

* A. Bos, Legal Adviser, Ministry of Foreign Affairs, The Hague. The views expressed are those of the author and do not necessarily reflect either the policy or the opinion of the Dutch Government.

I.F. Dekker and H.H.G. Post, eds., The Gulf War of 1980-1988

United Nations patrol boat to accompany it or a naval vessel from member states authorized by the Council to carry out this function.

This United Nations approach would guarantee that these ships may not become involved in hostilities. The Vance-Richardson proposal has been made to escape from the reflagging of ships, for instance the substitution of the Kuwati flag by the USA flag.

It is my opinion that the reflagging of Kuwaiti ships was legally not necessary since the relevant point is the neutrality of the flag state. Furthermore, the coordination of protection given to ships of different nations by an escorting warship under the flag of a third state is another possibility. In that case it is advisable to inform the belligerents that such kind of protection will be given, in order to avoid any misunderstanding. The belligerent states may, upon receiving that information, challenge the neutral status of any of the flag states of escorting warships.

Ships flying a United Nations flag only are not a new phenomenon. There have been a few precedents of such ships which were involved in minesweeping operations in the Suez canal and in transporting Yougoslavian troops for UNEF.

Such a United Nations approach would in practice avoid the question whether or not it is allowed to exercise the right of visit and search in relation to merchant ships sailing in convoy under the protection of neutral warships and it might make other rules of neutrality superfluous.

Such activities can be compared with the peacekeeping operations of the United Nations. Conditions for peacekeeping operations are: a) They need an authorization of the Security Council; b) They will take place under the authority of the Secretary-General; c) Consent of the states participating will be necessary and d) no force will be used. The aim will be to bring an end to the hostilities. In the case of the Gulf War one may ask whether the consent of the belligerents would have been necessary, if those operations only took place in the high seas.

The Kuwait crisis affirms that the impact of the United Nations on the rules of neutrality is evident. The binding resolutions of the Security Council dealing with transport by vessels to and from Iraq is just one example. The question who will be neutral in case a war breaks out becomes more pertinent.

In discussing the relevance of the rules of neutrality in case of binding Security Council measures, Professor Bothe himself rightly pointed out that such measures may deviate from the rules of neutrality.

Furthermore, I would like to add also on a few points with respect the impact of the new law of the sea. The Street of Hormuz is a very important passage for navigation in the Gulf. In principle free transit through straits should be guaranteed by bordering states. If a coastal state bordering an international strait is at the same time a belligerent state in a conflict, like Iran, that does not change the legal position of that state with respect to navigation under neutral flag.

The exclusion by a coastal state of neutral shipping from its territorial sea which is part of an international strait would, as I see it, in practice result in a sort of blockade, sort of since it hinders all shipping, neutral and enemy from entering or leaving the ports or the coasts of the belligerent state. Such a 'blockade' can however never be justified if also neutral states will be cut off by it.

It is important to distinguish between the rights and duties of neutral states and the activities of the ships flying their flag. There is no duty for the neutral states to prevent commercial ships flying the their flag from transporting contraband to the ports of the belligerent states. However, the involvement of a flag state becomes more prominent when it sends warships to escort ships of neutral states in convoy. Also in that case the strait-state has no right to prevent the passage of such a convoy.

In essence the escorting warship is only obliged to give the necessary information in case of suspicion of abuse of the neutral nature of the convoy and the task of the warships cannot be seen as prejudicial to the peace, good order or security of the coastal state.

I do realize, however, that in the *Corfu-channel* Case the International Court of Justice considered the sweeping of mines by British naval vessels in the Strait of Corfu as an infringement of the sovereignty of the coastal state over its territorial sea. Such activity can however also be seen as a contribution to the freedom of navigation.

Chapter 7

THE LAW OF NEUTRALITY:
THIRD STATES' COMMERCIAL RIGHTS AND DUTIES

A. Gioia[*] and N. Ronzitti[**]

INTRODUCTION

The armed conflict between Iran and Iraq was, to a large extent, a classic example of
a post-1945 conflict situation. The United Nations Organization failed to make an
objective determination as to the cause of the conflict and to identify the aggressor.
Both Iran and Iraq accused each other of having started the war and claimed to be
acting in self-defence under Article 51 of the United Nations Charter.[1] No formal
declaration of war was effected by either party and, until 2 October 1987, Iran and Iraq
did not even formally sever diplomatic relations.[2] For its part, United Nations Security
Council Resolution 598(1987) confined itself to determining that there existed a 'breach
of the peace' and demanded that 'Iran and Iraq observe an immediate ceasefire,
discontinue all military actions on land, at sea and in the air, and withdraw all forces to
the internationally recognized boundaries without delay.'[3] As a consequence, the
attitude of third states reflected, on the one hand, this legal lack of clarity as to which
was the aggressor state and, on the other, provided a significant test as to the viability
of the old law of neutrality and its applicability to the so-called 'non-belligerents' or
'states not parties to the conflict'.[4] There is, in fact, substantial agreement that, if the
United Nations Security Council is not in a position to take any binding decisions in

---

* A. Gioia, Researcher in International Law, University of Trent, Italy.
** N. Ronzitti, Professor of International Law, University of Pisa, Italy.

1. See 34 *Yearbook of the United Nations* (1980), pp. 312 *et seq.*
2. See 33 *Keesing's Contemporary Archives* (1987), p. 35601.
3. S/RES/598(1987), adopted unanimously on 20 July 1987 under Articles 39 and 40 of the UN Charter.
Text reprinted in 26 *ILM* (1987), pp. 1479-1480. On this resolution, see Tavernier, P., "Le caractère
obligatoire de la résolution 598(1987) du Conseil de Sécurité relative à la guerre du Golfe", 1 *European
Journal of International Law* (1990), pp. 278 *et seq.*
4. For an analysis of the issue of the law of neutrality in the Iran-Iraq War, see, generally and among
others: David, E., "La guerre du Golfe et le droit international", 20 *Rev.belge* (1987), pp. 153 *et seq.*; Orford,
T.M., *The Iran-Iraq Conflict. Recent Developments in the International Law of Naval Engagements*, Cape
Town 1988, pp. 24 *et seq.*; Russo, F.V., "Neutrality at Sea in Transition: State Practice in the Gulf War as
Emerging International Customary Law", 19 *Ocean Development and International Law* (1988), pp. 381 *et
seq.*; Boczek, B.A., "Law of Warfare at Sea and Neutrality: Lessons from the Gulf War", 20 *Ocean
Development and International Law* (1989), pp. 239 *et seq.*

I.F. Dekker and H.H.G. Post, eds., The Gulf War of 1980-1988
© 1992, T.M.C. Asser Instituut, The Hague

case of armed conflict or if it does not call upon a particular state to take part in enforcement measures, third states may remain neutral.[5] According to one view, third states may also adopt a position of so-called 'non-belligerency', as opposed to strict neutrality, favouring, in varying degrees, one of the parties to the conflict.[6]

Four main questions will be dealt with in this chapter: the right of neutrals to trade with belligerents; limitations on that right; measures taken by belligerents interfering with neutral commerce; measures taken by neutrals in order to enforce freedom of commerce.

I   THE RIGHT OF NEUTRALS TO TRADE WITH BELLIGERENTS

The right of neutrals to engage in trade with belligerents, subject to certain limitations, was recognized by the traditional customary law of war. The existence of this right was confirmed by the most highly-qualified international legal writers[7] and could be inferred from a number of instruments of treaty law. For example, Articles 2 and 3 of the 1856 Paris Declaration Respecting Maritime Law[8] state, respectively, that 'the neutral flag covers enemy's goods, with the exception of contraband of war' and that 'neutral goods, with the exception of contraband of war, are not liable to capture under enemy's flag.' The Declaration, therefore, presupposes that the goods which Articles 2 and 3 refer to are the object of commerce between neutrals and a belligerent state. Article 2 of the 1907 Hague Convention No. VIII on the Laying of Automatic Submarine Contact Mines[9] says that 'it is forbidden to lay automatic contact mines off

---

5. On the law of neutrality in the era of collective security, see, generally and among others: Wright, Q., "The Present Status of Neutrality", 34 *AJIL* (1940), pp. 391 *et seq.*; Lalive, J.-F., "International Organization and Neutrality", 24 *BYIL* (1947), pp. 72 *et seq.*; Komarnicki, T., "The Place of Neutrality in the Modern System of International Law", 80 *Hague Recueil* (1952, I), pp. 395 *et seq.*; Castrén, E., *The Present Law of War and Neutrality*, Helsinki 1954, pp. 421 *et seq.*; Tucker, R.W., *The Law of War and Neutrality at Sea (Naval War College, International Law Studies 1955)*, Washington 1957; Henkin, L., "Force, Intervention and Neutrality in Contemporary International Law", *Proceedings of the American Society of International Law* (1963), pp. 147 *et seq.*; Schindler, D., "Aspects contemporains de la neutralité", 121 *Hague Recueil* (1967, II), pp. 221 *et seq.*; Fenwick, C.G., "Is Neutrality Still a Term of Present Law?", 63 *AJIL* (1969), pp. 100 *et seq.*; Blix, H., *Sovereignty, Aggression and Neutrality*, Stockholm 1970; Norton, P.M., "Between the Ideology and the Reality: The Shadow of the Law of Neutrality", 17 *Harvard International Law Journal* (1976), pp. 249 *et seq.*; Seidl Hohenveldern, I., "Der Begriff der Neutralität in den befaffneten Konflikten der Gegenwart", *Festschrift für F.A. Freiherr von der Heydte*, Berlin 1977, pp. 593 *et seq.*; Bindschedler, R.L., "Neutrality, Concept and General Rules", 4 *Encyclopedia of Public International Law*, Amsterdam/New York/Oxford 1982, pp. 9 *et seq.*; Dinstein, Y., "The Laws of Neutrality", 14 *Israel Yearbook on Human Rights* (1984), pp. 80 *et seq.*

6. See *infra* note 26.

7. See, for example, Oppenheim, L., *International Law. A Treatise*, Vol. II, *Disputes, Law and Neutrality*, 7th ed., by H. Lauterpacht, London/New York/Toronto 1952, pp. 659, 674, 677; Balladore Pallieri, G., *Diritto bellico*, 2nd ed., Padua 1954, pp. 381-382; Castrén, *op.cit.* (note 5), p. 470; Berber, F., *Lehrbuch des Völkerrechts*, Vol. II, *Kriegsrecht*, Munich/Berlin 1962, pp. 221, 223.

8. Text reprinted in Ronzitti, N. (ed.), *The Law of Naval Warfare. A Collection of Agreements and Documents with Commentaries*, Dordrecht/Boston/London 1988, pp. 61 *et seq.*

9. Text reprinted *ibidem*, at pp. 129 *et seq.*

the coast and ports of the enemy, with the sole object of intercepting commercial shipping.' Again, freedom of commerce between belligerents and states not parties to the conflict is implied. The 1907 Hague Convention No. XIII, Concerning the Rights and Duties of Neutral Powers in Naval War,[10] does not embody any general rule prohibiting commercial intercourse between belligerents and neutrals. In this connection, it only forbids the supply of certain goods, which will be considered later.

During the Iran-Iraq war, the question of freedom of neutral commerce came into prominence almost exclusively within the framework of the more specific question of freedom of navigation. This is not surprising since both belligerents, given the relative inconclusiveness of the war on land, soon concentrated on a campaign of economic warfare against each other, which posed a serious threat to navigation in the Persian Gulf and through the Strait of Hormuz. Especially as from 1984, Iraq started the so-called 'tanker war', beginning to attack tankers carrying Iranian oil through the Gulf, in a deliberate attempt to discourage foreign oil trade with Iran and, therefore, reduce Iran's revenues for propagating the war. As a result of Iran's success, earlier in the war, in closing down Iraqi ports and persuading Syria to shut off the Iraqi-Syrian oil pipeline to the Mediterranean Sea, Iraq had been unable to export significant quantities of oil in 1981 and 1982; however, the Iraqi Government had gradually built up new export facilities, using pipelines in Turkey and Saudi Arabia, and was no longer dependent on shipping for its oil experts. Unable to strike at Iraq's overland exports, Iran's retaliatory measures, which consisted in attacks on merchant vessels, were thus directed against non-belligerent shipping travelling to and from the ports of the moderate Gulf States, especially Saudi Arabia and Kuwait, which supported Iraq. As a consequence of the belligerents' campaign of economic warfare, the right of neutrals to trade with belligerents was severely curtailed. This campaign was deliberately aimed at impeding foreign trade with the enemy and little attention was paid to the principle of freedom of neutral commerce. This does not necessarily mean, however, that, *as a matter of law*, that traditional principle ought to be regarded as obsolete.

On the contrary, the entry into force of the United Nations Charter has, if anything, strengthened the right of neutrals to trade with belligerents: the abolition of the traditional right to wage war has, in fact, somewhat limited the right of belligerents to resort to those measures, such as visit and search and blockade, which were connected with a state of war and which have now to be reconciled, as we shall see, with the right of self-defence.[11] As a consequence, states not parties to an armed conflict have more ground for claiming that a state of war is not in existence and that traditional peacetime rules, such as that of freedom of navigation on the high seas or that of freedom of passage through international straits, apply.[12]

This interpretation is confirmed by the practice of third states during the Gulf War and by United Nations resolutions. The United States, for example, repeatedly stressed

---

10. Text reprinted *ibidem*, at pp. 193 *et seq.*
11. See *infra* paragraph III.
12. On the status of international straits in time of international armed conflicts, see, in particular, Ronzitti, N., "Passage Through International Straits in Time of International Armed Conflict", in: *International Law at the Time of its Codification. Essays in Honour of Roberto Ago*, Vol. II, Milan 1987, pp. 363 *et seq.*

the necessity to ensure the 'free flow of oil' from the Gulf as well as freedom of navigation for 'neutral' and/or 'non-belligerent' shipping in the Gulf and through the Strait of Hormuz.[13] The United Kingdom also declared that it upheld 'the principle of freedom of navigation on the high seas',[14] as did several other states.[15] Attacks on merchant vessels and the mining of international and neutral waters were strongly condemned.[16] United Nations Security Council Resolution 540(1983) affirmed 'the right of free navigation and commerce in international waters'.[17] Security Council Resolution 552(1984) did the same, with special reference to shipping 'en route to and from all ports and installations of the littoral states that [were] not parties to the hostilities.'[18] This latter resolution also condemned attacks on commercial ships, as did Security Council Resolutions 582(1986) and 598(1987).[19] Neither third states nor United Nations resolutions made a clear distinction between peace-time and war-time as far as the right of free navigation and commerce was concerned.[20]

In this light, the traditional war-time rule which forbade attacks on merchant vessels on sight, should still be regarded as valid and attacks by both Iran and Iraq of merchant vessels travelling to and from belligerent and, *a fortiori*, non-belligerent ports should be considered illegal.[21] This is particularly true for neutral merchant vessels, since

13. See, for example, 85 *Department of State Bulletin* (May 1985), p. 46; 86 *Department of State Bulletin* (December 1986), p. 72; 87 *Department of State Bulletin* (July 1987), p. 62; *ibidem* (August 1987), pp. 78 and 82; *ibidem* (September 1987), p. 39.

14. See, for example, 57 *BYIL* (1986), pp. 629, 635, 644; 58 *BYIL* (1987), p. 638; 59 *BYIL* (1988), pp. 581, 582.

15. See, for example, the discussions preceding the adoption of S/RES/552(1984): *UN Docs*. S/PV.2541, S/PV.2542, S/PV.2543, S/PV.2545, S/PV.2546 (25 May to 1 June 1984).

16. See *loc.cit* (notes 13-15). See also: 84 *Department of State Bulletin* (August 1984), p. 73; 87 *Department of State Bulletin* (June 1987), p. 70; 88 *Department of State Bulletin* (September 1988), p. 42.

17. S/RES/540(1983), adopted on 31 October 1983. Text reprinted in 37 *Yearbook of the United Nations* (1983), p. 239.

18. S/RES/552(1984), adopted on 1 June 1984. Text reprinted in 38 *Yearbook of the United Nations* (1984), p. 234.

19. S/RES/582(1986), adopted unanimously on 8 October 1986. As for S/RES/598(1987), see *supra* note 3.

20. Apart from the United Nations, several other international bodies dealt with the question of freedom of navigation and neutral commerce during the Iran-Iraq War. For example, the North Atlantic Council underlined the importance of maintaining freedom and security of navigation on 12 December 1980 and again on 11 December 1987: see, respectively, 81 *Department of State Bulletin* (February 1981), p. 51 and *1987 NATO Communiqués*, p. 27. At the European level, a declaration issued in The Hague on 19 April 1988 by the Foreign and Defence Ministers of the Western European Union stressed 'the necessity of respecting the principle of free navigation' and called for 'an immediate end to all mining and hostile activities against shipping in international waters, taking into account that such activities can call for measures of self-defence': see 34 *Keesing's Contemporary Archives* (1988), p. 36106 (the full text of the statement has been kindly provided by the Secretariat of the W.E.U. in London).

21. Some, though by no means all, Iraqi attacks on non-belligerent merchant vessels were directed against ships travelling in convoys escorted by Iranian naval vessels: see, for example, 28 *Keesing's Contemporary Archives* (1982), p. 31850; 30 *Keesing's Contemporary Archives* (1984), p. 32689. On the legality of attacks against ships travelling under enemy convoy, see, for example, Kalshoven, F., "Commentary on the 1909 London Declaration Concerning the Laws of Naval War", in: Ronzitti (ed.), *op.cit*. (note 8), pp. 257 *et seq.*, at pp. 265, 268, 272, 273, 275.

there is an undeniable tendency in recent practice to diminish immunity from attack for enemy merchant vessels. It is open to question whether this practice, which finds some support in a passage of the Nuremberg judgment which expressly condemns attacks only on neutral vessels,[22] has been transformed into law. A case could be made that Iraqi attacks on Iranian flagged ships were justified on the ground that these were otherwise integrated in Iran's war-sustaining effort by transporting oil that financed Iran's military operations. However, the traditional criterion to be taken into account in order to establish whether a merchant ship loses its immunity is that of its participating in the flag state's war-fighting effort, for example by signalling the position of an enemy warship. On the contrary, the criterion of participation in the enemy's war-sustaining effort, even though it finds some support in state practice and is advocated by a number of lawyers, is not unquestionable and does not yet seem to have gained the status of a principle of customary international law.[23]

Another question is whether the traditional rule on freedom of neutral commerce only applies to the strictly neutral states or to all states not parties to an armed conflict. During the Gulf War, Iranian attacks were mainly directed against ships en route to and from the ports of Saudi Arabia and, especially, Kuwait and one of the arguments referred to by Iran when trying to justify its attacks was that the moderate Arab Gulf States were not in fact strictly neutral but partial to Iraq, since they extensively subsidized the latter's war effort and could not, therefore, avail themselves of the benefits of the law of neutrality.[24] From a more general point of view, it should be stressed that, as we shall see later, other states, even when officially adopting a policy of strict neutrality, did not always abide by their duty to abstain from acts of partiality towards one of the belligerents.[25]

It has already been observed that, according to one view, modern international law recognizes and protects an attitude of so-called 'non-belligerency', as distinct from strict neutrality, on the part of those states which, while not directly taking part in the hostilities, assist one of the parties to an armed conflict and discriminate against the

---

22. See "International Military Tribunal (Nuremberg), October 1, 1944, Judgment", 41 *AJIL* (1947), pp. 172 *et seq.*, at pp. 303 *et seq.* (findings made in respect of charges against K. Dönitz and E. Raeder).

23. On the legality of attacks against merchant vessels, see, for example, Nwogugu, E.I., "Commentary on the 1922 Washington Treaty Relating to the Use of Submarines and Noxious Gases in Warfare, *etc.*", in: Ronzitti (ed.), *op.cit.* (note 8), pp. 353 *et seq.* According to Chapter 8.2.2.2 of the 1987 U.S. Navy *Commander's Handbook on the Law of Naval Operations NWP9*, it would be legal to attack and destroy, 'either with or without warning' enemy merchant vessels which are 'integrated into the enemy's war-fighting/war-sustaining effort' when 'compliance with the rules of the 1936 London Protocol [which obliges states to assure the safety of passengers and crew] would, under the circumstances of the specific encounter, subject the surface warship to imminent danger or would otherwise preclude mission accomplishment.' For the text of the 1936 London Procès-Verbal Relating to the Rules of Submarine Warfare Set Forth in Part IV of the Treaty of London of 22 April 1930, see Ronzitti (ed.), *op.cit.* (note 8), pp. 349 *et seq.*

24. See, for example, *UN Docs.* S/16585 (25 May 1984) and S/18557 (5 January 1987).

25. See *infra* paragraph II.

other.[26] During the Gulf War, several states, such as, for example, the United States and the Netherlands, made it clear that they regarded the Arab Gulf States, Saudi Arabia and Kuwait included, as non-belligerent states, since they did not take part in the hostilities.[27] If 'non-belligerency', as distinct from neutrality, were to be considered as a lawful attitude of third states in their relations with the parties to an armed conflict, it would follow that these states could not reasonably be expected to bear negative consequences for violations of the duty of impartiality, which would only pertain to neutrality in the strict sense.[28] According to this view, the so-called 'rights of neutrals' – the right to trade with belligerents included – should be considered to apply to *all* states not parties to an armed conflict.[29] Security Council resolutions relating to the Gulf War, which affirmed the right of free navigation and commerce in international waters and condemned attacks on merchant ships en route to and from the ports of states that were not parties to the hostilities, would seem to support this assumption.[30]

II LIMITATIONS ON THE RIGHT TO TRADE WITH BELLIGERENTS

In the traditional law of war, the right of neutrals to trade with belligerents was not absolute, but was limited by a number of duties stemming from the 1907 Hague Conventions or from customary law, such as the general duty of impartiality or the duty to tolerate certain measures imposed by belligerents.

Leaving aside the question of belligerents' restrictions on neutral trade, which will be dealt with later,[31] the traditional law of war did not allow neutral states to supply services and goods, especially arms and war materials, to belligerents.[32] A neutral Power was not, however, bound to prevent its nationals from supplying arms or other war materials to belligerents. Article 7 of the 1907 Hague Convention No. V Respecting

26. See, especially, Schindler, *loc.cit.* (note 5), pp. 261 *et seq.* and bibliography therein quoted; Schindler, D., "Commentary on the 1907 Hague Convention XIII Concerning the Rights and Duties of Neutral Powers in Naval War", in: Ronzitti (ed.), *op.cit.* (note 8), pp. 211 *et seq.*, at pp. 211-214. For modern state practice, see especially Norton, *loc.cit.* (note 5), at pp. 254 *et seq.*

27. See 87 *Department of State Bulletin* (August 1987), p. 80; *ibidem* (October 1987), p. 41; 19 *NYIL* (1988), pp. 390, 391.

28. According to Schindler, *loc.cit.* (note 5), at pp. 275-277, 'non-belligerency' is a factual situation to which international law attaches no specific legal consequences. It follows that, whereas 'non-belligerent' states are not protected *vis-à-vis* belligerents by the rules on neutrality, they enjoy certain rights and, in particular, those deriving from the United Nations Charter.

29. See, in particular, Schindler, *loc.cit.* (note 26), at pp. 213-214. The author points out that the so-called 'rights of neutrals' are not in fact 'rights in the proper sense', but 'consist, on the one hand, in the duty of belligerents to respect neutral territory and, on the other hand, in the negation of duties of neutrals which might be presumed if they were not expressly denied'.

30. See, in particular, S/RES/540(1983), *op.cit.* (note 17), paragraph 3; S/RES/552(1984), *op.cit.* (note 18), paragraphs 2, 4 and 5; S/RES/582(1986), *op.cit.* (note 19), paragraph 2; S/RES/598(1987), *op.cit.* (note 3), preamble.

31. See *infra* paragraph III.

32. See, for example, Oppenheim, *op.cit.* (note 7), at pp. 675, 738-745; Balladore Pallieri, *op.cit.* (note 7), at pp. 407 *et seq.*; Castrén, *op.cit.* (note 5), at pp. 474 *et seq.*

Rights and Duties of Neutral Powers or Persons in Case of War on Land[33] states that 'a neutral Power is not bound to prevent the export or transit, for one or the other of the belligerents, of arms, munitions of war, or, in general, of anything which can be of use to an army or fleet.' A neutral state could, of course, prohibit the supply of war materials to belligerents, if it so desired. However, if it chose so to do, it was bound to prevent the trade in arms or war materials with *both* belligerents, in order to comply with its duty to remain impartial.[34]

Similar rules also applied to naval warfare. Article 6 of the 1907 Hague Convention No. XIII[35] provides that 'the supply, in any manner, directly or indirectly, by a neutral Power to a belligerent Power, of war-ships, ammunition or war material of any kind whatever, is forbidden.' However, constraints on private individuals were stricter in maritime warfare than in land warfare: Article 8 of the same Convention states that 'a neutral Government is bound to employ the means at its disposal to prevent the fitting out or arming of any vessel within its jurisdiction which it has reason to believe is intended to cruise, or engage in hostile operations' against one of the belligerents. The difference between these provisions and those on land warfare has been explained by the fact that ships could have a decisive effect on the outcome of the war and that they could be easily identified, so that the ban on export could be more effectively monitored.[36]

As a result of the entry into force on the United Nations Charter, the right of third states to trade with states engaged in an armed conflict may further be limited by the United Nations Security Council. Leaving aside the case in which enforcement action is taken under Article 42 of the Charter, the Security Council can decide, under Article 41, to impose an embargo concerning all trade relations or the export of certain goods to all belligerents. An embargo can also be imposed against one belligerent only, which is considered to be the aggressor. The resolution recently adopted by the Security Council concerning a trade embargo against Iraq because of its aggression against Kuwait is an example of this latter category.[37] During the Iran-Iraq war, however, no such decisions were taken by the Security Council. After the adoption of Resolution 598(1987),[38] some states, such as the United States,[39] pressed for a follow-up resolution to penalize Iran through an arms embargo for its unwillingness to accept and implement that resolution, but such attempts were not crowned with success. On the other hand, Security Council resolutions during the Gulf War, Resolution 598(1987)

---

33. Text reprinted in 2 *AJIL* (1908), Supplement, pp. 117 *et seq.*
34. See, for example, the authors quoted *supra* note 32.
35. *Supra* note 10.
36. See, for example, Schindler, *loc.cit.* (note 26), at p. 218.
37. See S/RES/661(1990), adopted on 6 August 1990 'under Chapter VII' of the UN Charter.
38. *Supra* note 3.
39. See, for example, 87 *Department of State Bulletin* (October 1987), p. 41; 88 *Department of State Bulletin* (March 1988), pp. 74-75; *ibidem* (June 1988), p. 44; *ibidem* (October 1988), p. 61.

included, called upon all states that were not parties to the conflict to refrain from acts which might lead to a further escalation and widening of the conflict.[40]

As for the traditional limitations on trade with belligerents, the old distinction between state and private activity is regarded by some as obsolete, as a result of governmental control and regulation of international arms trade in most countries. Consequently, the view is sometimes put forward that, since states control exports of arms and munitions, neutral states would have a *duty*, as opposed to a mere faculty, to take measures to prevent private persons from supplying war material and other assistance to belligerents.[41] On the other hand, if 'non-belligerency', as opposed to strict neutrality, were nowadays to be regarded as a lawful attitude of third states in their relations with belligerents, it would follow that those limitations would only apply to the states which chose to adopt a strictly neutral attitude and not to the other 'non-belligerent' states: according to this view, these latter would have no duty to abstain from supplying belligerents with goods and services, nor would they have a general duty of impartiality towards belligerents.[42]

During the Gulf War, several states, such as France and most Arab States, especially Saudi Arabia and Kuwait, clearly adopted an attitude of 'non-belligerency' and did not feel bound by traditional neutrality obligations. France, in particular, despite its traditional policy not to supply arms to states involved in an armed conflict, soon became one of Iraq's major suppliers of arms and military equipment during the conflict.[43] Other states officially adopted an attitude of strict neutrality, but it may be

40. See, for example, S/RES/479(1980), adopted unanimously on 28 September 1980 (text reprinted in 34 *Yearbook of the United Nations* (1980), pp. 318-319), paragraph 3; S/RES/540(1983), *op.cit.* (note 17), paragraph 6; S/RES/552(1984), *op.cit.* (note 18), paragraph 3; S/RES/582(1986), *op.cit.* (note 19), paragraph 7; S/RES/598(1987), *op.cit.* (note 3), paragraph 5.

41. On the modern aspects of limitations on neutral trading activities, see, especially, Stone, J., *Legal Controls of International Conflict*, Sydney 1954, pp. 408 *et seq.*; McDougal, M.S./Feliciano, F.P., *Law and Minimum World Public Order*, New Haven/London 1961, pp. 437 *et seq.*; Friedman, W., *The Changing Structure of International Law*, London 1964, pp. 346-349; Williams, W.L. "Neutrality in Modern Armed Conflict: A Survey of the Developing Law", 90 *Military Law Review* (1980), pp. 9 *et seq.*, at pp. 31-33. See also Boczek, *loc.cit.* (note 4), at p. 256. On the modern aspects of the international arms trade, see, for example, Delbrück, J., "International Traffic in Arms – Legal and Political Aspects of a Long Neglected Problem of Arms Control and Disarmament", 24 *German Yearbook of International Law* (1981), pp. 114 *et seq.*; *Le droit international et les armes*, Paris 1983, at pp. 93 *et seq.*

42. See, especially, Schindler, *loc.cit.* (note 26), at pp. 214, 217.

43. On France's attitude with respect to the Iran-Iraq War and on arms sales to Iraq, see, for example, Rousseau, C., "Chronique des faits internationaux", 85 *RGDIP* (1981), at p. 177; 27 *AFDI* (1981), p. 859; 28 *AFDI* (1982), p. 1095; 29 *AFDI* (1983), pp. 853-854 and 909; 29 *Keesing's Contemporary Archives* (1983), p. 32595; 30 *AFDI* (1984), pp. 951-952 and 1012-1013; 31 *AFDI* (1985), pp. 962-963; 31 *Keesing's Contemporary Archives* (1985), p. 33562; 32 *Keesing's Contemporary Archives* (1986), p. 34515; 34 *AFDI* (1988), p. 901; 33 *Keesing's Contemporary Archives* (1988), p. 35863. Even before the outbreak of the conflict, France had been the main Western benefactor of Iraq's policy to try and move away from dependence on the Soviet Union for its arms supplies. France, therefore, justified some of its early deliveries to Iraq by referring to the necessity to honour previously signed contracts. The same justification was given for the announced delivery to Iran of missile-launchers craft ordered under the Shah, which had been detained under European sanctions since the time of the United States hostages crisis: see 27 *Keesing's Contemporary Archives* (1981), p. 31013; 27 *AFDI* (1981), p. 859.

questioned to what extent their factual behaviour was in accordance with their officially declared policies. Only a few examples will be given here.[44]

The United States immediately adopted, at the outbreak of hostilities, and periodically reaffirmed, throughout the conflict, an official policy of neutrality, implying 'strict and absolute impartiality', and stressed that it would not supply arms to either side, 'either directly or indirectly'.[45] However, quite apart from direct arms sales, a specific policy to deny arms and war materials was adopted against Iran only, a country which, under the Shah, had been supplied largely with United States military equipment. The United States had imposed an embargo on the sale of all United States goods to Iran on 7 April 1980, in retaliation for the seizure of the United States embassy staff in Teheran.[46] An arms embargo had also been imposed on Iran, in April 1980, by the member states of the European Communities,[47] but this was lifted on 20 January 1981, a few months after the outbreak of hostilities, as a result of the release of the United States hostages.[48] The United States, for its part, revoked its more general restrictions on trade with Iran, but an arms embargo was said to continue, even after the outbreak of the so-called 'Iran-Contra affair'.[49] In addition, as from 1983, the United States adopted a policy 'to attempt to discourage arms supplies' to Iran through bilateral consultations with other states (the so-called 'Operation Staunch'). This policy was said to be justified by Iran's 'stubborn' refusal to discuss the end of the war except on terms 'clearly unacceptable to the Iraqi side'.[50] Finally, Iran was subject to specific controls on certain exports, as were other countries which were thought to provide

---

44. On the arms trade during the Iran-Iraq War, see, generally, Ohlson, T./Brzoska, M., "The Trade in Major Conventional Weapons", 15 *SIPRI Yearbook* (1984), at pp. 195 *et seq.*; Brzoska, M./Ohlson, T., "The Trade in Major Conventional Weapons", 17 *SIPRI Yearbook* (1986), at pp. 344-345; Ohlson, T./Sköns, E., "The Trade in Major Conventional Weapons", 18 *SIPRI Yearbook* (1987), at pp. 203-205; Goose, S.D., "Armed Conflicts in 1986, and the Iraq-Iran War", 18 *SIPRI Yearbook* (1987), pp. 297 *et seq.*, at pp. 306-307.

45. See, for example, 81 *Department of State Bulletin* (July 1981), p. 17; 82 *Department of State Bulletin* (July 1982), pp. 45, 82; 83 *Department of State Bulletin* (July 1983), p. 89; 85 *Department of State Bulletin* (April 1985), p. 57; 86 *Department of State Bulletin* (March 1986), p. 41; 87 *Department of State Bulletin* (July 1987), pp. 59, 62; 88 *Department of State Bulletin* (July 1988), p. 61.

46. See 80 *Department of State Bulletin* (May 1980), pp. 1-2. On 17 April, additional measures were adopted, including a ban on all imports from Iran: see *ibidem*, at p. 8.

47. See 26 *Keesing's Contemporary Archives* (1980), p. 30530. On 18 May 1980, the E.C. Foreign Ministers further decided to impose full-scale trade sanctions on Iran, but only with respect to contracts signed after the seizure of the United States hostages: see *ibidem*, at pp. 30535-30536.

48. See 27 *Keesing's Contemporary Archives* (1981), p. 31087.

49. See, for example, 28 *Keesing's Contemporary Archives* (1982), p. 31521; 81 *Department of State Bulletin* (February 1981), pp. 11, 13. With special reference to the 'Iran-contra affair', whose aspects were mainly of internal United States concern and which, therefore, will not specifically be dealt with here, see, for example, 87 *Department of State Bulletin* (January 1987), pp. 67, 68, 69, 72; *ibidem* (February 1987), p. 23; *ibidem* (March 1987), p. 19.

50. See, for example, 86 *Department of State Bulletin* (March 1986), p. 41; *ibidem* (December 1986), p. 72; 87 *Department of State Bulletin* (January 1987), p. 73; *ibidem* (March 1987), p. 19; *ibidem* (June 1987), p. 70; *ibidem* (July 1987), p. 65; *ibidem* (August 1987), p. 81; *ibidem* (October 1987), p. 41; 88 *Department of State Bulletin* (March 1988), pp. 75-76.

support for acts of international terrorism.[51] Iraq, which was not affected by 'Operation Staunch',[52] was, since February 1982, no longer subject to anti-terrorism export controls and, on some occasions, 'non-military' equipment, which could easily be converted into military equipment, was sold to Iraq by the United States.[53]

The Soviet Union also adopted, at the outbreak of hostilities, an official attitude of neutrality.[54] This notwithstanding, after at first attempting to improve its relations with Iran by proposing the sale of Soviet military equipment, the Soviet Union soon resumed, after the first year and a half of the war, its arms deliveries to Iraq, a country which, before the war, had been largely dependent on the Soviet Union for its military supplies.[55] By July 1987, the Soviet Union was described by a United States official as 'Baghdad's largest supplier of military equipment and a key source of economic aid.'[56]

A more coherent attitude was adopted by the United Kingdom. From the start, the British Government declared that sales of arms and military equipment, which were subject to licensing procedures, would be subject to 'neutrality obligations' and that 'arms or ammunition' and/or 'lethal equipment' would not be sold to either side.[57] In

---

51. See, for example, 51 *Federal Register* 199 (15 October 1986), pp. 36702-36703. With respect to Iran, anti-terrorism controls were extended in 1984 and 1986 and required a license, which would not normally be granted, for any export of aircraft and helicopters, regardless of value and weight, and for exports of outboard motors of 45 horsepower and above; exports of goods and technology subject to control for national security purposes, regardless of value, were also subjected to a denial policy, if destined 'for a military end-use or end-user'. Further export controls were imposed on Iran on 1 October and 27 November 1987: these covered self-contained underwater breathing apparatus and related equipment, as well as certain marine and battlefield-useful commodities, and were said to be a response to Iran's conduct of, or support for, underwater attacks against shipping or installations in the Persian Gulf and, more generally, to Iranian actions directed at United States and neutral shipping in international waters. See 84 *Department of State Bulletin* (November 1984), p. 68; 49 *Federal Register* 190 (28 September 1984), pp. 38243-38245; 51 *Federal Register* 108 (5 June 1986), pp. 20468-20469; 52 *Federal Register* 190 (1 October 1987), pp. 36749, 36756-36757; 52 *Federal Register* 228 (27 November 1987), pp. 45309-45311.

52. See, for example, 87 *Department of State Bulletin* (October 1987), p. 43. On the contrary, on some occasions, United States spokesmen admitted that the United States had 'an important stake in Iraq's continuing ability to sustain its defences' (87 *Department of State Bulletin* (July 1987), p. 66).

53. See, for example, 32 *Keesing's Contemporary Archives* (1986), p. 34515, which refers to the delivery of 48 U.S. Bell 214 ST troop-carrying helicopters, which were subsequently fitted with rocket launchers. On 27 August 1987, the United States and Iraq signed a five-year trade agreement aimed at expanding commercial ties between the two countries: see 34 *Keesing's Contemporary Archives* (1988), pp. 35863-35864. Apart from commercial relations, it is worth mentioning that United States satellite information was made available to Iraq at least in 1985 and 1986: see Boczek, *loc.cit.* (note 4), p. 256.

54. See, for example, 27 *Keesing's Contemporary Archives* (1981), p. 31011.

55. See, for example, 27 *Keesing's Contemporary Archives* (1981), p. 31012; 28 *Keesing's Contemporary Archives* (1982), pp. 31521, 31522, 31851; 29 *Keesing's Contemporary Archives* (1983), p. 32100. See also Goose, *loc.cit.* (note 44), p. 306.

56. Armacost, M.H., "U.S.-Soviet Relations: Testing Gorbachev's 'New Thinking'", 87 *Department of State Bulletin* (September 1987), pp. 36 *et seq.*, at p. 39.

57. See, for example, 52 *BYIL* (1981), p. 520; 53 *BYIL* (1982), p. 559; 54 *BYIL* (1983), p. 549; 55 *BYIL* (1984), p. 597; 56 *BYIL* (1985), p. 534; 57 *BYIL* (1986), p. 644; 58 *BYIL* (1987), pp. 638, 639. On 24 September 1987, the United Kingdom signed an export credit agreement with Iraq, but it denied that the agreement would help Iraq in its war with Iran, since it related to capital goods, machinery and services, as well as to medical and other humanitarian goods: see 34 *Keesing's Contemporary Archives* (1988), p. 35863.

October 1985, the British Government made public certain guidelines on the delivery of 'defence equipment' to Iran and Iraq. While maintaining its refusal 'to supply any lethal equipment to either side', the British Government declared that, subject to that refusal, it would 'attempt to fulfil existing contracts and obligations', but added that it would not, in the future, 'approve orders for any defence equipment which, in [its] view, would significantly enhance the capability of either side to prolong or exacerbate the conflict.'[58] These guidelines were apparently narrowly interpreted to allow the sale of spare parts for tanks and aircraft to belligerents.[59]

With reference to chemical warfare, the so-called 'neutral' states seem to have abided more strictly by their neutrality obligations. Controls on the export to both Iran and Iraq of certain chemicals, which were capable of being used to manufacture chemical weapons, were imposed by several Western European States,[60] as well as by the United States.[61]

III   MEASURES TAKEN BY BELLIGERENTS INTERFERING WITH
      NEUTRAL COMMERCE

The right of neutrals to trade with belligerents was subject, according to the traditional law of war, to measures that the latter could lawfully take in order to stop the flow of goods to the enemy: these were visit and search and blockade.

Visit and search of neutral merchant vessels could lawfully be effected in order to ascertain whether those vessels were carrying goods considered to be contraband of war. Belligerents had the right to board vessels bound for an enemy port, as well as those bound for a neutral port from which goods were presumed to be shipped to the enemy (doctrine of 'continuous voyage'). It is worth pointing out that, under the doctrine of contraband of war, only goods *bound for* enemy territory, and not those

58. 56 *BYIL* (1985), p. 534. See also 57 *BYIL* (1986), p. 644; 58 *BYIL* (1987), p. 638.

59. See, for example, 28 *Keesing's Contemporary Archives* (1982), p. 31522; 32 *Keesing's Contemporary Archives* (1986), p. 34515; 33 *Keesing's Contemporary Archives* (1987), p. 35160.

60. See, for example, 31 *Keesing's Contemporary Archives* (1985), p. 33562; 57 *BYIL* (1986), pp. 633-634; 19 *Rev.belge* (1986), pp. 431-432. It was reported in 1983 that the British Government had supplied Iraq with equipment for defence against chemical weapons; on the other hand, the British Government strongly denied in 1984 Iranian accusations that it was supplying Iraq with chemical weapons; see, respectively, 30 *Keesing's Contemporary Archives* (1984), pp. 32689, and 33058; see also 55 *BYIL* (1984), p. 588.

61. See, for example, 30 *Keesing's Contemporary Archives* (1984), p. 33058. For the text of the United States Rule of 30 March 1984 imposing foreign policy controls on the export from the United States to Iran and Iraq of certain chemicals used in producing chemical weapons, see 49 *Federal Register* 65 (3 April 1984), pp. 13135-13136. Foreign policy controls were subsequently expanded to the export of additional chemicals: see 49 *Federal Register* 180 (14 September 1984), pp. 36079-36080; 52 *Federal Register* 147 (31 July 1987), pp. 28550-28552; 53 *Federal Register* 129 (6 July 1988), pp. 25325-25326. All United States rules were said to further, *inter alia*, United States policy of maintaining neutrality in the Iran-Iraq war.

coming from enemy territory could be seized. This rule was a corollary of the general principle according to which trade with belligerents was permitted.[62]

Practice in the Gulf War has clearly demonstrated that belligerents still enjoy the right to visit and search neutral merchant vessels in order to ascertain whether they are carrying contraband of war. From 1985 especially, the Iranian navy systematically visited and searched neutral ships of various nationalities, which were suspected of carrying contraband.[63] Iraq was not in a position to do the same, since most of its warships had been destroyed in the early stages of the war.[64] As no neutral vessel was in a position to reach Iraqi ports, Iran concentrated on visiting vessels travelling to the ports of non-belligerent Gulf States, especially Kuwait, which was suspected of acting as Iraq's intermediary, partly because of the exceptional growth of Kuwaiti imports during the war.

Iran's decision to exercise the traditional right to visit and search was widely acquiesced in by third states. The United States expressly recognized that 'there is a basis in international law for ships searches by belligerents'.[65] The United Kingdom also recognized that 'under Article 51 of the United Nations Charter there is a specific and inherent right of self-defence by stopping and searching foreign merchant ships on the high seas' and that Iraq was using 'that specific right' to stop merchant ships.[66] The Netherlands, for its part, only seemed to recognize a belligerent's right to visit and search on the high seas with respect to ships travelling 'to and from' ports of the other belligerent.[67] This notwithstanding, the traditional doctrine of continuous voyage should still be regarded as valid.

With respect to the nature of contraband, the traditional distinction between 'absolute contraband' (*i.e.*, articles exclusively used for war) and 'conditional contraband' (*i.e.*, articles susceptible of use in war as well as for purposes of peace), as well as the so-called 'free list' (*i.e.*, articles which are not susceptible of use in war), are widely regarded as obsolete by legal writers, mainly because of recent belligerent practice to enlarge the category of goods liable to capture in order to comprise all goods considered to be useful for the enemy's war effort.[68] However, it is equally true that neutrals have an opposite interest and that their policy is to limit the right of belligerents

---

62. On the traditional doctrine of contraband of war and on visit and search, see generally Oppenheim, *op.cit.* (note 7), pp. 799 *et seq.* and pp. 848 *et seq.*; Balladore Pallieri, *op.cit.* (note 7), pp. 414 *et seq.* and pp. 448 *et seq.*; Castrén, *op.cit.* (note 5), pp. 545 *et seq.* and pp. 577 *et seq.*

63. See, for example, 32 *Keesing's Contemporary Archives* (1986), p. 34514; 33 *Keesing's Contemporary Archives* (1987), p. 35160. On 17 November 1987, Iran adopted legislation concerning prize law: see Momtaz, D., "Le droit de la guerre maritime: la pratique de l'Iran", to be published in a forthcoming volume on the maritime aspects of the Iran-Iraq War, edited by A. de Guttry and N. Ronzitti, at p. 7 (of the manuscript).

64. In addition, what remained of Iraq's naval forces could not leave Iraqi waters as a consequence of Iran's 'blockade' of Iraqi coasts: see *infra* in this paragraph.

65. See, for example, 86 *Department of State Bulletin* (March 1986), p. 41; 88 *Department of State Bulletin* (July 1988), p. 61.

66. See 57 *BYIL* (1986), p. 635; 59 *BYIL* (1988), pp. 580-581.

67. See *UN Doc.* S/PV.2546 (1 June 1984), p. 13.

68. See, for example, Kalshoven, *loc.cit.* (note 21), at pp. 272 and 274.

to seize goods. During the Gulf War, Iran treated as contraband of war all goods which could sustain, directly of indirectly, the enemy's war effort.[69] On the other hand, the United Kingdom only seemed to allow for interference with the supply of arms to the other belligerent for use in the conflict.[70] The United States also stressed, when explaining measures taken to protect its shipping, that its flag vessels were not carrying contraband since they carried 'no war material for Iraq' and would not 'serve belligerent ports'. On some occasions it was emphasized that United States flag ships only carried crude oil and oil products; on this latter point, however, United States officials also stressed that United States ships were not 'carrying oil from Iraq'.[71] An extensive interpretation of the doctrine of contraband would run counter to the right of neutrals to trade with belligerents. The United Kingdom position, according to which the exercise of traditional belligerent rights has nowadays to be reconciled with the right of self-defence under Article 51 of the United Nations Charter, carries with it the consequence of limiting the rights of belligerents and of enhancing those of neutrals. In addition, it is worth pointing out that the doctrine of contraband of war could certainly not justify Iran's frequent attacks on non-belligerent merchant vessels bound for non-belligerent ports or, even more so, attacks on vessels coming from such ports.[72]

The other traditional method for interfering with neutral trade with the enemy was blockade. Blockade, which, in order to be binding had to be declared and maintained by a naval force sufficient effectively to prevent access to the ports of the enemy, implied that commercial intercourse with the blockaded ports or coasts was totally forbidden; therefore, unlike the doctrine of contraband of war, blockade was a valid means for stopping *any* flow of goods bound for or coming from the blockaded ports or coasts. Trade relations, of course, could continue with ports which remained open.[73] For a number of reasons, mainly related to developments in the techniques of naval and aerial warfare, the traditional rules on naval blockade are widely regarded as being nowadays of rather limited interest.[74] This notwithstanding, blockade can probably still be regarded as a lawful measure, even though it has to be reconciled with Article 51 of the United Nations Charter. At the beginning of the Gulf War, on 22 September

---

69. According to the 1987 Iranian law (*supra* note 63), all goods belonging to states at war with Iran become the property of Iran; as for goods belonging to neutral states or to neutral or enemy nationals, two categories of goods are liable to capture: those the transport of which to enemy territory has been prohibited and those destined, directly or indirectly, to enemy territory if they effectively contribute to sustain the enemy's war effort. During the Iran-Iraq War, since no vessels were able to reach Iraqi territory, Iran's visits were mainly directed, as has already been pointed out, at vessels travelling towards Kuwait.

70. See *loc.cit.* (note 66).

71. See 87 *Department of State Bulletin* (July 1987), pp. 60-61; *ibidem* (October 1987), p. 42; 88 *Department of State Bulletin* (June 1988), p. 44.

72. See the authors quoted *supra* note 62.

73. On naval blockade, see generally Oppenheim, *op.cit.* (note 7), at pp. 290 *et seq.*; Balladore Pallieri, *op.cit.* (note 7), at pp. 428 *et seq.*; Castrén, *op.cit.* (note 5), at pp. 768 *et seq.*

74. See, for example, Kalshoven, *loc.cit.* (note 21), at pp. 272 and 274.

1980, Iran announced that it would prohibit all transportation of cargo to Iraq[75] and, thanks to the superiority of its naval forces and to the shortness of Iraq's coastline, effectively succeeded in preventing access to Iraqi ports throughout the conflict. On 1 October 1980, Iran issued another declaration concerning the 'closure' of the Shatt-al-Arab.[76] It is not clear whether these measures entirely satisfied all the traditional criteria for the lawfulness of a maritime blockade; Iran itself did not expressly refer to the traditional law of war at sea in order to justify its conduct, but rather pointed out that 'Iraq by its aggression to Iran [had] strongly endangered the safety of navigation.'[77] Be that as it may, it is worth recalling, with respect to the attitude of third states, that at least the United Kingdom, when referring to the exercise of traditional belligerent rights, expressed its opinion that the right of self-defence would not 'extend to the imposition of a maritime blockade' or to forms of economic warfare other than the visit and search of merchant ships.[78]

Apart from visit and search and, possibly, blockade, it is very doubtful that other belligerent measures interfering with neutrals' trading rights could be justified by having recourse either to the traditional law of war or to the law of self-defence. The main examples of such additional measures are the so-called 'war zones' and/or 'total exclusion zones': merchant vessels entering such zones are usually declared to be liable to be attacked on sight, without any attempt to determine, by a procedure of visit and search, whether they are carrying contraband of war. As a result of the setting up of such a zone, the right of neutrals to trade with belligerents is almost completely suppressed in the maritime area concerned.[79] The lawfulness of such zones, however, has not been validated by state practice, at least as far as neutral merchant vessels are concerned. Suffice it to recall, in this respect, the Nuremburg judgment and particularly

75. See 27 *Keesing's Contemporary Archives* (1981), p. 31006. Momtaz, *op.cit.* (note 63), at p. 4, note 13, refers to a 'Notice to Mariners No. 17/59', dated 22 September 1980.

76. See Momtaz, *op.cit.* (note 63), at pp. 5-6. The author refers (note 15) to a 'Notice to Mariners No. 18/59', dated 1 October 1980 and rightly observes that, since Iran's 'blockade' of the Iraqi coastline also covered the mouth of the Shatt-al-Arab, the reasons for this second proclamation were not very clear. It is worth pointing out, in this respect, that, at the outbreak of hostilities, some seventy-one neutral vessels were trapped in the Shatt-al-Arab and that, whereas Iran at some point agreed to enabling them to leave under the United Nations flag, Iraq refused to allow for the implementation of the plan, 'since these vessels must fly the Iraqi flag as long as they are in the Shatt-al-Arab': see 27 *Keesing's Contemporary Archives* (1981), p. 31014; *UN Doc.* S/14221 (16 October 1980).

77. See Momtaz, *op.cit.* (note 63), at p. 5.

78. See 59 *BYIL* (1988), p. 581.

79. On the practice of 'war zones' or 'exclusion zones', see, among others, Oppenheim, *op.cit.* (note 7), at pp. 680 *et seq.*; Castrén, *op.cit.* (note 5), at pp. 309 *et seq.*; Fenrick, W.J., "The Exclusive Zone Device in the Law of Naval Warfare", 24 *Can.YIL* (1986), pp. 91 *et seq.* With specific reference to the Iran-Iraq War, see also Jenkins, M., "Air Attacks on Neutral Shipping in the Persian Gulf: The Legality of the Iraqi Exclusion Zone and Iranian Reprisals", 8 *Boston College International and Comparative Law Review* (1985), pp. 517 *et seq.*; Leckow, R., "The Iran-Iraq Conflict in the Gulf: The Law of War Zones", 37 *ICLQ* (1988), pp. 629 *et seq.*

the passage condemning the German policy of sinking on sight neutral vessels venturing into a 'war zone'.[80]

During the Gulf War, Iran established a maritime 'war zone' which was restricted to its territorial waters outside the Strait of Hormuz. This zone was not a 'total exclusion zone' inasmuch as Iran did not formally prohibit access to all vessels, regardless of their hostile nature, but only subjected passage of foreign vessels to previous authorization for security reasons.[81] Apparently, the United States expressed its willingness to exercise the right of innocent passage in Iran's territorial sea and Iran referred to the works of the third United Nations Conference on the Law of the Sea, as well as to Article 19 of the 1982 United Nations Convention on the Law of the Sea, in order to claim the right to subject innocent passage of warships through its territorial sea to previous authorization.[82] In so doing, the United States blurred the distinction between the exercise of navigational rights in time of peace and in time of war. In effect it is to be assumed that, in the latter case, a belligerent has more penetrating powers as far as the control of its maritime belt is concerned. Be that as it may, and leaving aside the question of innocent passage by warships and, more generally, of the exercise of navigational rights in time of armed conflict,[83] it could be argued that Iran's 'war zone', inasmuch as it was confined to Iran's territorial sea and did not extend into the Strait of Hormuz, was a reasonable measure justified by the law of self-defence under Article 51 of the United Nations Charter.[84] As such, however, Iran's 'war zone' could not have justified Iranian attacks on merchant vessels, which, in any case, were mainly directed against vessels navigating on the high seas and outside the zone. As for the Strait of Hormuz, Iran's repeated threats to close the strait[85] were never put into practice, possibly because of third states' prompt and strong reactions.[86]

80. See "International Military Tribunal (Nuremberg), October 1, 1944. Judgment", *loc.cit.* (note 22), at p. 304 (findings made in respect of charges against K. Dönitz).

81. See Momtaz, *op.cit.* (note 63), at pp. 2-3, who again quotes the 'Notice to Mariners No. 17/59' of 22 September 1980. Iran's 'war zone' comprised all Iranian coastal waters between the border with Iraq and a line joining points situated at twelve miles south of Abu Musa and Sirri islands, south of Cable Bank Light and south-west of Farsi island. Thus, despite allegations to the contrary, Iran's 'war zone' did not affect waters in the Strait of Hormuz. See also the map published in 87 *Department of State Bulletin* (October 1987), p. 40.

82. See Momtaz, *op.cit.* (note 63), at pp. 16-17. On Iran's position, see also *UN Doc*. S/20525 (15 March 1989) and Iran's declaration made upon signature of the 1982 United Nations Convention on the Law of the Sea on 10 December 1982 (United Nations, *Multilateral Treaties Deposited With the Secretary-General. Status as at 31 December 1988*, New York 1989, p. 782).

83. On the relationship between the law of war and conventions on the law of the sea, see Ronzitti, *loc.cit.* (note 12), at pp. 363-365, and bibliography therein quoted.

84. On the legality of Iran's 'war zone' see, for example, Leckow, *loc.cit.* (note 79), at pp. 638-639; Russo, *loc.cit.* (note 4), at p. 389; Boczek, *loc.cit.* (note 4), at p. 251.

85. See, for example, 29 *Keesing's Contemporary Archives* (1983), p. 32595; 33 *Keesing's Contemporary Archives* (1987), pp. 35160, 35598.

86. On the attitude of third states, see, for example, 85 *Department of State Bulletin* (May 1985), p. 46; 86 *Department of State Bulletin* (August 1986), p. 71; 87 *Department of State Bulletin* (April 1987), p. 52; *ibidem* (June 1987), p. 70; *ibidem* (July 1987), pp. 59, 66; 27 *AFDI* (1981), p. 895; 33 *AFDI* (1987), p. 849; 13 *NYIL* (1982), p. 259. With reference to the regime of passage, it is well-known that the 1982 UN Convention on the Law of the Sea grants a right of 'transit passage', encompassing a right of overflight and

Iraq, for its part, established a maritime 'exclusion zone' on 12 August 1982. This zone extended from the Shatt-al-Arab into the high seas up to 65 km. from Kharg Island, on which was an important Iranian oil terminal. On 15 August President Hussein warned that foreign shipping companies 'had only themselves to blame' if their ships approached Kharg Island.[87] As a matter of fact, most Iraqi attacks on foreign shipping were directed against oil tankers travelling to and from Iran and inside the exclusion zone.[88] Iraq relied on both the law of self-defence and the law of war at sea in order to justify its maritime exclusion zone. On the one hand, Iraq stressed the limited nature of its zone, which was said to have been imposed in order to cope with the difficulty of identifying the nationality of ships and to be justified by 'the right of legitimate self-defence'. On the other hand, Iraq also stressed that the zone was justified on the ground of the existence of 'war' and invoked the law of war at sea. According to Iraq, this allowed it to impose a blockade of enemy ports and conduct military operations against all vessels trading with the enemy, especially in the light of Iran's attacks on foreign shipping travelling to and from the ports of non-belligerent Gulf States.[89] It seems clear, however, that the traditional law of blockade would not have justified Iraq's exclusion zone. Apart from other considerations, the law of blockade did not allow for attacks on sight of vessels breaking or attempting to break blockade, but only for their capture and condemnation. Even from the point of view of evolving customary law, it would seem that, while it is doubtful that the setting up of an 'exclusion zone' might justify attacks on enemy merchant vessels, it would certainly not allow for attacks on neutral merchant vessels.

Third states' reactions against belligerent restrictions on neutral trade were mainly directed against attacks on neutral shipping on the high seas and outside the declared 'war/exclusion zones'. It has already been pointed out that attacks on neutral shipping

---

the liberty for submarines to pass submerged, through straits, such as the Strait of Hormuz, which are used for international navigation between one part of the high sea or an exclusive economic zone and another part of the high sea or exclusive economic zone (Articles 37 *et seq.*). It seems that the United States assumed, throughout the conflict, that all nations enjoyed a right of unimpeded transit passage through the Strait of Hormuz in accordance with the 1982 Convention, this being regarded, on this point, as declaratory of existing customary law: see, for example, 78 *AJIL* (1984), pp. 884-885. According to Iran, on the other hand, the regime of transit passage, as opposed to the traditional regime of non-suspendible innocent passage, was not based on customary law, and would only be brought to force, for states parties, as a result of the entry into force of the 1982 Convention: see, for example, United Nations, *op.cit.* (note 82), p. 762; *UN Doc.* S/20525 (15 March 1989). On this question see, for example, Leanza, U., "The Delimitation of Marine Areas in the Persian Gulf and the Right of Passage in the Strait of Hormuz", 1 *Yearbook of the University of Rome II, Department of Public Law* (1988), pp. 388 *et seq.*, at pp. 400-402 and, more generally, Ronzitti, *loc.cit.* (note 12), at pp. 377 *et seq.*

87. See 28 *Keesing's Contemporary Archives* (1982), p. 31858; Rousseau, C., "Chronique des faits internationaux", 86 *RGDIP* (1982), pp. 812-813. On 26 February 1986, Iraq extended the 'exclusion zone' to include areas close to Kuwait: see Rousseau, C., "Chronique des faits internationaux", 90 *RGDIP* (1986), p. 678. See also the map published in 87 *Department of State Bulletin* (October 1987), p. 40.

88. See, for example, 30 *Keesing's Contemporary Archives* (1984), pp. 32689, 33058; 31 *Keesing's Contemporary Archives* (1985), p. 33560; 32 *Keesing's Contemporary Archives* (1986), p. 34514.

89. See, for example, 28 *Keesing's Contemporary Archives* (1982), p. 31850; *UN Docs.* S/16590 (27 May 1984), S/16972 (20 February 1985).

are to be considered as totally illegal, even from the standpoint of the traditional law of war. The question of reprisals remains to be dealt with, however. Both belligerents tried to justify restrictions on neutral commerce, including the setting up of exclusion zones and attacks on neutral shipping, by referring to arguments which clearly resemble the traditional doctrine of belligerent reprisals affecting the rights of neutrals. However, the question of reprisals will be dealt with elsewhere in this volume.[90]

IV MEASURES TAKEN BY NEUTRALS IN ORDER TO ENFORCE FREEDOM OF COMMERCE

The traditional law of warfare provided neutral states with certain means of enforcing their right to trade with belligerents. Neutral states could protest against wrongful measures taken by belligerents and could resort to reprisals. However, protests and reprisals did not protect their merchant shipping from the actual danger of wrongful acts by belligerents. The 1909 London Declaration Concerning the Laws of Naval War[91] recognized the right of convoy: Articles 61 and 62 of the Declaration specified that 'neutral vessels under national convoy are immune from search': and that, if the commander of a belligerent ship had reason to suspect that the confidence of the commander of the convoy had been abused and communicated his suspicions to him, it would be for the commander of the convoy alone to investigate the matter and, in the event, withdraw protection from one or more vessels. However, the 1909 Declaration never entered into force and at least one major maritime Power, the United Kingdom, does not seem to consider convoy as a right rooted in customary international law.[92] Convoy apart, a policy of denying visit and search by duly commissioned ships of belligerents should be regarded as unlawful.

The Gulf War has shown that neutrals are entitled to take measures in order to protect their shipping. Several states did not confine themselves to protesting against attacks on neutral merchant vessels and against the mining of international waters, but took concrete steps in order to ensure freedom of navigation and the 'free flow of oil' from the Gulf and the Strait of Hormuz. These steps consisted in the deployment of naval units in the region of the Gulf and of the Strait of Hormuz in order to protect international shipping and/or to carry out minesweeping operations.

Leaving aside the question of minesweeping operations on the high seas, the legality of which seems beyond question,[93] the protection of neutral shipping was effected in

---

90. See Chapter 3, III, in this book.

91. Text reprinted in Ronzitti (ed.), *op.cit.* (note 8), pp. 224 *et seq.*

92. For the traditional British position on convoy, see Oppenheim, *op.cit.* (note 7), at pp. 849-851, 858-859.

93. On this question, see Ronzitti, N., "La guerre du Golfe, le déminage et la circulation des navires", 33 *AFDI* (1987), pp. 247 *et seq.*, at pp. 650-651. A different question is, of course, whether the illegal mining of the high seas can give rise to self-defence under Article 51 of the United Nations Charter and thus justify attacks on mine-laying vessels: on this latter question, see also, for example, Nordquist, M.H./Wachenfeld, M.G., "Legal Aspects of Reflagging Kuwaiti Tankers and Laying of Mines in the Persian Gulf", 31 *German Yearbook of International Law* (1988), pp. 138 *et seq.*, at pp. 161-164.

different ways. Some states, such as the United Kingdom and France, decided not to resort to the rules on convoy in order to protect their flag ships. The function of the British 'Armilla Patrol' was at first simply one of providing a visible naval presence in the area in order to encourage British shipping to continue to transit the Strait of Hormuz; as from 1987, British warships began to accompany ships in transit.[94] French naval vessels were said to be authorized to assist merchant vessels 'according to circumstances' and 'in accordance with international law'.[95] It is interesting to note, in this connection, that, whereas the United Kingdom, as we have seen, expressly allowed for the visit and search of merchant vessels by Iranian warships,[96] France at first attempted to prevent visit. It seems, however, that France's attitude was subsequently abandoned.[97]

The United States and Italy decided to adopt the technique of convoy in order to protect their merchant ships. The United States specified, that, in case a belligerent tried to exercise the right to visit and search for contraband with respect to United States flag ships in convoy, the United States escort would certify the absence of contraband.[98] The Italian Government expressly referred to Articles 61 and 62 of the 1909 London Declaration, thereby indicating that it regarded them as declaratory of existing customary law.[99] However, when the Italian naval unit did in fact reach the Gulf, at the end of September 1987, it was reported that a note issued by the Ministry of Defence itself specified that, if the commander of an Iranian warship insisted on visiting an escorted ship in order to ascertain the true nature of its cargo, he could be allowed to visit the ship, unarmed and accompanied by the commander of the Italian escort.[100] It seems clear that this attitude was not required by the 1909 London Declaration, which, as already noted, gives the convoying officer the exclusive power to investigate allegations that a vessel under his convoy carries contraband.

---

94. See House of Commons, *Third Special Report from the Defence Committee, Session 1986-1987. The Protection of British Merchant Shipping in the Persian Gulf*, London 1987; 58 *BYIL* (1987), pp. 638-639; 59 *BYIL* (1988), p. 582.

95. See 27 *AFDI* (1981), p. 895; 33 *AFDI* (1987), p. 948; 34 *AFDI* (1988), p. 964; Rousseau, C., "Chronique des faits internationaux", 92 *RGDIP* (1988), pp. 142-143.

96. See *supra* note 66 and accompanying text.

97. See, for example, 32 *Keesing's Contemporary Archives* (1986), p. 34514; Rousseau, C., "Chronique des faits internationaux", 90 *RGDIP* (1986), pp. 233 and 677-678; 91 *RGDIP* (1987), p. 139; Ronzitti, N., "The Crisis of the Traditional Law Regulating International Armed Conflicts at Sea and the Need for its Revision", in: Ronzitti (ed.), *op.cit.* (note 8), pp. 1 *et seq.*, at p. 8. A similar attitude was allegedly adopted by the Soviet Union, whose decision to station naval combat vessels in the Persian Gulf and to provide escorts for its merchant vessels was said to be a response to Iran's decision to stop, search and detain a Soviet arms-carrying vessel in September 1986: see 87 *Department of State Bulletin* (July 1987), pp. 62 and 64; *ibidem* (October 1987), pp. 39 and 42. Be that as it may, it seems that Iran subsequently avoided exercising its right to visit and search with respect to Soviet vessels: see Boczek, *loc.cit.* (note 4), at p. 261.

98. See 26 *ILM* (1987), p. 1458; 88 *Department of State Bulletin* (March 1988), p. 74; *ibidem* (June 1988), p. 44.

99. See Camera dei Deputati, *X Legislatura, Bollettino delle Giute e delle Commissioni Parlamentari, IV Commissione Permanente, martedì 8 settembre 1987*, at p. 5.

100. See *Corriere della Sera* (10 October 1987), p. 4 and *ibidem* (12 October 1987), p. 4.

With respect to convoy, it is also interesting to note that the Dutch Government, which did not send naval units to the Gulf in order to protect its merchant shipping, had also referred to Articles 61 and 62 of the 1909 London Declaration as a possible basis for protection under international law when answering questions raised in Parliament in 1980. However, the Dutch Government had added that it was a 'vexed question' whether or not those rules might still be considered to apply.[101] On the whole, given that the practice of the United States and Italy was not seriously challenged, it seems reasonable to conclude that convoy has gained currency as a lawful means of protecting neutral shipping.

The deployment of naval units in the Gulf proved to be a rather effective deterrent against attacks on non-belligerent merchant vessels. However, the great majority of merchant ships passing through the Strait of Hormuz (even excluding Gulf States vessels) sailed under the flag of states which had no naval presence in the Gulf. The Gulf States themselves were not in a position effectively to protect merchant ships flying their flag. They were the particular target of Iranian attacks.

Western warships in the Gulf area were at first only allowed to protect their own flag vessels and to provide assistance to foreign ships only after an attack had occurred. This policy changed towards the end of the conflict when the United States announced that it would also 'provide assistance under certain circumstances to ships in distress in the Persian Gulf': such assistance would be provided to 'friendly, innocent neutral vessels flying a non-belligerent flag' that were not carrying contraband.[102] The United Kingdom, for its part, announced that its warships would protect foreign flag ships having a clear majority United Kingdom or dependent territory interest in the ownership,[103] while France declared that the situation of foreign flag ships on which French seamen were employed was being 'clearly scrutinized'.[104] This policy was usually considered to be a 'humanitarian outgrow' of the intensification of the 'tanker war' and to be consistent with neutrality obligations. It is a moot point, however, whether a right to protect foreign vessels can be based on the right of collective self-defence.

One of the most striking features of the Gulf War from the point of view of the protection of neutral shipping was undoubtedly the practice of reflagging Kuwaiti tankers.[105] As a result of escalating attacks on its shipping, Kuwait decided, in 1986, to seek assistance from the permanent members of the United Nations Security Council

---

101. See 13 *NYIL* (1982), p. 259.

102. See 88 *Department of State Bulletin* (July 1988), p. 61; *ibidem* (September 1988), p. 42; *ibidem* (October 1988), p. 62.

103. See Lowe, A.V., "United Kingdom Practice in the Gulf Conflict" to be published in de Guttry/Ronzitti (eds.), *op.cit.* (note 63), at p. 11 of the manuscript.

104. See 34 *AFDI* (1988), p. 964.

105. On this practice, see, for example, Nordquist/Wachenfeld, *loc.cit.* (note 93), at pp. 140 *et seq.*; Mertus, J., "The Nationality of Ships and International Responsibility: The Reflagging of the Kuwaity Tankers", 17 *Denver Journal of International Law and Policy* (1988), pp. 207 *et seq.*; Davidson, S., "United States Protection of Reflagged Kuwaiti Vessels in the Gulf War: The Legal Implications", 4 *International Journal of Estuarine and Coastal Law* (1989), pp. 173 *et seq.*; Wolfrum, R., "Reflagging and Escort Operations in the Persian Gulf: An International Law Perspective", 29 *Virg.JIL* (1989), pp. 387 *et seq.*

in protecting its vessels and maritime commerce. The Soviet Union responded to this request by allowing Kuwait to charter three Soviet-registered tankers, which would thereby become entitled to Soviet naval protection. The United States went further and agreed to re-register eleven of Kuwait's state-owned oil tankers under the United States flag.[106] The United States Government said that the reflagging of Kuwaiti tankers in the United States was 'an unusual measure to meet an extraordinary situation', but stressed that, while the vessels in question would have to meet ownership and other technical requirements under United States laws and regulations, the reflagging was consistent with both domestic and international law and would entitle the reflagged vessels to the same type of protection as that accorded other United States flag vessels operating in the Gulf. At the same time, the United States Government also stressed that the reflagging would not change its official position of neutrality in the conflict, as all ships under United States protection would 'adhere strictly to the rules of neutrality' and none of them would 'carry contraband or serve belligerent ports'.[107]

Apart from the United States, the United Kingdom also agreed to re-register three Kuwaiti oil tankers under the British flag and emphasized the purely commercial and administrative nature of reflagging, not requiring Government approval.[108] The practice of reflagging was not, as such, seriously challenged by Iran.[109]

CONCLUSIONS

The Iran-Iraq War has demonstrated that the old concept of neutrality still plays a certain role in modern situations of armed conflict where the United Nations Security Council fails to determine that an act of aggression has taken place and to identify the aggressor. However, it is necessary to assess if and how far the rules on neutrality have been influenced by the entry into force of the United Nations Charter.

With respect to neutral states' commercial *rights*, practice in the Iran-Iraq War has clearly shown that neutrals still enjoy the right to trade with belligerents, and that attacks by belligerents on neutral merchant vessels, as well as the mining of neutral

---

106. See 33 *Keesing's Contemporary Archives* (1987), pp. 35597, 35598.

107. See, for example, 87 *Department of State Bulletin* (June 1987), p. 70; *ibidem* (July 1987), pp. 60-62; *ibidem* (August 1987), pp. 78 *et seq.*; *ibidem* (October 1987), pp. 42-43, 44; 88 *Department of State Bulletin* (June 1988), p. 44.

108. See 33 *Keesing's Contemporary Archives* (1987), p. 35599; Gray, C., "The British Position in regard to the Gulf Conflict", 37 *ICLQ* (1988), pp. 420 *et seq.*, at pp. 424-425.

109. For example, on 10 July 1987, an Iranian spokesman said that, although Iran did not approve of the United States flagging of ships belonging to a regional country, it did not have 'the right to interfere in the affairs of others' (33 *Keesing's Contemporary Archives* (1987), p. 35598). Iran did object, however, to the presence of non-belligerent naval forces in the Gulf. In particular, quite apart from specific incidents, Iran accused the United States of having violated its neutrality and of supporting the aggressor by its naval presence in the Gulf. Iran also referred to, Security Council Resolution 598(1987), *op.cit.* (note 3) – which, however, it had not yet itself accepted – and accused the United States of violating its paragraph 5, which called upon all states not parties to the conflict to refrain from acts which might lead to an escalation of the conflict: see, for example, *UN Docs.* S/19161 (29 September 1987), S/19202 (9 October 1987), S/PV.2818 (14 July 1988). On this latter point, it seems clear, however, that paragraph 5 of resolution 598(1987) did not prohibit the exercise of freedom of navigation in the Gulf: see Ronzitti, *loc.cit.* (note 93), pp. 651-652.

waters, are to be considered unlawful. The mining of large areas of the high seas, within no definite limits, should also be regarded as prohibited. On the other hand, the mining of a limited portion of the high seas could be regarded as lawful, provided that the requirements of the 1907 Hague Convention No. VIII are complied with.[110]

The right of neutrals to trade with belligerents implies the exercise of freedom of navigation on the high seas and freedom of passage through internationals straits, whereas innocent passage in the territorial sea of belligerent states can be subject to limitations.

In the face of belligerents' resort to unlawful measures of economic warfare aimed at preventing neutral trade with the enemy, neutral states, in addition to raising protests and resorting to reprisals, are entitled to take measures in order to protect their shipping: the deployment of naval units on the high seas in the area of hostilities in order to protect merchant vessels and/or to carry on minesweeping operations in undeclared minefields, has to be regarded as lawful. It is more doubtful whether a neutral state can take active steps in order to protect merchant ships flying the flag of other states. On the other hand, the practice of 'reflagging' other states' merchant vessels does not seem to raise serious legal objections.[111]

With respect to neutral states' commercial *duties*, practice in the Iran-Iraq War has shown that neutral states still have a duty to tolerate the exercise of certain measures of belligerents which interfere with neutral commerce on the high seas. In particular, belligerents still enjoy the right to visit and search neutral merchant vessels in order to ascertain whether they are carrying contraband of war: resistance to search is not permitted unless neutral merchant vessels are travelling under national convoy. However, with respect to the notion of contraband of war, the Gulf War has confirmed that, whereas neutral states are interested in limiting the right of belligerents to seize goods considered to be contraband of war, belligerent states tend to enlarge the category of goods liable to capture, in order to comprise all goods considered to be useful for the enemy's war effort.

Another controversial question is that of the so-called 'exclusion zones'. The setting up of such zones, which cannot be justified by the old rules on naval blockade or by other traditional rules of naval warfare, should still be regarded as unlawful, at least in so far as it implies indiscriminate attacks on neutral merchant vessels.

The Iran-Iraq War has also revived the controversial question of whether the old rules on neutrality are to be applied to all states not parties to an armed conflict or only to those states which choose to adopt an attitude of strict neutrality towards belligerents. Practice in the Gulf War seems to have added some credibility to the theory according to which the states not parties to an armed conflict are no longer under any obligation

---

110. For the text of the Convention, see *supra* note 9. According to Chapter 9.2.3. of the 1987 U.S. Navy *Handbook NWP9*, *op.cit.* (note 23), 'Mining of areas of indefinite extent in international waters is prohibited. Reasonably limited barred areas may be established by naval mines, provided neutral shipping retains an alternative route around or through such an area with reasonable assurance of safety' (paragraph 8).

111. In addition to the authors quoted *supra* note 105, see also Migliorino, L., "Il trasferimento di bandiera in tempo di guerra: la guerra Iran-Iraq e il re-flagging delle petroliere del Kuwait", 92 *Il Diritto Marittimo* (1990), pp. 868 *et seq.*

to adopt a strictly neutral attitude, but may discriminate among belligerents without losing their 'non-belligerent' status. According to this view, the traditional duty of impartiality, as well as the traditional duties of prevention and of abstention, such as, for example, the duty not to supply belligerents with arms or other war material, would only concern the states desiring to adopt an attitude of strict neutrality. What is still not very clear is whether the so-called 'non-belligerent' states would still enjoy the traditional rights of neutrals, such as the right to trade with belligerents, with all its implications, without being molested or, on the contrary, would have to tolerate the exercise of more stringent measures interfering with their shipping on the part of belligerents. In other words, and from a more general point of view, it is still necessary to clarify what, if any, are the legal consequences of an attitude of 'non-belligerency', as opposed to strict neutrality.

COMMENTS

Ove Bring[*]

I.   Probably the most important point made in the contribution written by Dr. Gioia and Professor Ronzitti concerns the impact of the United Nations Charter on the law of naval warfare and neutrality. Today, traditional belligerent rights associated with the Paris Peace Treaty of 1856, the Hague Conventions of 1907 and the unratified London Declaration of 1909 have to be reconciled with the post World War II regulation of the use of force associated with the cities of San Francisco and New York.

The entry into force of the United Nations Charter has produced a legal regime – today also possessing the status of customary law – which presents a number of constraints on the rights of parties to a conflict to engage in acts of war or other military actions. This will be underlined by the making of three points.

First, attempts to exercise belligerent rights in conflicts falling *short* of war cannot be accepted in a legal system where all members of the international community shall settle their disputes by *peaceful* means (in accordance with Article 2(3) of the United Nations Charter). Reliance on the concept of belligerent rights *before* war has actually broken out is in direct contravention of the principle that states should do everything feasible in terms of crisis management and the avoidance of crisis escalation (a principle which flows from Articles 2(3), 2(4) and 33 of the United Nations Charter).

Second, the exercise of belligerent rights in an *ongoing* conflict, against states not party to the conflict, will in principle always contravene the prohibition of the threat or use of force in Article 2(4) of the Charter. The relationship between a belligerent state and a neutral or non-belligerent state is characterized by a condition of peace, and the fundamental rule of the law of peace is the almost absolute prohibition of the use of force. The only possible justification for military action against a state hitherto outside the armed conflict is the argument that such action is legitimate under the concept of self-defence.

Third, although the justification of self-defence may be valid against the opponent state party to the conflict, it does not follow that conflict-related activities of third states readily give rise to an extensive right to counter-measures. Legitimate counter-measures involving the use of force may only be taken within the ambit of the right of self-defence and not as any form of reprisal which cannot at the same time be described as self-defence. Reprisals in the law of peace cannot involve the use of force.[1] Further-

* O.E. Bring, Legal Adviser, Ministry for Foreign Affairs, Stockholm, Sweden. The views expressed in these comments are those of the author and do not necessarily reflect the policy or the opinion of the Swedish Government.

1. See the consensus interpretation of Article 2(4) of the United Nations Charter in the Declaration on Principles of International Law concerning Friendly Relations and Co-operation among states in accordance with the Charter of the United Nations, A/RES/2625(XXV) annex of 24 October 1970.

I.F. Dekker and H.H.G. Post, eds., The Gulf War of 1980-1988
© 1992, T.M.C. Asser Instituut, The Hague

more: not only does Article 51 of the United Nations Charter imply that self-defence is subject to the important customary law restriction of proportionality – *i.e.* the force used must not exceed what is necessary under the circumstances – the Charter moreover represents a general constraint on any conflict-escalation policy that would involve, or would risk involving, additional states in the hostilities. The Charter's ambition of collective security, and the corresponding obligation of member states to settle their disputes peacefully, is just as valid in time of war as in peace. The General Assembly confirmed in the Friendly Relations Declaration that one of the legal principles of the Charter was the duty to co-operate with other states in the maintenance of international peace and security. If hostilities have broken out between certain states, the maintenance of peaceful relations with other states (they may call themselves neutral or non-belligerent), is still an overriding principle.

The conclusions to be drawn from these observations are:

(1) that the protection afforded third party shipping under the traditional law of neutrality has increased in the post-1945 world as a consequence of the law of the United Nations Charter; and

(2) that the concept of neutrality, as a concept for preserving peaceful relations, is of manifest and continued relevance in modern international law in situations where the Security Council has not taken a decision indicating the contrary.

II.   A related issue, touched upon by Gioia and Ronzitti in their contribution, is that the development referred to above is reinforced or parallelled by the recent development of the law of the sea. Even though the 1982 Law of the Sea Convention (UNCLOS) has not been a success from a ratification point of view, it has managed to confirm and strengthen the customary law principles with regard to the uses of the sea. The freedoms of the high seas are laid down in Articles 58 and 87 of the Convention and, in this context, the freedom of navigation is given a prominent position. Since the law of the United Nations Charter makes war an abnormal condition and since the law of the sea is basically a peacetime regime, the peacetime scope of application of the principle of freedom of navigation has increased at the expense of traditional belligerent rights.

But, in addition, it has to be underlined that freedom of navigation is a principle which is also applicable in war, even if its war-time application has to be reconciled with the 'imperative exigencies of war and the legitimate needs of national defense'.[2] The strengthening of the principle in peacetime, however, could be presumed to have a 'spill-over effect' with regard to time of war, thereby – compared to previous decades – striking a slightly different balance between civilian and military interests, and thus benefiting commercial shipping.

III. Having concluded that the legal protection of neutral shipping has a prominent place in modern international law, one has to ask (as Gioia and Ronzitti do), whether the distinction between 'neutrality' and 'non-belligerency' implies different levels of

---

2. The phrase is borrowed from Howard S. Levie, in: Ronzitti, N. (ed.), *The Law of Naval Warfare,* Dordrecht 1988, p. 141.

protection for ships of different nationalities. Modern world history is full of examples of states not party to a conflict which do not regard themselves as neutral in the sense of the 1907 Hague Conventions. During the 'Winter War' between Finland and the Soviet Union in 1939-1940, Sweden regarded its own position as one of non-belligerency (and not neutrality), thereby setting aside the Hague law requirement of strict impartiality and supporting Finland in a number of ways, including non-hindrance of individuals who wished to join the Finnish forces as volunteers. During the Gulf War of 1980-1988, third parties may have declared themselves 'neutral', but it is not very likely that they did so with the intention of bringing the traditional *law* of neutrality into focus as *the* applicable legal regime.[3]

Dietrich Schindler has pointed out that while, before 1914, third states could only choose between joining one belligerent side or remaining neutral in accordance with the Hague Conventions, after the entry into force of the collective security systems of the League of Nations and the United Nations, international law has recognized an intermediate position – that of non-belligerency.[4] In the numerous armed conflicts which have taken place since 1945, the law of neutrality has seldom been applied. Third states may regard themselves as strictly neutral under the law of the Hague, or they may take an attitude of qualified neutrality or non-belligerency. While 'neutrals' are those states which apply the law of neutrality in its entirety and expect to receive all the benefits of this legal regime, 'non-belligerents' are states which may assist one of the parties to the conflict and thereby discriminate against the other party. Since non-belligerents could be expected to deviate from the law of neutrality, they cannot reasonably expect to receive all the protection that flows from it.

On the other hand, the state practice of non-belligerence on the part of Kuwait and Saudi-Arabia during the Iraq-Iran War (*i.e.* the partiality of these states in favour of Iraq), did not lead the Security Council to conclude that these non-belligerent states were less entitled than others to the benefits of freedom of navigation. This principle of non-discrimination was evident in Security Council Resolution 552 (1984) of 1 June 1984, and in Security Council Resolution 598 (1987) of 20 July 1987. At the same time, in these and other resolutions, the Security Council called upon all states not parties to the conflict to refrain from acts which might lead to a further escalation of the conflict. The Council seemed to recognize that states which were not strictly impartial had to bear a heavier burden of risk than others.

IV. Although in many respects inconclusive, a legal evaluation of the Iraq-Iran War and the status of the law of neutrality in relation to belligerent rights will reveal some interesting points. Gioia and Ronzitti have shown that the establishment of 'war zones' in the Gulf was not, as such, condemned or disputed by states not parties to the conflict.

---

3. The UK Government was first reported to have stated that 'we are neutral in the war between Iran and Iraq.' See Chr. Greenwood, "The Concept of War in Modern International Law", 36 *ICLQ* (1987), p. 294, quoting Marston (ed.), "United Kingdom Materials in International Law", 53 *BYIL* (1982), p. 559, but the Foreign and Commonwealth Office later made clear that the statement had the following wording: 'we are impartial in the war between Iran and Iraq' (statement by Greenwood at the Gulf War Colloquium).

4. D. Schindler in: Ronzitti, N. (ed.), *The Law of Naval Warfare, op.cit.* (note 2), pp. 211-214.

At a Round Table of experts on international humanitarian law applicable to armed conflicts at sea, held in Toulon in October 1990, it was stated in the concluding draft document that a belligerent state 'cannot gain any additional rights under the law of armed conflict by establishing zones which might adversely affect the legitimate uses' of the sea. The establishment of zones was regarded as an exceptional measure in naval warfare and it was concluded that 'the same body of law applies both inside and outside the zone'. This means, *inter alia*, that attacks on neutral merchant vessels are *a priori* prohibited within such zones. The Toulon document also includes the following accumulative requirements with regard to the establishment of zones:

1. The extent, location and duration of the zone shall not exceed what is strictly required by military necessity and the principle of proportionality.
2. Due regard shall be given to the rights of all states to legitimate uses of the seas.
3. Necessary safe passage through the zone shall be provided in some cases where normal navigation routes are affected.
4. The commencement, duration, location and extent of the zone shall be publicly declared and appropriately notified.[5]

Nothing in the relevant Security Council Resolutions adopted during the Iraq-Iran War contradicts the legal assessment attempted by the Toulon expert meeting.

An interesting feature of state practice during the war was, of course, the reflagging of tankers and the deployment of naval units and convoys to protect international shipping. When a neutral or non-belligerent state protects its own ships through a military presence this does not give rise to any specific legal problems. The right of self-defence is applicable at sea. If ships of other flag states are convoyed this could be seen as preparations for collective self-defence. The seeming acquiescence in the United States policy of reflagging Kuwaiti tankers could perhaps be seen as an innovative form of a collective self-defence arrangement. Be that as it may, Gioia and Ronzitti point out that the demonstrated will and capacity to protect non-belligerent merchant shipping in the Gulf proved to be a rather effective deterrent against attacks. It is a recurring paradox in the development of international law, that violations of existing law (and we had many of these in the Iraq-Iran War) tend to give rise to responses and reactions which lead to a progressive development of the law. It remains to be seen whether this is actually the case with regard to the Gulf War of 1980-1988.

5. Round Table of Experts on International Humanitarian Law Applicable to Armed Conflicts at Sea, Results of the Second Meeting of the Madrid Plan of Action held in Toulon, France, October 1990, p. 8.

Part IV

Criminal Responsibility

* * *

An Islamic International Legal Order?

Chapter 8

CRIMINAL RESPONSIBILITY AND THE GULF WAR OF 1980-1988: THE CRIME OF AGGRESSION

Ige F. Dekker*

INTRODUCTION

During the Gulf War between Iran and Iraq both countries claimed to be victims of an act of aggression by the other party. Iran especially considered – from the very beginning and for a long time – the condemnation by the international community of the Iraqi aggression as a condition for its co-operation in the attempts of the United Nations to resolve the conflict.[1] It made the accusation that the Iraqi regime and, more particularly, President Saddam Hussein in person, should be held responsible for this war and, consequently, demanded the prosecution and trial of those guilty of 'a premeditated act of aggression'.[2] Iraq, on the other hand, took a more defensive attitude in this respect, although it strongly opposed the view that it would have committed an act of aggression against Iran. On the contrary, Iraq claimed that it acted in self-defence against Iranian aggression.[3]

The main question to be dealt with in these pages will be whether the Iraqi military activities and points of view provide sufficient grounds in international law for the Iranian demands with regard to the criminal responsibility of Iraq and the Iraqi regime

---

* I.F. Dekker, Lecturer in Public International Law, Faculty of Public Administration, University of Twente, Enschede, The Netherlands. The author would like to thank Dr. Harry H.G. Post and Professor Dick W.P. Ruiter for their comments on a draft of this contribution and Mr Maarten Bisseling for his research assistance.

1. See the first Iranian letter to the Secretary-General of the United Nations on this issue, signed by the President of Iran at the time, Bani-Sadr, on 1 October 1980, *UN Doc*. S/14206 and the Iranian *note verbale* of 4 October 1982 to the Secretary-General of the United Nations, *UN Doc*. S/15448. This condition has been reiterated in several other Iranian communications on the Gulf War to the United Nations; see, for instance, the letter dated 25 November 1986 from the Foreign Minister of the Islamic Republic of Iran to the Secretary-General, *UN Doc*. S/18480, Annex 3, and the Annex to the letter dated 11 August 1987 from Iran to the Secretary-General of the United Nations concerning the 'Detailed and official position of the Islamic Republic of Iran on the Security Council Resolution 598(1987)', *UN Doc*. S/19031.

2. Declaration of the Iranian representative in the Security Council of 23 October 1980, *UN Doc*. S/PV.2252, p. 37. See for later statements Legal Department of the Ministry of Foreign Affairs of Iran, *A Review of the Imposed War by the Iraqi Regime upon the Islamic Republic of Iran*, Tehran 1983, pp. 53, 69, 78; *UN News Digest*, Press release WS/1277, 27 March 1986, pp. 4-5.

3. See notes 40-52 *infra* and accompanying text.

I.F. Dekker and H.H.G. Post, eds., The Gulf War of 1980-1988
© 1992, T.M.C. Asser Instituut, The Hague

for the 'crime of aggression.'[4] In a complicated conflict such as this one, it is by no means easy to assess the validity of the justifications of the parties, if only because the facts are extremely difficult to determine objectively. For purposes of international law this problem regarding the facts can be partially avoided by analysing the conflict mainly on the basis of the viewpoints raised during discussions of the conflict in the Security Council of the United Nations.

Besides this problem regarding the facts, there is also the problem of the applicable law. The criminal responsibility of states and persons for the 'crime of aggression' is still an emerging and controversial issue of international law. The first endeavours in this century[5] towards criminalizing the use of force in (positive) international law took place between the two world wars, though only in non-binding resolutions of the Assembly of the League of Nations and in treaties which never entered into force.[6] Just after the Second World War the Charters and Judgments of the International Military Tribunals of Nuremberg and Tokyo accepted the criminal responsibility of persons for crimes against peace: the planning, preparation, initiation or waging of a war of aggression.[7] In a resolution adopted unanimously at its first session, the General Assembly of the United Nations affirmed 'the principles of international law recognized by the Charter of the Nuremberg Tribunal and the judgment of the Tribunal'.[8] More

---

4. For the assessment of the other conditions which may be relevant from the perspective of criminal responsibility – including the Iranian demand for the condemnation of Iraq for serious breaches of the humanitarian law of armed conflicts – see David, E., "La guerre du Golfe et le droit international", 23 *RBDI* (1987), pp. 161-169; Tavernier, P., "La Guerre du Golfe: quelques aspects de l'application du droit des conflits armés et du droit humanitaire", 30 *AFDI* (1984), pp. 41-64; Tavernier, P., "Les Problèmes de Responsabilité International et la Guerre du Golfe", in 20 *Thesaurus Acroasium* (1989), to be published; and Chapters III en IV of this volume.

5. Under traditional international law the concept of criminal responsibility of states has been accepted, but faded during the 18th century. See Munch, F., "Kollektivschuld und Staatenstrafe", *Internationales Recht und Diplomatie* (1967), pp. 37 *et seq.*

6. See the resolutions of the Assembly of the League of Nations of 25 September 1925 and 24 September 1927; the Draft Treaty of Mutual Assistance, 1923, and the Geneva Protocol for the Peaceful Settlement of International Diputes, 1924. All these documents are contained in Ferencz, B.B., *Defining International Aggression: The Search for World Peace*, Dobbs Ferry 1975, vol. 1, pp. 77 *et seq.* For further details see Brownlie, I., *International Law and the Use of Force by States*, Oxford 1963, pp. 66 *et seq.*, and Rifaat, A.M., *International Aggression. A Study of the Legal Concept: Its Development and Definition in International Law*, Stockholm 1979, pp. 50 *et seq.*

7. With regard to the Nuremberg Judgment, reference is made below to "Judgment and Sentences", 42 *AJIL* (1947), pp. 172 *et seq.* (hereinafter: Nuremberg Judgment), and with regard to the judgment of the International Military Tribunal for the Far East to Röling, B.V.A./Rüter, F.C. (eds.), *The Tokyo Judgment*, 3 vols., Amsterdam 1977-1981 (hereinafter: Tokyo Judgment). For a concise outline of the historical background, organisation and judgments of these Tribunals and for further literature on this subject, see Jescheck, H.-H., "Nuremberg Trials", in: Bernhardt, R. (ed.), *Encyclopedia of Public International Law*, vol. 4, Amsterdam 1982, pp. 50-57; Röling, B.V.A., "Tokyo Trial", in: *ibidem*, pp. 242-245. See also Ginsburgs, G./Kudriavtsev, V.N. (eds.), *The Nuremberg Trial and International Law*, Dordrecht 1990.

8. A/RES/95(I), 11 December 1946. In A/RES/177(II), 21 November 1947, the General Assembly directed the International Law Commission to formulate these principles. During its second session in 1950, the ILC adopted the formulation of the principles, which, however, were never accepted by the General Assembly. The text of the 'Nuremberg Principles' is published in *The Work of the International Law Commission*, New York 1980, p. 116.

recently, the General Assembly of the United Nations accepted (without a vote) its well-known Declaration on the Principles of International Law, in which it recognized that 'A war of aggression constitutes a crime against the peace, for which there is responsibility under international law.'[9] The same principle is, in roughly identical words, embodied in the General Assembly's Definition of Aggression of 1974.[10] However, the extremely general formulation of these provisions conceals a profound difference of opinion between states as to the recognition or the lack of recognition of criminal responsibility for serious breaches of the prohibition of the use of force of states and/or individuals.[11]

This difference of opinion does not seem to have disappeared, as is shown in the discussions on the work of the International Law Commission of the United Nations concerning the drafts on State Responsibility and the Code of Crimes against the Peace and Security of Mankind.[12] Both drafts have in view the regulation of the 'crime of aggression'; the first as an international crime which gives rise to state responsibility,[13] the second as a crime against peace which gives rise to criminal responsibility of individuals.[14]

The significance of the recognition, in the instruments of international law referred to, of the responsibility of states and persons for the international crime of aggression and the crimes against peace lies above all in a strengthening of the view that aggressive wars are unlawful and unacceptable.[15] However, it is still very doubtful whether the criminal responsibility of states and persons for these crimes has been sufficiently elaborated in generally recognized international norms so as to be suitable for application by way of positive international law. Nevertheless, such instruments do provide a normative framework for assessing the use of armed force in international relations, notably for the United Nations, in the exercise of its tasks and competence relating to the maintenance of peace and security. Above all, they mark the development of the international legal order towards an order in which there is a real possibility

9. A/RES/2625(XXV) Annex, 24 October 1970, principle I, par. 2.

10. A/RES/3314(XXIX) Annex, 14 December 1974, Article 5(2). This principle is, pointedly, left out in the 'Declaration on the Enhancement of the Effectiveness of the Principle of Refraining from the Threat or Use of Force in International Relations', A/RES/42/22 Annex, 18 November 1987.

11. See Broms, B., "The Definition of Aggression", 154 *Hague Recueil* (1977), pp. 299, 356. See also Ferencz, B.B., "Aggression", in: Bernhardt, R. (ed.), *Encyclopedia of Public International Law*, vol. 3, Amsterdam 1982, pp. 1-6.

12. See especially the discussion held in 1983 in the Sixth Committee of the General Assembly of the United Nations on the Draft Code. *UN Doc.* A/C.6/38/SR.37 *et seq.* The ILC decided in 1984 to begin its work on the Draft Code with the responsibility of individuals and to decide at a later stage whether this Code should contain also rules relating to the responsibility of states. See *Yearbook ILC* (1984), vol. II, pt. 2, p. 17.

13. See "ILC Draft Articles on State Responsibility", Article 19(3)(a), *Yearbook ILC* (1976), vol. II, pt. 2, p. 118.

14. See "Draft Articles on the Draft Code of Crimes against the Peace and Security of Mankind", Article 12, in: *Report ILC* (1988), *UN Doc.* A/43/10, p. 172.

15. See Röling, B.V.A., "International Law and the Maintenance of Peace", 4 *NYIL* (1973), pp. 1, 80 and 100 (for the Dutch, adapted version, see Röling, B.V.A., *Volkenrecht en vrede*, Deventer 1985, pp. 157, 195).

of a collective worldwide security system, and in which 'armed force shall not be used, save in the common interest.'[16]

I   STATE RESPONSIBILITY: THE CRIME OF AGGRESSION

A   The applicable law

The concept of state responsibility for international crimes is still a very controversial subject of international law.[17] It seems that a great majority of states accepts in principle that there are international wrongful acts of a very serious nature which thereby can and should be qualified as 'international crimes'. But the crucial and much debated question is: what legal consequences should be attached to such international crimes, and in particular, what 'penal' sanctions can or should be taken by third states which are not directly affected?

The Draft Articles on State Responsibility drawn up by the International Law Commission have, until now, not solved this question.[18] Article 19, paragraph 2 of Part I of the Commission's Draft provides:

> 'An internationally wrongful act which results from the breach by a state of an international obligation so essential for the protection of fundamental interests of the international community that its breach is recognized as a crime by that community as a whole constitutes an international crime.'[19]

In Article 19, paragraph 3 a non-exhaustive list of international crimes based on 'the rules of international law in force' is given. The first example mentioned is that of 'a serious breach of an international obligation of essential importance for the maintenance of international peace and security, such as that prohibiting aggression.'[20] Thus,

---

16. Charter of the United Nations, 1945, preamble.

17. On this subject see, *inter alia*, Brownlie, I., *System of the Law of Nations, State Responsibility*, Oxford 1983, Part I, especially pp. 32 *et seq.*; Dinstein, Y., *War, Aggression and Self-Defence*, Cambridge 1988, pp. 107-111; Gilbert, G., "The Criminal Responsibility of States", 39 *ICLQ* (1990), pp. 345-369, 369; Weiler, J.H.H./Cassese, A./Spinedi, M. (eds.), *International Crimes of State. A Critical Analysis of the ILC's Draft Article 19 on State Responsibility*, Berlin/New York 1989 (with a systematic bibliography 1946-1984). See also Hofmann, R., "Zur Unterscheidung Verbrechen und Delikt im Bereich der Staatenverantwortlichkeit", 45 *ZaöRV* (1985), pp. 195 *et seq.*; Marek, K., "Criminalizing State Responsibility", 14 *RBDI* (1978-1979), pp. 460 *et seq.*; Mohr, M., "The ILC's Distinction between 'International Crimes' and 'International Delicts' and its Implications", in: Spinedi, M./Simma, B. (eds.), *United Nations Codification of State Responsibility*, New York 1987, pp. 115 *et seq.*; Triffterer, O., "Prosecution of States for Crimes of State", in: Bassiouni, M. Cherif (ed.), *International Criminal Law*, Springfield 1987, vol. III, pp. 99-107.

18. One author concludes that 'International crimes fail to satisfy the requirements of any definition of crime, Article 19 itself does not add any clarity to the concept, the examples in Article 19(3) diverging widely as to their suitability for criminalisation and, finally, the whole idea is inappropriate in contemporary international law.' Gilbert, *loc.cit.* (note 17), p. 369.

19. *Yearbook ILC* (1976), vol. II, pt. 2, p. 118.

20. *Idem.*

according to the International Law Commission, the international crime of aggression is one of those international wrongs 'which are more serious than others and which as such, should entail more severe legal consequences.'[21] The legal consequences of state responsibility are the subject of Part 2 of the Draft Articles which is, for the greater part, still under consideration.[22] In particular, the 'severe legal consequences' of international crimes are far from being clear.[23] The former Special *Rapporteur*, Mr Riphagen, proposed some general provisions in that regard, with 'only' a reference to the Charter of the United Nations as the framework for the special legal consequences of aggression.[24] He underscored that – just as the determination of the existence of an international crime could not be left to any individual state – a 'single state cannot take upon itself the role of "policeman" of the international community.'[25] The newly-appointed Special *Rapporteur*, Mr Arangio-Ruiz, has planned to dedicate a separate chapter to the consequences deriving from an international crime.[26] He stressed at the same time the great difficulties involved in determining by what means punitive or otherwise afflictive measures in reaction to international crimes could be justified.[27]

Even the most passionate critics of the concept of criminal responsibility of states recognize aggression as a 'potential' international crime.[28] Firstly, there is, at least to some extent, a consensus among states on a definition of the crime of aggression. As will be remembered, the question of when there is aggression formed the object of lengthy and difficult negotiations in the United Nations for many years, which finally resulted in the adoption – by consensus – of a Definition of Aggression, annexed to General Assembly Resolution 3314(XXIX) of 14 December 1974.[29] However, the legal status of this recommendation by the General Assembly is still not very clear. In accepting the Definition of Aggression, some delegates declared that they considered it to be a non-binding explanation of the Charter. On the other hand, others, including

21. *Yearbook ILC* (1976), vol. II, pt. 2, p. 109.

22. In 1986 the ILC provisionally adopted draft articles 1 - 5 of Part II. Article 5(3) provides that '"injured State" means, if the international wrongful act constitutes an international crime (...), all other States.' See *Yearbook ILC* (1986), vol. II, pt. 2, p. 38.

23. See Simma, B., "International Crimes: Injury and Countermeasures. Comments on Part 2 of the ILC Work on State Responsibility", in: Weiler/Cassese/Spinedi (eds.), *op.cit.* (note 17), pp. 283-315.

24. See "Sixth report on the content, forms and degrees of international responsibility", section I, Articles 14 and 15, *Yearbook ILC* (1985), vol. II, pt. 1, pp. 13-14.

25. *Yearbook ILC* (1982), vol. II, pt. 1, p. 45.

26. See *Report ILC* (1989), *UN Doc.* A/44/10, p. 191. The principles relating to the settlement of disputes will be the subject of Part 3 of the Draft.

27. *Ibidem*, pp. 197-198.

28. See, for instance, Gilbert, *loc.cit.* (note 17), p. 363. See also the contributions by T.L. Stein and A. Cassese to the general discussion on "Crimes of State", in: Weiler/Cassese/Spinedi (eds.), *op.cit.* (note 17), pp. 194-213.

29. For a description of the creation of the Definition of Aggression and all relevant documents on this matter, see Ferencz, *op.cit.* (note 6). For a critical discussion of this resolution, see Broms, *loc.cit.* (note 11); Röling, B.V.A., "Die Definiton der Agression", in: Delbrück, J., *et.al.* (eds.), *Recht im Dienst des Friedens*, Berlin 1975, pp. 387-403; Stone, J., *Conflict Through Consensus, United Nations Approaches to Aggression*, Baltimore/Londen 1977, especially pp. 123-152.

the Iraqi representative,[30] considered it to be a legally binding interpretation of the Security Council's powers and of the rights and duties of the member states. The practice of the Security Council does not give a definite answer to the question of the legal status of this resolution. In the small number of cases in which the Council identified an act of aggression since 1974, the relevant resolutions never – and the discussions on such cases seldom – explicitly referred to the Definition of Aggression.[31]

Moreover, there are some confusing elements in the relation between the Definition and the Draft Articles on State Responsibility.[32] The Definition seems to start from a stricter concept of criminal responsibility than the Draft Articles, because it only marks 'a *war* of aggression' as an international crime, whereas aggression in the preamble of the Definition is already considered as 'the most serious and dangerous form of the illegal use of force'.[33] Article 19(3)(a) of the Draft Articles mentions aggression as such as an international crime.

Secondly, the coercive measures on which the United Nations' Security Council, which has a primary responsibility for the maintenance of peace and security, is competent to decide with regard to an 'act of aggression'[34] may not be penal sanctions in the true sense, but they might well be seen as a first step in that direction. According to the above-mentioned Definition of Aggression, the rules set forth in this document were intended in particular as guidelines for the Security Council. If only for this reason, the Iranian demand that the Security Council should condemn the Iraqi military action as an act of aggression is significant from the point of view of international law.[35] However, the weak point in this respect is, of course, that the Security Council is a political organ and not a judicial one. Under the Charter of the United Nations – and

---

30. The Iraqi representative at the Sixth Commission of the General Assembly of the United Nations, Mr. Yasseen, stated, *inter alia*, that the acceptance of the Definition of Aggression by the General Assembly would entail the acceptance of the content as an interpretation of 'the exact meaning' of the Charter of the United Nations and that therefore the Definition 'must be binding on all states and even on the Security Council, which derived its authority from the Charter and could not fail to be bound by it.' However, at the same time he noted that 'legally, the Definition (...) would take the form of a General Assembly resolution and would therefore only have the force of a recommendation.' See *UN Doc*. A/C.6/SR.1478, p. 6.

31. *Cf.*, Bassiouni, M. Cherif/Ferencz, B.B., "The Crime Against Peace", in: Bassiouni, M. Cherif (ed.), *International Criminal Law*, Springfield 1986, vol. I, p. 167, at p. 191. Moreover, it is noteworthy that in the cases where the Security Council has identified an act of aggression, these tend to be armed incidents rather than armed conflicts. See, in particular, S/RES/393(1976), S/RES/527(1982), S/RES/567(1985), S/RES/581(1986) in connection with the South African attacks on neighbouring states and S/RES/573(1985) regarding the condemnation of the Israeli attack on the PLO headquarters in Tunisia. For further details on the practice of the Security Council, see Cot J.P./Pellet, A. (eds.), *La Charte des Nations Unies*, Paris 1985, pp. 659 *et seq.*; Wellens, K.C. (ed.), *Resolutions and Statements of the United Nations Security Council (1946-1989). A Thematic Guide*, Dordrecht 1990.

32. *Cf.*, Gilbert, *loc.cit.* (note 17), p. 360.

33. A/RES/3314(XXIX) Annex, preamble, para. 5.

34. See Charter of the United Nations, 1945, Articles 39-43. The powers of the General Assembly of the United Nations, with regard to determining whether aggression has taken place, will be left out of consideration here. Iran has never explicitly requested this body to condemn the Iraqi action as an act of aggression.

35. See note 1 *supra* and accompanying text.

this is repeatedly confirmed by the Definition of Aggression – the Security Council has complete discretion in determining the existence of an act of aggression and in taking coercive measures.[36] As mentioned before, in the practice of this organ, little use is made of its far-reaching powers in regard of acts of aggression.[37]

B   The initial use of force and the right of self-defence

The Definition of Aggression uses a straightforward starting point in determining the concept: aggression is the first use of armed force in contravention of the Charter of the United Nations.[38] The Security Council may deviate from this principle where the extent of the use of force and its consequences are slight, or – as western states are particularly fond of emphasizing[39] – the party resorting to force has no aggressive motives.

The facts seem clear to the extent that a large-scale military action took place on the part of Iraq against Iran on 22 September 1980 and that within a week Iraq had occupied large areas of Iran. In the first letters to the United Nations with regard to the conflict, the Minister for Foreign Affairs of Iraq, Hammadi, refers to the military action as an exercise of the right of self-defence necessitated by circumstance,[40] a justification also given in a note of the Ministry of Foreign Affairs of Iraq to the Embassy of Iran at Baghdad of 17 September 1980.[41] Obviously this right obtains within international law, but it may be exercised only when certain conditions have been met. The most essential condition laid down in Article 51 of the Charter of the United Nations is that an armed attack must have taken place.[42] Such an armed attack should be 'substantial' on the score of its scale and effects and may not include mere frontier incidents.[43] However the Iraqi communications to the Security Council, certainly up

---

36. *Cf.*, A/RES/3314(XXIX) Annex, of 14 December 1974, Articles 2 and 4. The proposals made during the creation of the Charter of the United Nations to include a definition of aggression in this treaty as well as an automatic obligation for the Security Council to take coercive measures in such cases, were expressly rejected at that time. See *United Nations Conference on International Organization*, vol. 12, pp. 296, 348, 381, 445 and 507. For further details see Cot/Pellet (eds.), *op.cit.* (note 31), p. 645; Schaeffer, M., *Die Funktionsfähigkeit des Sicherheitsmechanismus der Vereinten Nationen*, Berlin 1982, p. 34.

37. See note 31 *supra*.

38. A/RES/3314(XXIX) Annex, of 14 December 1974, Article 2.

39. See Stone, *op.cit.* (note 29), pp. 40-45.

40. See letters dated 21 and 24 September 1980 from the Minister for Foreign Affairs of Iraq to the Secretary-General and the President of the Security Council, *UN Doc.* S/14191 and S/14192.

41. *UN Doc.* S/14272, Annex 1.

42. See Brownlie, *op.cit.* (note 6), pp. 278-279; Dinstein, *op.cit.* (note 17), pp. 172-190. See in this context also Malanczuk, P., "Countermeasures and Self-Defence as Circumstances Precluding Wrongfulness in the International Law Commission's Draft Articles on State Responsibility", 45 *ZaöRV* (1983), pp. 705-803.

43. See the Judgment of the International Court of Justice of 27 June 1986, "Military and Paramilitary Activities in and against Nicaragua (Nicaragua v. United States of America) (Merits)", *ICJ Reports* (1986), p. 103. In this context it is also said that *an act of aggression* in the form of an armed attack has taken place. See, *e.g.*, Rifaat, *op.cit.* (note 6), pp. 124-125.

to 24 October, do not contain any such allegation.[44] The central issue in the Iraqi justification is the – alleged – breaches by Iran of the Algiers Agreement of 6 March 1975 and the Treaty concerning the State Frontier and Neighbourly Relations of 13 June 1975 between the two states.[45]

International law literature has defended the position that in addition to their *inherent* right to self-defence in the case of an armed attack, states may also have a right to self-defence in other circumstances.[46] Regardless of the merits of the arguments for and against this position, it suffices in the present case to point to the generally-accepted condition with which the exercise of the right to self-defence must comply in any case: the response must be proportional.[47] The large-scale military action commenced by Iraq on 22 September 1980 and continued throughout the following months certainly does not comply with this condition, irrespective of the other arguments put forward by Iraq in its first communications to the United Nations, such as Iran's alleged admission and support of sabotage or threats to Iraq's internal security.

The untenability of the Iraqi position was apparently even realized in Baghdad, as can be gathered from the letter of 24 October 1980 to the Secretary-General,[48] that introduced a change in the justification of the by now large-scale hostilities.[49] Minister Hammadi claimed that Iran, and not Iraq, had commenced hostilities. Reference was made to Iranian military actions having begun on 4 September 1980. This date, rather than 22 September 1980, was now held to be the beginning of the war, and Iran was alleged to have started the war against Iraq. In this context it is curious that 22 September 1980 was then described as the day '... on which Iraq exercised *preventive* self-defence to defend its people and territories.'[50]

---

44. Substantial military actions by Iran were mentioned in a letter dated 24 October 1980 from the Minister of Foreign Affairs of Iraq to the Secretary-General, *UN Doc.* S/14236. In a note dated 16 November 1980 addressed to Iran, contained in *UN Doc.* S/14272, Iraq links its military activities to '... the escalation of Iranian aggression against Iraq ...' It can be added that even the available surveys of events contain no mention of any sizeable Iranian military activities against which Iraq would have had to defend itself in the manner adopted on 22 September 1980. See Amin, S.H., "The Iran-Iraq Conflict: Legal Implications", 31 *ICLQ* (1982), pp. 167-168; Hünseler, P., *Der Irak und sein Konflikt mit Iran*, Bonn 1982, pp. 63-69; Pipes, D., "A Border Adrift: Origins of the Conflict", in: Tahir-Kheli, S./Ayubi, S. (eds.), *The Iran-Iraq War. New Weapons, Old Conflicts*, New York 1982, pp. 3-4.

45. Text of the Agreement and the Treaty in 1017 *UNTS*, no. 14903. See further Chapter 1 of this volume.

46. *Cf.*, for example, Kelsen, H., *The Law of the United Nations*, New York 1951, p. 269, or Kunz, J.L., "Individual and Collective Self-Defence in Article 51 of the Charter of the United Nations", 41 *AJIL* (1947), p. 878, and Brownlie, *op.cit.* (note 6), p. 273. A position favouring a wider right to self-defence is advocated, *inter alia*, by Bowett, D.W., *Self-defence in International Law*, New York 1958, pp. 185-186 and by McDougal, M.S./Feliciano, F.P., *Law and Minimum World Public Order*, New Haven 1961, pp. 232-241.

47. See Brownlie, *op.cit.* (note 6), pp. 261-265 and 279; Dinstein, *op.cit.* (note 17), pp. 190, 216-219; Rifaat, *op.cit.* (note 6), p. 127. See also the Judgment of the International Court of Justice of 27 June 1986, "Military and Paramilitary Activities in and against Nicaragua", *ICJ Reports* (1986), pp. 94, 122.

48. This letter was annexed to a letter dated 27 October 1980 from the representative of Iraq to the Secretary-General. See *UN Doc.* S/14236.

49. See also Tavernier, P., "Le conflit frontalier entre l'Irak et l'Iran et la guerre du Chatt-el-Arab", 4 *ARES Défense et Sécurité* (1982), pp. 352-353.

50. *UN Doc.* S/14236 (emphasis added).

In itself the right to preventive self-defence is accepted by some authors on international law.[51] However, according to these authors, the conditions with which preventive self-defence should comply in order to be justified are stringent. For example, Rifaat states:

'Hence, if the danger of an armed attack is grave and imminent, the state against which such an attack would be directed is warranted, by Article 51, to exercise its inherent right of self-defence to prevent such an attack from taking place.'[52]

He immediately adds that even a state acting in preventive self-defence in its response is bound by the principle of proportionality. In view of the extent of Iraqi activity, a large concentration of Iranian troops on the frontier and a manifest threat of attack should have been noted, at least for those who allow for the possibility of preventive self-defence in international law. However, neither in Iraqi communications to the United Nations nor in any other report is there a trace of such instances.

Quite apart from its tardiness, Iraq's claim to preventive self-defence is extraordinary, because it *followed* the earlier observation that Iran had started the war. It is not inconceivable that this contradictory argument results from the fact that even Iraq would find it difficult to demonstrate that the Iranian military activities between 4 and 22 September 1980 fulfilled the requirements for exercising the right to self-defence.

C   Territorial ambitions

On the basis of the foregoing it must be assumed that Iraq was the first to use armed force and that this initial use of force is difficult to justify in terms of international law and of the Charter of the United Nations in particular. Moreover, it is possible to point to some aspects of the Iraqi action that could be qualified as aggravating rather than mitigating circumstances in the light of the Definition of Aggression. In addition to the extent of the military operation, these aspects concern above all the territorial ambitions that accompanied it.

Iraq has repeatedly stressed in its communications to the Secretary-General and the Security Council that its military actions were not aimed at territorial expansion.[53] But

---

51. See, *e.g.*, Rifaat, *op.cit.* (note 6), pp. 126-127, Bowett, D.W., "Economic Coercion and Reprisals by States", 13 *Virg. JIL* (1972) p. 4. Brownlie, *op.cit.* (note 6), p. 275 and p. 278, like many other authoritative authors, considers that preventive self-defence is not permitted. In its Judgment of 27 June 1986, "Military and Paramilitary Activities in and against Nicaragua", the International Court of Justice did not express its view on the issue of the lawfulness of a response to the imminent threat of an armed attack. See *ICJ Reports* (1986), p. 103. But Judge Schwebel rejected in his Dissenting Opinion in the Nicaragua case rejected a reading of the text of Article 51 of the Charter which would imply that the right of self-defence under this Article exists 'if, and only if, an armed attack occurs.' *Ibidem*, p. 347.

52. Rifaat, *op.cit.* (note 6), p. 127.

53. The Minister of Foreign Affairs of Iraq, Hammadi, states in a letter of 21 September 1980, *UN Doc.* S/14191, that his Government '... has no territorial ambitions in Iran', and in a letter of 24 September 1980, *UN Doc.* S/14192, that '... my Government has on no more than one occasion made it clear that we harbour no expansionist territorial designs against Iran. This policy was clearly stated in the statements emanating from the highest authorities of my Government.'

at the same time Iraq was clear about its territorial objectives. In the much quoted letter of 21 September 1980, the Minister for Foreign Affairs of Iraq, Hammadi, indicated that the Iraq-Iran frontier, particularly in the Shatt-al-Arab, was now redrawn in accordance with the *pre* 6 March 1975 situation, *i.e.*, before the Algiers Agreement.[54] He added that this river '... shall again be, as it has always been throughout history, an Iraqi river subject to the full control and sovereignty of Iraq.'[55]

As is explained elsewhere,[56] the 1975 Algiers Agreement, in so far as it concerns the Shatt-al-Arab frontier, was certainly no territorial improvement for Iraq. However, before 1975 the Shatt-al-Arab was by no means under the exclusive control of Iraq. The Turkish-Persian Protocol of Constantinople of 1913 had established in a legally quite unambiguous way that the left bank and a number of islands in the river comprised a part of Iranian territory. And it is by no means unlikely that the application of the *Thalweg* principle – which usually refers to the ideal shipping route from the point of view of navigation – had thus become binding with respect to some parts of the river area.

In this light it seems that the military actions of September 1980 were aimed at territorial expansion *vis-à-vis* Iran. In view of the importance of the Shatt-al-Arab for both states, the relatively small territorial changes apparently aspired to by Iraq cannot be brushed aside as being of secondary importance. Subsequent communications to the United Nations reinforced the impression that Iraq did have territorial ambitions.[57]

D   The attitude of the Security Council of the United Nations

It may thus be concluded that there are sufficient grounds for the submission presented by the Iranian representative in the Security Council that

'... the invasion of Iran by the Iraqi armed forces constitutes a premeditated act of aggression as defined in the Annex to the General Assembly Resolution 3314 (XXIX).'[58]

54. See *UN Doc.* S/14191.

55. *Idem.* See also the Memorandum of Iraq of 17 September 1980, included in *UN Doc.* S/14272.

56. See Dekker, I.F./Post, H.H.G., "The Gulf War from the Point of View of International Law", 17 *NYIL* (1986), pp. 76-83. See also Chapter 1 of this volume.

57. In the letter of 27 October 1980, *UN Doc.* S/14236, Minister Hammadi wrote that '[I]n order to guarantee our full sovereignty over Shatt-al-Arab, our national river, and to be in a position enabling us to actually exercise that sovereignty, it is imperative to secure the eastern bank of the river after Iran refused to recognize our sovereignty and used force to close it to navigation. Shatt-al-Arab is our only water outlet to the outside world.' He added that Iraq could not recall its troops until Iran had fully recognized Iraq's sovereignty over the river *de facto* and *de jure*, and that '[O]n the basis of military considerations and topography, there may be better positions forward for defensive purposes, but there are none backward.' Finally, the Iraqi Minister indicated that as regards frontier agreements, only the Protocol of Constantinople was now in force between the two states, '... the views of Iraq and Iran notwithstanding.' It is noteworthy that none of the available publications reveal that Iraq interprets this Protocol to mean that the entire Shatt-al-Arab, including the islands and the left bank, is Iraqi territory. See also Chapter 1 of this volume.

58. *UN Doc.* S/PV.2252, p. 37.

The Iraqi attack falls within the terms of the first instance of an 'act of aggression' in the Definition:

> 'The invasion or attack by the armed forces of a state of the territory of another state, or any military occupation, however temporary, resulting from such invasion or attack, or any annexation by the use of force of the territory of another state or part thereof.'[59]

Even the official Iraqi viewpoints reveal little more than a common war of aggression, in which expansionist ambitions at least play a role. However, this Iraqi military action, unlawful from the point of view of international law, has never been condemned by the Security Council (or the General Assembly) as an act or a crime of aggression. During one of the first debates on the Gulf War in the Security Council, only the Ambassador of the United States to the United Nations, Mr McHenry, stated unequivocally that 'the national integrity of Iran was threatened by the Iraqi invasion.'[60] This opinion, which was in itself quite remarkable in view of the hostage drama still taking place in Tehran at that time, was not contested by any of the other representatives present, except of course by the Iraqi delegate.[61] The French representative supported the American view to some extent by declaring that in order to ensure its security 'one of the protagonists has placed its hopes in weapons'. However, he then asked: 'But, as for the other, has it always refrained from using weapons against its neighbour?' and added: 'Once again, that is not for the Council to decide.'[62]

This conclusion is characteristic of the Security Council's attitude to the issue.[63] Its first resolution with respect to the situation between Iran and Iraq, adopted on 28 September 1980, called upon both parties 'to refrain immediately from any further use of force and to settle their dispute by peaceful means in conformity with principles of justice and international law.'[64] In Resolution 540(1983) of 31 October 1983 the Security Council affirmed 'the desirability of an objective examination of the causes of the war', but it did not indicate in what manner this examination should be implemented. The Security Council expressed its view at the beginning of the Gulf War for the first time on 24 February 1986, and then in very carefully worded or even disguised terms, and certainly did not question the legality of the Iraqi attack. In Resolution 582(1986), the Security Council '[d]eplores the initial acts which gave rise to the conflict between Iran and Iraq and deplores the continuation of the conflict'.

---

59. A/RES/3314(XXIX) Annex, 14 December 1974, Article 3(a).

60. *UN Doc.* S/PV.2252, p. 16.

61. *Ibidem*, p. 36.

62. *UN Doc.* S/PV.2254, p. 6.

63. See also Chapter 2 of this volume, and especially the contribution of Marc Weller.

64. S/RES/479(1980), 28 September 1980. See also S/RES/514(1982), 12 July 1982 and S/RES/522(19-82), 4 October 1982. The General Assembly adopted on 22 October 1982 Resolution 37/3 concerning "Consequences of the prolongation of the armed conflict between Iran and Iraq", in which it, *inter alia*, reaffirmed 'the principles that no state should acquire or occupy territories by the use of force, that whatever territories had been acquired in this way should be returned, that no act of aggression should be committed against any state, that the territorial integrity and the sovereignty of all states should be respected ...' This resolution too was, in fact, rejected by Iran.

The famous Resolution 598(1987) of 20 July 1987 is in fact equally disappointing. In this resolution the Security Council determined the existence of 'a breach of the peace as regards the conflict between Iran and Iraq' and mandatorily demanded[65] that the parties 'observe an immediate cease-fire (...) and withdraw all forces to the internationally recognized boundaries without delay' under the supervision of the United Nations.[66] However, these are typical provisional measures which, according to Article 40 of the Charter of the United Nations, 'shall be without prejudice to the rights, claims, or position of the parties concerned'. Instead of taking a decision as to the violation of the prohibition of aggression, the Security Council again simply deplored 'the initiation and continuation of the conflict', and requested the Secretary-General, in paragraph 6 of this resolution, 'to explore, in consultation with Iran and Iraq, the question of entrusting an impartial body with inquiring into responsibility for the conflict and to report to the Security Council as soon as possible.' Some representatives in the Security Council stressed the importance of this paragraph but they did not indicate in what manner this non-committal and unspecified request could be implemented.[67]

At first Iran rejected this resolution because 'pronouncement of Iraq as the aggressor and the party responsible for the conflict as well as determining damages and war reparations are essential for a thorough study of the conflict and formulation of a final solution.'[68] But one year later, on 17 July 1988, Iran accepted this resolution, without the Security Council condemning Iraq for committing aggression.[69] The reports of the Secretary-General on the implementation of Resolution 598(1987) up till now do not mention any progress in respect of paragraph 6 thereof. In a letter dated 30 July 1990 to the President of Iran concerning the resolution of all the outstanding issues between the parties, President Saddam Hussein proposed 'to drop paragraph 6 of Security Council Resolution 598(1987) from the discussion (...), because it obstructs rather than

65. See Tavernier, P., "Le caractère obligatoire de la résolution 598(1987) du Conseil de sécurité relative à la guerre de Golfe", 1 *European Journal of International Law/Journal européen de droit international* (1990), pp. 278-285. See also Chapter 2 of this volume.

66. The United Nations Iran-Iraq Military Observer Group (UNIIMOG) was established by the Security Council under the terms of its Resolution 619(1988) of 9 August 1988. See also S/RES/620(1988) of 26 August 1988, S/RES/631(1989) of 8 February 1989, S/RES/651(1990) of 29 March 1990, S/RES/671(1990) of 27 September 1990 and S/RES/685(1991) of 31 January 1991. The mandate of UNIIMOG came to an end on 28 February 1991. See the Report of the Secretary-General of 26 February 1991, *UN Doc.* S/22263, p. 5.

67. See *UN Doc.* S/PV.2750, p. 16 (United Kingdom), p. 27 (FRG), p. 32 (Italy) and p. 41 (Ghana). The representative of Ghana believed that the determination of responsibility for the war and its consequences 'will not only constitute an act of justice, but will be a useful precedent in deterring future aggression by any country.'

68. See the Annex to the letter dated 11 August 1987 from Iran to the Secretary-General of the United Nations concerning the "Detailed and official position of the Islamic Republic of Iran on the Security Council Resolution 598(1987)", *UN Doc.* S/19031, para. 14.

69. See Letter dated 17 July 1988 from the President of the Islamic Republic of Iran addressed to the Secretary-General, *UN Doc.* S/20020.

promotes progress towards peace.'[70] At present no reaction by Iran on this proposal is available.

The conclusion must be that the neutral attitude of the Security Council towards the conflict between Iran and Iraq was obviously based on political considerations, since there did not seem to be any obstacles in international law to the Security Council condemning the Iraqi attack as an act of aggression. On these grounds the Council could in fact have intervened more directly in the armed conflict between Iraq and Iran.

II   INDIVIDUAL RESPONSIBILITY: CRIMES AGAINST PEACE

A   The applicable law

From the point of view of international law, the fact that individuals have been made responsible for crimes against peace can be considered as an important precedent in international jurisprudence.[71] In their judgments the International Military Tribunals of Nuremberg and Tokyo explicitly stated that the Charters on which their jurisdiction was based should be considered as 'the expression of international law existing at the time of its creation'.[72] This position has been criticized by various scholars of international law, particularly regarding crimes against peace.[73] Subsequently these crimes have up till now not been elaborated in generally recognized rules applicable to

70. Enclosure II to Letter dated 15 August 1990 from the Permanent Representative of Iraq to the Secretary-General, *UN Doc.* S/21528.

71. On this subject, see in particular E. David, "L'actualité juridique de Nuremberg", in: *Le Procès de Nuremberg. Conséquences et actualisation*, Actes du Colloque international Université Libre de Bruxelles, Brussels 1988, pp. 89 *et seq.*; Green, L.C., "International crimes and the legal process", 29 *ICLQ* (1980), pp. 567 *et seq.*; Jessup, P.C., "The Crime of Aggression and the Future of International Law", 69 *Political Science Quarterly* (1947), pp. 1 *et seq.*; Lukashuk, I.I., "International Illegality and Criminality of Aggression", in: Ginsburgs, G./Kudriavtsev, V.N. (eds.), *The Nuremberg Trial and International Law*, Dordrecht 1990, pp. 121-140; Murphy, J.F., "Crimes against Peace at the Nuremberg Trial", in: *ibidem*, pp. 141-153; Rifaat, *op.cit.* (note 6), pp. 193 *et seq.*; Röling, B.V.A., "The Nuremberg and the Tokyo Trials in Retrospect", in: Bassiouni, M.C./Nanda, V.P. (eds.), *A Treatise on International Criminal Law*, Springfield 1973, pp. 590 *et seq.*

72. Nuremberg Judgment, *op.cit.* (note 7), p. 216. In exactly the same sense see the Tokyo Judgment, *op.cit.* (note 7), p. 28. Three of the eleven judges in the Tokyo Tribunal – the French judge, Bernard, the Indian judge, Pal and the Dutch judge, Röling – made dissenting opinions, partly because, though for different reasons, they could not agree with the view of (the majority of) the Tribunal regarding crimes against peace; see Tokyo Judgment, *op.cit.* (note 7), pp. 488, 551, 1048 respectively. In connection with determining the place of crimes against peace in international law today, especially the argument of the Dutch judge continues to be relevant. He considered that a war of aggression is prohibited by international law but does not constitute a 'true crime' under that law. Crimes against peace could in his opinion at most be described as crimes in *statu nascendi*: 'Where the decisive element is the danger rather than the guilt, where the criminal is considered an enemy rather than a villian, and where the punishment emphasizes the political measure rather than judicial retribution.' See Tokyo Judgement, *op.cit.* (note 7), pp. 1059-1062.

73. *Cf.*, David, *loc.cit.* (note 71), p. 95; Jessup, *loc.cit.* (note 71), p. 1; Röling, *loc.cit.* (note 71), p. 590; Rifaat, *op.cit.* (note 6), p. 177. But see Lukashuk, *loc.cit.* (note 71), p. 129 and Murphy, *loc.cit.* (note 71), p. 152.

all states,[74] although various attempts to that effect have been made and are being made in the United Nations.[75] Moreover, we have to keep in mind that, despite scores of international wars have been waged after the Second World War, no one has been officially held responsible for committing crimes against peace since Nuremberg and Tokyo.[76]

If a tribunal were to be established in accordance with Iran's demands,[77] in order to try the most prominent Iraqi leaders for crimes against peace, this tribunal would likewise be confronted with the question to what extent, according to current international law, a war of aggression is a crime that can be attributed to individual persons. Nevertheless, such a tribunal would be able to answer this question in the affirmative with greater justification than its illustrious predecessors. In contrast with the period preceding 1945 a prohibition of the use of force is now recognized as a fundamental norm of international law which, in the opinion of many scholars, has the character of *ius cogens*.[78]

With regard to the criminal responsibility of individuals for violations of this norm, one can point to several documents affirming the principle. In the first place, there is Resolution 95(I) of 11 December 1946 of the General Assembly in which it endorsed 'the principles of international law recognized by the Charter of the Nuremberg Tribunal and the judgment of the Tribunal.'[79] The International Law Commission elaborated these principles, but the General Assembly failed to approve the latter document.[80] Such was the fate of the 1954 Draft Code of Offences against the Peace and Security of Mankind of the International Law Commission. Consideration of this Draft Code was postponed by the General Assembly because of problems closely related to that of the definition of aggression. Seven years after reaching a consensus about the definition of aggression, the General Assembly invited the International Law Commission in 1981 to resume its work on the Draft Code.[81] In 1987 its (English) title was changed into 'Draft Code of *Crimes* against the Peace and Security of Mankind'.[82]

---

74. But see Brownlie, I., *Principles of Public International Law*, 4th ed., Oxford 1990, p. 562. He considers that 'whatever the state of the law in 1945, Article 6 of the Nuremberg Charter has since come to represent general international law.'

75. See notes 79-84 *infra* and accompanying text.

76. On this subject, see David, *loc.cit.* (note 71), p. 160. See also the statement by Mr Shevardnadze, Minister for Foreign Affairs of the USSR, at the forty-fifth session of the General Assembly of the United Nations, in which he declared that 'the principle of suppressing aggression and threats to peace should, in our view, be complemented with the principle of individual responsibility and commensurate punishment.' *USSR Press Release*, 25 September 1990.

77. See the documents mentioned in note 1, *supra*.

78. See Akehurst, M., *A Modern Introduction to International Law*, 6th ed., London 1987, pp. 41, 259; Brownlie, *op.cit.* (note 74), p. 513; Nguyen Quoc, D./Daillier, P./Pellet, A., *Droit International Public*, 3rd ed., Paris 1987, p. 190; Verdross, A/Simma, B., *Universelles Völkerrecht. Theorie und Praxis*, 3rd ed., Berlin 1984, p. 332. See also Judgment of the International Court of Justice of 27 June 1986, "Military and Paramilitary Activities in and against Nicaragua", *ICJ Reports* (1986), p. 101.

79. See note 8 *supra*.

80. *Idem.*

81. See A/RES/36/106 of 10 December 1981.

82. See *Yearbook ILC* (1987), vol. II, pt. 2, p. 13, and A/RES/42/156 of 7 December 1987.

At the end of its forty-second session (1990), the Commission had, on the basis of the eight reports of its Special Rapporteur Mr Thiam, provisionally adopted eleven articles on general principles and seven articles on specific crimes.[83] However, in view of the very broad scope and some highly controversial subjects, such as the problem of the implementation of the Draft Code, it seems unlikely that this venture will succeed within a measurable space of time.[84]

Evaluations of the Iraqi military action against Iran in the light of the standards applied by the Nuremberg and Tokyo Tribunals for crimes against peace will also meet with serious problems of substance. In the decisions of both tribunals the constitutive elements of these crimes were only sketchily outlined. Generally speaking, in the view of the tribunals, German and Japanese military action, before and during the Second World War, obviously met the criteria of crimes against peace so that it was rarely necessary to specify the constitutive elements of the crimes.[85] The question which concerned the courts above all at that time was who could be held responsible for the commission of these crimes.[86]

Shortly after participating in the Tokyo Tribunal, Röling remarked that an objective assessment of crimes against peace immediately after the war was an 'almost superhuman task'.[87] Extreme caution is even more called for if one would try, as in the present case, to arrive at such an assessment of an armed conflict, virtually exclusively on the basis of the facts as derived from United Nations documents. These facts are obviously insufficient for a full answer to the question whether there are adequate grounds for the Iranian accusation in this respect.

83. Article 1 (Definition); 2 (Characterization); 3 (Responsibility and punishment); 4 (Obligation to try or extradite); 5 (Non-applicability of statutory limitation); 6 (Judicial guarantees); 7 (*Non bis in idem*); 8 (Non-retroactivity); 10 (Responsibility of the superior); 11 (Official position and criminal responsibility); 12 (Aggression); 13 (Threat of aggression); 14 (Intervention); 15 (Colonial domination and other forms of alien domination); 16 (International terrorism); 18 (Recruitment, use, financing and training of mercenaries); X (Illicit traffic in narcotic drugs). See *Report ILC* (1990), *UN Doc.* A/45/10, p. 54.

84. Beside the principles and crimes mentioned in the previous note the following principles and crimes are also proposed for inclusion in the Draft Code of Crimes: complicity, conspiracy, attempt, breach of a treaty designed to ensure international peace and security, war crimes, genocide and apartheid. For the question concerning the establishment of an international criminal jurisdiction, see "Eighth Report on the Draft Code of Crimes against the Peace and Security of Mankind", *UN Doc.* A/CN.4/430/Add.1 (1990); and *Report ILC* (1990), *UN Doc.* A/45/10, pp. 36 *et seq.*

85. *Cf.*, Nuremberg Judgment, *op.cit.* (note 7), p. 186; also see Brownlie, *op.cit.* (note 6), p. 195; Rifaat, *op.cit.* (note 6), p. 156; Röling, *loc.cit.* (note 29), p. 390, in which he raises the questions whether an international judge actually needs a definition of a war of aggression and is inclined to answer this in the negative.

86. On this matter see Brownlie, *op.cit.* (note 6), p. 195; David, *loc.cit.* (note 71), p. 105; Röling, B.V.A., "Crimes against Peace", in: Bernhardt, R. (ed.), *Encyclopedia of Public International Law*, vol. 3, Amsterdam 1982, p. 135.

87. Röling, B.V.A., *Strafbaarheid van de agressieve oorlog* (Criminality of aggressive war), Inaugural lecture, Groningen 1950, p. 4.

B   War of aggression

The first question to be answered is whether there are relevant indications that the Iraqi military action against Iran falls within the terms of the concept of crimes against peace as applied by the post Second World War Tribunals. Such crimes are defined as follows in the Nuremberg Charter:

> 'Planning, preparation, initiation or waging of a war of aggression, or a war in violation of international treaties, agreements or assurances, or participation in a common plan or conspiracy for the accomplishment of any of the foregoing.'[88]

The element of 'war in violation of international treaties, agreements or assurances' was not elaborated by the Tribunals as an independent substantive basis of the crime. They stated that even with regard to such a war, the aggressive nature must be proved as an indication of unlawfulness, fault and liability.[89] Modern ideas on crimes against peace are also concerned with qualified violations of the prohibition of the use of force or of other international obligations. The International Law Commission generally agreed that 'seriousness' constitutes the essential element of all the crimes to be defined in the Draft Code of Crimes.[90] The Commentary to Draft Article 1 on the Definition of these crimes states that the element of seriousness 'can be deduced either from the nature of the act in question (...), or from the extent of its effects (...), or from the motive of the perpetrator (...), or from several of these elements.'[91]

The Tribunals did not produce a general definition of a 'war of aggression'. However, their lengthy consideration of German and Japanese foreign policies leading to the Second World War, induces to the conclusion that there is indeed a 'war of aggression' when extensive armed force is used by one state against another, as long as it is not a reaction to a similar action by that state, and cannot be legally justified on other grounds, and which is aimed at occupying or controlling the territory of that state.[92] The Draft Code of Crimes seems to start from a less confined content of the crimes against peace for it incorporates in Article 12, under the heading of 'Aggression', the main provisions of the Definition of Aggression as adopted by the General Assembly in 1974.[93] As explained above, this Definition concerns aggression as such,

---

88. Charter of the International Military Tribunal, 1945, Article 6(a). The Charter of the Tokyo Tribunal, Article 5 contains a virtually identical description of crimes against peace. *Cf.*, also the Allied Control Council Law nr. 10, Article 11(1)(a), see note 7 *supra*, for where to find these references. Also *cf.*, the formulation by the International Law Commission of the 'Nuremberg Principles', see note 8 *supra*.

89. *Cf.* Nuremberg Judgment, *op.cit.* (note 7), p. 214.

90. See *Yearbook ILC* (1987), vol. II, pt. 2, p. 13.

91. *Idem.*

92. This appears to be a 'safe' interpretation of the twelve 'acts of aggression' and 'wars of aggression' identified by the Nuremberg Tribunal in the German action. See Nuremberg Judgment, *op.cit.* (note 7), p. 186. In principle Brownlie, *op.cit.* (note 6), p. 50, 209, arrives at the same interpretation although he also considers that the judgment allows for considerable latitude on this point. Also see *History of the United Nations War Crimes Commission*, New York 1948, p. 254.

93. See A/RES/3314(XXIX) Annex, 14 December 1974.

which has, also in the context of the Definition, a broader meaning than 'a war of aggression'.[94] However, in view of the general definition of the crimes against the peace and security of mankind,[95] it must be assumed that only 'serious' forms of aggression are crimes against peace. And one of the main criteria for the determination of the seriousness of aggression is, indisputably, whether or not the use of armed force is aimed at occupying or controlling the territory of another state.[96]

In the light of these descriptions the conclusion that the Iraqi military action of 22 September 1980 was a 'war of aggression' seems justified. This action, which began with airraids on ten Iranian airfields, and was soon afterwards directed against other objectives using land and sea forces, assumed a large-scale character.[97] Earlier in this paper it was explained that the official Iraqi justification for this action could not be upheld in international law,[98] and that – even on the basis of official Iraqi documents – it may reasonably be assumed that the attacks were, *inter alia*, inspired by expansionist ambitions.[99]

This conclusion would still be valid even if it were only possible to show that the Iraqi intentions were merely to achieve the disputed claim for sovereignty over the entire Shatt-al-Arab. Admittedly such an intention is of a completely different order from that of the wars of aggression judged by the Nuremberg and Tokyo Tribunals. But the judgments do not contain any indication that more limited objectives of the use of force should not therefore allow it to be termed a 'war of aggression'. On the contrary, the judgments suggest that any large-scale military action as an instrument of foreign policy, even for the settlement of border disputes, can constitute a crime against peace.[100] In more concrete terms it should be noted that the Tokyo Tribunal also termed the limited and short-term Japanese action against the Russian troops at Lake Khassan in 1938, a 'war of aggression'.[101] This was an instance of a military action – in fact a separate issue from the other Japanese wars of aggression – with limited aims in an area where the frontier was not clearly determined.

94. As will be remembered, Article 5(2) of the Definition of Aggression provides (only) that 'A war of aggression is a crime against international peace' and that 'Aggression gives rise to international responsibility'. Because Article 5 is left out of Article 12 of the Draft Code of Crimes, there is no reference at all in the Draft Code to the concept of 'a war of aggression'!

95. See note 90 and accompanying text.

96. Article 12(4) of the Draft Code of Crimes (= Article 3 of the Definition of Aggression) mentions as the first example of acts of aggression '[T]he invasion or attack by the armed forces of a state of the territory of another state, or any military occupation, however temporary, resulting from such invasion or attack, or any annexation by the use of force of the territory of another state or part thereof.' See *Report ILC* (1988), *UN Doc*. A/43/10, p. 173.

97. On this subject, see in detail Staudenmaier, W.O., "A Strategic Analysis", in: Tahir-Kheli, S./Ayubi, S. (eds.), *op.cit.* (note 44), pp. 27, 36.

98. See notes 40-52 *supra* and accompanying text.

99. See notes 53-57 *supra* and accompanying text.

100. See Nuremberg Judgment, *op.cit.* (note 7), p. 218. Also see note 92 *supra*.

101. See Tokyo Judgment, *op.cit.* (note 7), p. 320.

C   The responsible persons

In the case of crimes against peace the crucial issue is the criminal responsibility of *individuals* for a 'war of aggression'. To that end it must be proved that the individuals concerned have deliberately planned, prepared, initiated or waged the war of aggression or have consciously participated in such activities in one way or another.[102] The circle of persons who can in principle commit such crimes is limited, but cannot be exactly determined because of the strongly casuistic and in some cases remarkably inconsistent character of the Nuremberg and Tokyo decisions in this respect.[103] With regard to the Draft Code of Crimes the question what category of individuals can be involved is also still unsettled. The Commentary on the article concerning aggression states:

> 'It remains to be decided whether only government officials are concerned, or also other persons having political and military responsibility and having participated in the organization and planning of aggression. It will also have to be decided whether the article applies to private persons who place their economic and financial power at the disposal of the authors of the aggression.'[104]

Moreover, the issue here is not only who can commit a crime against peace as such, but also who can participate in the commission of such a crime ('complicity') or who can participate in a common plan to commit such a crime ('conspiracy').[105]

Yet it is clear that the true political leader of a state planning and initiating a war of aggression may be the first to be held responsible for such action. In addition, all persons who actively participate in the determination of war policy, as well as those who have specific knowledge of such policy and yet retain their high position should in principle also be held responsible. Further, all the relevant documents in this respect contain the principle that the official position of the individual who commits a crime against peace, whether as Head of State or as government official, does not relieve him of criminal responsibility.[106]

To the extent that it is possible to define the circle of persons who can be held responsible, there seems to be no great problem in the case concerned here, as Iran's accusations were limited to the Iraqi regime, and President Saddam Hussein in

---

102. See note 88 *supra* and accompanying text.

103. See the literature mentioned in note 86 *supra*.

104. *Report ILC* (1988), *UN Doc.* A/43/10, pp. 187-188.

105. See for the content and the application of these complex 'related offences', "Eighth Report on the Draft Code of Crimes against the Peace and Security of Mankind", *UN Doc.* A/CN.4/430(1990), pp. 3-16; and *Report ILC* (1990), *UN Doc.* A/45/10, pp. 15-28.

106. *Cf.,* Article 7 Charter of the Nuremberg International Military Tribunal (see note 7 *supra*); Article 6 Charter of the International Military Tribunal for the Far-East (*ibidem*). See also Principle III of Principles of International Law Recognized in the Charter of the Nuremberg Tribunal and in the Judgment of the Tribunal (see note 8 *supra*), and Article 11 Draft Code of Crimes against the Peace and Security of Mankind (see *Report ILC* (1988), *UN Doc.* A/43/10, p. 184).

particular.[107] From what is known of the political system of Iraq,[108] all the important decisions leading to the beginning of the Gulf War in September 1980 were taken by the Revolutionary Command Council (RCC), the highest political organ of the state since the Iraqi revolution of July 1968 brought the Ba'ath Party into power. Saddam Hussein, who had already been a powerful vice-president for some years, became on 12 July 1979 President of the Republic, Chairman of the RCC and Chairman of the Regional Command Council of the Ba'ath Party. He was also Prime Minister and Commander-in-Chief of the Iraqi armed forces.

Proving 'intent' or 'guilt' as an element of a crime against peace is a more difficult matter. The Nuremberg and Tokyo Tribunals tended to a more or less 'objective' method of proving the existence of this requirement. In his analysis of the Nuremberg Tribunal Brownlie notes:

'Acts of participation in the planning of specific wars were *par excellence* a basis of guilt. In particular, attendance at the conferences at which Hitler revealed his plans, on 5 November 1937 and 23 November 1939, was given significance. Presence at one or other of these conferences was a decisive factor in the conviction of Goering, Raeder and von Neurath. (...) Apart from participation in these conferences, the planning of specific aggressive wars created responsibility.'[109]

Most members of the International Law Commission are also of the opinion that the intention to commit a crime against peace 'follows objectively from the acts themselves' and that there is 'no need to inquire whether the perpetrator was conscious of a criminal intent.'[110] According to some members, on the other hand, intent 'may not be presumed, but must always be established.'[111]

To the extent that evidence of an intention to commit a crime against peace can be derived from the circumstances, the United Nations documents give some evidence for the conclusion that the Iraqi regime, and President Saddam Hussein in particular, could be held responsible for this crime. In the above-mentioned letters to the United Nations, Iraq denied any intention of initiating a war of aggression or that it had territorial ambitions. On the other hand, on 17 September 1980, the Iraqi Minister for Foreign Affairs informed the Iranian Ambassador that, because of Iran's attitude, Iraq considered that it was obliged to use force in order to recover areas which it considered unjustly occupied by Iran.[112] Subsequent communications from Iraq also give the impression that this denial is, at the very least, of a questionable nature.[113] But the

---

107. See, in particular, the declaration of the Iranian Prime Minister, Mr Rajai, in the Security Council of 17 October 1980, *UN Doc.* S/PV.2251, p. 2.

108. See Khadduri, Majid, *The Gulf War. The Origins and Implications of the Iraq-Iran Conflict*, New York/Oxford 1988, pp. 64 *et seq.* See also al-Khalil, Samir, *Republic of Fear. The Politics of Modern Iraq*, London 1989, pp. 110 *et seq.*

109. Brownlie, *op.cit.* (note 6), p. 197.

110. *Yearbook ILC* (1987), p. 13.

111. *Idem.*

112. See notes 54-57 *supra* and accompanying text.

113. See especially the Note, appended as an annex to the letter of 25 November 1980, *UN Doc.* S/14272.

documents which may furnish the conclusive evidence on this point, such as the minutes and decisions of the meetings of the Iraqi RCC in the period preceding the military attack of 22 September 1980, are not available yet.

In its letters to the United Nations, Iran never indicated how the Iraqi political and military leaders should be tried for crimes against peace. It is clear that the basic principles of fair trial require that the prosecution takes place before an independent court of justice.[114] In the absence of a permanent international criminal court, the only reasonable option is to establish an *ad hoc* international penal tribunal, composed of judges of both parties to the conflict and judges of some neutral states. This could be done by a (multilateral) treaty or, perhaps, by a decision of the General Assembly of the United Nations. Although the trial of individuals for crimes against peace by a domestic court is not excluded by international law 'the nature of crimes against peace is such that no domestic proceedings can conceivably dispel doubts regarding the impartiality of the judges. As a matter of law, jurisdiction over crimes against peace is universal.'[115]

III   CONCLUSION

In terms of the principles of international law regarding the criminal responsibility of states for the crime of aggression, an analysis of, in particular, the documents of the Security Council furnishes a remarkable picture of the Iraqi action in the first stage of the Gulf War of 1980-1988. The official justification of the large-scale military action which began against Iran on 22 September 1980 appears not to be able to stand the test of the – by no means strict – rules relating to self-defence. As the available documents show that the Iraqi action was apparently also inspired by territorial ambitions, this action can be placed within the scope of the concept of aggression. On these grounds the Security Council could have ordered coercive measures against Iraq of an economic or even a military nature.

In the light of the analysis, the Iranian demand that the Iraqi leaders and President Saddam Hussein in particular should be tried for crimes against peace thus reveals itself in a rather remarkable international law perspective. The available United Nations documents do contain some relevant indications that they could be held responsible for these crimes under the Nuremberg and Tokyo rules.

However, the fact that not one of these possibilities has been applied in practice, reveals also that the concept of criminal responsibility of states as well as of individuals for one of the most serious violations of international law, the crime of aggression, does not at present occupy a very strong position in the international legal and political order.

114. See Principle V of 'The Principles of International Law Recognized in the Charter of the Nuremberg Tribunal and in the Judgment of that Tribunal', as adopted by the ILC in 1950 (see note 8 *supra*) and Article 6 of 'Draft articles of the draft Code of crimes against the peace and security of mankind', in: *Report ILC* (1990), *UN Doc.* A/45/10, p. 56.

115. Dinstein, *op.cit.* (note 17), p. 139.

COMMENTS

Eric David[*]

The issue of criminal responsibility in the Gulf War in terms of international law raises the question of whether or not the resort to this war, and/or the acts committed during this war constitute international crimes. We know that the violation of the rules prohibiting aggression in international relations and certain sorts of behaviour in time of armed conflict are prohibited by international criminal law, either as crimes against peace, or as war crimes. Ige Dekker, in his excellent paper, dealt with the crime of aggression. I should like to make a few comments on this issue (violations of *ius contra bellum*) and to add a few words about war crimes (violations of *ius in bello*) in the Gulf War.

I THE VIOLATIONS OF *IUS CONTRA BELLUM* IN THE GULF WAR

Mr Dekker seems somewhat cautious about the international prohibition of the crime of aggression. In the introduction to the paper he holds:

> 'The criminal responsibility of states and persons for "the crime of aggression" is still an emerging and controversial issue of international law.'

And again in the conclusions to the study:

> '... the concept of criminal responsibility of states as well as of individuals for one of the most serious violations of international law, the crime of aggression, does not at present occupy a very strong position in the international legal and political order.'

I partly agree and partly disagree with this view, especially from a *legal* perspective. For example, with regard to the conclusion, I agree with the idea that the crime of aggression does not occupy a very strong position in the present *international order* (not the *legal order*), because it is true that since Nuremberg and Tokyo, states (or people) have never really been able to prosecute leaders of a state for crimes against peace. However this is more a factual or a political problem than a legal one. On a strictly legal plane, I consider that for some aspects, the penalization of aggression is not controversial at all, whereas for other aspects, it is indeed a matter of discussion.

I should like to deal with each of these issues but I shall reverse the order of presentation which has been followed by Ige Dekker. I prefer to begin with what is, in my opinion, the less controversial issue, that is, the individual responsibility for crimes

---

* Eric David, Lecturer in International Law, Université Libre de Bruxelles.

I.F. Dekker and H.H.G. Post, eds., The Gulf War of 1980-1988

against peace, before going into the more controversial issue, *i.e.*, the state responsibility for the crime of aggression.

A   Individual responsibility for crimes against peace

There could be a crime against peace if the resort to force in the Gulf War amounted either to a war of aggression, or to aggression. If resort to force is a *war of aggression*, there is not the slightest difficulty in asserting that the people who planned, initiated and waged this war are guilty of a crime against peace. This conclusion is founded

- on the Nuremberg and the Tokyo precedents;
- on the confirmation of the Nuremberg principles by the General Assembly of the United Nations (A/RES/3(I) and A/RES/95(I));
- on the specific wording of the General Assembly's resolutions 2625(XXV)[1] and 3314(XXIX)[2], the legal and customary character of which has been recognised by the International Court of Justice.[3]

Therefore, we believe that the rule according to which 'a war of aggression is a crime against the peace' is a *de lata rule* which can entail for the authors of such a war all the consequences revealed by the Nuremberg and the Tokyo cases.

If resort to force is a mere *aggression* and not, strictly speaking, a *war of aggression*, then I agree with Ige Dekker that the criminal responsibility of its authors is not so clearly established as in the case of a war of aggression. We must remember, indeed, that

- at Nuremberg, the *Anschluss* was considered as an 'aggressive act', not as an 'aggressive war',[4] and its authors were not condemned for this act;
- during the debates relating to the definition of aggression, the socialist states wanted to penalize any 'act of aggression', but it is the restrictive view confining the crime against peace to a 'war of aggression' which prevailed.[5]

Consequently, the fact that the penalization of 'aggression' as such appears only in the Draft Code of Offenses against the Peace and Security of Mankind made by the

---

1. 1st Principle, 2nd para.: 'A war of aggression constitutes a crime against the peace, for which there is responsibility under international law.'
2. Article 5 § 2: 'A war of aggression is a crime against international peace. Aggression gives rise to international responsibility.'
3. *Military and paramilitary activities in and against Nicaragua, ICJ Reports* (1986), pp. 101, 103, §§ 191, 195.
4. International Military Tribunal, Judgment of 1 October 1946, in: *AJIL* (1947), p. 284.
5. Broms, B., "The definition of aggression", *Hague Recueil* (1977), I.T. 154, pp. 356-357.

International Law Commission (1954 and today)[6] shows that this penalization is just a *de lege ferenda* rule.

In all events, as Ige Dekker demonstrated, in the present case, it is difficult to argue that the resort to hostilities was only an act of aggression and not a war of aggression.

B   Criminal state responsibility for aggression

I agree with Ige Dekker that criminal state responsibility for aggression is much more debatable than an individual's responsibility for crimes against peace and for the following reasons:

1° the only source of this so-called criminal responsibility of states remains a mere draft: Article 19 of the draft articles on state responsibility of the International Law Commission;[7]
2° according to Article 19, criminal responsibility would be attributable to a state for 'aggression'; this provision does not specify that the act of the state should be a 'war of aggression'; consequently, if, as we have seen above, the existence of a rule of criminal *individual* responsibility for a 'mere' aggression is already debatable, *a fortiori*, the existence of a rule of a criminal *state* responsibility for aggression is doubtful;
3° all the consequences of Article 19 have not yet been drawn by the International Law Commission, and the members of the Commission at present disagree about the question whether or not the provision on strictly penal consequences will be retained.[8]

For these reasons, I think that Article 19 remains a *de lege ferenda* rule, except if one can show that the measures which were taken against Japan and Germany after the Second World War (military occupation, territorial amputations, war damages) are comparable to some kind of penal sanctions, and therefore, constitute a precedent. If this is the case, criminal state responsibility for aggression is less debatable as it seems to be at first sight.

In the Gulf War, we might wonder if the issue of criminal responsibility, of either of individuals or of the state, is not purely theoretical as the Security Council did not designate any culprit. We do not think so taking into account that the Security Council expressly reserved the question.[9]

---

6. 1954 Draft Code, Article 2 § 1, *Yearbook ILC* (1954), vol. II, p. 151; 1988 Draft Code, Article 12, *Rapport C.D.I.* (1988), *UN Doc.* A/43/10, p. 141.
   7. *Annuaire C.D.I.* (1976), Vol. II, pp. 2, pp. 89 *et seq.*
   8. *Rapport C.D.I.* (1989), *UN Doc.* A/44/10, pp. 94-202.
   9. S/RES/598 of 20 July 1987, § 6.

II   THE VIOLATIONS OF *IUS IN BELLO* IN THE GULF WAR

Numerous violations of international humanitarian law have been committed by each side.[10] Each of these violations during this war which can be construed as a grave breach, according to the 1949 Geneva Conventions which bind both states, entails individual criminal responsibility for the author of the breach.

However, this conclusion only concerns the violations of the so-called 'Law of Geneva' which regulates the treatment of persons in the power of the enemy. What about the violations of the rules which govern the conduct of hostilities, *i.e.*, the so-called 'Law of The Hague'? What about the bombing of towns and civilian targets? What about the use of gas?

We know that making the civilian population the object of an attack is a grave breach according to Article 85 of the 1977 Additional Protocol I, but that neither Iraq, nor Iran ratified this instrument. In the same way, we know that the use of gas is prohibited by the 1925 Geneva Protocol but that the violation of this prohibition is not penalized by any instrument. *A fortiori*, the use of gas in a non-international armed conflict, which could have been the case when civilians were bombed in the Iraqi town of Halabadja in Kurdistan is not penalized either.

Does this mean that it would be impossible to prosecute the people who committed such acts? I do not think so. Firstly, these acts are offenses against the municipal law of all nations (murders, destructions), and, as violations of the laws of war, they cannot be justified by the existence of a state of war.[11] Consequently, their authors can be prosecuted before a domestic tribunal for a breach of municipal law. However, as these offenses are not international crimes, the jurisdiction of the tribunal would depend on the traditional bases of competence which are in force in most states: the territorial, personal or protective principles. Failing the applicability of these principles, the prosecutions would be impossible – hence there is a need to find a basis of universal jurisdiction.

Such a basis exists since these acts, if they are not *stricto sensu* war crimes, are, in all events, crimes against humanity. On the one hand, these acts can be construed as 'inhumane acts committed against any civilian population (...) during the war' (Article 6(c) of the Statute of the International Military Tribunal of Nuremberg). On the other hand, the International Law Commission has observed that the distinction between war crimes and crimes against humanity is 'porous',[12] and, in the *Barbie* Case, the French *Cour de Cassation* has recognised that a war crime could also be a crime against humanity if it was committed with a political and ideologocial goal.[13] Even if, in the Gulf War, technically speaking, no 'war crime' has been committed as has been shown above, there have been nevertheless violations of the laws of war, and I see no difficulty

10. *Cf.* David, E., "La guerre du Golfe et le droit international", *R.B.D.I.* (1987), pp. 161-169. See also chapters 3 and 4 of this book.

11. *Cf.* David, E., "L'actualité juridique de Nuremberg", in: *Le Procès de Nuremberg; conséquences et actualisation*, actes du colloque du 27 mars 1987, Brussels 1988, p. 145.

12. *Rapport C.D.I.* (1987), *UN Doc.* A/42/10, p. 31.

13. Cass. fr. 20 Dec. 1985, *Barbie, J.D.I.* (1986), p. 402, note Edelman.

in transposing to these violations the reasoning of the French supreme court relating to war crimes.

If this conclusion might still seem doubtful, I like to add that, after all, the Nuremberg Judgment is in itself a justification to prosecute facts such as wanton bombing of civilians, or wanton use of gas. Nuremberg would be a precedent not because of the substance of the rules which were stated by the Tribunal, but because of the way in which these rules were brought to light. In other words, it is not the conclusions of the judgment which matter, but the reasoning followed to reach those conclusions. It is this reasoning which constitutes a precedent enabling the penalization, here and now, of acts and behaviour which, otherwise, would not strictly appear to everyone as crimes under international law in force.

It would, indeed, not be more difficult, absurd or excessive to prosecute people who bear the responsibility for attacks against civilians or for the use of gas in the Gulf War than it was to prosecute the German leaders in Nuremberg for crimes against peace on the basis of instruments which were not in force (a *draft* Treaty of Mutual Assistance sponsored by the League of Nations in 1923, the 1924 Geneva Protocol), were not binding (resolutions of the League of Nations 1927 and of the Pan-American Conference of 1928), or which did not strictly incriminate war such as the 1928 Kellog-Briand Pact.[14]

In the same way, it would not be more excessive to prosecute the Iraqis and the Iranians implicated in these crimes than to prosecute the Nazis for crimes against humanity without any other foundation than a close link with the other categories of crimes provided for by the Statute of the International Military Tribunal.[15] Like the Nuremberg judges, who would be entrusted with the task of judging any author of the above-mentioned acts could say that he

'must know that he is doing wrong, and so far from it being unjust to punish him, it would be unjust if his wrong were allowed to go unpunished.'[16]

---

14. *Cf.* David, *loc.cit.* (note 11), pp. 95-96.
15. *Ibidem*, pp. 99-104.
16. International Military Tribunal, *op.cit.* (note 4), p. 217.

COMMENTS

Peter Malanczuk[*]

The issues related to the topic of 'criminal responsibility' under international law are difficult to deal with in general and particularly delicate in the context of assessing the conduct of Iraq during the war with Iran. The difficulty of the topic in general is reflected in continuing fundamental disagreement – despite new chances of enhanced international cooperation – during the discussions held at the end of 1990 in the Sixth Committee of the UN General Assembly concerning the Report of the International Law Commission (42nd session 1990) and the 'Draft Code of Crimes Against the Peace and Security of Mankind'.[1] The delicacy of analyzing the conduct of Iraq in the war against Iran in terms of 'criminal responsibility' becomes apparent when the rather different attitude of member states of the United Nations and of the Security Council is taken into consideration with regard to the war unleashed by Iraq against Kuwait. Thus, the rapporteur had no easy task and his cautious approach, both in limiting the scope of his investigation to the question of aggression and in the way he developed the argument, is to be commended. In the following comments only three observations are made in the hope of stimulating discussion.

The first observation concerns the history of 'crimes against peace' which Bert V.A. Röling, the distinguished Dutch international scholar, who also had practical experience in the area, has adequately described as 'complex'.[2] It is interesting to note that already after the Napoleonic wars the idea was at least considered – although not implemented for political reasons – to put Napoleon on trial for the wars he had commenced. Furthermore, it is worthwhile recalling that the envisaged trial of the German Kaiser after World War I, on the basis of the compromise reached in the Versailles Peace Treaty, 'for a supreme offence against international morality and the sanctity of treaties',[3] did not take place because the Dutch refused to extradite Wilhelm II. Thus, the Nuremberg and Tokyo trials after World War II should be seen in a broader historical perspective. However, the fact that the Nuremberg and Tokyo Tribunals, leaving aside the legal objections raised with respect to their authority and certain

---

* P. Malanczuk, Professor of Public International Law, University of Amsterdam (the Netherlands).
1. See *UN Doc.* A/CN.4L.456 of 6 February 1991, containing a "Topical summary of the discussion held in the Sixth Committee of the General Assembly during its forty-fifth session, prepared by the Secretariat" on the Report of the International Law Commission on the Work of its Forty-Second Session (1990), pp. 11 *et seq.*

2. Röling, B.V.A., "Crimes Against Peace", in: Bernhardt, R. (ed.), *Encyclopedia of Public International Law*, Instalment 3, Amsterdam 1982, pp. 132 *et seq.*, at p. 133.

3. Quoted by Röling, *idem.*

I.F. Dekker and H.H.G. Post, eds., The Gulf War of 1980-1988
© 1992, T.M.C. Asser Instituut, The Hague

aspects of their decisions,[4] have not been followed by any other precedents in later state practice makes it difficult to determine their true significance for establishing customary international law.

The second observation addresses the question whether Iraq, in attacking Iran, can invoke grounds upon which its action can be justified in international law. In view of the factual circumstances, the only legal doctrine seriously available to justify the attack on such a large scale is the doctrine of preventive or anticipatory self-defence. It is well-known that many authorities reject this doctrine as an admissible defence and do so for good reasons. A closer analysis of the literature and of practice – for example, of the debate in the Security Council in June 1981 concerning the Israeli preventive military action against the nuclear reactor in Iraq – does not unequivocally support this view.[5] However, even if one assumes that anticipatory self-defence against an imminent armed attack by another state continues to be legal under the criteria established by the Caroline incident ('necessity of self-defence, instant, overwhelming threat, leaving no choice of means, and no moment for deliberation' with the additional requirement that the action taken must not be 'unreasonable or excessive' and 'limited by that necessity and kept clearly within it'), it is apparent that Iraq's attack on Iran cannot be justified on the basis of those criteria.

The third and final observation is of a more fundamental nature. 'Criminal responsibility' under international law in general, and, as witnessed by an article published in the first issue of the new 'European Journal of International Law',[6] the problems related to universal criminal jurisdiction and to establishing an International Criminal Court in particular, appear to receive more attention recently. However, it remains necessary to emphasize the inherent limitations of this discussion in view of the horizontal and decentralized nature of international law as a 'primitive' legal system. In short, the proposition – certainly not a new one – is that, although there is clearly criminal responsibility in certain cases of individuals under international law, the term 'criminal responsibility' makes no sense when applied to the conduct of states. As far as certain internationally-wrongful acts are named 'crimes', as in Article 19 of the ILC's Draft Articles on State Responsibility, there may be a case for arguing that there should be responsibility of states for 'international crimes' to indicate the seriousness of the act in question and to stress the importance of the protected value for the international community as a whole. If, however, there are no separate legal consequences following from the commission of an 'international crime', in the end we may be left only with misleading terminology, unless it is possible, first, to avoid associations with individual

---

4. See, for example, the recent summary given by Ipsen, K., *Völkerrecht*, 3rd. ed., 1990, pp. 531 *et seq.*

5. Malanczuk, P., "Countermeasures and Self-Defence as Circumstances Precluding Wrongfulness in the International Law Commission's Draft Articles on State Responsibility", in: Spinedi, M., Simma, B., (eds.), *United Nations Codification of State Responsibility*, New York 1987, pp. 197 *et seq.*, at pp. 246 *et seq.*, with references.

6. Graefrath, B., "Universal Jurisdiction and an International Criminal Court", *European J. of Int. Law* (1990), pp. 6 *et seq.*

punishment under highly-developed national criminal legal systems with their substantive and procedural safeguards and, second, to focus attention on the issue of the rights of third states not directly affected by the act allegedly constituting an 'international crime'. If one looks at the relevant work of the ILC, this still remains an open question.[7]

---

7. For an excellent analysis see Simma, B., "Bilateralism and Community Interest in the Law of State Responsibility", in: Dinstein, Y., (ed.), *International Law at a Time of Perplexity*, Dordrecht/Boston/London 1988, pp. 821 *et seq.*

Chapter 9

THE GULF WAR OF 1980-1988 AND THE ISLAMIC CONCEPTION OF
INTERNATIONAL LAW

Mohammed Bedjaoui[*]

'Never before had I lived in a city where no call to prayer rose up, punctuating time, filling
space, reassuring men and walls.' (Amin Maalouf, *Léon l'Africain*, Ed. J.C. Lattès, Paris
1986, p. 295) (Translation)

'Here we are in the land of Islam and proudly wear our faith like a diadem. Let us not be too
harsh with those who carry their religion like a hot coal in the hand.' (Ibidem, p. 124)
(Translation) (The reference is to those Andalusian Muslims who were forced to convert to
Christianity or leave Spain.)

'Wherever you may be, some will be inquisitive about your skin and your prayers. Be sure
not to encourage their instincts, my son! Be they Muslim, Jewish or Christian, they will have
to take you as you are or lose you. When people seem narrow-minded, remind yourself that
God's earth is vast, and vast are His hands and His heart. Never hesitate to remove yourself
beyond all seas, all frontiers, all native lands, all creeds.' (Ibidem, p. 365) (Translation)

INTRODUCTION

Though fully conscious of the honour bestowed on me by an invitation to take part in
this colloquium, situated as it was bound to be on a high plane of scholarship, I
hesitated for a long time before accepting. Everything I represent, in one *persona* or
another, urged me to abstain from intervening in this debate, if only out of sensitive
regard for the countries involved, concerned or affected by that grave and long-drawn-
out conflict in the Gulf: the *jurist* within me suffered from the obliteration of
international law in the unleashing of armed might; the *Arab* in me could hardly bear
the involvement of an Arab State in that war; the *Muslim* that I am could not endure the
clash of two Muslim States; as an *Algerian* I could not but mourn the passing of the
1975 Algiers Agreements that had bound the belligerents; as an offspring of the Third
World I was rudely shaken by a nightmare vision of a temple wrecked, of idols
trampled underfoot, of shattered convictions; while as an *international judge* bound by
the duties of his office I was most reluctant to concern myself in public with a quarrel
between states.

---

[*] Judge M. Bedjaoui, Member of the International Court of Justice.

I.F. Dekker and H.H.G. Post, eds., The Gulf War of 1980-1988
© 1992, T.M.C. Asser Instituut, The Hague

Yet here I am, as you have prompted and urged, to present my communication. I shall do so, however, without even mentioning the name of the two belligerents. That is as delicacy dictates. Need I add that, if at any point I appear to stray outside this self-denying ordinance, I shall have done so quite unintentionally and that I fully respect all the peoples of the region, and all others too?

This paper comprises three parts of unequal length and importance. In the first part I shall approach the Gulf War of 1980-1988 with the tools of analysis provided by the international law which governs the whole of the international community today, that is to say, the law of the Charter of the United Nations, which is the one continuously applied by the high judicial organ of which I have the honour to be a member.

In doing so, however, I shall play the purely passive part of an observer taking care not to pronounce any individual judgment. I shall simply take cover behind the body of learned and authoritative writers who, on the strength of the principles and rules of international law, as wielded on their own responsibility as legal scholars, have been driven to compile a weighty catalogue of violations. As a working postulate, *i.e.*, as a starting-point which I have neither to approve nor deny, I shall take the virtually unanimous conclusion of legal scholars that the international law of the community of nations was a *major victim* of this War.

And since the normal key for deciphering the Gulf situation, *i.e.*, the international law to which all are subject, opens the door to pessimism and condemnation, I shall confine myself to seeing whether there might not be some other key, some other possible reading of the War, another system of references drawn from Islamic international law, and whether that legal order can provide some elements enabling the situation to be understood and dealt with in a coherent and effective way.

That inquiry will be the subject of my second part, where I shall be going in quest of the legal tools of analysis to be derived from the Islamic conception of international law and applying them on the conditions and within the limits imposed on me by my personal and professional constraints. I hope to reach various conclusions, which I shall submit to you with the genuine humility of the jurist who knows he knows nothing, the judge who knows he seeks nothing, and the man who knows he can do nothing.

In the third and last part I shall endeavour to draw conclusions from the previous analyses resulting from the two parallel decoding operations, and inquire successively into the areas of convergence between the universal conception of international law and the Islamic conception, the circumstances in which there might come into being a genuine renaissance of Islamic law in the service of peace within a pluralist world, and the possible place and role of such a law at the regional level, bearing in mind the provisions of the United Nations Charter on regional arrangements.

I THE 1980-1988 GULF WAR AND UNIVERSAL LAW: THE SEVERE JUDGMENT OF WORLD LEGAL SCHOLARSHIP UPON THE BELLIGERENTS

A The catalogue of violations of international law drawn up by legal scholars

In the eyes of world legal opinion, this war did not appear to give rise to any complex problems so far as concerned fact-finding, the discernment of the applicable principles and rules, the consequent legal assessment of the facts and the identification of the belligerent or belligerents responsible for particular breaches of international law. Jurists have been virtually unanimous in considering that, when all was said and done, the problems raised by the war for foreign ministries, their legal advisers and public opinion, could be reduced to simple, classic terms: breach of the prohibition on the use of force, rejection of the rules on peaceful settlement of disputes between states, non-compliance with Security Council decisions, violations of the principles and rules of humanitarian law, infraction of the rights and obligations of neutral states, encroachments upon the freedom of navigation on the high seas, *etc.*

In order the better to circumscribe, reconnoitre and come to grips with the legal arena of the wartime events, scholars have set down certain marker beacons. Their beams of light, generated by the batteries of today's universal law, have naturally enough been trained on the conduct of the belligerents. I must however confess that in this time of *glasnost* I find myself sometimes regretting that the searchlights have not been swung round to show up in the same harsh glare the shadow side of the conduct of certain international organs and neutral states.

In analyzing the premonitory signs of war, scholars have shown how all the ingredients of the impending bloodshed were present in the actions and pronouncements of the future belligerents, who mutually accused each other of violations of treaties, warlike goings-on, meddling in each other's domestic affairs, openly vowing to overturn each other's internal regime with a view to liberating its people, territorial expansionism, expulsion of each other's nationals, virulent press campaigns, inflammatory speeches, *etc.* But perhaps these omens have not themselves been sufficiently analyzed with a view to characterizing them in relation to the international order and, if need be, the regional Islamic order. If that had been done, many things would perhaps have appeared in a clearer light.

Almost unanimously, legal scholars deplored the outbreak of hostilities and concentrated on the question of identifying the aggressor with reference to customary and conventional law and, more particularly, the provisions of the United Nations Charter and the Resolution on the definition of aggression.

The war's terrifying progress and the difficulties of securing a cease-fire throughout so many agonizing years have also been subjected to impartial analysis in the light of modern international law.

The conduct of the hostilities and the treatment of persons in enemy hands led jurists to draw up a fearful catalogue of violations of humanitarian law: the bombardment of civilian populations; retaliation by way of (legally prohibited) reprisals against similar civilian targets; serious and sometimes irreversible damage to the environment, especially when offshore oil installations were targeted; use of prohibited weapons; recruitment and combat use of adolescents;[1] improper treatment of prisoners-of-war and persons in enemy hands, *etc.*

For eight long years, nearly as long as the First and Second World Wars combined, the belligerents waged total war against each other, with nearly a million dead, about 150,000 prisoners and material destruction estimated to exceed the entire combined national debts of the Third World countries (over one million million dollars in 1988), accompanied by the most shocking violations of humanitarian law.

Faced with this horror, the International Committee of the Red Cross, making use of a procedure to which it resorts only in exceptional cases, felt obliged on 7 May 1983 to appeal to all states parties to the four Geneva Conventions of 12 August 1949, reminding them that they had solemnly undertaken not only to respect but also *to ensure respect for* those Conventions. The appeal called upon states systematically to raise the question of the observance of humanitarian law in any contact with either of the belligerents, and to make special efforts to have that law respected.

This unusual procedure was again resorted to nine months later, on 13 February 1984, when a second memorandum from the ICRC emphasized that:

> 'The violations of law determined and described in its two memoranda are *fundamental* in character [and] not only endanger the life and liberty of tens of thousands of victims of the present conflict but (...) undermine the *essence* and principles of international humanitarian law. In time they may lead to the *discredit* of the rules of law and universal principles whereby states have agreed to provide the human person with a better defence against the rigours of war.' (Emphasis added; Translation from French)

B   **The muted and desultory criticisms levelled at the slack conduct of international organizations and third states during the war**

In fairness it must be said that world legal opinion did not wholly ignore these problems. When the belligerents carried out armed actions against neutral shipping (bombing, machine-gunning, interception, seizure) and more generally against freedom of navigation and neutral maritime commerce, culminating in the mining of waters used by international shipping, these actions were seen as breaches of international law and as justifying the measures of protection taken by third states to ensure the safety of their vessels and of international navigation in general.

---

1. Lamentably, children have in all ages been the innocent victims of the madness of adults. At the present moment (in 1990), the International Committee of the Red Cross, in its Geneva museum, is showing a timely exhibition on 'Children in War'. This heartrending exhibition shows how children have been mutilated in body and soul in Timor, Cambodia, Afghanistan, Iran, Iraq, Viet-Nam, China, Rhodesia and elsewhere. It shows, for example, a child, during the Chinese civil war in 1946, leading a line of blind persons in the traditional long robe, each with a hand placed on the shoulder of the one in front of him. It shows another child in a cap raising his hands under the threat of Nazi weapons at the entrance to the Warsaw ghetto. It shows that shattering image of the toddler and the little girl fleeing in panic along a road in Viet Nam under napalm bombardment in June 1972 (see Vichniac, Isabelle, *Le Monde*, 1 November 1990).

However, there are two aspects of the war which, paradoxically, did not arouse a great deal of scholarly curiosity.

1   *The assistance provided by third states to the belligerents*

In any armed conflict between two states, it is always of course possible that one or more third states may, at one time or another, adopt a political or diplomatic position, or even take material steps, in favour of one or other of the belligerents, and if they actually provide arms they can no longer be regarded as neutral states. This is commonly the case, and the 1980-1988 Gulf War was no exception.

But the spectacular feature of this conflict, a 'first' perhaps in the entire history of warfare, was the involvement of states which, without any actual sympathy for the cause of either state, massively sold arms, gave technological assistance and provided military intelligence *simultaneously to both camps*. This was surely something more than just the ruthless application of the laws of the international arms trade. For there were strong signs that behind this indiscriminate delivery to both belligerents of the means of mutual destruction there lay a strategy for weakening both to the point of their common extinction. This strategy appears to have begun by a preconditioning of the latent adversaries for the ferocious war in which they eventually engaged and, according to its own logic, to have continued with the intention of prolonging the conflict until the strength of both regional giants was entirely sapped.

The question is, were such phenomena, such a scenario, a fit or proper subject for legal analysis? Could the multifarious material encouragement lavished on either camp to pursue the use of force in international relations escape such analysis? If it could, and if international law in consequence has to turn its back on such situations, international law would no longer be the vehicle either of peace or justice. If it could not, that analysis has still to be carried out in terms of international law.

The most that emanated from the Security Council was an occasional request that third states 'refrain from any action likely to intensify or widen the conflict.' One could hardly be more culpably mild.

2   *The poor showing of the Security Council*

This is the second aspect about which jurists have had little to say. Here was a deadly, devastating war raging which dramatically set back the clock of progress for both belligerents. The Security Council was incapable either of identifying its initiator, abbreviating its duration, imposing a cease-fire or exacting compliance with international humanitarian law from either belligerent.

There is thus absolutely no getting away from the comparison between the 1980-1988 Gulf War and the present crisis in the Gulf. Now the Security Council has taken in ten weeks more decisions than it took in eight years previously, when an actual war was raging.

If modern international law, the work of man, remained powerless to forestall, limit, discipline and halt that war, could Islamic international law, the work of the divine legislator, prevent, explain or condemn this immensity of chaos and desolation?

Let us ascertain whether, and in what way, the war could be analyzed in terms of Islamic international law.

II   THE 1980-1988 GULF WAR AND THE ISLAMIC CONCEPTION OF INTERNATIONAL LAW (THE SEARCH FOR ANOTHER CIPHER KEY TO THIS WAR)

A   Preliminary observations

I have two preliminary observations to make.

1   *Does intertemporal law come into play?*

From the methodological point of view, there is a certain ambiguity in applying to a 20th century war an Islamic law of divine origin, which was revealed in the 7th century, *i.e.*, thirteen and a half centuries earlier.

Intertemporal law forbids us to analyze a past situation with the legal tools of the present. Conversely, no doubt, one ought not to analyze a contemporary situation by setting aside prevailing law (universal public law) and making use of ancient norms (the Islamic law of the 7th century).

Intertemporal law amounts in fact to a warning to jurists to characterize a historical situation only by reference to the standards of its time, and a present-day situation only by the application of contemporary law.

Perhaps, however, the problem before us here is not actually a problem of intertemporal law. The peoples and rulers of the belligerent states are Muslims; the Islamic international law which may govern them is of divine origin and was revealed at the beginning of the 7th century. By virtue of its sacred origin, it is an immutable law whose provisions are intangible. Hence to analyze the 1980-1988 Gulf War in the light of Islamic international law must necessarily amount to reading a contemporary situation in the mirror of ancient sacred texts. The chronological gap is immense but inevitable at the level of the analysis. Hence it appears necessary at least to draw attention to it here. It is as if it were necessary to issue a peremptory and irrevocable condemnation of abortion in secular modern societies by making use of the canon law of mediaeval Europe. The law belongs to one age and the abortion to an entirely different one.

2   *A law ahead of its time?*

My second observation somewhat tempers the scope of my first. Looking in broad outline, as I propose to do, at the Islamic conception of international law, one realizes that one is in the presence of a law incredibly ahead of its time, so that its principles and rules, in particular so far as the conduct of war is concerned, fully stand comparison with those of present-day humanitarian law.

In what follows I thus intend to expound the Islamic conception of war in relation to the 1980-1988 Gulf War. The full range of that conception will be appreciated if at each stage of the analysis it be borne in mind that it arose at the beginning of the 7th century. In various astonishing ways it nevertheless resonates strongly through to our own era. This reminder of the remote origin in time of a legal system enables one to measure the extent of what Islam introduced into a dimming mediaeval West. It will also enable us to realize the still vital relevance of this *corpus juris* laid down, if I may be forgiven for saying so in present company, one thousand years before Grotius, Gentilis, Ayala or Pierre Bayle.

Islam's vision of human society underlies its conception of international law. Man, created by God, is born good. The Koran maintains him in this elective quality. Islam accordingly considers war as contrary to human nature, for the essential foundation of man's passage on this earth is peaceful, fraternal and civilizing co-existence. Mutual slaughter is a fundamental deviation from the natural behaviour of peoples and the mission of Man upon earth. There is no irresistible urge to war in human societies. On the contrary, they tend towards peace, which constitutes the *dhahira as-sahiha, i.e.,* their primal health and authentic stamp.

But war, *jihad,* a reprehensible act for believers, may nevertheless be an unavoidable evil once it is necessary to repulse an aggression, to defend Muslims in order to protect their faith when under threat, to thwart plots by their enemies to oppress or despoil them or, finally, to promote the reign of divine justice upon earth.

Fundamentally, therefore, Islam regards war as a *pis-aller.* Citing the attitude of the Prophet Muhammad during the Hodaibya expedition, Sheikh Mohammed Draz has written:

'In the eyes of Islam, an international arrangement which is somewhat disadvantageous for Muslims but is likely to avoid bloodshed is better than a bloody victory for the just cause.'[2]

B   The unlawfulness of war between two Muslim States, in the Islamic conception of international law

1   *There is no place for war in the Dar ul-Islam*

The war we are considering was between Muslim belligerents on either side. But Islamic law makes a cardinal distinction between *Dar ul-Islam* and *Dar ul-Harb, i.e.,* between the world of Islam and the world of war. It is inadmissible that the community of the faithful, the *umma,* should engage in internecine, indeed fratricidal wars, which would destroy its social fabric.

---

2. Draz, Mohammed Abdallah, "Le droit international public et l'Islam", *Revue égyptienne de droit international,* 1949, Vol. 5 and *Revue de la Croix Rouge internationale,* 1950, pp. 194-209; quotations in the present paper will be based on the latter publication (here, p. 200) and are translated by the author.

2   *Exceptions to the principle of the banishment of war within the Dar ul-Islam*

In the 1980-1988 Gulf War, each side put forward 'modern' reasons in order to justify resort to force. There were allegations of, among other things, interference in internal affairs, assistance lent by one regime to the opponents of the other, breaches of treaties and international commitments, *etc*. But some of these justifications may also be interpreted in terms of the rules and principles of Islamic law.

a   The incompatible features of the neighbouring political regimes

Under this heading I shall mention various acts and attitudes alleged by one or other belligerent against the other: hostile broadcasts, assistance to opposition forces, expulsion of opponents, unfriendly propaganda, mutual accusations of dividing the Muslim community or abandonment of Islamic principles, down to accusations of apostasy justifying war against the apostate, *etc*.

If such actions and attitudes would certainly not justify the unleashing of a war according to modern international law, in the Islamic law of the seventh century it was a duty to fight apostates, tyrants, the impious and any Muslim authorities guilty of either abandoning Islam or violating its precepts. The 'bad' Muslims within the *umma* had to be fought and the internal enemy extirpated from Islam.

Need I explain that such an outlook, aimed as it was at bolstering the Islamic internal front, was historically understandable in the seventh century when Islam had just come into being and had to be protected in a hostile or aggressive environment?At the same time, it must be recalled that Muslims take pride in a spirit of tolerance. They have not conferred upon themselves 'the right, or even the duty, according to their sacred Book, to take up arms, either to impose their doctrine or to annihilate those who do not adopt it. (Otherwise) the concept of "international law" would be meaningless in Islam, since non-Muslims would have no right to liberty or even to life (...) On the contrary, the Koran lays a moral prohibition on placing the conscience of others under duress.'[3] *Surat* I, verse 257, admonishes the believer that 'there should be no constraint in matters of faith', and the Koran recalls that God did not will that there should be only one religion: 'It is by a kind of divine decree that there will always be differences of view between men' (*Surat* XI, verse 118).[4]

If therefore Muslim peoples accept this plurality of religious convictions in respect of non-Muslim peoples, why should they not admit that neighbouring Muslim peoples should simply be imbued with differing schools of thought? But perhaps this question is not as watertight as it appears, for it comes more easily to a man to accept a difference in a foreigner than in his brother.

---

3. Draz, *op.cit*. (note 2), p. 197.
4. *Translator's note*. Given the controversial nature of some English translations, the quotations from the Koran have here been rendered indirectly via the French.

However that may be, it is one of the essential achievements of contemporary international law to have proclaimed each people's right to choose its own political regime and the principle of non-interference in the internal affairs of a state.

The second series of alleged justifications of the 1980-1988 Gulf War can be assembled under the head of breaches of treaties and international undertakings.

b   The accusation of violation of the 1975 Algiers Agreements

This is not the place for me to analyze the Algiers Agreements of 1975 or to determine whether, when and by whom they were violated. It is sufficient for present purposes to note that an accusation was made in that sense.

Islamic international law is clear on this subject.

Absolute respect for treaty commitments was one of the strongest of the original features of this law in the seventh century. The question of treaties was approached on a very precise religious basis, through the Koran and the *hadiths* of the Prophet.[5] The view taken of the absolute necessity of respecting treaties and other undertakings can be gauged from the punishment laid down for their violation. This sanction was the most shattering and therefore the most deterrent which the historical circumstances of that area could conceive in a time of religious fervour, namely divine retribution. In that century marked by Islamic piety, any violation of an undertaking was held to incur a punishment in the afterlife, accompanied by exclusion from Paradise.

The realm of treaties was made the subject of elaborate and in many ways exquisitely crafted rules. The purpose of treaties, the conditions of their validity, the circumstances justifying their denunciation, and their classification (in particular by Sheikh Muhammad Abu-Zahra) were codified and constitute a legal monument which in many respects has remained astonishingly relevant today.

c   A celebrated example of the stress laid on honouring treaties

The leading historical example of emphasis placed on the honouring of undertakings is provided by the letter which the Prophet Muhammad sent to Honayna and the inhabitants of Khaybar and Moqna, a letter in the form of an agreement with the Jews of Medina, where the Prophet had taken refuge (*hijra*) to escape pursuit by the Qoreish tribe from Mecca.

---

5. The foundations of Islam are the Koran, the sacred Book of Divine Revelation and the *sunna*, which is the collection of '*hadiths*'. A *hadith* is a 'saying' or 'the word' of the Prophet. Hence Islam reposes on the word of God (Koran) and the word of the Prophet (the *sunna* made up of *hadiths*). The accuracy and validity of the *sunna* is verified through the degree of certainty of the various chains of transmission. Muslim society was essentially a community of oral traditions. The *sunna* began to be written down between the first and third centuries after the death of the Prophet and was based on oral traditions going back to witnesses who had lived in the Prophet's immediate entourage. Hence the *sunna* is the explanation, case by case, of the principles of the Koran, of the manner in which the Prophet himself applied the Koranic norms in concrete situations.

In this letter of agreement, the Prophet mentions in particular:
- the protection of the Jews, of their religion, their form of worship, their property and their slaves;
- their exemption from taxes;
- a promise that they should not be concentrated into a particular district;
- a guarantee that they should not suffer any injustice or any prohibition on the wearing of their vestments or holy-day clothes, or on their going on horseback;
- an acknowledgment of their right to fight any who declare war upon them;
- equality of penal treatment as between Jews and Muslims;
- free access of Jews, as a people of the Book, to any mosque;
- their right of audience with any Muslim dignitary.

The Prophet had solemnly enjoined Muslims to honour the undertakings contained in this document. He had promised rewards to those who treated Honayna and the inhabitants of Khaybar and Moqna well and condign punishment to whoever infringed any part of this letter of agreement. He had added, in an altogether exceptional sign of unwavering firmness, that he would call down God's curse upon all violators, that he would consider himself personally as their enemy and that he would not ask God for any leniency in their favour.[6]

d   The content of the alleged breach of a conventional undertaking

The above analysis of the value of a treaty in Islamic law would be incomplete and indeed misleading without a proper reference to the content or subject matter of the treaty. Accordingly it will be as well to recall that the 1975 Algiers Agreements bore essentially upon a *territorial dispute*. The alleged breach has to be analyzed in terms of rival claims of sovereignty over various areas of territory. The alleged breach was therefore of a *territorial* nature.

This brings up the question of what is understood in Islamic international law by *the concept of territory*. In this law elaborated in the seventh century, there was a 'Dar ul-Islam' with a *single territory* covering the entire community of the faithful (the *umma*). Islam was not conceived on the model of a European State (which for that matter did not exist at the time even in Europe), with interstate frontiers, which would have raised the problem of territorial claims in acute conflictual terms.

Today, of course, the European State model does exist in the lands of Islam. Frontiers do exist. This, however, does not prevent various Arab national legislations from, for example, recognizing the right of any Arab to acquire the nationality of another Arab country in which he may reside.

6. This letter was taken down word for word by Ali Ibn Abi-Taleb from the Prophet's dictation on Friday 3 Ramadan of the year 5 of the Hegira in the presence of Ammar ben Yasser, Salman el-Farissi and Abou Dar el-Ghaffari. Written in Arabic and Hebrew, and described as a treaty, it was discovered in Egypt. It is at present in the Cambridge Museum and has been published. The specialist Mohamed Hamidullah deals with this important document in the *Recueil des documents politiques datant de l'époque du Prophète et des Califes Rachidoun*, Al-Irshad Publication and Distribution House, 3rd edition Beirut, 1389, corresponding to 1969 AD, pp. 93-95.

Modern international law, while imbued with respect for the separate sovereignty of state entities, does not accept that these entities are entitled to settle a territorial dispute by the use of force, which has been proscribed in international relations. *A fortiori*, I find it clear that Islamic international law, which does not admit the concept of a territorial dispute within the Muslim world, cannot authorize resort to war for the settlement of any such dispute.

Each system possesses its own internal logic. Anyone taking it upon himself to invoke Islamic international law must surely realize the minor importance attached by it to territorial questions as between Muslims. Islamic law is fundamentally constructed upon *the traditional model of the unity of the community* and not on *the territorial model of the European States in relation with other states*.

C   The outbreak of the war as perceived through the filter of Islamic international law

(i)   *Before starting a war*, Muslims are under a duty to send their opponent a warning and to invite him to reach a peaceful arrangement. Only if that warning is rejected may war be unleashed.

(ii)   The question of the *identification of the aggressor* and the international responsibility incurred by him was raised continually throughout the long duration of the 1980-1988 Gulf War. The Security Council of the United Nations was seized of it but never succeeded in designating the aggressor.

Right from the seventh century, Islamic international law laid down rules whereby war could be lawful *only on very strict conditions*. Thus, extraordinary as it may seem, it was able to place the discretionary power to wage war under severe restrictions 13 centuries before modern international law actually abolished that power – if that is indeed the case. Islamic law declared that a just war[7] could be waged in only five

---

7. Much has been written in the West as in the East on the meaning of 'holy war' (*jihad*). It must first be stressed that the notion of 'holy war' does not apply within the Islamic world itself. In mediaeval Europe it was only a question of 'holy war' against the 'infidels' (first Muslims and, secondarily, Jews), as can be seen from the writings of scriptural commentators and ecclesiastics, from decisions of Councils of the Church and papal bulls, both before and after the period of the crusades which were themselves perfect examples of holy wars. According to a 'hadith', the word of the Prophet Muhammad in the seventh century, 'the greatest holy war for man is the struggle to conquer his own passions'! In a remarkable essay published in Arabic in 1987 and translated into French in 1989 under the title *L'Islamisme contre l'Islam* (Maspéro, Paris), a senior member of the Egyptian judiciary, Mohammed Saïd Al-Ashmaoui, had several observations to make on the notion of *jihad* (pp. 67-73), including the following passages: 'Of all the key-concepts of Islam, *jihad* is certainly the most controversial. Non-Muslims can take it to mean a holy war declared against them. Most Muslims regard it as a religious imperative implying that non-Muslims are to be won over by good example and persuasion, while an extremist minority views it as a thinly veiled religious imperative whereby Islam must be imposed on non-Muslims. In Arabic, the etymology of *jihad* suggests an effort towards a given objective. It thus has several connotations: to harness oneself resolutely to a task, stubbornly to resist adversity, or simply to struggle to survive, if need be by fighting an opponent (...) (Over and above the historical evolution of the meaning), the deep meaning of *jihad* remains: that is to say, as the Prophet has explained, the soul's unrelenting effort against negative elements so that it may gain in strength and serenity. This is the major *jihad*, whereas holy war is only the minor *jihad* (...) To sum up, *jihad* has two meanings:

situations and no more:
- *self-defence* and counter-attack in the event of *aggression*;
- war declared and waged on *those who break treaties* or international undertakings;
- war for the *defence of the oppressed*, which for the Koran is a war waged essentially in the service of God. *Surat* IV, verse 75, declares: 'Why do you not fight as God would have you, to defend the weak, men, women and children who cry: "Lord! Deliver us from this tyrannical city; give us an ally and protector to act in thy name!"?';
- war upon an enemy who *foments and sustains division* within the Islamic community (*umma*) with the intention of destroying its foundations and unity; and finally
- war to repulse *armed religious persecutions*, aggressive manifestations of intolerance and the stifling of the freedom of thought and belief, a type of conflict considered analogous to self-defence or counter-attack.

Thus we see that the case of self-defence and action to counter aggression was held to be the primary hypothesis justifying war. According to one of the *hadiths* of the Prophet: 'He dies best who perishes to uphold his right'. And *Surat* II clearly states in verse 190: 'Commit no aggression! God does not love aggressors!' And in verse 194: 'Strike back at him who commits an aggression against you.' *Surat* II, verse 39, says: 'The cry of those who have been attacked shall be heard. They have been unjustly treated and God is mighty enough to make them victorious; those who were driven from their homes for no just cause, simply for having said "God is our Lord"'.

Hence, if it be asked whether Islamic international law contained any rules on self-defence, aggression and punishment, the answer, unsurprisingly, is positive. But one caveat must be added: the counter-attack must be proportionate to the aggression; the Koran requires Muslims to show moderation.

D   The conduct of warfare

In Islam, the conduct of warfare is subject to an impressive array of rules. To give a brief idea, simply setting a body of soldiers on the march is governed by no fewer than seven major principles (each of which comprises a series of rules) that the 'emir of the war', *i.e.*, the commander-in-chief, must scrupulously observe. I need only mention the first of these principles:

---

the original one, which is of a religious character, and the one acquired in the course of history, which is political in nature and notably imprecise. In its first acceptation, *jihad* is an individual ethical condition; in its acquired sense it is a war against non-Muslims, or indeed in many cases against Muslims. We do not doubt that *jihad* is meant as an instrument of justice and clemency, not a weapon of violence and war.' (Translation from French).

'Have the troops march only at a speed compatible with the strength of the weakest warriors while keeping up the strength of the strongest, and do not demand forced marches likely to prove fatal to the former and exhausting to the latter.'[8]

1   *The distinction between combatants and non-combatants and the protection of civilians*

The 1980-1988 Gulf War raised in acute form the key question of the distinction between combatants and non-combatants and the protection of civilian populations, especially from deliberate bombardment, and subsequent reprisals.

In the Islamic tradition, international law designated strictly military targets and drew a distinction between combatants and non-combatants. Muslims must confine their targets to enemy combatants, military installations and the depots of combatant forces. Only the enemy's regular army should be fought.

Civilians must be not only spared but also protected by Muslims, according to a hadith of the Prophet, especially women, the aged, children, the disabled, and workers or wage-earners employed as servants, the peasants in their fields and monks and hermits in their cells.

Muslim combatants must never ill-treat the non-combatant civilian population of an occupied territory. An Islamic army must not set up camp in places likely to cause significant distress to the civilian population. It should not bar roads and passages to the population or countryfolk.

Religious sites and edifices, and all places of worship, were immune from attack unless the enemy himself attacked Muslims in a sacred place. *Surat* II, verse 191, says: 'Do not fight them in the vicinity of the Holy Mosque until they fight you there.'

In his meticulous exegesis, Mawerdi envisages countless situations. For example, he focuses on the following example of the immunity of civilians and non-combatants, which is not without a certain echo today: 'Should the enemy use women and children as his shield during the battle, they must be respected and one should aim to kill only the men.'[9]

In this intricate work of regulation, showing that scrupulous respect for non-combatants was already a feature of Islamic law in the seventh century, one Muslim jurist, during the Middle Ages, went even so far as to forbid a combatant to kill his enemy's horse, which he should carefully avoid trying to hit.[10]

Here again is a *hadith* which Harith ben-Nebhan of Basra had handed down from Aban ben-Othman (the son of the Caliph Othman ben-Affan) who enjoyed great religious, moral and political authority:

---

8. Abdul-Hassan Ali Mawerdi, Al-Mawerdi, or El-Mawerdi, died in Baghdad in 1058, *Al-Ahkam as-Sultaniya*, (*The Rules of the Sultanate*), translated into French by E. Fagnan as *Les statuts gouvernementaux ou règles de droit public et administratif*, Beirut 1982 (584 pages), p. 71.

9. Mawerdi, *op.cit.* (note 8), p. 84.

10. *Idem.*

'Prevent your soldiers from doing evil (...) for a company of soldiers never does evil without God implanting fear in the hearts of its members;

Prevent your soldiers from committing fraud (...) for a company of warriors never committed fraud without God making them the plaything of a handful of men;

Prevent fornication among your soldiers (...) for no company of soldiers ever committed it without God sending them an epidemic.'

This text, and various others which cannot possibly all be quoted here, protect the civilian and non-combatant population from theft, pillage, rape, *etc.*, but do just as much to protect the enemy's combatants from similar exactions.

2   *Prohibition of degrading or inhuman practices*

The Koran condemns the torturing of the enemy or his subjection to unduly harsh ordeals. This rule that combatants should be spared unnecessary suffering, together with the rules for the protection of the civilian population and the fundamental distinction between combatants and non-combatants, already featured in seventh-century Islam, constitute one of the foundations of humanitarian international law as codified in the 20th century.

The disciplinary instructions given by the Prophet Muhammad to the heads of expeditions abound in such injunctions as the following: to inflict on the enemy the lightest losses compatible with the aims of the war, not to kill by treachery or ruse, not to mutilate combatants, to leave their mortal remains intact and not to take reprisals on those who are guilty of such degrading or inhuman practices.[11] Well known to Muslims is the episode of the profanation of the mortal remains of Hamza, the uncle of the Prophet, who died at the battle of Ohad. Muhammad's response to this profanation was to pardon the offence.

On account of their general behaviour towards their adversaries on the battlefield as elsewhere, Muslim fighters were described by Voltaire as 'the most clement of all the conquerors of the earth.'[12]

11. One cannot but be struck by the progressive nature of these regulations from the seventh century, when on other continents, before, during and after that period, wars were the occasions of horrible mutilations. In particular, the European chroniclers of the crusades, often men of the Church, have left gruesome accounts of the behaviour of the crusaders among the Muslims. *Cf.* Rechid, Ahmed, "L'islam et le droit des gens", *Hague Recueil* 1937, II, Vol. 60, pp. 373-506, *passim* and particularly pp. 449-461 ("Les Lois de la Guerre"). Rechid quotes various passages from outraged Christian chroniclers such as Bernard-le-Trésorier, Baudin Archbishop of Dol, Jacques de Vitry, Archbishop of Acre, Guillaume de Tyr and Canon Anquetil, *etc.* Let us not forget, either, the shocking conditions on fields of battle elsewhere, even between combatants of the same religion, before, during and after the Islamic precepts of the seventh century, which may be gleaned from the extensive bibliography attached by Ahmed Rechid to his course of lectures.

12. Voltaire, *Essai sur les moeurs*, Ch. XXVII.

3   *The choice of weapons. The prohibition of weapons likely to cause victims indiscriminately*

The Koran and *hadiths* of the Prophet command on the one hand that Muslim fighters should never overstep certain bounds in waging war and, on the other hand, that they should never, in particular, widen the scope of the battle, either in a territorial sense or by stepping up the nature of the weapons employed.

Thus, as a corollary of the principle that operations should be restricted to the actual military objectives, Islam forbade the use of weapons of mass destruction, including actions likely to have devastating effects over a wide area, such as *flooding* or *fire-raising*.[13] In general terms *Surat* II, verse 186, had exhorted: 'Fight as God would have you against those who make war upon you. But do not overstep the bounds of justice and equity.' A prohibition on poisoning wells or springs came to be added to the ban on flooding and arson. In his campaign orders, Caliph Abu-Bakr exhorted his troops to overcome their enemies by bravery and never by poison.[14]

Here in a nutshell is the idea which eventually gave rise to the modern principle of the prohibition of weapons of mass destruction such as strike indiscriminately against both combatants and civilians.

4   *Ban on blockading food supplies or attacking nature, the work of God*

The case of Thomama, a noble of the Beni-Hanifa tribe, is frequently on the lips of Muslim doctors of the law. With all the new-found ardour of a recent convert, Thomama had decided to put a stop to the export of grain from his region (Al-Yamama) to Mecca, which was at war with Muhammad. When however the Prophet heard of this, he ordered Thomama to raise this blockade and allow the inhabitants of Mecca to continue with their ordinary trade including, in particular, their imports of grain. This episode seems strangely relevant to the very complex situation of the times we live in.

At the same time, suggesting that Islam was concerned to protect the environment and nature, the work of God by which man is sustained, Muslim fighters were forbidden to set fire to harvests, destroy crops, kill domestic animals or damage civilian property.[15]

---

13. See Draz, *op.cit.* (note 2), p. 202.

14. *Cf.* Rechid, *op.cit.* (note 11), p. 481.

15. All the laws of war are in fact encapsulated in the orders in question, which Muhammad's first successor, the Caliph Abu Bakr, issued to the army at the time of the campaign in Syria, which was the first country to accept Islam: 'Remember', he told his generals, 'that you are at all times under the eyes of God and on the eve of death; that you will be called to account on the last day (...) When you fight for the glory of God, conduct yourselves as men, without turning your back, but let not your victory be sullied with the blood of women, children or the aged. Do not destroy the palm-trees, do not burn the dwellings, the fields of wheat or barley, never chop down the fruit-trees and never kill cattle unless you need to for food.' Omar, Abu Bakr's successor as Caliph, summed up good conduct in the following words: 'Do not be cowards in the fight or cruel in the use of force, and do not abuse victory.' (For further details, see Rechid, *op.cit.* (note 11), *passim* and pp. 451-453.)

5   *Treatment of prisoners-of-war and persons in enemy hands*

A series of rules were decreed to ensure that prisoners-of-war were treated with respect. Here the chivalrous learnings of Islam were a strong influence. According to the jurist and theologian Abu Dawud,[16] prisoners must be treated humanely and those who were acquainted with each other should not be separated during their captivity. Another Muslim jurist, Tirmidi, drew up a set of rules illustrating the idea that a prisoner should receive better treatment than the captor would accord himself. The great doctor of Islamic law, whose name is honoured throughout the Muslim world, Al-Bukhari, taught that if a Muslim took charge of a prisoner he should feed and clothe him in the same way as himself. Many other jurists considered that ill-treating a prisoner-of-war was a very grave sin meriting punishment and entitling victims to immediate release without ransom.

More generally speaking, Islam prescribes that a prisoner should never be killed and that he should be released if circumstances preclude his receiving the good treatment to which he is entitled. In that connection, history relates that Salah ed-Deen el-Ayoubi, known in the West as the doughty warrior Saladin, once released some prisoners because he could no longer continue to feed them. A few days later he was surprised to find himself face-to-face with them on the battlefield. He then declared that it was good that this should be so, and that, rather than leaving them to starve, it was preferable to risk having to fight them again and to see them seeking death in a fair fight.

Islamic scholars often recall the contrasting behaviour of the crusaders who gave their Muslim prisoners short shrift; they also recall how Napoleon Bonaparte exterminated all his Muslim prisoners after the battle of Acre.

Concern for humane conduct was also illustrated by, *inter alia*, the following incident narrated, after other authors before him, by Sheikh Mohammed Draz:

'After the siege of Khaybar had ended in favour of the Muslims, Bilal took two Jewesses prisoner.[17] He took them back to the headquarters across a battlefield strewn with Jewish bodies. One of the two prisoners broke down at the sight. When the Prophet learned what Bilal had done, he sternly upbraided him in the following terms: "Have you no human feeling in your heart, Bilal? How could you subject women to the spectacle of the corpses of their menfolk?".'[18]

16. Abu Dawud, *Kitab al-Jihad* (The Book of War).

17. I presume that they had taken part in the fighting. Bilal was a slave who was among the very first to convert to Islam and to share the epic life of the Prophet Muhammad.

18. Draz, *op.cit.* (note 2), p. 202.

6   *Truces, cease-fires, peace*

These can take place in the following circumstances, according to the Koran and the *hadiths*:

A *truce* in Islamic law is compulsory four times every year, during the four holy months of Dou al-Qaada, Dou al-Hija, Moharram and Rajab.

A *cease-fire* and *peace* are instituted
-   if the Muslims consider that they have attained their war objectives, or
-   if the enemy surrenders, or
-   if the enemy requests a cease-fire, on condition that this is not a ruse and that he does not occupy any of the territory of the Muslims.

Generally speaking, Muslims must always be on the alert to seize any opportunity of making peace.

7   *The Muslim's duty of humility and humanity in the event of victory*

It is the duty of Muslims not to glory in their victory, in order to spare their enemies' dignity. On the contrary, the enemy must be treated with respect and benevolence, which is conducive to the elimination of the enmity between the combatants and the creation of ties of trust between the Muslims and their erstwhile foes.

III   THE UNIVERSAL LEGAL ORDER AND THE ISLAMIC LEGAL ORDER

It would be possible to study many other questions, such as the attitude of neutral states, in the light of the Islamic legal order of the seventh century. But the time has come to consider, in this third and last part, what is common to both of the two legal analyses of the 1980-1988 Gulf War that can be made in the light either of modern international law or of seventh-century Islamic law. However, such a comparison between solutions provided on the one hand by the universal legal order and, on the other, by an Islamic legal order of a regional nature, immediately suggests other questions, some retrospective, some prospective. In the first place, it calls into question the very *existence* of an Islamic legal order today, when that order not only appears to have undergone no evolution since the seventh century but also transpires in practice to have found little favour with Muslim States in their respective relations. Then there is the question of how this Islamic legal order, were it to be recognized, updated and applied, might co-exist with the universal legal order, in accordance with the relevant provisions of the United Nations Charter.

A   Does there still exist any Islamic regional legal order?

The 1980-1988 Gulf War has given me the opportunity of outlining here certain aspects of the Islamic conception of international law which emerged after the seventh century, on the basis of the Koran and the *hadiths* of the Prophet. Since those beginnings, Islamic schools of law have been established and have enriched this *corpus islamicus juris* with their commentaries. But since the Middle Ages the world has evolved, and power and potential have gradually moved to other, non-Muslim centres. Many centuries ago, the Arabo-Muslim Orient began its slow decline. This decadence can be seen in every field. More particularly, Islamic international law still remains, regrettably, a law of speculation pursued for purely academic purposes: what we are doing here today is no exception. There are several causes of this situation.

1   *International law, of Western origin, has always ignored or overlooked Islamic international law*

In his book, *La fascination de l'Islam*, Maxime Rodinson, with immense scholarship and a superb wealth of documentation, retraced the various historical stages of the Western attitude to the Muslim world. A prickly attitude at the best of times! In the Middle Ages it was the perception of 'two worlds in conflict (...) To the Christian West, the Muslims were a danger but grew into a problem.'[19]

The oldest known *Code of International Law* is the *Kitab al-Majmu* of Zaid ibn-Ali, who died in 738 AD. It contains a long chapter entitled 'Siyar' concerning the rules governing war and peace as between Muslims and non-Muslims. The great jurist Sarakhsi (died 1090 AD), who produced a four-volume treatise on international law, defined 'siyar' as follows: 'The word *siyar* (conduct) is the plural of *sira* (...), the conduct of Muslims towards non-Muslims in the state of war and in the state of peace; also towards non-Muslims subject to the Islamic State; (...) towards apostates, who are the worst of non-Muslims on account of their having renegued after having professed; (...) towards Muslim rebels whose situation is less grave than that of non-Muslims.'[20]

Despite this, the West has either remained ignorant of the contribution of the Arabs and Islam to international law or has disregarded it. With the exception of a few highly specialized historians, Western scholars who have sought to trace back the history of international law have done so after their fashion without hardly ever thinking of the Islamic contribution. All over the world, even today, the great majority of treatises and manuals of international law short-circuit the history of international law by mentioning the contribution of Greco-Roman Antiquity and then calmly passing over the contribution which Islam made from the seventh to the 15th century.

Let me give just one example among hundreds. One might have expected that Ernest Nys, the Belgian jurist, who had devoted over 400 pages to 'the origins of international

---

19. Rodinson, Maxime, *La fascination de l'Islam*, suivi de *Le Seigneur bourguignon et l'esclave sarrasin*, Paris 1989, p. 200 (Translation from French).

20. Quoted by Hamidullah, Muhammad, "Contribution musulmane au droit international", in: *L'Islam dans les relations internationales*, IVe Colloque franco-pakistanais, Paris 1984, 1986 (pp. 138-143), p. 139 (Translation from French). Simply within this period immediately following upon the rise of Islam in the seventh century, one could refer to numerous Islamic works of exegesis and codification on international law which reveal Muslim thinking about international relations at the time. Thus each of the following great jurists produced a *Kitab as-Siyar* or treatise on international law: Zaid ibn Ali, already cited (died 738), Abu Hanifa, his disciple (died 767); Zufar (died 775); Abu Yusuf (died 789); Muhammad ash-Shaibani (died 804); al-Auza'i (died 774); al-Waqidi (died 822); Malik (died 795); *etc.*

law'[21] and had moreover published some 15 historical studies on diplomacy, the law of war and theories of international law,[22] would allot a few pages to the Islamic contribution. But no: this is how, in the introduction to the book to which I have just referred, he casually makes a giant leap forward in time, eclipsing six to eight centuries in the history of the Mediterranean world which were in large measure dominated by international relations between Islam and Europe: 'The civilization of Antiquity', he writes, 'disappeared in the sixth century. The birth of the European spirit occurred somewhere around the 12th or 13th century. In the intervening period the vehicle of intellectual tradition was what is generally termed (!) Arab scholarship [*la science arabe*].'[23] Nothing more in 414 pages: and so the Muslim contribution to international law and international relations was summed up in one faintly dismissive sentence.

Open any treatise or manual of international law today and you will find little improvement. But who could complain when, as we shall see, even Arab and Muslim jurists themselves are completely unaware of the lslamic conception of international law or confine it to the ghetto?

B   Islamic legal writers, so fertile in private law, are sterile when it comes to public international law

This persistent reality is not hard to explain. After a long decline followed by a very long period of existence as colonies or protectorates, the Arab and Muslim countries had ceased to be protagonists on the international scene. This situation naturally dried up their creativity in an area, that of interstate relations, from which they were excluded by their diminished or suppressed political status. In such circumstances Muslim jurists could only display their scholarship and expertise in the politically innocuous area left to them by their colonial masters or protectors: the private law of persons and property.

This law, which in particular covered the personal status of the individual, was governed by the Koran and the *hadiths*. For that reason it was not a secular law but, despite this, the extensive exegesis and interpretation (*ijtihad*) to which it was subjected by Muslim jurists led not only to its development and adaptation but also to its partial secularization.

The fact remains that, as a matter of history, the primal Islamic law was subjected to tensions which resulted, on the one hand, in running its public law branch into the sands and, on the other, in leading its private law branch into a development which, while appreciable, does not exceed certain limits. Just as a machine which has been stopped for too long tends to seize up or rust, or an organ without a function atrophies, or for that matter a legal rule which is not applied falls into desuetude, so any internal public law, and still more any international public law which goes unused will wither. To put the matter briefly, the Islamic law which rose out of the religious revolution of the seventh century has historically suffered from the brake being applied in the public

---

21. Nys, Ernest, *Les origines du droit international*, Brussels 1894, and Paris 1894, 414 pp.
22. See the list at the front of the above-mentioned book.
23. *Op.cit.* (note 21), pp. II-III (Translation from French).

domain and from being kept in leading strings in the private domain. This has resulted in an unbalanced evolution, in that its public (international) law limb has been virtually amputated and its private law limb allowed to develop only in a somewhat ingrowing manner.

This precisely reflects the political situation of the Islamic peoples in their long subjugation.

Unfortunately, since acquiring independence, these peoples have still not succeeded in reviving the public international law limb. With a few rare exceptions, jurists from the newly independent Muslim countries have succumbed to the easy temptation of lazily imitating the West instead of meeting the more demanding needs of creativity. From the Atlantic to the Sunda Islands, the great majority of treatises and manuals of international law published in the Muslim world are western works translated into the local language by those jurists, who are thus reduced to the role of translators and copyists.

This is also a situation which reflects the minor political status and subdued, ineffectual role of these underdeveloped countries on the international scene. But the fight against underdevelopment, no matter how important the lever of economics, remains to a large extent conditioned by the cultural factor. And I can restrain myself no longer from *appealing to all jurists in the Muslim world to take greater personal responsibility and mobilize more efficiently in a decisive effort of creativity, instead of confining themselves to an attitude of slavish imitation which often results in strapping lifeless articial limbs of foreign legal origin on living human communities.*

I consider moreover that my appeal deserves the endorsement of non-Muslim, especially Western jurists, once they realize the benefit that such a revival could confer on pluralism and democracy in the world.

1   *The institutions of the newly independent Islamic countries were moulded in*
        accordance with culturally alien models which distanced them from Islamic
        law

a   The creation of states in accordance with the 'common' model (the standard
        of the twentieth century)

In the case of the Muslim peoples the culmination of the decolonizing process followed the habitual stereotype. Up to now, peoples who have won their freedom have sought to exercise their right of self-determination by endowing themselves with a state corresponding on paper to the standards of the twentieth century. The decolonization process has thus flowed into this familiar mould of the state, in accordance with a sort of 'universality principle' applied to the contemporary organization of state power, when in fact the state is the 'historic product' of an entire civilization and the Muslim States had been organized in accordance with the model of a *community.* And so the state as we know it has been the form assumed by all the successful examples of national liberation. But was that the only form? Was there no other way in which self-determination could be realized at the institutional level? I cannot say. I would simply observe that it was impossible for this creation of states in accordance with the 'common' model, though it doubtless constituted progress, to maintain those states under the governance of traditional Islamic law.

However that may be, this generalized and uniformly followed evolution predetermined and marked out the itinerary in advance. Each newly created state had to assume its own rights and obligations, of a similar nature to those already familiar to and practised by the other states.

b   The adherence of Muslim States to the Charter of the United Nations, their membership of international organizations, and the significance of both for the survival of Islamic law

In accepting the Charter of the United Nations and other constitutions of specialized agencies, by actually joining the United Nations and other organizations of the system as members and, finally, by ratifying a large number of multilateral treaties, the Muslim States have undertaken to apply modern international law and, what is more, have participated in its development and codification in various international bodies since 1945. They have subscribed to the purposes and principles of the Charter, which lays upon them the obligation to act 'in conformity with the principles of (...) international law' (Article 1, Charter of the United Nations). And so it is not Islamic law but this universal law which is supposed to govern the international relationships of each of the Muslim States with the other members of the international community.

But do the consequences of the Muslim States' adherence to the Charter of the United Nations and their admission to membership of worldwide organizations stop there? Do they not include the very abandonment of Muslim law for the benefit of global law? Or do they not rather include the opportunity for Muslim law to make whatever contribution it may to the development of a more genuinely universal law, one bearing the stamp of the participation of all?

This question is inextricable from that of the weight exerted by Muslim States in the world, *i.e.*, of the extent of their influence in international relations. That weight and that influence, it seems, are still very modest.

Nevertheless, becoming party to the Charter of the United Nations did not deprive the Muslim States of the possibility of setting up their own regional organs within which Islamic law could have enjoyed every opportunity of a revival.

c   The Islamic regional groupings and the missed opportunities of a revival of Muslim law

For the last decade the Islamic world has been regrouped in its own regional organization, the Organization of the Islamic Conference. The creation of this regional institution is in conformity with Chapter VIII, Articles 52-54, of the Charter of the United Nations. But so far that Organization does not appear to have produced any clear undertaking to ensure the development and modernization of Muslim public international law by adapting it to the new structure of the international community and having it applied in inter-Islamic relations.

d   The numerous references, during the 1980-1988 Gulf War to the Charter of the
           United Nations and international law, and recourse to the United Nations for
           the purpose of ending the conflict

No Islamic regional institution took the settlement of the Gulf conflict in hand or could
indeed have done so. In passing, I would recall that the 1975 Algiers Agreements
concluded by the belligerents in order to settle their territorial dispute were registered
at the United Nations for want of a purely Islamic institution that could receive them.
It was also on an organ of the United Nations, the Security Council, that the task of
attempting to end the conflict devolved, even though the Charter contains provisions
whereby it could have conferred primary, but not of course exclusive competence on
any appropriate regional institution with a view to finding a solution before the Council
itself took over.

When the Security Council took the war onto its agenda, one of the belligerents, it
is true, showed some mistrust towards it, in a manner corresponding to its usual line of
conduct. But on either side, what was invoked, both within the Council and outside it,
was international law, not Islamic law.

All these factors, and many others that one might mention, have led to the situation
where Islamic law has remained more or less in the same condition as it was in the
seventh century and has suffered from the indifference which has nearly always been
shown towards it whether by the international community or the Muslim States
themselves.

That being so, the possibilities of the co-existence of this law with universal law
remain intact only in theory, but are in fact nil.

C   **The possibilities of the co-existence of a universal order and an Islamic
           regional order**

1   *Some untried possibilities*

Article 52 of the Charter of the United Nations clearly provides that nothing in that
Charter precludes the existence of regional agencies for dealing with such matters
relating to the maintenance of international peace and security as are appropriate for
regional action.

What prevented making use of this provision to bring peace to the region was the
incapability of the only existing and appropriate regional forum to take the settlement
of the conflict in hand, not any incompatibility of Muslim law or that Islamic forum
with the purposes and principles of the United Nations.

2   *The total compatibility between the principles of universal law and those of
           Islamic law, and the entire agreement of their analyses of the 1980-1988 Gulf
           War*

Though certain aspects could have been taken much further, the above survey should
have sufficed, as it stands, to show how one arrives at virtually the same legal analysis

of the 1980-1988 Gulf War whatever 'key' be used, whether that of public international law or that of Islamic law.

SELECTED BIBLIOGRAPHY

Almond jr., H.H., "Neutral Shipping, the Persian Gulf War, and Recovery for Damage arising in that War", 14 *Syracuse Journal of International Law and Commerce* (1988) Special Issue, pp. 849-863.

American Society of International Law, "Neutrality, the Rights of Shipping and the Use of Force in the Persian Gulf War (Part I, Part II)", *Proceedings of the 82nd Annual Meeting*, Washington 1990, pp. 146-172, 394-613.

Amin, S.H., "The Iran-Iraq Conflict: legal implications", 31 *International and Comparative Law Quarterly* (1982), pp. 167-188.

Boczek, B.A., "Law of Warfare at Sea and Neutrality: Lessons from the Gulf War", 20 *Ocean Development and International Law* (1989), pp. 239-271.

Boyle, F.A., "International Crisis and Neutrality: U.S. Foreign Policy toward the Iraq-Iran War", in Leonhar, A.T./Mercuro, N. (eds.), *Neutrality. Changing concepts and practices*, Lanham/New York/London 1989, pp. 59-95.

Costello, T.W., *Persian Gulf Tanker War and International Law*, Newport, RI 1987.

David, E., "La guerre du Golfe et le droit international", 23 *Revue Belge de Droit Internationale* (1987-1), pp. 153-183.

Davidson, S., "United States Protection of Reflagged Kuwaiti Vessels in the Gulf War: The Legal Implications", 4 *International Journal of Estuarine and Coastal Law* (1989), p. 173 ff.

Decaux, E., "La résolution 598(1987) du Conseil de Sécurité et les efforts de paix des Nations Unies entre l'Iran et l'Irak", 34 *Annuaire Francais de Droit International* (1988), pp. 62-90.

Dekker, I.F. & Post, H.H.G, "The Gulf War from the Point of View of International Law", 17 *Netherlands Yearbook of International Law* (1986), pp. 76-105.

Dutli, M.T., "Enfants-combattants prisonniers", 72 *Revue Internationale de la Croix-Rouge* (1990), pp. 456-470.

El-Dakkah, S., "Le droit international humanitaire entre la conception islamique et le droit international positif", 72 *Revue Internationale de la Croix-Rouge* (1990), pp. 111-125.

Fenrick, W.J., "The Exclusive Zone Device in the Law of Naval Warfare", 24 *Canadian Yearbook of International Law* (1986), pp. 91-126.

Fleck, D., "Rules of Engagement for Maritime Forces and the Limitation of the Use of Force under the UN Charter", 31 *German Yearbook of International Law* (1988), pp. 165-186.

Gehrke, U. & Kuhn, G., *Die Grenzen des Irak*, Stuttgart 1963.

Giegerich, Th., "The German Contribution to the Protection of Shipping in the Persian Gulf: staying out for political or constitutional reasons?", 49 *Zeitschrift für ausländisches öffentliches Recht und Völkerrecht* (1989), pp. 1-40.

Gray, Chr., "The British Position in regard to the Gulf Conflict", 37 *International and Comparative Law Quarterly* (1988), pp. 420-428.

Gray, Chr., "The British Position with regard to the Gulf Conflict (Iran-Iraq): Part 2", 40 *International and Comparative Law Quarterly* (1991), pp. 463-473.

Hecker, H., "Iraner als Opfer des Völkerrecht", 26 *Archiv des Völkerrechts* (1988), pp. 464-469.

Hünseler, P., *Der Irak und sein Konflikt mit Iran*, Bonn 1982.

Jenkins, M., "Air Attacks on Neutral Shipping in the Persian Gulf: the Legality of the Iraqi Exclusive Zone and Iranian Reprisals", 8 *Boston College International and Comparative Law Review* (1985), pp. 517-549.

Kaikobad, K.H., "The Shatt-Al-Arab River Boundary: a legal reappraisal", 56 *British Yearbook of International Law* (1985), pp. 49-109.

Kaikobad, K.H., *The Shatt-Al-Arab Boundary Question: A Legal Reappraisal*, Oxford 1988.

Lagoni, R., "Gewaltverbot, Seekriegsrecht und Schiffahrtsfreiheit im Golfkrieg", in Fürst, W./Herzog, R./Umbach, D.C. (Hrsg.), *Festschrift für Wolfgang Zeidler*, Berlin/New York 1987, pp. 1833-1867.

Leckow, R., "The Iran-Iraq conflict in the Gulf: The Law of War Zones", 37 *International and Comparative Law Quarterly* (1988), pp. 629-644.

Linnan, D.K., "Iran Air Flight 655 and beyond: free passage, mistaken self-defence, and State responsability", 16 *Yale Journal of International Law* (1991), pp. 245-289.

Mann, H., "International Law and the Child Soldier", 36 *International and Comparative Law Quarterly* (1987), pp. 32-57.

McCormack, T.L.H., "International Law and the Use of Chemical Weapons in the Gulf War", 21 *California Western International Law Journal* (1990), pp. 1-30.

Momtaz, D., "Le statut juridique du Chatt El-Arab dans sa perspective historique", in *Actualités Juridiques et Politique en Asie*, Paris 1988, pp. 59-67.

Mertus, J., "The Nationality of Ships and International Responsibility: The Reflagging of the Kuwaity Tankers", 17 *Denver Journal of International Law and Policy* (1988), pp. 207-233.

Nordqvist, M.H & Wachenfeld, M.G., "Legal Aspects of Reflagging Kuwaiti Tankers and Laying of Mines in the Persian Gulf", 31 *German Yearbook of International Law* (1988), pp. 138-164.

Orford, T.M., *The Iran-Iraq Conflict. Recent Developments in the International Law of Naval Engagements*, Cape Town 1988.

Post, H.H.G., "Comments, with particular reference to the Gulf War", to M.C.W. Pinto, "The Prospects for International Arbitration: Inter-State Disputes", in Soons, A.H.A (ed.), *International Arbitration: Past and Prospects*, Dordrecht/Boston/London 1990, pp. 189-193.

Ramazani, R.K., *The Persian Gulf and the Strait of Hormuz*, Alphen a/d Rijn 1979.

Ronzitti, N., "La guerre du Golfe, le déminage et la circulation des navires", 33 *Annuaire Francais de Droit International* (1987), pp. 647-662.

Russo, F.V., "Neutrality at sea in transition: state practice in the Gulf War as emerging international law", 19 *Ocean Development and International Law* (1988), pp. 381-399.

Sandoz, Y., "Appel du CICR dan le cadre du conflit entre l'Irak et l'Iran", 29 *Annuaire Francais de Droit International* (1983), pp. 161-173.

Schofield, R.N., *The Evolution of the Shatt Al-' Arab Boundary Dispute*, Wisbech 1986.

Singer, S., "La Protection des Enfants dans les Conflicts Armés", 68 *Revue Internationale de la Croix-Rouge* (1986), pp. 135-172.

Tavernier, P., "Le conflit frontalier entre l'Irak et l'Iran et la guerre du Chatt-el-Arab", 4 *ARES* (1981), pp. 333-370.

Tavernier, P., "La guerre du Golfe: Quelques aspects de l'application du droit des conflicts armés et du droit humanitaire", 30 *Annuaire Francais de Droit International* (1984), pp. 41-64.

Tavernier, P., "La guerre du Golfe: les grandes puissances et les autres ou le triomphe de l'ambiguité", 7 *ARES* (1984/1985), pp. 529-560.

Tavernier, P., "La guerre du Golfe: l'argumentation irakienne", in Guilhandis, J.F./Torelli, M. (eds.), *Force armée et diplomatique*, Dordrecht 1985, pp. 211-222.

Tavernier, P., "Le Conflit entre l'Irak et l'Iran", 9 *ARES* (1987), pp. 307-325.

Tavernier, P., "La Résolution 598 du 20 Juillet 1987 et le rôle du Conseil de Sécurité dans la guerre entre l'Irak et l'Iran", 10 *ARES* (1988), pp. 209-222.

Tavernier, P., "Le caractère obligatoire de la résolution 598(1987) du Conseil de Sécurité relative à la guerre du Golfe", 1 *European Journal of International Law* (1990), pp. 278-285.

Wolfrum, R., "Reflagging and escort operations in the Persian Gulf: an International Law perspective", 29 *Virginia Journal of International Law* (1989), pp. 387-399.

TABLE OF DOCUMENTS

TABLE OF ARBITRATIONS AND JUDGMENTS

INDEX